GATEWAYS

ENTERING THE ARGUMENT

Alan Ackmann
Dana Dunham
Amy Hornat-Kaval
Erin MacKenna-Sandhir
Eileen Seifert

DePaul University

Cover photo © 2010 Sebastián Morales. Cloud Gate, 2004, Anish Kapoor. Stainless steel, 33 ft. **X** 66 ft. **X** 42 ft. Millennium Park, Chicago. Used by permission of the artist Anish Kapoor and of the photographer Sebastián Morales.

Kendall Hunt
publishing company

www.kendallhunt.com
Send all inquiries to:
4050 Westmark Drive
Dubuque, IA 52004-1840

Copyright © 2011 by Alan Ackmann, Dana Dunham, Amy Hornat-Kaval, Erin MacKenna-Sandhir and Eileen Seifert

ISBN 978-0-7575-9621-6

Printed in the United States of America
10 9 8 7 6 5 4 3 2

ACKNOWLEDGEMENTS

We are all deeply committed to teaching and to First-Year Writing, and we hope that this text will help both our students and our colleagues meet their educational objectives.

We are very appreciative of the support we've received while writing this book.

We'd like to thank the Department of Writing, Rhetoric, and Discourse, and particularly our Director of First-Year Writing, Dr. Darsie Bowden, and our Department Chair, Dr. Peter Vandenberg.

Our fellow faculty members and students were the inspiration for this text and the source of valuable feedback. We would especially like to recognize our colleague Michael Moore for his important contribution on electronic portfolios.

We would like to acknowledge Michelle Bahr, Christine O'Brien, and Clay Johnson at Kendall Hunt Publishing Company.

Finally, we would like to thank our families and loved ones. We are very grateful for their continuous support during this project.

Alan Ackmann
Dana Dunham
Amy Hornat-Kaval
Erin MacKenna-Sandhir
Eileen Seifert

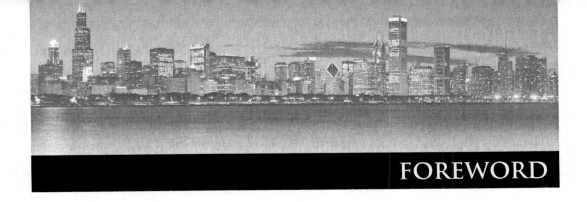

FOREWORD

TO STUDENTS

We wrote this book with you in mind. We hope it will give you a practical and helpful tool kit of ideas and practices for writing arguments based on research. We've tried to anticipate the parts of the process where you might need advice and encouragement, and we have suggested approaches that have worked for our own students.

Writing is hard, so we've thought about motivation. Why put in the effort? What is the point beyond the grade and the credit hours? We think that people argue because it's a necessity of life. Our albums of readings show writers arguing at points of crisis, at times when decisions will have crucial results for the authors and their communities. We include George Washington trying to keep his army together as the Revolutionary War winds down, and we see doctors and patients responding to a disease that destroys the ability to breathe.

Our message is that your ideas and your writing matter, too. Your education is preparing you to be leaders. At the point when the "they" who should protect children, preserve the environment, and prosecute injustice turns out to be you, we want you to have the research and writing skills that will make your ideas count.

Our book has two parts. Part One takes you step by step though the process of understanding assignments, planning and researching an argument, and revising and critiquing your paper. Part Two consists of a flexible group of readings with albums that allow your class to see connections between the selections. Each class and professor is different, but our book will give you a good foundation for understanding your class work and for working independently.

We hope that you will find your writing course empowering and challenging. You're coming to this stage of your education with experience, ideas, and a lot of school behind you. When you leave this course, we hope you will be a clearer thinker and a more self-assured and powerful writer.

TO FACULTY

No book can take your place. We designed our book to be a helpful partner to classroom teachers. Our text is short because we know that you want to customize your course with your own materials. We hope this book will reinforce the principles of argumentation and research that you want your students to learn. We approach teaching this course with the hope of reducing anxiety and creating strong motivation, and we think you do, too. Our tone is encouraging, but our standards are high. We think students should get to know major figures like Aristotle and Quintilian, and we want them to see how writers in our own era carry on the rhetorical heritage. Our readings are alphabetically arranged so that you can shape them into units that work for your course design. The albums suggest groupings that can help you to show students how knowledge and writing practices connect authors and audiences. As you construct a gateway to argument and research for your students, we are honored to be your companion for the journey.

CONTENTS

TRACKING THE PROJECT   xi

CHAPTER 1: GETTING STARTED   1
    The Big Picture   1
    Understanding Argument   2
    Surveying Your Interests   6
    Composing Summaries   17
    Critiquing the Rhetoric   20

CHAPTER 2: MANAGING INFORMATION   31
    Finding Your Stance   31
    Finding and Evaluating Sources   35
    Annotating Your Bibliography   39

CHAPTER 3: PUTTING IT TOGETHER   43
    Drafting Your Argument   43
    Deciding on a Structure   45
    Integrating Your Research   47
    Employing the Appeals   51
    Testing Audience Response   53
    Revising Your Argument   54
    Developing Your Style   56
    Designing Your Document   60

CHAPTER 4: INTRODUCTION TO READINGS   67
    Rhetorical Literacy   68
    Public Relations Literacy   68
    Political Literacy   68
    Technological Literacy   69
    Scientific Literacy   69
    Medical Literacy   69
    Academic Literacy   70

READINGS

Excerpt from *Rhetoric*   71
    Aristotle

Give Employees Facebook Time   75
    Traci Armstrong

Queen Elizabeth's Image Repair Discourse:
Insensitive Royal or Compassionate Queen?   78
    William L. Benoit and Susan L. Brinson

President Bush's Image Repair Discourse on Hurricane Katrina   87
    William L. Benoit and Jayne R. Henson

Excerpt from *The Closing of the American Mind*   97
    Allan Bloom

Malignant Mesothelioma Mortality—United States, 1999–2005   105
    Center for Disease Control

How the Scapegoats Escaped   110
    William D. Cohan

Diffuse Malignant Pleural Mesothelioma: Symptom Management   112
    Mary Ellen Cordes and Carol Brueggen

Reading Philosophy with Background Knowledge and Metacognition   127
    David W. Concepción

God vs. Science   141
    Dan Cray

Visceral Has Its Value   149
    Maureen Dowd

Do You Pass the Social Media Recruitment Test?   151
    Boris Epstein

A Kind Word for Bullshit: The Problems with Academic Writing   154
    Philip Eubanks and John D. Schaeffer

The Floyd Landis Doping Scandal: Implications for Image Repair Discourse   165
    Mark Glantz

The Median Isn't the Message   175
    Stephen Jay Gould

Cut This Story! Newspaper Articles are Too Long   179
    Michael Kinsley

The Case for Short Words   183
    Richard Lederer

Chapter XVII from *The Prince,* "Concerning Cruelty
And Clemency, And Whether It Is Better To Be Loved Than Feared"   186
    Niccolò Machiavelli

George Washington's Tear-Jerker 188
    John R. Miller
Senate Bill 561 190
    Ben Nevers
Greetings from Idiot America 194
    Charles P. Pierce
Excerpt from *Institutio Oratoria Book XII, Chapter 1* 204
    Quintilian
Writing for the Public 208
    Mike Rose
A Modest Proposal 215
    Jonathan Swift
What the Public Doesn't Get About Climate Change 220
    Bryan Walsh
Newburgh Address 222
    George Washington
Colombia Uses Ads to Persuade Rebels to Turn Themselves In 225
    Laurel Wentz
The Dawkins v. Collins Debate 228
    Gary J. Whittenberger

TRACKING THE PROJECT

For many students, an argumentative, multi-source research paper is the most complicated academic task they've undertaken at this point in their education. Unlike shorter papers—the kind that can be cranked out in a weekend, an evening, or even (in some cases) on the train ride into campus—multi-source research papers can take the entire term to write and revise. Consequently, it is important to develop some initial strategies for organizing your material and keeping tabs on your thought process. Here are some practical steps to get you started.

KEEP YOUR INFORMATION IN ONE PLACE

As you work, you're going to accumulate a lot of stuff: articles, drafts, Post-its with impulsive observations, lecture notes from class, and so forth. It will be useful, therefore, to have all of it in one place. So make a decision, early on, about where you're going to keep the stuff you acquire. You can use a three-ring binder, an accordion folder, or even a designated thumb drive or computer file (though you should also have a hard copy of the most important items). Whatever you choose, however, be sure to have one section where you can keep your paper materials—like copies of your articles—and one where you can take notes to yourself about how the project is evolving. Having all of this material in one spot will be an invaluable resource as your project develops.

TRACK YOUR LONG- AND SHORT-TERM GOALS

There are several reasons for this. First, one of the easiest ways to lose track of your goals is not to have any in the first place. Conversely, one of the easiest ways to self-assess your progress step-by-step is to remain aware of how (and how well) you're meeting the challenges you've set for yourself. This applies to your larger goals (like crafting a well-supported argument) and your shorter ones (like writing an introduction or reading a single article). This kind of consistent, ongoing reflection is quite helpful in managing the recursive tasks inherent in a long project.

TRACK YOUR STRUGGLES AND SUCCESSES

One of the advantages of record keeping is that you become aware of what you instinctively do well, and what you could probably do better. Whenever you find yourself clicking on all cylinders (or sputtering out) make a note of why you think this is, and what you could potentially change about your strategy in the future. After all, writing a single research paper is great—but the larger goal here is to acquire transferable skills of research and argumentation, and that requires isolating and reflecting on patterns in your process.

TRACK YOUR INDIVIDUAL WRITING EXPERIENCE

You're going to learn a lot about yourself as a writer in the next several weeks—among the things you'll learn, hopefully, is what makes you unique. The idea that every writer operates in the same fashion, and that learning how to write is somehow a process of figuring out what everybody else does, is a myth. The fact is that no two writers in this class—or maybe even no two writers, period—will write in precisely the same way. Each will have different styles, work habits, and processes. Part of learning how to write, therefore, involves learning how *you* write. So the higher awareness you can gain of your own idiosyncratic processes and patterns, the better off you'll be.

Periodically throughout the next few chapters, you'll find other suggestions of things to track in your notebooks or netbooks (whatever the case may be). In the meantime, just keep the above suggestions in mind.

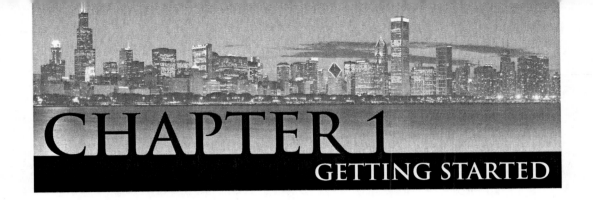

CHAPTER 1
GETTING STARTED

THE BIG PICTURE

Think of the most memorable arguments you've had throughout your life. For one reason or another, you were compelled to enter into those arguments. Perhaps you feared you would lose a long-held conviction if you didn't fight for it. Or, maybe your certainty on the subject matter at hand provided the impetus. Perhaps you've had one argument thrust upon you and avoided another for years. Invitations into argument can range from subtle to glaring. A polite but misguided remark might be enough in one context, whereas a metaphorical punch in the face may not render you ready in another. Just as there are multiple ways of getting into an argument, there is no one way to argue. Argument is an art form. Still, if your goal is to move your audience toward a certain action or conviction, some methods, over the centuries, have proven more effective than others. Just as there is more than one way to argue, there is more than one way to learn how to argue.

In your Writing, Rhetoric, and Discourse 104 class, your instructor may assign a number of different types of assignments. What you do in your class might be quite different from what your roommate is doing in her section of WRD 104. However, the classes are likely to share two important goals: learning to write a strong argument and practicing research techniques to help you support that argument.

Whatever project becomes your focus, remember that it will most likely not be accomplished in one sitting, or as a single activity. Argumentative writing, like most writing, takes place in stages, with multiple overlapping tasks that sometimes occur both independently and as part of an ongoing process of composition. You will spend some time writing, some planning, some imagining, some drafting, some erasing, some tweaking, and some editing. Frequently, you might find yourself engaging in some of these tasks simultaneously—or depending on your process, you might not do some of them at all. Additionally, consider that you will undoubtedly discover things about yourself as a writer in the next few weeks that are unique to your own skills and experiences, and that some of the notions we explore here will be straightforward and accessible, while others will seem murky and abstruse. As a consequence, there will be times you rejoice about how profound and meaningful your writing is, and other times when (probably unnecessarily) you want to delete everything and start from scratch.

You will probably not go through all of these aspects in the neat little sequence described above—nor should this be expected. Every writer has his or her quirks and foibles and will almost certainly spend more or less time on one aspect or another than the writer one seat over. The important point, though, is that you should not expect to complete an argumentative, research-based project quickly or without challenge. This makes you no different than any other writer. If the assigned project seems intimidating, though, it may help you to think of it not as a single, daunting endeavor but instead as a series of smaller, manageable tasks.

Finally, it's important to consider that everything we're about to cover works toward yet another, larger goal: to prepare you for life outside of college. If you leave the class able to write a research paper based on multiple sources, that's great. If you leave with critical reading and analysis skills that allow you to evaluate whatever ideas you encounter post graduation...well, that's even better.

UNDERSTANDING ARGUMENT

WHY START AN ARGUMENT?

As you begin a class that features argumentation and research, you may be wondering why you need to take this course. After all, you've been arguing throughout your life without any help from textbooks. Sometimes you win, sometimes you lose, and sometimes the whole thing seems like a waste of time. Argument can have a bad reputation. Just as rhetoric, something that relates closely to argument, is often thought to consist of manipulative tricks that get in the way of honest decisions and productive action, argument is often associated with uncomfortable conflict.

Yet, colleges and universities take argument quite seriously, connecting skill in argumentation with clear thinking and effective leadership. In public and private life, students of argument have skills that make a difference. On the other hand, you may feel that you've been manipulated or tricked by good arguments. Well, one of the benefits of a course in argument is that you will no longer feel powerless—you'll be able to analyze other people's positions as well as confidently express your own.

Here are some of things that argumentative skill can help you do:

- Evaluate alternatives to make good decisions
- Figure out how to define a complex concept
- Set priorities when resources are scarce
- Convince a group to unite behind the best course of action
- Decide what values will guide your life

As you move through the chapters in this book, you will soon notice that the field has a history that goes back thousands of years and crosses continents and cultures. At first, it may be daunting to hear references to Aristotle's *Rhetoric* and Toulmin's work on enthymemes. But the existence of profound philosophers and an extensive technical vocabulary is really good news. You don't have to figure it all out for yourself; instead, you can draw on the best of centuries of study and experience so that you know how to make a difference in your own life.

For example, when:

- cars are sailing at high speeds past the corner of your block, you'll know how to craft an argument for a traffic light to your town council.
- an instructor asks you to take a stand on global warming, you'll know how to organize the evidence and make your case.
- you have to decide if a job in a dynamic world capital is worth living far from your family, you'll have a structure for sorting out your conflicting desires.
- you are sitting in the waiting room of an intensive care unit, and a surgeon asks you to choose which heart valve will go to someone you love, you'll have the skills to make a life or death choice.

Now that you've seen some examples of what argument can offer, let's begin by establishing some of the heritage at your disposal when crafting an argument.

TIPS

on Getting Organized

When you start an argument-based composition and rhetoric course, one of two things is likely to happen. Either your instructor will give you topic areas to write about, or your instructor will tell you to find a topic that interests you.

Before you do anything else, invest time in understanding the assignments for the whole course. Though they share a theoretical foundation and compatible end goals, there is significant opportunity for variety in the way that specific courses are developed. To make the whole term a little more cohesive, many argument-based rhetoric courses have assignment sequences, which means all the assignments work toward a final goal and build the necessary skills along the way. If you have written descriptions of the assignments, go over them and mark the key descriptions. Ask your instructor questions so that you are clear about the terms and time line. This is the point to work out a preliminary schedule in your calendar so that you hit all of the little mile markers that get you from gunshot to finish line.

GETTING STARTED: CONCEPTS AND DEFINITIONS

When you start a course that combines argumentation with writing complex research papers, you will most likely start by building a foundation in major concepts about argument. You'll learn the terms that rhetoricians use to describe arguments, and you'll practice applying them to published work. You also may be searching for a research topic according to the guidelines established by your instructor. Understanding arguments and finding good topics benefit from a foundation in organizational skill, conceptual knowledge, and a willingness to delay taking a stance (for a while) in favor of critical thinking.

CONCEPTUAL KNOWLEDGE

There is no single definition of argument. Here's a list of several ways to define the term. Argument is:

- a claim supported by evidence.
- a dispute or quarrel.
- the main idea of an extended discussion.
- a course of reasoning that demonstrates truth or falsehood.

In addition, fields like computer science and mathematics use the term to express ideas about numbers and procedures. These definitions are not abstract; they come from real situations that people encounter. Their common ground is that argumentation uses words and ideas to solve problems. People don't argue when they agree and everything is clear. Since there are so many ideas about what an argument *could be,* it's helpful to find some ways of classifying the arguments that you read and write.

One strategy is to figure out the nature of the claim.

Here are three ways of classifying claims by the purpose of the argument:

Classification	Explanation	Examples
Definition	When people are trying to figure out what something is or even whether it exists, they make claims of definition.	• Life begins at conception. • There is no obesity epidemic. • Spanking is a form of child abuse.

Classification	Explanation	Examples
Value	When people are trying to compare the merits of the two choices, they make claims of value.	• It's better to spend school funds on arts programs than on driver education. • Love is more important than money. • Free speech matters more than the protection of people's feelings.
Procedure	When people are trying to decide how to act given a conflict, they make claims of procedure.	• We should allocate two million dollars to build a new pool. • The village government should ban pit bulls. • Schools should remove soft drink machines from their premises.

Other classification systems look at how arguments are arranged. Two of the most famous are the Classical and Toulmin models. Please see "Critiquing the Rhetoric" later in this chapter for descriptions of these models.

FORGET THE THESIS (FOR A WHILE)

Finding the claim and identifying its purpose works well when you want to *analyze* an argument. This approach isn't nearly as helpful when you want to *compose* an argument in an academic setting. Have you ever gotten the advice to start a paper by having a thesis? Or to start an argument by composing a claim? Perhaps you've heard that your first job as a writer is to choose a thesis, present it in your introduction, develop it in the body, and reinforce its importance in the conclusion.

The problem is that you may not be sure what you think, or you may not have enough information to offer convincing support for your view. If you don't know what other people have written on the subject, you can't be sure how your ideas fit in to the conversation. Also, starting with a thesis or fixed position shuts down the creation of new ideas as you write. Rigidly defending a thesis, come what may, changes the way you explore an idea, reducing it to a process of finding people (or sources) who agree with you, and rejecting people or sources that do not. But research, like writing itself, is about discerning new truths even more than confirming old ones, and beginning with a thesis resists this fact.

So, maybe you shouldn't start with a thesis at all. Instead, consider starting with a question framed as a hypothesis, a kind of educated guess about the direction your argument *might* take. Think of this like a hypothesis in traditional scientific research. Before you combine those red and blue liquids in their respective beakers, scientific method dictates that you develop a theory about what will happen. If you predict that the two liquids combined will create a dangerously unstable compound that will bubble over the sides of the tube, it doesn't inherently matter whether you are wrong or right (except on the level of safety, perhaps). What *does* matter is that you spend some time critically evaluating what you expect to find through your research, so that when something *actually* happens you have a lens through which it can be interpreted. Similarly, a hypothesis in non-scientific research allows you to take stock of your understanding at the beginning of a project, providing a starting position which future pieces of information can affirm or contradict. Therefore, we recommend you start with question-based explorations and make predictions about the likely outcomes.

When you've explored your subject, you should be able to answer the following key questions:

Who is interested in my topic?
What events triggered interest in this topic?
When did the conversation about my topic begin?
Where do discussions of my topic take place?
What kinds of arguments are people or groups making about my topic?
What authorities have published opinions or studies about my topic?
What kinds of evidence do people use when they argue about this topic?
Who has the power to make something happen in my topic area?
Has this topic been unjustly ignored or dismissed?
Have distinct sides or points of view emerged about the topic?
What fields of expertise have connections to my topic?

SURVEYING YOUR INTERESTS

FINDING YOUR TOPIC

If your instructor has offered it to you, take advantage of the invitation to connect with your own interests. Maybe you have been waiting for the chance to explore an issue or to advocate for a position. Or, if you have been assigned a topic or asked to choose from a list of topics, search for the angles or focuses within that topic that interest you. Either way, you might need to make some lists or brainstorm to discover your interests.

BRAINSTORMING

Brainstorming consists of several different activities designed to elicit ideas, possibilities, and connections between what you already know and what you'd like to find out. There is no one correct or approved way to brainstorm. Rather, brainstorming—how it's done as well as how much of it is done—often depends on the unique and individual process of each writer.

Nevertheless, there are some guidelines that may help brainstorming work for you. Try giving your brainstorm structure:

> Step 1: Write down words that connect to your topic.
> Step 2: Select a word from the first list and brainstorming about that concept.
> Step 3: Group the words from the second list that have common elements or concerns.

You can brainstorm on your own or as a group activity.

Here's an example of a student's structured brainstorm on the topic of gun violence in neighborhoods:

> Step 1: like a war, innocent kids die, neighborhood fear, silence, hopeless, gangs, police reactions, news stories, memorials with teddy bears, getting worse
> Step 2: (on "innocent kids die"): incidents in Chicago, the boy who was shot thirteen times, baby shot in stroller, children shot sitting on their couches, students shot in school, what does innocent mean?, injuries as well as deaths, beatings as well as shootings, ages of victims, reactions of families, relation to school achievement, kids can't play outside, relation to obesity
> Step 3: (common elements of concern): no place is safe, extent of the human damage, ripple effect to other problems

Brainstorming has helped this student to sort out what he knows and to find out what issues keep drawing him deeper into the argument about how to stop community violence and protect children. Notice that he is not interested in issues like the reasons for the violence. His brainstorm also locates his interest in the victims more so than the perpetrators. Another writer might go in a completely different direction, but this student has found his gateway into the argument.

TROUBLESHOOTING

Even once you find your way into an argument, you may encounter certain roadblocks. Three problems to watch for are topics with little room for debate, topics with insufficient available research, and topics steeped in technical language that is inaccessible to you. In the case of some medical issues, for example, there is a well-accepted standard of care with little room for debate, or you might find out that the causes of a disease are well-known with little disagreement among experts. Given this roadblock, you might shift directions a bit to find a heated discussion of the best treatments. While titles in databases will guide you to the most discussed and best-documented areas of your subject, sometimes you will discover that an issue or figure doesn't actually have a substantial amount of source material behind it. In history, for example, Lucrezia Borgia, legendary Renaissance noblewoman, and her poison ring seem intriguing, but the material goes back to the limited number of available primary sources, so you quickly reach a dead end in research. Finally, there are some subjects that may require linguistic or technical resources that you don't have yet. Try reading an article or two in the field to see if you can follow the discussion.

As you read, try to envision yourself as a participant in the subject you are exploring. This will help you access the debate. In order to do this, pay attention to your reactions while reading. If you find yourself agreeing or disagreeing passionately with a text, that could be a way to gain access to the conversation. Similarly, if during your reading you note an issue that seems unresolved, or a problem or solution that is not being considered but should be, that too is another point at which you can enter the discussion.

Once you've gained access to a debate and discovered the areas in your subject where reasonable people can disagree, ask yourself why readers would benefit from reading your argument. Also ask yourself what you would get out of investing your time in this area.

You may worry that many people would not be interested in your subject and may never have even heard of it. That is actually not a problem. Some powerful arguments work to convince audiences that a problem exists and that they should pay attention to it. In the beginning of the AIDS crisis, many people did not understand that there was an epidemic, and early writers in the field worked to convince people that a public health crisis was in progress.

As you work toward a claim, ask the following questions:
- Is my issue general or specific? Global or local?
- Am I trying to get people to recognize and understand an issue, or do I want them to do something about it?
- Is there an existing position that I want to support?
- Do I want to explain why a current viewpoint is wrong?
- Do I want to propose modifications to a current argument?

As you investigate further, you'll find the answer to these questions, and your claim will start to emerge. Mainly, you'll want to learn as much as possible, make a genuine effort to understand multiple viewpoints, and be willing to change your mind along the way. Throughout this process, write down your ideas. You will save time and preserve valuable thoughts if you keep a notebook to document your research process.

GENERAL READING

So you know that brainstorming and looking for an entry point to a debate are important initial steps to finding your topic. General reading is another key to getting a good start. You need a trustworthy overview of your subject so that you will know how to read and evaluate more specific readings as you progress. This section offers tips on how to track down general reading on your topic.

General reading is meant to help you determine the:

- current issues in your field.
- points where people disagree or have different approaches.
- benefits that could come from working on a particular question.
- availability of material on your subject.
- readability of scholarly and professional materials in the field.

In daily life, many people use search engines like Google for general knowledge, and they often end up reading Wikipedia. For academic or professional work, this approach has limitations. Wikipedia is an open platform—anyone can post on it. Similarly, internet search engines access a wide range of materials, but they are not always selective about quality. When you are new to a field, you need information that you can trust. So we suggest a different approach. Your college library will have lists of specialized reference books and databases that have credibility in an academic setting. *CQ Researcher* is a fine starting point that offers unbiased overviews of topics recently debated on the floor of Congress. You might also try *LexisNexis* to find periodical articles on your topic. (Note that these will not necessarily be disinterested, so you'll need to work to achieve balance across your sources.) Further, you can look for an encyclopedia entry, an introductory chapter in a book, or a magazine article that surveys an issue rather than takes a side in a controversy. Keep in mind that there are general encyclopedias like the *Britannica* as well as specialized references like the *Encyclopedia of Philosophy*, the *Encyclopedia of Bilingual Education*, and the *Encyclopedia of Gender and Society*. Some instructors see the general encyclopedias as good for getting background information on your topic, but not suitable as sources for a works cited. Check with your instructor for guidelines and expectations.

TAKING *notes*

Keeping track of this information will prepare you to formally propose your topic to your instructor or to an audience of your peers. Some research guides still seem to believe that you are going to take notes on index cards with careful summaries and paraphrases of your research. This traditional method has the strength of requiring you to read carefully and to put the material in your own words. The truth is that a lot of people just don't do it. Instead, they photocopy books and print online sources and then go back and underline them. This approach can work if you are careful to annotate the printouts or to enter ideas and questions in your course notebook as you read. At a very minimum, make sure to write a full citation of the source on the top of each printout and record this citation in your research notebook. Check a citation guide to make sure that you have all the required information.

As you make judgments about how to invest your time, be aware that many instructors will start the grading process of a research paper by looking at the Works Cited page to check the quality of the sources. They know that a paper with good sources is more likely to contain a strong argument than a paper derived from the first three articles that appeared in a popular search engine. (See "Finding Your Stance" in Chapter 2 for a demonstration of how source material contributes to a project's merits or flaws.)

READING CRITICALLY

An important part of the preliminary research process, of course, involves critical reading. As students, you are often asked to read to prepare for a class or as part of a homework assignment. Yet, for as often as you are told to read, it's likely that you are rarely told *how* to read a text critically. You already know that you read differently in different contexts. For example, the way you read a novel on the beach differs from the way you read your notes the night before a chemistry exam. Similarly, the way you read the take-out menu at your local taco joint differs from the way you read a love letter written to you by an old flame. But did you realize that the way you read for one class should differ from the way you read for another? For this class, you're asked to read critically, but what does that mean? This book includes an essay by David W. Concepción titled "Reading Philosophy with Background Knowledge and Metacognition" that provides a method for critical reading relevant to a rhetoric class. Borrowing some strategies from Concepción, this section outlines a two-step approach to facilitate a critical understanding of assigned readings and texts you track down during your research process. First, you'll want to establish background knowledge and basic information. Next, you'll evaluate the essay by analyzing the author's methods.

HOW TO ESTABLISH BASIC INFORMATION AND BACKGROUND KNOWLEDGE

In a rhetoric class, nearly all the assigned readings will submit arguments, which means they will include claims (either written or implied), support, and analysis. As you encounter the readings in this book, you'll want to keep in mind the rhetorical triangle, which demonstrates that the key elements of a given rhetorical situation are in a dynamic interplay with one another; the writer/communicator, reader/audience, text/message and context combine to create the text's overall effect.

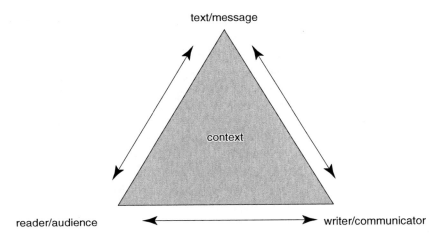

Ask yourself the following questions to determine key information about the writer, audience, topic, and context:

Questions about the **writer/communicator**	• Who is this text's writer? • To what communities does the writer belong? • What is the writer's stake in this topic? • What is the writer's purpose?
Questions about the **reader/audience**	• For whom is the text intended? • Where does the text appear, and who reads this publication? • What are the values, interests, assumptions, and shared knowledge of this audience?
Questions about the **text/message**	• What is the text's primary message? • What appeals are used to convey the text's message? • What formal and stylistic conventions are used to discuss this topic?
Questions about the **context**	• What event compelled this writer to produce this text? • In what larger social context can you situate this text? • What is taking place beyond the text that makes this conversation relevant to its audience?

As you answer these questions, you'll notice that critical reading *involves* the reader and requires an active interchange between reader, writer, and text. For example, when you agree or disagree with a writer's ideas, you're comparing her way of thinking to your own and exchanging thoughts. Further, if you revisit the rhetorical triangle, you'll notice that the reader shares equal prominence with the writer and message in constructing the rhetorical situation, which means that—as its reader—you are vital to the reading's context and the determination of its effectiveness. Nonetheless, getting involved with a text can be harder than it sounds, especially if the text expects you to have background knowledge you lack.

Concepción states that "background knowledge helps us make inferential links among the sentences that are written on the page." He further notes that "we need background information to construct and retain a text's gist." But you won't always have the necessary knowledge on every assigned reading. Here are some ways to combat this problem:

Reposition the text

Consider how the reading fits into the context of your class. As mentioned earlier, rhetorical texts mean to persuade a defined audience toward a particular conviction or action. Fortunately, you don't need to know everything about the topic to determine how well the piece functions rhetorically. Your instructor will provide background information on argumentation—this is more important than having a fully developed understanding of mesothelioma, for example.

Be patient

Though it may seem oddly timed, some of the background knowledge you'll need to comprehend the readings will emerge during the class discussion *after* you've completed the reading. A comment shared by another student or by your instructor might allow you to make certain connections in the text. For this reason, try to stay engaged with a text throughout both your individual reading and the class discussion about it.

Be resourceful

Use dictionaries and encyclopedias to establish working definitions of unfamiliar terms and concepts.

How to Evaluate Texts

Establishing basic information and background knowledge will help you explore the text as a rhetorical situation, but you're not reading the essay critically until you evaluate the author's various claims, instances of support, and methods of analysis. Evaluative reading not only asks what the author is doing, but also judges how well those moves work on a defined audience. Furthermore, evaluation involves metacognition (meaning you think about how you're thinking). In his essay, Concepción writes, "If a student is truly engaged in reading she will be evaluating and making arguments." Here's how you'll begin evaluating and making arguments in the context of your rhetoric class:

The first step is to show you understand a reading, which you can demonstrate through summary. (For more information on writing summaries see "Composing Summaries" later in this chapter.) Once you can prove you understand a text, you've earned the right to state whether you think the writer is likely to convince his or her given audience.

Next, you'll need to support your argument by describing *how* a writer convinces (or fails to convince) her audience. To do this, you'll track down the writer's support and determine how likely it is to compel its defined audience toward an action or conviction. Now you're evaluating the text. (For information on how to judge a text's effectiveness, see "Critiquing the Rhetoric" later in this section.)

Finally, metacognition comes in when you think about how your own values and position on the topic guide your responses to the author's views. For example, do you assume that scientific certainty and faith are incompatible? If so, you might be unwilling to accept that Francis Collins, who debates Richard Dawkins in the *TIME* article included in Part 2, is credible as a Christian scientist. Remain aware of how your own latent philosophical leanings seep into your reading of a text. If an author's ideas threaten to undo your own, you might unwittingly produce an evaluation that directs your views out of harm's way.

HOW TO ANNOTATE TEXTS TO FACILITATE CRITICAL READING

In his article's appendix, Concepción discusses the importance of flagging, which is a method of abbreviated note taking. He differentiates between flagging and highlighting, stating that, unlike highlighting, flagging lets you "do more than just distinguish important from unimportant." For a rhetoric class, you might flag assigned readings in the following ways:

1. In your own words, write in the margin an abbreviated version of the topic the reading addresses. Place this near the sentence where the writer first announces his subject matter.
2. Identify the author's claims by writing **AC** in the margin. Then, briefly describe her argument—particularly the main argument—in your own words. Know that the main argument might be implied rather than stated directly, in which case you'll need to put it into words for the writer.
3. Note claims the author disputes by writing **OC** (opponent's claim) in the margins.
4. Write **R** when the author provides a rebuttal for opponents' claims.
5. Identify support (data, evidence, examples, testimonies) by writing **S** in the margins; you can then add a more detailed annotation to note the type of support.
6. Keep track of moments of analysis by placing **AN** in the margins. Remember, the author might use analysis to prove her position or to refute opposing viewpoints.

Here's a sample flagging of an article you'll find in Part 2.

Maureen Dowd

Visceral Has Its Value

AC.

Topic: Sarah Palin's surprising endurance in the political realm.

It's easy to dismiss Sarah Palin.

She's back on the trail, with the tumbling hair and tumbling thoughts. The queen of the scenic strip mall known as Wasilla now reigns over thrilled subjects thronging to a politically strategic swath of American strip malls.

S. Example that supports the initial claim, "it's easy to dismiss Sarah Palin" by showing her "Yoda-like syntax."

The conservative celebrity clearly hasn't boned up on anything, except her own endless odyssey of self-discovery. And she still has that Yoda-like syntax.

"And I think more of a concern has been not within the campaign the mistakes that were made, not being able to react to the circumstances that those mistakes created in a real positive and professional and helpful way for John McCain," she told Bill O'Reilly.

AC. Democrats have something to learn from Palin.

Yet Democrats would be foolish to write off her visceral power.

S. Testimony to Palin's appeal.

As Judith Doctor, a 69-year-old spiritual therapist, told *The Washington Post's* Jason Horowitz at Palin's book signing in Grand Rapids, Mich., "She's alive inside, and that radiates energy, and people who are not psychologically alive inside are fascinated by that."

S. Supports claim that Democrats have something to learn from Palin.

Barack Obama, who once had his own electric book tour testing the waters for a campaign, could learn a thing or three from Palin. On Friday, for the first time, his Gallup poll approval rating dropped below 50 percent, and he's losing the independents who helped get him elected.

AC. More specific version of the earlier claim—Obama could benefit from emulating Palin's method of connecting with her audience. This is the author's main claim.

He's a highly intelligent man with a highly functioning West Wing, and he's likable, but he's not connecting on the gut level that could help him succeed.

The animating spirit that electrified his political movement has sputtered out.

People need to understand what the president is thinking as he maneuvers the treacherous terrain of a lopsided economic recovery and two depleting wars.

Like Reagan, Obama is a detached loner with a strong, savvy wife. But unlike Reagan, he doesn't have the acting skills to project concern about what's happening to people.

S.

Obama showed a flair for the theatrical during his campaign, and a talent for narrative in his memoir, but he has yet to translate those skills to governing.

AN. Three sections of analysis further the claim that Obama could learn from Palin's approach to politics.

As with the debates, he seems resistant to the idea that perception, as well as substance, matters. Obama so values pragmatism, and is so immersed in the thorny details of legislative compromises, that he may be undervaluing the connective bonds of simpler truths.

Americans who are hurting get angry when they learn that Timothy Geithner, as head of the New York Fed before becoming Treasury secretary, caved to the insistence of Goldman Sachs and other A.I.G. trading partners that they get 100 cents on the dollar when he could have struck a far better bargain for taxpayers.

AN. Analyzes current socio-political environment.

If we could see a Reduced Shakespeare summary of Obama's presidency so far, it would read:

Dither, dither, speech. Foreign trip, bow, reassure. Seminar, summit. Shoot a jump shot with the guys, throw out the first pitch in mom jeans. Compromise, concede, close the deal. Dither, dither, water down, news conference.

It's time for the president to reinvent this formula and convey a more three-dimensional person.

Palin can be stupefyingly simplistic, but she seems dynamic. Obama is impressively complex but he seems static.

She nurtures her grass roots while he neglects his.

He struggles to transcend identity politics while she wallows in them. As he builds an emotional moat around himself, she exuberantly pushes whatever she has, warts and all — the good looks, the tabloid-perfect family, the Alaska quirkiness, the kids with the weird names.

Just like the disastrous and anti-intellectual W., this Visceral One never doubts herself. The Cerebral One welcomes doubt.

On Afghanistan, Palin says, W-like, that the president should simply give Gen. Stanley McChrystal a blank check. But Afghanistan is a wrenching decision, and we do need the closest exit ramp. So the president should get credit for standing back and studying the issue, and for not rubber-stamping the generals' predictable urge to surge. But the way he has handled the perception part has allowed critics — including generals — to cast him as indecisive.

McChrystal and Gen. David Petraeus should have been giving their best advice to Obama — and airing their view against scaling down in Afghanistan — in confidence. Instead, McChrystal pushed his opinion in a speech in London, and Petraeus has discussed his feelings in private sessions with reporters. This creates a "Seven Days in May" syndrome, where the two generals are, in effect, lobbying against the president and undercutting him as he's trying to make a painfully complex, life-and-death decision.

This time, Obama should adopt Palin's straight-from-the-gut approach, call the generals into the Oval and tell them, "Your pie-holes you will shut or rise higher you will not. Because, dang it, the president I am!"

AC. Elaborates on earlier claim that Obama can learn from Palin.

Four sections of AN further the main claim.

AC. Obama's cerebral approach is appropriate for complex policy decisions.

AC. Palin's visceral approach works best when the public perception of a crisis is at stake.

S. Example

AN. Furthers the main claim.

S. Example of a policy decision where Obama could borrow Palin's approach.

ROADBLOCKS

Now that you've established the relevant basic information and background kr ⸱o-tated the text, and evaluated the author's methods, you're interacting with th critically. Still, common roadblocks in the form of negative thoughts can ⸱ progress. Here are some examples of common problematic thoughts them:

The Problem	Why It Happens	What To Do About It
This reading is boring.	You might feel a reading is "boring" when it doesn't relate directly to your experiences or when it addresses unfamiliar subject matter. Perhaps the author imagines a different audience, one with specialized knowledge in the field.	Remember, college is a time to explore new ideas. You'll soon discover that no topic is boring once you look at it through the right pair of glasses. Be open to new ideas and trust that the author's intention is to broaden your perspective and invite you into the discussion.
This reading is too long or repetitive.	Lengthy academic writing will shift from claim to evidence and into analysis with little or very subtle indication of these transitions. Further, complicated arguments might require several fairly similar—though not duplicative—examples (or other types of evidence) in order to be well supported, credible, and convincing.	As you read, carefully trace the writer's argument through its various parts: claims, evidence, and analysis. This way you won't mistakenly believe distinct parts are the same. If you still believe a work is repetitive, ask yourself why. Is the writer making a particularly risky or unpopular claim? Excessive support might be the writer's way of anticipating and refuting criticism.
This author uses unnecessarily big words.	Academic writing hopes to capture complex ideas, and often simple language can fail to adequately convey the author's meaning.	Always read with a pen in your hand, and keep track of terms that elude or confuse you. Look up unknown words as they appear so that you can review their definitions alongside their context in the reading. If a term still doesn't make sense, don't worry. You don't need to know every term's meaning to grasp the text. Over time, you'll start to notice that certain terms will reappear in the work of an academic subject; your comprehension of these terms will increase over time.
I don't understand this reading.	Not understanding a reading can combine elements of the three problems above. When a text is unfamiliar, lengthy, and cryptic, it will likely be difficult for any reader. It's okay to have trouble understanding a reading, particularly the first time you read it. When you run into this problem, know you're not alone, as many other students in your class are likely having the same experience.	When you become frustrated with a reading, don't give up. Instead, take a break and try to summarize what you've read so far. Instead of asking, "what does this mean," try asking, "what is the writer doing here?" Then move forward, handling small sections of the text at a time. Luckily, one of the goals of class discussion is to demystify complicated texts. Come prepared to facilitate your own and others' increased comprehension by reading the text multiple times and marking places in the text where the writer loses you.

COMPOSING SUMMARIES

WHAT IS A SUMMARY?

As you read through your preliminary research, you'll no doubt find yourself needing to summarize, which is a skill that will also come in handy as you transition into the writing phase of your project. A summary is an objective, brief, and accurate recreation of a larger source (or sources) that is used to enhance and support a writer's own argument in academic writing. Since much academic discourse is part of a larger discussion, one of the first steps in writing an academic paper is learning how to effectively summarize.

ISN'T SUMMARIZING SUPPOSED TO BE EASY?

Though you do it every day, summarizing is not as straightforward as it might initially appear. In fact, students often come to class believing that summary requires less focused attention than other elements of argumentative discourse; after all, the root of a successful summary can be loosely characterized as repetition and is easily dismissed as simply spitting back condensed information to an unfamiliar reader, like a glorified mimic. Far from creating a simplistic echo, though, summarizing requires careful and critical reading and analysis in order to internalize an often complicated source and to represent that source accurately. It's no easy feat, actually, and a good summary rises well above the level of simple parroting.

WHY WILL SUMMARIES BE USED IN AN ARGUMENT?

Summaries have multiple functions in argumentative writing. Here are some of the more common situations.

You might summarize to:

- describe major events or incidents that prompted you to make the argument.
- provide necessary context for a position or source, so your opinion rests sec͏   in the larger conversation.
- articulate key sources or arguments to which you are responding.
- prove that you understand the opinions of those who disagree with yͨ
- include important evidence or reasons necessary to prove your poiͫ
- demonstrate the authority of one of your sources.

This is by no means a comprehensive list of all the occasions in
marize, but it does cover some of the most frequent circumstͣ

How do I summarize something?

There are many ways to successfully summarize. If you find yourself struggling, consider the following process:

Begin by reading the source text in full. This may sound self-evident, but many students (in an attempt to save time, perhaps, or write things down while the moment is fresh) try to write a summary while reading for the first time. This creates challenges because it is difficult to summarize something you don't fully comprehend or have not internalized. These kinds of summaries, written as a student grips tightly to the source material like a novice swimmer clutching the side of a pool, often result in extended paraphrases rather than clear renditions of the full argument. Furthermore, summarizing involves separating superordinate points (like main ideas or major subtopics) from subordinate ones (like transitional elements or secondary evidence). Until you read through a text in its entirety, it is sometimes difficult to know what part of it falls into which category.

Next, try to write a one or two sentence summary of the entire source. Sometimes you can find a summary sentence in the text. Otherwise, you'll need to ask, what is its main idea—the primary objective? If it is an informational source, what main idea or concept does it try to impart? If it is a persuasive source, what does it want the reader to believe or to do? As comprehensively as possible, describe what (in an ideal world) the source will have accomplished. Clearly and accurately identifying this main point will give you a lens through which to view the rest of the text, and have something against which to assess that work's organizational and rhetorical decisions.

Once you have the main idea in mind, identify the source's major subtopics, reasons, or phases of thought. Every piece of writing has subtopics—phases of the writing that enhance the main idea by addressing one particular angle or dimension of the discussion. In longer works, like books, these are often identified by chapters. In medium-length works, like academic articles, section headers are frequently (though not exclusively) employed. In shorter works, paragraph breaks are sometimes sufficient. In any case, look for moments in the source where the writer leaves behind one major dimension of the discussion and takes on another. If the moment within your own paper requires a lengthier summary, develop the summary by adding additional sentences describing each phase of thought.

If an even lengthier summary is required, go back through the original source and add significant details or quotations to the subtopics until the desired length and elaboration is achieved.

So how long should my summary be?

Unless your instructor specifies one, there is no set length for a summary, and no objective standard for detail and level of development. Trying to define the length of a successful summary in absolute terms is difficult, since it deemphasizes the fact that summary plays an active role in argumentation. Like most decisions in writing, the length of a successful summary is determined by the immediate needs of a writer's rhetorical moment and the summary's level of importance and relevance to the paper's primary objective.

If what you're summarizing is just a glancing item in the overall argument (an episode of a television series, for example, or a brief biography of a major player in your topic) you can get away with a sentence or two. If, however, the main idea of your paper is that scholar X's ideas are newly relevant to the larger discussion based on recent discoveries, and deserve more attention, you may spend several pages of the paper doing nothing but summarizing scholar X's work. Either level of development is fine because each is appropriate to the moment. In other words, rather than asking how long a summary should be, ask how long it should be in order to be effective.

Perhaps without realizing it, you already make situational decisions about how comprehensively you will summarize something. Imagine that it's thirty seconds before class begins, and a less than prepared classmate sitting next to you asks you to describe the day's assigned reading—you'd give a very efficient summary lasting no more than a few sentences, covering the reading's main claim with perhaps only a few supporting reasons. Now imagine you're with this same classmate in the elevator of the Lewis center on your way up to class. Having a sixteen floor ascent with a few stops thrown in allows you to cover some of the finer details of that same reading. The student is still interested, so you take your time. In each situation, you assessed the needs of your audience and tailored a summary to meet those needs by using variables like available time, familiarity with subject matter, and relevance to larger goals. Writing a summary in an academic paper requires precisely the same skill set.

What do you mean by objectivity?

One of the trickier points to latch onto in summarizing is the idea of objectivity, which means that an effective summary will be unbiased, revealing nothing about the writer's attitude toward the material being summarized. A good summary will treat the material fairly and without commentary. In argumentative writing, which places such a high premium on presenting an opinion, this can be somewhat counterintuitive. So think of it like this: when summarizing, you are laying a neutral foundation on which you can build future argumentative discussion. Before you get into analysis of a given topic, it is often necessary to give an unbiased overview of the relevant information or opinions. This way, readers can have an objective set of information against which to compare your subjective interpretation.

It is important to realize, however, that you can sometimes reveal bias by what you do *not* say, in addition to what you *do* say. If you are writing a paper that compares two proposals for running a home for wayward youth, for example, and in the course of summarizing the two views you spend significantly more time outlining one proposal at the expense of the other, your bias will be made clear before you even get to the analysis section of your paper, which might subsequently damage your credibility. It is vital that you initially treat all perspectives of the controversy with an appropriate balance.

This raises the larger question of whether total objectivity in summaries is even possible. The matter is complicated by the fact that many people and institutions that claim to be objective are in fact anything but. News channels, periodicals, and (yes) even instructors consistently paint a skewed version of the world—sometimes innocently and sometimes quite maliciously. Academic discourse, however, relies on being able to accurately characterize the ideas of people who disagree with you—and the first step toward this is being able to write an objective summary.

SO WHAT MAKES A SUMMARY SUCCESSFUL?

A successful summary will enhance the effectiveness of an academic argument by providing an objective overview of one of that argument's foundational ideas. It will be concise yet thorough, unbiased yet confident, and accurate to the source yet connected to the writer's larger goals.

CRITIQUING THE RHETORIC

Whether you're writing a three-page rhetorical analysis or a ten-page research paper, making an argument requires you to analyze other writers' use of rhetorical appeals. At times, you'll acknowledge the merits of a writer's methods; in other cases, you'll work to reveal the flaws in an argument.

This section will outline an approach for analyzing a writer's use of the appeals and establish three common methods for critiquing rhetoric: the Toulmin Model, Rogerian Method, and identifying the logical fallacies. Understanding these methods will not only enhance your ability to read a text, it will also enable you to spot the flaws and opportunities in your own argument.

The Toulmin Model

In 1958 British philosopher Stephen Toulmin published *The Uses of Argument*. In this text, he outlines a method for analyzing the strength of practical arguments in judicial settings. The Toulmin Model was soon adopted by rhetoricians to test the strength of arguments in their field.

Toulmin established six interrelated parts of argument hinging around an assumption called the warrant, which the audience would need to accept for the argument to move from its grounds to its claim.

Often writers will not announce their warrant, and readers may not even notice that they are being asked to accept this assumption. When you uncover a writer's warrant, you also uncover the strength of the argument. Take a look at the following example alongside definitions of the six parts.

Part	Definition	Example
Claim	The conclusion of an argument that requires the arrangement of support.	The neighbors' barbeque will be cancelled.
Grounds	The verifiable information relied upon to support the claim. You can begin your grounds with the phrase "given that."	Given that there is a tornado passing through Chicago…
Warrant	The inferential leap necessary to move from the grounds to the claim. You can begin your warrant with the phrase "and since."	and since one cannot cook outside during a tornado…
Backing	Information supplied to support the warrant. Elements of the backing could begin with the term "because."	because being outside can be dangerous…
Rebuttal	Exceptions to your claim that your argument must accept in order to stand. A rebuttal could begin with the term "unless."	unless the weather clears up before the barbeque or the party is moved inside…
Qualifier	A term or phrase that allows you to manage the degree of risk you take on with an argument.	one could argue, possibly, certainly, we must conclude that, and necessarily

If we put these six pieces together, the argument reads as follows:

Given that there is a tornado passing through Chicago, and since one cannot cook outside during a tornado because being outside can be dangerous, unless the weather clears up before the barbeque or the party is moved inside, certainly, the neighbors' barbeque will be cancelled.

Remember that the argument will not be written in this form, as the audience is often only provided the grounds and the claim. It would most likely read:

Given that there is a tornado passing through Chicago, the neighbor's barbeque will be cancelled. The formal name for this kind of statement is an enthymeme, an argument that leaves out information the audience is likely to assume. Using the Toulmin model has allowed us to uncover the argument's warrant, which means we can evaluate its strength.

Let's test out this concept. Do you think the rhetor's audience is likely to accept the assumption that one cannot cook outside during a tornado? If so, the argument is likely to be effective.

The Rogerian Method

Not all argument ends with a winner and a loser. Psychologist Carl Rogers imagined effective argument as finding and maintaining common ground. Rogerian argument employs empathetic listening and willingly concedes some ground to the opposing view in favor of winning its audience's support.

To use this approach as a method of analysis, consider how well a writer or speaker reaches his or her audience. Here are some questions you can ask to determine if a text effectively employs the Rogerian method of argumentation:

- Does the writer look for shared ground with her opponents?
- Does the writer present an argument objectively and without biased language?
- Does the writer attempt to find a compromise between opponents and proponents of the issue?

The Logical Fallacies

A logical fallacy is an error in reasoning. It happens when the writer suggests that the information in an argument's premise is logically connected to the information in its conclusion, when it is not. If you can uncover fallacies in the work you're analyzing, you'll have a legitimate critique of the writer's rhetoric.

For our purposes, we'll focus on the fallacies that occur most often in the types of arguments you'll encounter in a writing class. Here are the usual suspects with brief definitions and examples that demonstrate the faulty reasoning at work:

Fallacy	Definition	Example
Faulty Cause and Effect or *post hoc, ergo propter hoc*	Causal claims can be tricky given the many variables that can be at work in a given equation. Without exploring other possibilities, this fallacy simplifies the relationship between two events by claiming that the first caused the second.	Ever since *Gossip Girl* became a popular show, teen promiscuity has increased.
Non Sequitur	This fallacy fails to move logically from the premise or reason to the conclusion, suggesting a logical relationship between two points where no such relationship is proven.	Plastic surgery for pre-teens is a dangerous trend. Have you noticed how much work has been done on the faces of members of Congress lately?
Hasty Generalization	An argument that moves to its conclusion without sufficient evidence commits a hasty generalization.	My neighbor's cat hissed at me when I walked past her porch. Cats don't like people.
Straw Man	A straw man fallacy constructs a weaker, superficial version of an argument and then attacks it, rather than attacking the real argument.	The American family is in terrible trouble today because there is no respect for older generations. Think about young adults who would push their grandparents off the sidewalk if they got in the way.
Stacking the Deck (Special Pleading)	This fallacy provides information that supports the rhetor's view while ignoring or sublimating any information that supports contrary opinions.	Rod Blagojevich was an excellent state governor. He expanded health programs for children, instituted statewide smoking bans, and signed a comprehensive death penalty reform bill.
Begging the Question	This line of reasoning employs as evidence the very information being challenged by the argument.	Forcing students to write research papers is a waste of time because research papers are dumb and useless.
Appeal to Majority	When a rhetor argues in favor of a position based on its popularity with others, an appeal to majority is at work.	Most people believe that poison ivy is contagious, so we had better keep Decker home from school today.

Fallacy	Definition	Example
Dogmatism	The argument here is that only one acceptable view exists, and those who disagree are simply wrong—no debate necessary. Dogmatic phrases are easy to recognize; if you've ever been told that *everyone who has studied the topic knows*…or *anyone informed on the matter agrees*, you've experienced dogmatism.	No one who has watched him play baseball believes he's not on steroids.
Moral Equivalence	This fallacy makes minor misdeeds comparable to major offenses.	Questioning the attendance policy is just like saying you don't value a university education.
Ad Hominem	Latin for "to the man," *ad hominem* arguments attack the individual making the argument rather than the argument itself.	Don't vote for the Tea Party candidate; he's a xenophobic bigot.
Either-Or Choices	At times, only two choices are available. The either-or proposition becomes a fallacy when a complex issue with more than two courses of action is presented as an ultimatum with only one acceptable choice and one highly undesirable option.	In his speech after 9/11, President Bush stated, "either you are with us or you are with the terrorists."
Slippery Slope	The slippery slope fallacy begins by accepting that a first step is not harmful on its own, but insists that the danger lies in the doom that is sure to follow.	If we pull our troops out of Afghanistan, we'll help spread tyranny across the globe.
Scare Tactics	Relying on our imaginative capacity, scare tactics discourage us from verifying the factual basis of an argument by playing on our fears.	Potential changes in federal law demand your immediate attention! You may be in danger of losing your student loan unless you send this reply card to Robber Baron National Bank today.
Bandwagon Appeal	This appeal encourages an action based on its presumed popularity with others. It asks us to get on board, lest we be left behind.	Everyone is on Facebook!

Of course, not every text you critique will lend itself to all of the above analytical methods. If a text works strictly within the Toulmin model of argumentation, for example, you won't consider how well it employs the Rogerian model, but you can certainly evaluate the rhetor's use of the appeals and uncover fallacies of reasoning.

Now that you've got some ways to objectively summarize and critically analyze the rhetorical effectiveness of your source material, you may be thinking about formally proposing a topic for your research paper.

Writing the Proposal

Once you've chosen a topic, your instructor might require you to submit a research proposal to prove that your idea is suitable for the larger paper assignment. A proposal or prospectus for a research project is a unique academic convention distinct from the typical academic paper in a few key ways. First, you're probably used to writing academic papers that begin with an argument represented by your thesis statement and supported by adequate detailed evidence, right? Well, for the research proposal, you get to take a break from these common requirements. While the proposal does assert that the topic you've chosen is appropriate for the assignment your instructor has given, you're not yet making an argument on that topic. After all, you still have a lot of research to do before you determine what position to take in the larger debate, and in the meantime, you'll want to remain unbiased and open to all points of view. However, you do want to describe the exigency or controlling reason that compelled you to write about this topic.

HOW WILL I KNOW IF I'VE CHOSEN A WORKABLE TOPIC?

If your instructor has allowed you the creative license to select your own research topic for your project, you've also been given a tremendous responsibility. Choosing the right topic takes careful thought and some preliminary research. DePaul's library database provides some helpful starting points like *CQ Researcher* and *Academic Search Premiere*, but any topic you find will need to be carefully tailored to the demands of the assignment. Therefore, the best way to test a topic's viability is to review the assignment prompts provided by your instructor and make certain that you can fulfill the demands described there with your chosen topic.

Here are some additional ideas to help you determine whether you've selected a viable topic:

Scope

Can this topic be treated fairly in the page limit given by your instructor? For example, you can't adequately address steroids in sports in only 6–8 pages, but maybe you can focus on one professional sport and the steroids commonly used by its players within a given time period. Let's say you limit to cycling and even a particular competitive event in that sport, like the Tour de France. Now you've narrowed to a topic that you can research with strategic focus and write about with adequate detail.

Argument

Does a legitimate debate exist here? A viable topic for a complex academic research paper must include intelligent and informed points of view on at least two sides of an issue. Returning to the topic mentioned above, a question like, "should steroids be allowed in professional sports," might lead you away from a legitimate debate. The question requires one side to reply with an affirmative, yes. But does anyone take this view? And, if so, are supporters well balanced to their opposition? Repositioning the question to "Are rhetorical strategies used by convicted dopers able to repair their public images"—the question addressed in Mark Glantz's essay appearing in Part 2—leads toward a paper better suited to academic research and debate.

Complexity

Does answering your research question—the central question your research paper poses—require the collection and analysis of material from multiple credible sources, or can it be answered by simply tracking down and arranging straightforward facts and relevant observations? If the latter is true, your topic may not result in an interesting and productive argument. If you can detect a central problem or tension among scholars who address this topic in your preliminary research, the topic probably has the complexity to sustain a lengthy research paper.

WHO IS THE AUDIENCE FOR MY RESEARCH PROPOSAL?

If your instructor has asked that you write for a given audience, be sure to think carefully about that group's assumptions and values as they relate to your topic. In general, you can pretend that you are presenting your ideas to a panel of academic judges who are knowledgeable about your topic, and who will determine whether your project has the potential to contribute meaningfully to the ongoing conversation about it. In order to convince this panel that your work deserves its support, you'll want to show knowledge of this conversation, including important moments—both historical and recent—in the conversation's life cycle. Note that the judges sitting on your imaginary panel may have different positions on your topic among them, and your goal is to win their trust by appearing as a neutral, knowledgeable, and credible writer interested in illuminating dark moments in the conversation's history and lighting the corridors to its future.

WHAT SHOULD MY PROPOSAL INCLUDE?

Given that you're not submitting and supporting an argument (except that your topic is worth investigating), you might wonder what should be in your proposal. You should consult your instructor's assignment prompt and guidelines to determine this, but proposals commonly include the following parts:

- An announcement of your topic
- Your research question
- Identification of stakeholders
- Background information that contextualizes your topic
- An outline of the debate scholars have on your topic
- Summaries of the views held on all sides of the debate
- A statement of your proposed project's academic merit

In sum, you'll want to think of your research proposal as a map for the journey your research project will take to its final destination. The clearer the map, the more likely you are to get there.

Here is a sample paper from a student proposing a final research paper on the efficacy of methods intending to reduce teen pregnancy rates in America.

Samantha Ford

WRD 104

Erin MacKenna

8 May 2009

Final Paper Proposal

The United States has the highest teenage pregnancy rate of any Western industrialized nation, and "approximately three million teens acquire a sexually transmitted infection each year" (Sendziuk 55). Democrats and Republicans believe that teen pregnancy and teenage STI rates are epidemics that need solutions; however, the two parties have different opinions how schools should go about preventing teenage pregnancy and STI. Those on the right contend that we should teach students an abstinence-only program and only mention contraceptives in regards to their faults and ineffectiveness in preventing pregnancy and Sexually Transmitted Infections. Social Liberals, however, argue that it is irresponsible not to provide our youth with a comprehensive sex education program, which promotes abstinence, but also gives teens medically accurate information about contraceptives. This debate continues to flourish as both sides offer evidence to support their claims.

Since 1991, the rate of teenage pregnancies in this country has declined. Conservatives claim this is due to the success of abstinence-only programs in high schools. When George W. Bush became president, there was an escalating increase in federal funds directed towards abstinence-only sex education programs. Federal funding for abstinence only programs jumped from "$60 million in 2000 to $176 million in 2008" (56). Right-wing groups such as the Heritage Foundation assert that these millions of dollars are well spent, saying that abstinence only programs influences teenage sexual behavior and postpone sex among teens until later on in life.

There has been one recent study in which the evidence suggests that these beliefs are accurate. Performed by Dr. Stan Weed, and published in the American Journal of Health Behavior, conservatives use Dr. Weed's findings to show that abstinence only programs "cut the rate of sexual activity among students roughly in half" (Shaw-Crouse par. 2). Adding to the study's credibility, in the state of Georgia, for example, pregnancy rates have been dropping steadily for 11 years since abstinence only programs were mandated (Huber par. 3). Backers of abstinence only programs also say:

> Abstinence programs offer a holistic approach, teaching teens how to build healthy relationships, increase self-worth and set appropriate boundaries in order to achieve future goals. Abstinence education shares the realities of sexually transmitted diseases and the best way to prevent them. Accurate information about contraception is provided, but always within the context of abstinence as the healthiest choice. The realistic limitations of condoms are shared but without the explicit demonstration and advocacy that characterizes "comprehensive" programs. (Huber par. 2)

Supporters of abstinence-only programs also cite positive outcomes for abstinent teens versus the negative outcomes one could experience if they are sexually active. Those on the right contend that abstinent teens "have, on average, higher academic achievement and better psychological well-being than those who are sexually active" (Shaw-Crouse par. 10). Teenage sex is usually a negative experience and most teenagers who have sex later regret it, says some conservative advocates of abstinence only sex education. With all the apparent successes of abstinence-only programs in our high schools, conservatives continue to stand by this policy.

The social liberals, on the other hand, completely disagree and are quick to point out flaws in the other side's methods of research. They claim that there is strong evidence to support that abstinence-only programs are failing and, may in fact, be counterproductive in preventing teenage pregnancy and Sexually Transmitted Infections. "A recent review of abstinence programs in the United States found that pregnancy rates among partners of young male abstinence-program participants were no lower than those among the partners of nonparticipants" (Sendziuk 56). Another argument made is that European countries have a significantly lower rate of teenage pregnancies than the United States, and they teach a comprehensive sex education program in their schools. Liberals argue that America should be following their example and by teaching abstinence only we are going "backwards." Furthermore, liberal organizations such as SIECUS or (the Sexuality Information and Education Council of the United States) call studies that claim abstinence-only programs are effective (these studies are also usually funded by conservative programs that support abstinence-only education such as the Heritage Foundation) "garbage science." Many supporters of a comprehensive sex education program in our schools, such as William Smith, vice president of public policy at SIECUS, believe that:

> The ideologues [on the right] want more and more emphasis on the benefits of marriage. They're trying to craft an argument that marriage is a public health intervention, but beneath the surface there is a moral and religious argument. They [social conservatives] are trying to hijack a public health message (Friedman 765).

Liberals also believe that many of the federal dollars allocated towards abstinence-only programs often fund religious foundations, whose goal, along with abstinence, is to convert young people to Christianity (765). This would clearly violate separation of church and state. With this interpretation of evidence, Democrats continue to push for legislation to provide a more comprehensive sex education program in our high schools, which as of now has had little success.

CHAPTER 2
MANAGING INFORMATION

As you become more familiar with the conversation going on around your topic, you need to find methods of tracking and evaluating the information that you assemble. This task requires that you have the sense of direction that comes from defining not only your topic but also your stance.

FINDING YOUR STANCE

Your **stance** is the specific position that you take on your topic. Popular images of argument often envision the stance as simply pro or con. However, you actually have many more options. Your choice depends on numerous factors including the scope of available information, the nature of your priorities, and even the time available for the project. Thinking in terms of a popular metaphor first imagined by Kenneth Burke (1897–1993), an American literary theorist and philosopher, can help you navigate these choices and find your stance for your research topic.

Imagine that you are just arriving at a party where a conversation has been taking place for quite some time. You're not sure how long those involved have been talking, but it's clear that the topic is well established among them and a debate has emerged. Being the newcomer, you listen for a while to gain background information and to get a handle on the various positions. When you're ready, you contribute your thoughts on the matter. Are you likely to simply restate someone else's view? Probably not. Intuitively, you understand that this would be of little value to the group. You know you want to use what you've learned to contribute a new and original perspective that advances the discussion, but how can you, given the length and breadth of the discussion and your late arrival?

Luckily, academic discussions value nuance, so even a modest point can become an important contribution to the larger discussion. It's better to explain and support a single smaller point well than to make sweeping but unsupported or unproductive claims. Here are ways to contribute thoughtfully to an academic discussion:

- **Develop additional reasons.** You can support the same stance as another participant in the conversation, but for different reasons.
- **Adjust the scope.** You can offer local applications to a universal argument.
- **Make a comparison.** Show similarities or differences between two issues or points of view.
- **Demonstrate applicability.** You can offer a practical application to a theoretical argument.

The goal is to avoid reiterating a position already put forth by another partygoer in favor of contributing your own unique and thoughtful view to the discussion.

Review the three case studies below to see how these writers selected and developed their stances for arguments with multiple sources.

 CASE STUDY:

Demetrius never doubted the topic for his research paper. He wanted to write about closed brain injuries because his father, a junior high gym teacher, had sustained a life-threatening injury in the course of a fall on the basketball court. At first Demetrius wanted to argue that these brain injuries were serious and devastating for families. Then he realized that everyone agrees with this position. Who is going to come out in favor of brain injuries or say that they are minor health issues? On the other hand, Demetrius didn't feel that he had the time or education to deal with highly specialized medical arguments about the treatment of these injuries. He almost gave up on his topic. In his mind, he kept going back to what it was like for his mother and siblings to cope with so many questions and unknowns while they sat for hours in the ICU waiting room. He also remembered the happy but scary day that his Dad came home and the family had to handle his memory loss and physical challenges. Then it hit him that he was working towards a practical stance: he wanted to argue that the families of brain-injured patients need specialized information written in language they could understand. His argument became a proposal for a booklet and hotline.

 CASE STUDY:

Esther wanted to write about the motivations of celebrities who give money to charity. She suspected that many of them were not sincerely interested in the causes they supported, but rather were polishing their public images. As she thought through her stance, members of her writing group challenged her on how she could prove what these celebrities truly felt or intended. When Esther started to read about celebrity charities, she found that the press had already raised the issue of the effectiveness of celebrity charities, but they didn't deal with the issue of underlying motives. She still couldn't find any proof. On the other hand, she found that some celebrities were able to raise both consciousness and cash for a variety of worthwhile causes. She also discovered some charities that were in financial disarray because the celebrity was not well-versed in the management of the funds. She decided to take the stance that celebrities could be effective fund-raisers if they worked with professional non-profit managers.

CASE STUDY:

Eric's instructor had his class choose a paper topic that related to an aspect of education that interested them. Eric wanted to be an accountant, and his biggest interest was sports. Even though he was a good student, he felt despair over a whole term of reading about education policy. His first internet search seemed random and pointless. Remembering a clustering exercise from a previous writing course, he wrote education, money, and sports on a sheet of paper and tried to find lines of connection among his terms. As he worked, he remembered an argument he had with his roommate about whether it was fair that athletes got priority registration for classes. He began to look into the advantages offered to student athletes at colleges around the country, but he wondered if he would be able to find sources beyond the sports pages on his topic. When his class visited the library, he asked the librarian if there were sources that would give his argument academic credibility. Together they found studies in a number of fields about policies for student athletes. After doing some preliminary research, Eric narrowed his topic from the general subject of the advantages offered to student athletes to the varying GPA and academic achievement requirements for athletic eligibility and how they impact the athletes' career success after college. He successfully linked finances, education, and sports in an argument that mattered to him.

Like these students, you may arrive at your stance in stages. This is a positive thing. Uncertainty and changes of direction can be signs that you are pursuing real intellectual inquiry.

When you're trying to find a stance, it's helpful to return periodically to the following checklist:

✓   Is this argument necessary? Is there room for disagreement or at least multiple viewpoints?
✓   Are there accessible evidence, testimony, and examples to back up my stance?
✓   Can I handle the necessary research in the available time?
✓   Do I care enough about this topic to convince someone else?

Notice that Demetrius reframed his stance so that this argument had **exigency**, a reason for being. On the other hand, Esther recast her stance to a position that was provable from the available evidence.

Once you have indentified your stance, then you are ready to seek proofs in a targeted, effective search. Take the time to make a list of the kinds of evidence you'll need.

EXAMPLE: Demetrius' list of evidence:

- Find evidence that there really is a problem. Do other families report similar questions and concerns as my family?
- Do medical professionals report any problems in communicating with families?

- Is there any material already out there for families of closed brain injury patients?
- Is there similar material for other kinds of conditions?
- What media do medical institutions use to communicate with families who are dealing with brain injuries?
- How do current materials meet or fail to meet the needs of regular people?

STANCE AND CONTEXT: WILL YOUR STANCE FIT YOUR RHETORICAL SITUATION?

As you consider what stance to take on your topic, be sure you have a clear understanding of the assignment and select a stance that allows you to fulfill its requirements. Do you have enough space to fully discuss and develop the most important ideas in your argument? If not, you will find changing your stance can make this possible. If your paper is meant to be only 6–8 pages long, you won't be able to treat fairly a debate on abortion because there is not enough room to fully discuss such a big topic.

 EXAMPLE:

See the list below for an example of using stance to establish the parameters of your inquiry. Instead of working with the whole topic, you select a manageable segment of it. Note how a potential topic becomes much more manageable as we move down the list:

1. abortion
2. reproductive rights
3. conscience clause protecting pharmacists
4. conscience clause protecting pharmacists in Illinois

This process has reshaped a position on reproductive rights in general to a particular state's public policy. The resulting argument will be easier to explain and to support.

The way you articulate your stance will also help you find your audience. For example, if you want to argue that pharmacists who refuse contraception to patients should not be protected against legal action, your audience could be a congressional committee or an action group that might help draft public policy.

Until now, we've suggested that you remain neutral while choosing your topic and examining your preliminary sources. Once you have a stance, think of it as a new pair of glasses through which you'll review your initial sources and their arguments. Keep wearing your glasses as you look for and evaluate new sources.

FINDING AND EVALUATING SOURCES

Sources perform many valuable functions in your argument. The sources you consult in your preliminary research help you to understand the public conversation on an issue and help you to find where your concerns fit in to the larger picture. As your argument progresses, sources play an even larger role in your argument. They can provide:

- background and context for your argument.
- essential voices of the conversation in your field.
- credibility with your audience.
- evidence for your reasons.
- anecdotes and quotes to illustrate ideas.
- images and visuals that clarify and compel.

FINDING SOURCES

In daily life, when you need information, you may ask your friends and turn to your favorite search engine with a side trip to Wikipedia. However, when acting as a person of power and authority, you need to be more critical about your methods. We suggest that you use the resources of your college library. Academic institutions support databases that are far more specialized and selective than many of the popular databases we find on the internet search engines. In addition, college librarians have specialized training in how to help you find exactly the kinds of sources that your instructor requires, including scholarly journals or government documents. Your library will not only help you get better information, it will also save you time. If you are still skeptical, consider the following case studies:

 CASE STUDY:

Kevin is interested in body-building. He works out daily in his gym and he talks to some of the other body-builders about steroids. He decided he would like to write an argument for his rhetoric class defending steroid use. As the deadline for the annotated bibliography approached, he interviewed the most muscular people at his gym, and he did a quick search on steroids. He decided to use the first four or five articles that he found on the web. His professor commented that his sources were not authoritative or credible. One was a fourteen year old with his own blog and another was supported by a drug company in another country that sells substances that are not approved for sale in the U.S. He had a hard time sorting out the issues and he couldn't figure out the opposing views. After falling further and further behind on the drafts of the assignment, he got a C- on the paper.

CASE STUDY:

Neil also wanted to research steroids. He is a student athlete who is concerned about high performance, eligibility, and long-term health. Early in the course, he used his college library's online exercise to get an overview of resources in his field. He also checked with the reference librarian about the best databases and specialized reference books in the field. She suggested that he break his subject down into key words and subject areas so that he could target his research. In the course of his paper, Neil interviewed his coach and fellow athletes, but he also had a mix of government studies, a feature story in Sports Illustrated *on banned substances, a journal on sports medicine, and an article on violence associated with some banned substances. He ended up getting an A and having his paper accepted into the university's writing showcase.*

Although information you access through the library database is most likely to put you in a good position to craft a strong argument, other sources that are not traditionally considered "academic" may still have a place in your bibliography and can also help you build a strong argument. For example, you may find leaflets or information sheets that give the history of a building or organization when you do a site visit. The important things to consider when deciding on the sources you will include in your argument are the assignment parameters, what you are using the source for, and how it will be perceived by your audience.

IDENTIFYING AND CLASSIFYING SOURCES

Understanding the range of sources and how they work in your paper is crucial to your success in argumentation. Academic writing values balanced and varied sources, so you'll need to know how to identify and use them.

A traditional classification system divides sources into primary and secondary sources.

Primary sources come from first-hand participation or observation. Descriptions of a battle by soldiers on the front line or by civilians caught in the crossfire would be primary sources. The documentary film maker Ken Burns used this kind of material brilliantly in his television series *The Civil War* when he included letters and diaries from the Union and Confederate troops and from their families. Other kinds of primary sources would be documents like census records or the passenger lists of ocean liners.

Secondary sources are at one remove from the events themselves because they build their arguments on primary and other secondary sources by analyzing or interpreting them. An entry from a historical encyclopedia on Civil War weaponry would be a secondary source, as would an article in an academic journal analyzing the role of women's magazines in supporting and upholding the southern cause. Perhaps you know someone who has written a family history that uses city directories or church records to trace the movement of generations from one location to the next.

People who classify sources may apply different standards. The strictest standards might restrict primary sources to original documents, like the manuscript of a diary or letter. More inclusive standards might still count an edited and published version of a civil war diary or the Illinois Territorial Papers as a primary source. Online sources present opportunities for a lively debate about how to classify sources. The point is that you need to understand the distinction but that no set of rules can take the place of your own critical thinking and dialogue with your instructor.

Another approach to sources classifies them by type.

Data is material like statistics or measurements that can be independently verified. The population of Chicago at the time of the legendary fire or the height of Mount Everest would be data.

Testimony comes in two major categories:

> **Eyewitness accounts** from people who participate or observe an event: a parent who has triplets and a job as an airline pilot could give eyewitness testimony on work/life balance.

> **Expert opinions** from people with professional credentials: a behavioral psychologist could provide expert testimony on the effects of work/life balance issues on pilot alertness.

Laws, public policies, and regulations have a special status, especially in arguments about what is permissible and possible. These also represent a society's or community's established rules for governing behavior. A company's employee handbook would state what attire is appropriate for the workplace. A state law like the Illinois Workmen's Compensation Act might stipulate whether a particular injury is covered under Workmen's Compensation.

Images and recordings: Especially with the move to electronic documents, images and recordings allow you to show as well as tell about crucial aspects of your argument. You can share film footage of JFK's inaugural address or include close-ups of Roger Federer's serve.

DETERMINING THE QUALITY OF SOURCES

Even when you are sure that you can classify your source, you may still be wondering how good it is. Will it help your argument and convince your readers? Here are some key points to determining the value of a source:

Currency

In most cases, it is better to have the *most recent* sources available. In some cases, it is essential. For instance, if you are researching cancer treatment, you would want the most recent medical developments. Even if you are looking at something more scholarly or historical, like Aristotle's views on rhetoric, the most recent scholarship will often give an overview of major opinions that have come before. At the same time, eyewitness sources from the past may be highly valuable if you are making the point that the language of racism has consistent themes over a variety of historical periods.

Authority

You want sources who know what they are writing about. Either they should have been there or they should have studied and understood the material. Avoid sources that don't allow you to judge the credentials of the author. Especially with web publications, you may be dealing with an author who is simply cutting and pasting, or, even worse, deliberately misleading readers.

Balance

Instructors often require balanced sources. You can achieve balance in several ways. Some sources present an overview of the major positions that people may take on an issue. You can also use highly partisan sources as long as you can identify their stances and evaluate their evidence and methodology. Make sure that you cover the major sides or positions in the public conversation on your topic. Even if you are looking for support for your point of view, don't neglect opposing viewpoints.

WHOM DO YOU TRUST?

Your instructor tells you to find the most authoritative scholars in your field. But you're a beginner and you have no clue. You can't figure out which economic views are liberal or conservative or whose methodology is meticulous and whose is suspect. You don't want to base your whole paper on a shaky foundation, so what do you do?

Here are some factors that will help you decide if your source is trustworthy:

Look at the **publisher**. University presses and professional organizations seek the kind of well-documented sources that will support your argument.

Look at the **citations**. If an author gives credit to sources that support the claim and provides notes and a bibliography, you are on safer ground in citing the text.

Research the **author**. A few clicks of the button can tell you a lot about the educational background and publication history.

Use the **university library** and its **databases**. The librarians and the university faculty collaborate to create a collection that is worth your time and attention.

ANNOTATING YOUR BIBLIOGRAPHY

If your professor assigns an annotated bibliography during or after your research, you may be tempted to think that it's just another exercise rather than an integral part of your writing process. But try not to conceive of your annotated bibliography as something that's separate from your research paper—it isn't. Your annotated bibliography is a valuable initial step toward forming your own argument. Think of it as the foundation of your paper, rather than something distinct from it.

While your instructor may have special guidelines he or she wants you to follow, generally an annotated bibliography consists of an alphabetized list of sources you have read in your research. Each source is accompanied by an annotation, which consists of a brief unbiased summary and a short description of the purpose the source will serve in your paper.

 EXAMPLE of an annotation

Machiavelli, Niccolo. *The Prince*. Trans. N.H. Thompson. Mineola, New York: Dover, 1962.

This classic work was written in 1553 as a guide for rulers to seize and maintain power. It uses historical examples and the events of Machiavelli's time to give amoral and practical advice on subjects like the advisability of lying, the importance of avoiding flattery, and the need to control public opinion. The guidelines are purely pragmatic with little attention to conventional morality, as when Machiavelli accepts the value of torture. This book is an important document for the study of Italian politics in the sixteenth century, but students of government and

 **TIME** *saver*

When you make a judgment about a source, write it down. Label the bibliography entries for each source with the category of source and make notes about its authority and possible uses in your paper. Make sure to include all the information that your citation system requires.

Sample Bibliographical Label

Ehrenreich, Barbara.
Nickel and Dimed: On (Not) Getting By in America. New York: Henry Holt, 2001.
Primary Source. Investigative journalism by reporter who worked undercover in minimum wage jobs. Recognized as *New York Times* Notable Book. Great source of anecdotes and examples; also has well-cited research.

politics have also applied its concepts to other eras up to the present day. Readers debate both the ethics of the work's advice and of its author. Students of rhetoric cite it as an example of a powerful and enduring argument.

Collecting your research in an annotated bibliography serves several purposes. It allows you to catalogue the information, ideas, and perspectives you have read during your research. It also gives you the opportunity to analyze and evaluate your choice of sources for your argument. Here are some things to consider as you work on your annotated bibliography:

Guidelines of the assignment—Usually, your instructor will provide you with guidelines for the types of sources you should include in your bibliography. Look over these guidelines carefully as you research. Your instructor may require you to:

- cite a specific number of sources.
- choose sources that have been published after a certain year to ensure their currency.
- present balanced sources that represent multiple viewpoints.
- include a specific percentage of scholarly versus popular sources.
- avoid certain sources, such as Wikipedia.
- follow a specific policy for online sources.
- include or avoid categories of reference sources like general encyclopedias.

Keeping these guidelines in mind will help you to meet the requirements of an annotated bibliography assignment, as well as to build your ethos as a disciplined researcher.

Rhetorical Contexts—As you begin to compile your sources, consider the rhetorical context of each one. Who is the source's author, and what was his purpose for writing it? How would you describe the intended audience of the source? What sort of publication did you find it in? When was it published? Being aware of the elements of the source's original rhetorical context will allow you to judge how the source will function within your own rhetorical context. Would *your* audience consider the source credible? Will it help *you* be credible as a thinker and writer on your subject?

Summarizing—As you begin to select the sources you will include, take the time to read and analyze each of them carefully so that you can create a clear, accurate, concise, and unbiased summary. You may want to review the guidelines for writing a good summary in Chapter 1. Although scrutinizing multiple sources at once may seem daunting, doing a thorough job of it now will be immensely helpful when you begin to write your paper. The familiarity you will have gained with your sources will allow you to more effectively engage them in your own writing.

Format and Style—Check with your instructor about which citation format he or she would prefer. Each citation style—MLA, APA, etc.,—has its own format for citations and guidelines for document layout. Regardless of which citation style you use, be sure to follow the format carefully, taking into consideration elements like line indentations, spacing, and punctuation placement. Proper citation form will suggest to your reader that you are careful, thorough, and have an eye for detail. Refer to your handbook for formatting guidelines and examples.

Learning from the Overview—Once you have a draft of your annotated bibliography, take a step back and consider the sources you've compiled as a group. Taking a bird's eye view of your sources can help you gauge if you are prepared to enter into the debate going on within your topic and if you will function well in your rhetorical context. The following checklist will help you to decide if you are ready to enter your argument:

- ✓ Do you feel as though you are ready to enter your argument?
- ✓ Have you gathered enough background information?
- ✓ Have you familiarized yourself with enough perspectives on your topic?
- ✓ Are you up on the current ideas and well-known experts who write on your topic?

You can use your annotated bibliography as a litmus test to predict how successful your project will be, and to make adjustments accordingly.

When you've finished your annotated bibliography, and you are comfortable that it represents a good starting point for your argument, congratulate yourself. You've created a defined space within a larger conversation and given yourself the tools to step into that space with your own ideas and perspective.

CHAPTER 3
PUTTING IT TOGETHER

DRAFTING YOUR ARGUMENT

Almost every writer struggles with getting started. Just knowing that you need to produce written material can cause anxiety. Crafting a well-written argument—particularly a multi-source research-based one—is a complex and time-consuming task. While any anxiety you feel is understandable, it's important to remember that the longer you wait to begin, the more difficult your project will be to complete. This section will provide you with some ideas and suggestions that may help you take that initial step.

PREWRITING

Prewriting is the planning and work that happens before you begin to compose. This stage of writing is often overlooked, but it can be an important time to get organized and to think about your direction. Spending time planning before you start composing can make the journey easier. You will likely need to do some tweaking along the way, but these practices are a good way to get started.

- Organize all of your source materials and notes. Review them, noting common themes and ideas. What is the most important? The least important?
- Annotate the assignment instructions. Highlight and mark any areas of emphasis. Note any questions you may have and contact your instructor to resolve them.
- Focused brainstorming and list making are also part of the prewriting stage. You may want to focus on creating a traditional outline, or simply list the major claims in your argument.
- Consider your audience's knowledge, assumptions and attitude towards your topic. How will this affect your choice of rhetorical appeals? How can you reach this audience?

Spend some time reviewing the results of your prewriting. As you begin drafting, you will be juggling ideas (your own and others') along with materials.

DRAFTING

Drafting is actually one of the last stages of writing your argument. By the time you sit down to write a draft, you should have made decisions about your:

Audience	Who are you writing to? What do you want to tell them? How do you want them to react to your argument?
Appeals	What rhetorical appeals will you employ to best communicate with this audience?
Claims	What are your main ideas? How will they contribute to the conversation you've entered?
Sources	How will your sources support these main ideas?

Once you have thought about these components of your essay, you are ready to explore some ways of working with them. Good drafts are explorations, and explorations can be challenging and unpredictable. Don't worry—you will have the opportunity to make changes and corrections in the revision stage. The important thing now is to begin writing.

There are many ways to begin. The key is knowing what works for you. You'll want to think carefully about how you work best. Understanding your habits, your strengths, and what keeps you from writing can make a big difference. Some common "writing roadblocks" and solutions are listed below:

Roadblock	Solution
I need a quiet space to work.	Try working in a quiet section of the library or an empty classroom. You can also turn any space into a quiet space by buying a set of earplugs to keep the noise out.
I have trouble working alone.	Form a writers' group—connect with your classmates and set a weekly date to get together and work on your writing.
I get stuck at the beginning.	There is no rule that all writing must start at the beginning. Start in the middle. Start at the end. Write whatever you have to say; you can go back later and move things to the proper positions.
I lose my train of thought easily.	Experiment with prewriting and brainstorming exercises. Write down anything that comes into your head, even if it conflicts with the section you are composing. You can review and arrange later.
I procrastinate.	Try setting early deadlines for yourself. Make appointments with your instructor or a tutor to discuss your work. This will force you to stay ahead of schedule.
I don't know where to start.	Read the assignment instructions. Make a list of questions and check with your instructor for answers. See Chapter 1 for brainstorming ideas. Begin to outline or organize your main ideas before you start writing.

Once you have some ideas in writing, begin thinking about how to tailor them to the rhetorical situation.

DECIDING ON A STRUCTURE

Working with widely recognized models for argumentation will help you to organize the work that you have been doing on integrating your sources into a coherent whole. It may also help you to find holes in your research or gaps in your thinking. Maybe you're missing some key definitions or the history of the problem, or maybe you haven't thought enough about how your examples and data connect to your claim.

Your instructor may specify a model for your argument, or leave the choice to you. Here are some major forms of argument and some pointers about how they could connect with your purpose and your audience.

The Classical Model

This model gets its name from its origins in the rhetorical practices of classical Greece and Rome. If you are trying to move an audience, this system will help you to keep them involved and interested. Classical rhetoricians prized a high level of emotional literacy. You can see this in the excerpt from Aristotle's *On Rhetoric* in Part Two of this book.

Here are the elements of the classical model and a description of their functions:

- The **introduction** gets readers involved and interested as it builds to the announcement of your claim.
- The **background** helps readers to follow your discussion by explaining context and terms.
- The **outline** gives readers the steps or main stages of the argument so that they can follow its progress.
- The **presentation of your case** lays out the reasons that support your claim and backs them with evidence.
- The **presentation of opposing or alternative views** concedes points that the opposition may have right and rebuts major claims of the opposing argument.
- The **conclusion** makes a final appeal to the audience to accept and act on your argument by reinforcing its benefits and reminding of the consequences of failing to accept it.

This outline is just the beginning, though. Depending on your aims and circumstances, you can rearrange this argument in numerous ways. For instance, if you have reason to believe that your audience hates you or your stance, you might start with the rebuttal so that you can actively address the negative atmosphere. If your subject is confusing or highly technical, you will need to spend more time on the background and use the outline to break the big picture into easier steps. On the other hand, if the argument is on a well-known and popular subject, you will be able to move much more quickly to your reasons. You can find out what you need to do by user-testing the argument. See the section on "Testing Audience Response" later in this chapter for some ideas on how to get good feedback.

THE TOULMIN MODEL

Another important model for arguments is derived from the work the British philosopher Stephen Toulmin (1922–2009). Rhetoricians and writing instructors find his ideas helpful in understanding and explaining the support for a claim. His method is especially useful if you are arguing to clarify. Many academic arguments aim to create knowledge and to establish definitions rather than to create policies or move people to action. The Toulmin approach is particularly suited to assignments that analyze these types of arguments, but it also can provide a framework for organizing your own argument.

Here are some of the major features of Toulmin analysis:

- The **claim** states that something is true or a course of action is desirable.
- **Qualifiers** scale down a claim so that it corresponds with the available evidence. Claims may be true only in certain cases or under certain circumstances. Many arguments become vulnerable because they are too broad. Adding the right qualifiers puts your argument in a much more defensible position.
- The **warrant** is a bridge-like idea that the audience must accept to move from the grounds to the claim. A careful examination of warrants guards against the kind of argument that sounds good but falls apart under closer examination.
- The **backing** presents evidence such as data or testimony that supports the warrant.
- **Rebuttals** recognize and answer opposing views.

THE ROGERIAN MODEL

During the Cold War that followed World War II, the psychologist Karl Rogers (1902–1987) noticed that nations on opposite sides of the Iron Curtain had mirror images of each other as aggressive and destructive societies. He thought about how discussion can polarize participants and the public in a way that is dangerous in a world with nuclear weapons. In response, he explored forms of interaction that could allow individuals and groups to work through differences without becoming more and more hostile. His model is a foundation for the practice of mediation which occurs today in areas from international forums to school playgrounds. This framework also appeals to rhetoricians who want to make win-win arguments.

The Rogerian Model:

- expresses respect for the problem and the stakeholders.
- describes opposing views in a neutral and respectful manner.
- presents the benefits of speaker's position to all parties.
- establishes a mutually agreeable solution or at least to keeps the lines of communication open.

You can see that there is crossover among these three models, but the differences might help you to focus your argument on your goals. If your concern is to lead an audience to belief and action, the classical model may have more helpful ideas. If you are concerned with demonstrating how a line of reasoning works or breaks down, Toulmin may be the more useful structure. The Rogerian model reduces the idea of argument as a struggle between views or people and emphasizes the discovery of common ground.

INTEGRATING YOUR RESEARCH

Once you have begun writing your draft, you may be wondering about the best way to incorporate your research into your own argument. Considering the amount and variety of information that you may have gathered during your research, organizing and shaping it may seem like overwhelming tasks. Here we would like to present you with strategies for combining your research and your own ideas to produce an effective argument. As we move to the next stage, remember that the writing process isn't a straight line. You may need to return to some of the earlier stages of the project as you write.

As you start to work with the information you have collected, you will immediately start to reap the benefits of your careful selection and evaluation of your sources. If you've chosen good sources, analyzed their rhetorical context, and considered the role they will play in your argument, you are well on your way to integrating your research into your argument effectively.

 CONSIDER *this*

Don't abandon research yet! Beginning to integrate your sources into your writing, even in a complete initial draft, does not necessarily mean that you are finished with your research. In fact, your early efforts to put all the pieces of your argument together may allow you to see more clearly what information you lack, which aspects of your topic you could expand, and what questions remain unanswered. Sometimes research gives rise to more research—and that's okay. Thinking of your research as an ongoing process—even throughout the drafting and revision of your paper—will help you stay attuned to opportunities for making your paper even better.

PURPOSES AND LOCATION

One way to get started integrating your sources into your writing is to map out how you will use them. If you've written an annotated bibliography of your sources, you may have already addressed the relevance of each source for your project. Here are some of the reasons to use sources in an argument:

- To provide background or context
- To trace what other people have said before you
- To serve as evidence or support for the points you are making
- To serve as examples of the phenomenon you want to discuss
- To support your point of view
- To serve as a counterpoint to your point of view

As you think about what each source will do for you, you can begin to think about how you want to integrate it. One of the first things you'll need to decide is where the source should appear in your paper. This decision goes hand in hand with what you want to use the source for.

Does the source provide some background information that you believe your readers should know before they get very far into your argument? If a source provides information that you believe is the strongest point of support for your own view, should you present it early in your argument, or should you save the best for last? If one of your sources provides a view that goes against your own, where would be the most effective place for you to address that counterpoint? Regardless of your reason for using the source, *why* you are using it should inform *where* you integrate it into your own text. For some more ideas about structuring your text, review the next sections on "Deciding on a Structure" and "Drafting Your Argument" in this chapter.

METHODS FOR INCORPORATING SOURCES

If you have an idea of where each of your sources will make an appearance in your paper, the next thing to think about is how the source will be represented in your paper. There are three basic ways of incorporating material from your sources into your own writing: summarizing, paraphrasing, and quoting. Consult the chart on the next page for more information on how to incorporate these three forms into your writing.

You may choose a variety of these methods to incorporate information from a single source into your argument. You can think of yourself as a weaver, bringing threads and strands of thought together and entwining them in a way that creates a coherent whole.

In order to make a pleasing pattern, a weaver needs to be deliberate. The important thing is to consider what method of integration would best suit the information or ideas you want to integrate into your paper. Have a reason for why you choose to present your sources' ideas as you do:

	Definition	Purpose	Method	Considerations
Summarizing	A summary is a distilled overview of the most essential ideas or main argument of a source.	Use a summary of a source when it is important for the reader to understand the main argument or basic gist of the source.	For more information on writing a good summary, see Chapter 1 of this text.	• Remember to read the source carefully so you can offer the most accurate version of the ideas as possible. • In order to strengthen your ethos, make sure that you offer an unbiased version of the source's argument. That will demonstrate to your reader that you are an open-minded, critical thinker.
Paraphrasing	A paraphrase is a shorter passage or individual point or idea from a source that has been rewritten into your own words and sentence structures.	Use a paraphrase when you want to address a certain passage or section of a text, or an individual point or idea within the larger scope of that source's argument. Whereas a summary takes a step back and looks at the big picture, a paraphrase allows you to zero in on a smaller part of that whole.	To paraphrase well, reword the passage you've chosen *completely*. This means not just that you've changed the words, but also that you've reworked the structure of the sentence so that it sounds like something you would have written naturally. Consult your handbook for more information on how to write a good paraphrase.	As important as it is to change language to make it your own, it is equally important to make sure the ideas in your paraphrase are true to those in the original passage. Make sure you understand all the words in a passage—especially technical vocabulary and jargon—in order to accurately translate the author's ideas from her words to yours.
Quoting	A quote is a selection of exact words from the original text that you incorporate into your own writing using quotation marks.	Use a quote when the original author's words are particularly powerful or beautiful, or when you want your reader to hear the ideas in the author's own words for extra support or emphasis.	Make sure your quotation is punctuated correctly. Check your handbook for specific guidelines.	When you choose a quote to incorporate into your paper, ask yourself if you could communicate the information equally effectively in your own words. If you can, it would be better to paraphrase that passage.

ATTRIBUTING SOURCES

No matter what way you choose to incorporate your source material, it is very important to make sure that you attribute it to its original source. There are two ways to do this:

Signal Phrases

Signal phrases directly reference the writer of your source in the sentence itself, rather than citing his name only in a parenthetical citation. Signal phrases are especially valuable when you want to address another writer's perspective or ideas about your topic. Consult your handbook for examples of verbs you can use in signal phrases to help you put the spotlight on the conversation you have entered with your research.

 ### EXAMPLES OF SIGNAL PHRASES

In an op-ed column in The New York Times, *Maureen Dowd argued that* Barack Obama could learn from Sarah Palin's ability to engage her audience on an emotional level.

Philosopher and professor David Concepción urges professors to give students clear guidelines on how to understand and retain difficult reading material.

Formal citation

In most academic arguments, you must formally cite your sources regardless of how and where you choose to incorporate signal phrases. Formal citation includes things like parenthetical citation or footnotes, as well as your works cited page or bibliography. The method you use to incorporate formal citation into your paper will depend on which citation style you are using. Ask your instructor and consult your handbook for more information.

THE MOST IMPORTANT VOICE IS YOURS!

One of the most important things to remember about integrating your research into your argument is that despite having immersed yourself in texts written by other people, *you* are the writer of your argument. Consequently, your argument should above all else showcase your ideas in your own words. When you've been surrounded by sources written by experts who have spent a long time studying your topic, it can be tempting to rely on the information and ideas found in them, rather than on your own ideas. However, it's your argument, and your voice should emerge as the loudest in the conversation. It is good that you have learned from your sources, and it's natural to want to use them to demonstrate your extensive research on the topic. However, don't sell yourself short. Before you "hand over the mic" to another speaker, make sure that the quote or paraphrase adds something to the conversation. Your best tribute to the authors of your sources is to take their ideas and show why they are important, what you've done with them, and how you've advanced the conversation as a result.

EMPLOYING THE APPEALS

The rhetorical triangle envisions a text's writer, audience, and subject as the three sides. The writer, audience, and subject are each associated with an argumentative appeal. Traditionally they go by their Greek names of ethos, pathos, and logos.

- *Ethos* concerns how the audience feels about the writer or **speaker** and the type of credibility he/she manages to establish.
- *Pathos* involves the use of vivid language, examples, and anecdotes to arouse emotional involvement in the **audience**.
- *Logos* relates to the use of evidence about the **subject,** or message. It includes data, testimony, and reasoning.

Powerful writers understand the dynamic interplay among these appeals. You should consider how to incorporate the different types of appeals as you build an argument. Think about your own relationship to the subject and the audience.

For example, if you are arguing about lowering the drinking age to eighteen, and your audience is a congressional committee, know that your age might render your argument suspect. You'll want to take measures to bolster your credibility and head off accusations of a self-serving position.

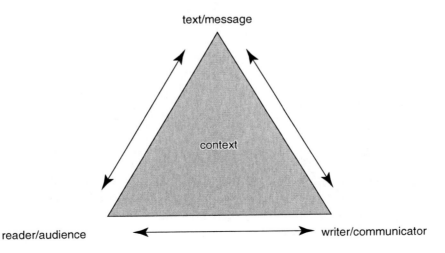

Of course, in some situations your age and experience might be very valuable. You have strong ethos as a representative of a new generation. Older people may be very eager to hear your views on college life or new media. In the end, there is almost always a way to manage the appeals to benefit your argument, but you'll need to be aware of the rhetorical situation.

The power of the appeals also means that you take on heavy ethical responsibilities when you construct them. If you present data and inspire trust, you have to be very sure that you are presenting accurate evidence that doesn't mislead your audience. If you tell vivid stories that arouse anger or fear, you need to think about the consequences and whether the reaction is productive and controllable.

The following case studies show writers shaping and revising the appeals in their arguments.

 CASE STUDY: A REVERSAL OF EXPECTED VALUES

Brittany is drafting an argument against factory farming. She develops three lines of argument: a vivid description of chickens living in a confined space with their beaks and claws maimed; a government report on viruses that can travel from factory-farmed animals to humans; and a description of the environmental damage caused by sewage from pig farms. Brittany loves animals. She is pretty sure that her description of the horrible living conditions in the crowded cages will be her most powerful reason.

She tests her list of reasons on her writing group and gets a surprise. They tell her that the chickens are going to die anyway, so their short stay in the cages hardly seems like the major issue. They also point out that they are students and that prices matter to them. If they can get cheaper food from factory farming, they are for it. However, they do worry about their health. If there is any chance that they can get an incurable disease that would make them look again at organic meats or even consider meatless diets.

Brittany is surprised, even shocked. She had never imagined readers who wouldn't take a chicken's suffering seriously. As she revises, she rearranges her material, placing more emphasis on the logos derived from information about health risks and less on the pathos of the animals' conditions. She goes back to her sources and looks at how they deal with a variety of audience reactions, and tries to find a way to make all the appeals count for a wider variety of readers.

 CASE STUDY: AN UNEXPECTED HOSTILE REACTION

Miguel is preparing a lecture aimed at students in residence halls about the dangers of binge drinking. He has pulled together statistics on its prevalence as well as examples of the risks to health and safety that are associated with this practice. He also finds evidence to link binge drinking with sexual assault and studies that correlate the drinking with failure to graduate. He feels like he has a strong case and solid ethos because he's a college student and residence advisor. Much to his surprise, his peer review group reacts to his

argument with hostility. They tell him that there is no drinking problem on his campus and that he is just one of those guys who don't want other people to have any fun. He's shaken by this experience but glad it happened before he actually gave the presentation. He decides that he may need to construct an argument that starts with refutation to deal with the negative emotions.

Here are some questions you can ask yourself to help you evaluate your use of ethos, pathos, and logos.

Use of Ethos	Use of Pathos	Use of Logos
Do you carefully match your writing style (diction, tone, syntax) to your audience?	Are you able to get the reader emotionally involved with the text's subject matter? Is this appropriate for the genre?	Are your claims well supported with evidence?
Do you employ credible source material?	Do you attempt to evoke emotions such as fear or sympathy from the audience? Are these appropriate strategies given the context, or are they more likely to raise suspicion?	Is the evidence you employ likely to convince the audience?
Do you demonstrate an understanding of the audience's values?	Is information conveyed imaginatively to the reader in the form of narratives or anecdotes? If so, what effect does this have on the audience?	Do you avoid fallacious steps in reasoning like faulty cause and effect arguments?
What assumptions do you expect the reader to accept? Are these reasonable?	Do you attempt to find emotional common ground with readers by appealing to shared values or beliefs?	Do you maintain coherent lines of reasoning in your argument? Do your points and ideas proceed logically and connect to one another?
How well do you maneuver within the standard usage conventions of the genre?	Do you include images that mean to evoke emotions?	Do you use visual representations of your data?

TESTING AUDIENCE RESPONSE

As you can see from the previous case studies, it's important to test your appeals to see how they work and to learn some of the possible repercussions of intense and controversial material.

You already may have gotten the advice to imagine your audience's reaction. To some extent this approach makes sense, but there are potential problems with this approach. Make sure that your imagined audience is not a stereotype.

Some examples of typical audience stereotypes include:

- Older people are conservative and prudish.
- Teenagers are empty-headed and impulsive.
- Midwesterners have no fashion sense.
- Real men don't eat arugula.

These stereotypes may lead you to alienate or insult portions of your audience. A better course of action is to test your argument on real readers. You can also get valuable clues to possible audience reaction when you research opposing views to your argument. As you work to understand and summarize them fairly, you'll be imaginatively reconstructing someone else's world. At this point, you'll start to understand better what might move them to accept your argument.

REVISING YOUR ARGUMENT

Revision is a crucial component of academic writing that most new writers make the mistake of skipping right over. Don't fall into the same trap. The revision portion of the writing process can dramatically enhance the quality of your essay (and usually your grade).

Before we go any further, it's important to note the distinction between revision and editing. Think of editing as a tune up. It normally focuses on spelling, grammar, proper formatting, and other details. Editing comes just before proofreading, where we examine our work for mistakes.

Revision goes beyond that. It's "big picture" thinking that results in substantial changes to a text. Revision considers audience, bolsters argument, connects ideas, plays with style, and more. Revision allows you to take a step back and mull over all the components of your essay in order to think about how they function together. In this phase, you may find yourself focusing on:

- your relationship with the audience.
- the quality of your argument.
- how well you've incorporated credible sources and information.
- your use of rhetorical appeals.
- how the paper cues the readers to move through the discussion.
- developing your personal style.
- diction (and how your vocabulary choices create a tone for the essay).

When you begin to revise, focus on arranging and developing your material in the most effective way possible. You will want to think about the decisions you've made as an author and make changes as needed. Consider the following revision moves and the methods you can use to achieve them:

The Moves	The Methods	Examples
Add	Develop definitions, examples, proofs, and documentation.	A student notices that a paragraph is full of generalizations. She adds a case study and some statistics.
Cut	Remove redundant language, irrelevant ideas or discussions, ineffective proofs.	Audience testing of a student's initial draft reveal that a discussion of plastic surgery in an essay on celebrity charities is beside the point, so the author cuts this section.
Change	Even out your diction, alter your appeals to better suit your audience, improve your integration of a certain source, or clarify the wording of your sentences.	A student uses a picture of a rapper spitting into the camera to open his portfolio. The instructor is offended, so the student picks a more user-friendly image.
Move	Relocate ideas, paragraphs, or even whole sections to enhance the logical coherence of your argument and to clarify its structure.	A peer reviewer notices that the conclusion of an essay is much better focused than the opening. The writer moves the final paragraph to the front of the essay.

This is also a great time to check and make sure you've met the expectations of the assignment. Each assignment has special requirements. In particular, good arguments skillfully combine many different components. Consequently, there are several revision strategies unique to argumentation. Consider the checklist below as you review and revise your argument.

✓ Did you discuss and develop all of the major points you'd like to make?
✓ Is there a balance of source materials? Make sure you have a broad array of credible sources. Don't depend on one or two sources for the bulk of your argument.
✓ Were you able to effectively acknowledge and respond to opposing views and different perspectives?
✓ Does the support you offer fully back up the claims you make?
✓ Is the organization of your argument effective? Does its order make sense? Would your essay work better if you rearranged sections?
✓ Consider your use of appeals. Is there a dominant appeal? Is it appropriate for your rhetorical situation?
✓ Would additional appeals strengthen your argument?

One essay can go through several revisions. You can review and change as much or as little of your work as you need to, over and over again until you are completely satisfied. You'll probably need to experiment a bit to find the revision techniques that work best for you. There are many different ways to approach this task. Below are some common techniques you may want to try:

Reading out loud	Reading your essay out loud will help you catch rough spots, spelling errors, and more. It's an easy way to quickly determine what areas need your attention.
Essay exchange	Alternatively, you can exchange essays with classmates and have them read your work to you while you make notes about potential changes.
Peer review	Peer review is a common activity in the writing classroom. It's a great chance to see many different styles of writing and get instant feedback from real audience members. Don't be afraid to get your own group together outside of the classroom!
Talk it out	Call a friend or family member and explain the nature of your argument to them. Allow them to ask questions. You'll rapidly uncover the weak spots in your essay.
Cut and paste	Experiment with the order of your text. Open a new version and move things around. What happens if your conclusion takes the place of the introduction? What if you delete your second paragraph, or swap it with your third?
Meet with a tutor	The University Center for Writing-based Learning is free and operates on all DePaul campuses. Tutors are trained to help you look at the big picture of your essay and evaluate what changes to make.
Meet with your instructor	Stop by office hours, make an appointment, or send an email. Your instructor is always able to offer additional feedback and support during the writing process.

DEVELOPING YOUR STYLE

Writing style is a synthesis of multiple elements that give an impression of the writer and makes an impression on the reader. A writer's style infuses her entire text and arises from things like:

- word choice
- length and structure of sentences and paragraphs
- use of creative language like metaphor, simile, and imagery
- use of humor
- level of engagement with the audience
- rhythm and sound
- visual elements included with the text

While style can be challenging to define, the best writers don't leave it up to chance. Given that it has an impact on how your audience will receive your argument, you should make an effort to craft your style so that it enhances your work.

CONSIDER *this*

Revision is a recursive process. This means that you will likely find yourself repeating the process more than once as you develop and refine your own style.

There is no one correct style, even for an established genre like academic research papers. A general guideline that works across contexts is that your style should be informed by your rhetorical situation. Elements of your rhetorical situation like purpose, audience, and publication should help you determine the kind of style that would be most effective.

In most cases, and for our purposes here, you should work toward creating a style that is clear, appropriate, and memorable.

CLEAR

In nearly all cases you should strive to be clear in your writing. This may seem like it goes without saying, but, especially when writing an academic argument, clarity can be a challenge for a number of reasons.

Some challenges to clarity are encountered by writers regardless of what genre they are writing in. Research on writing tells us that when you find yourself strongly focused on trying to articulate your ideas in the argument you are making, things like sentence fragments and run-ons, comma splices, and dangling modifiers are more likely to appear. For more information and practice with these topics, consult your handbook.

Another challenge to clarity is more particular to writing a research-based argument. Managing the complexity of your topic, the research you've done, and the argument you want to build can be difficult. Yet, being able to negotiate these complex ideas without oversimplifying them is an important writing skill.

Many students think that academic arguments are meant to be dry and difficult to read, and try to write theirs accordingly. It's true that the complexity of the content can make academic arguments challenging to understand (see Chapter 2 for advice about this). However, it's important to remember that the challenge you offer your own readers should not come in the form of deciphering lengthy sentences or difficult vocabulary, but rather from engaging with your ideas and evaluating your contribution to the conversation you've entered.

In fact, you could even say that as the complexity of your ideas increases, your sentence style should become more straightforward. After all, if you've gone to all the trouble to do good research and construct a solid argument, it would be counterproductive to distance yourself from your readers by trying to sound "academic."

On the other hand, using the terms that characterize a particular academic discipline may increase your authority and strengthen your ethos. Also, one of your goals in this class and in college should be to practice using language in more sophisticated, compelling ways.

But take care to be conscious of why you choose your words. Use words to showcase your analytical abilities and ideas, rather than for their own sake. As you write, think about what will draw your readers in and allow them to more easily consider and appreciate what you've accomplished.

For more discussion on these issues in academic writing, see the essays by Richard Lederer, Philip Eubanks, and John D. Schaeffer in Part 2 of this book.

Appropriate

Beyond clarity, your next challenge is to create an appropriate style for your rhetorical situation. Analyzing your rhetorical situation and determining an effective level of formality for your argument is an important step in achieving an appropriate style.

In our information-heavy society, we have grown used to shortcuts and abbreviations, especially when it comes to language. Day-to-day writing situations such as emails, text messages, and Facebook wall posts usually demonstrate low levels of formality in their vocabulary choice, spelling, grammar, and punctuation. These choices are fine because they are appropriate for that rhetorical situation. Your audience in these cases may even expect more relaxed prose—they might raise their eyebrows at a perfectly spelled, capitalized, and punctuated text message.

However, using this kind of relaxed prose for your argument may not be the most effective choice. It all depends on its rhetorical context. In determining the level of formality for your argument, you should consider:

- your audience
- your genre
- your argument's intended publication

For example, would your argument about the cost of textbooks be submitted for publication in your student newspaper? Or is it to be modeled after the arguments published in a journal on contemporary issues in education? Or, will it be written as a letter addressed to the textbook publishing company itself? In each of these cases, you may choose to use a different level of formality for maximum effectiveness.

The idea of level of formality goes beyond simply observing the conventions of standard English when it comes to spelling and punctuation. It involves other choices, too. Your diction, or word choice, as well as the presence of the speaker in the argument and the engagement with the audience also enter in to the level of formality of any text.

"Can I say 'I'?"

You may have been told that saying "I" in the papers you write for school—particularly research papers—is off-limits. It's always good to check with your instructor on this, but generally in college-level writing, using the word is not outlawed. In fact, respected thinkers and writers use "I" even in papers published in formal academic journals.

Speaking in the first person within your argument can be rhetorically appropriate, but it's a good idea to consider the rhetorical context before you do.

Think carefully about the potential consequences of using "I." How will your audience respond to your choice to use the first person? It may improve your ethos by allowing them to see you as knowledgeable and relatable. Or, it could have the opposite effect, distracting them from the objectivity of your evidence and casting doubt on whether you can present any support beyond your personal experience.

The same sorts of considerations should be applied to how you address your audience. Some arguments acknowledge the audience directly and frequently, saying "you" often. Others acknowledge their audience only by having considered their assumptions, knowledge, and potential objections as the argument was constructed.

There are few hard-and-fast rules as to what makes for an appropriate style. What *is* certain, though, is that you should be making deliberate choices and using your skills with language to respond effectively to your rhetorical situation.

MEMORABLE

It may seem difficult to reconcile the level of appropriate formality for your argument with your desire to write in your own voice and make a unique impression on your reader. But don't think that writing more formally means writing in a way that is impersonal or "soulless." Although constructing an academic argument may entail using more formal language than you normally would, that doesn't mean you can't use a powerful or creative style that resonates with your reader. In fact, that should be your goal.

Rhetorical Figures

In the history of rhetoric, figures of sound and sense have emerged as ways of capturing attention, focusing ideas, and creating memorable moments. Some of the figures, like chiasmus, require a great deal of stylistic skill. Others are well within the reach of any writer who wants to draw particular attention to a passage.

In the O.J. Simpson trial, his defense attorney Johnny Cochran was able to neutralize much of the prosecution case by holding up a blood-stained glove and chanting, "If it doesn't fit, you must acquit." The power of that rhyme, a figure of sound, has stayed in the public memory to this day. In John F. Kennedy's inaugural address, he captured the attention of the world with a figure called *chiasmus* when he said, "Ask not what your country can do for you; ask what you can do for your country." The idea was important, but the carefully balanced phrases with their contrasting ideas were simply unforgettable.

For more examples of rhetorical figures, consult your handbook, or visit www.americanrhetoric.com.

DESIGNING YOUR DOCUMENT

Although rhetoric is typically thought of as the study of language, it has never been exclusively confined to words alone—not even when rhetoric was primarily the study of the spoken word, as opposed to the written word.

The effectiveness of a verbal speech, after all, is determined not only by language-based decisions like syntax and diction but also by intonation, syllabic emphasis, volume, and intensity at a given moment in the speech, and the dress or expressions of the speaker—a host of visual and auditory cues in addition to text-based ones. Classical rhetoricians covered many of these elements under the canons of memory and delivery.

Similarly, the written word today is often enhanced and modified by visual elements of composition, ranging from font decisions to the formatting of a document to the integration of photographs, charts, or graphs. This is especially true as self-printing and publishing opportunities increase. The ease of technology invites growing numbers of communicators to blend their written words with visual components.

With that in mind, here are some guidelines to keep in mind when incorporating visual elements into your writing.

FONT AND FORMATTING

The following are tips to keep in mind when making basic formatting decisions for your documents:

Font and Formatting Guidelines	Explanation
No need to get fancy.	Aesthetic concerns are typically secondary to the main point you wish to make, and while a glamorous font might delight the eye, it often distracts the reader. A traditional serif-based font, like Times New Roman or Garamond, is usually sufficient. Check with your instructor to see if a particular font is required for the class.
Follow your own rules.	If you chose to use headers, footers, section labels, or other partitioning, make the formatting of these sections consistent within the document. A particular layout or formatting decision will set expectations for similar decisions throughout the work—and you should follow these expectations. Make sure that you play by the rules that you set for yourself.
Be careful with special formatting.	Whenever you put something in bold or in italics, or even put part of a sentence in ALL CAPITALIZATION LIKE YOU'RE SHOUTING, the eye is automatically drawn to that part of the writing you're singling out, over and above other moments. These formatting decisions are visual elements, not language elements, and if you're not careful, a readers' natural tendency to prioritize visuals over text can undercut how your argument is absorbed.
Know the conventions of your form.	You will rarely be called upon to simply invent formatting decisions from scratch. Almost always, your instructors will give you guidelines regarding font choices, layout decisions, and so forth. If they do not, simply study a few examples of the forms you want to emulate. You can make the work a lot easier on yourself by understanding the modes and practices of your form.

INTEGRATING PHOTOGRAPHS AND OTHER VISUALS

Many writers now pay attention to how visuals can enhance text in communication. This is especially true for web-based writing, as the conventions encourage visual design so viewers can grasp the main idea of a page quickly.

Similarly, an increasing number of professors are giving students the latitude to include visual elements in their own arguments.

Choose your visuals carefully.	Visual elements can carry the same argumentative and rhetorical weight as written ones. Not all visuals are created equal or can be used for equivalent purposes. Every well-imagined photograph is a blend between a subject and the photographer's interpretation of that subject. The visual you choose can add a dimension to the text that would have been lacking otherwise, reinforcing your claim.
Establish a connection with the text.	In many ways, since a photograph is most likely the first thing that a reader will notice when encountering your text, you are obligated to be more conscious of how the visual element fits within your prose. Don't simply slap a photograph somewhere in the text and leave the reader to fill in the dots—take the time to integrate the photograph or visual into your prose the way you would any other text-based source. Be sure to write a caption and give a photo credit directly below the image.

HIERARCHIES AND CONTRASTS

Readers have a natural tendency to group and categorize multiple visual elements, and to infer a total meaning from them that is sometimes perceived as greater than the individual elements themselves.

In other words, readers absorb visual aspects of a text as a whole—not in isolation from one another—and they assign relationships based on different design decisions. It simply means that you should try and respect the tendency towards holistic viewing in a reader by considering the following suggestions:

Let design reinforce your message.	When you design visual elements of a document, you are not only tinkering with appearances. You are also sending subtle clues about the information communicated through these devices. A reader will draw conclusions from the ways in which you organize information. A break from consistency in formatting is generally thought to be accompanied by a break in logical or argumentative progression. Respect a reader's natural tendency to draw inferences from your document's design, and make your decisions appropriately.
Keep colors complementary.	You may get the opportunity to work with color and formatting. If this is the case, your color choices should be designed around contrasting elements—choices too close to one another can be difficult to separate visually. Don't overpower a reader with color—a color palette of five or fewer contrasting colors is generally sufficient.

So, you've got a lot to think about. If you're feeling a bit overwhelmed, that's normal. Writing is a complex process and there are many factors to consider. One way to take a step back and evaluate what you've learned and how you will present it is by building a portfolio.

CONSIDER *this*

The specific ratio between image and text will vary with the medium in which you are working and with the purposes of a piece. If you are crafting a position based argument in a scholarly paper, you will typically rely on the text. If you are making the same argument in a flyer for commuters on their way to work, the visuals themselves might be needed to carry the argument's weight.

PORTFOLIOS

Portfolios play many roles in academic and professional life: artists use them to document and to showcase their work over time; architects use them to present drawings, media, and projects to clients; writers use them to make connections between the kinds of work that they do individually and collaboratively for any number of creative, academic, and professional goals and audiences.

In each case, purpose and audience help to guide your rhetorical selection of materials, your reflections on those materials, and their presentation. While some instructors may have you present your work in a paper portfolio, you may also be asked to create a digital portfolio.

FIRST-YEAR WRITING DIGITAL PORTFOLIO REQUIREMENTS

In the First-Year Writing Program at DePaul, we often use digital portfolios as a way for you to showcase your work and to show how you've met the learning outcomes of the course in which you are enrolled.

Your instructor will guide you through a process that begins early in the term for selecting, designing, reflecting on, assessing, and presenting the work you have done in the course. Your WRD Digital Portfolio will contain:

1. A Reflective Essay that introduces your work to your peers, your instructor, and writing-program administrators.
2. Samples of your work that show your progress on the program learning outcomes:
   - Rhetorical knowledge
   - Critical thinking, reading, and writing
   - Processes
   - Knowledge of conventions

The design and composition of your digital portfolio draw on the very same strategies and outcomes that you've been practicing in your WRD class: readers will attribute credibility and authority to you when your design and arrangement are done with care; thoughtfully integrated examples of your work will support your reflective essay's main points; and you will get practice in articulating and presenting your work in a rhetorically effective way.

GUIDELINES FOR THE COMPOSITION, DESIGN, AND PRESENTATION OF YOUR DIGITAL PORTFOLIO

These stages of portfolio development serve as a guide; they work differently for everyone, and no one moves through them at the same pace. Some writers reflect constantly, always making connections between assignments and pieces of writing. Others focus on organization, spending more time in recursive drafting/design. We offer these stages here not as a prescriptive how-to guide to follow, but as a way for you to gauge your own process and to help you plan ahead:

SELECTION

Keep everything you've worked on in this course in a safe, backed-up location—notes, early drafts, final drafts, journal entries, peer and instructor feedback, everything. You might not use all of these materials in your final portfolio, but your life will be easier if you know where they all are, and when they are easily accessible.

DESIGN

After you have made careful, judicious selections of the work that you want to include in your portfolio, you can make good use of an organizing principle. You'll want to think through some rhetorical decisions in advance: how to label your links; how to present long passages of text; where to incorporate visuals; how to represent different kinds of work — individual, collaborative, collective, reflective, academic, personal. Just as readers have certain expectations of an academic essay, conventions have developed around portfolios as well, including easy-to-follow navigation, readability, and accessibility.

REFLECTION

Reflection refers to the process that we engage in when we want to look back at some activity or decision we've made, to think about what we've learned from it, and how we might use it in the future. Reflection is a powerful tool in teaching and learning—think of it as a dot-connecting mechanism. Outside of academics, reflecting is a common tool among professionals and organizations as a way to establish values, goals, and future actions. The following questions are ways of reflecting:

- What did I do?
- What was important about what I did? Did I meet my goals?
- When have I done this kind of work before? Where could I use this again?
- Do I see any patterns or relationships in what I did?
- How well did I do? What worked? What do I need to improve?
- What should I do next? What's my plan?

Reflection is also difficult. It requires honesty, self-awareness, and the ability to think critically about the conditions of our work and its outcomes. Through this process of action-reflection-action, we can often assess our past action and efforts with an eye toward integrating it and improving it in the future.

If you're asked to compose a reflective essay, here are some questions to consider. You should be able to provide clearly labeled, specific examples in your responses.

How do you define revision? What steps have you taken this quarter to revise for different audiences and contexts?
To what degree does the target audience, purpose, or context impact the work in your portfolio?
How do you analyze texts (including the work of other students)?
What role(s) has peer review played in your development as a reader, writer, and thinker?
What do you consider to be the most important components to your writing process? Why? Has that changed over the course of the quarter?
How do you edit? How do you manage to ensure correct surface features: syntax, grammar, punctuation, and spelling? What considerations figure into your editing?
Describe your approach to writing in different genres.
Beyond the learning outcomes, what individual goals did you have for your reading and writing this term?
What have you accomplished that you feel proud of?
What would you like to continue to work on?

Feedback, Critique, Workshops

We recommend that you invite feedback and critique on your portfolio from peers, from your instructor, and from tutors in the DePaul University Center for Writing-based Learning. Some instructors will ask for mid-term portfolios to facilitate this process.

Reflection and Your WRD Digital Portfolio

Your WRD instructor may ask you to frame and to reflect upon your work in the context of the course's learning outcomes. She may ask you to reflect on your writing and revision process. He may ask you to make connections between the work you've done in this course and the writing you did in high school, with an eye toward future writing-intensive courses, and even your professional goals. The nice thing about portfolios is that they can be designed to do all of these kinds of reflecting and showcasing.

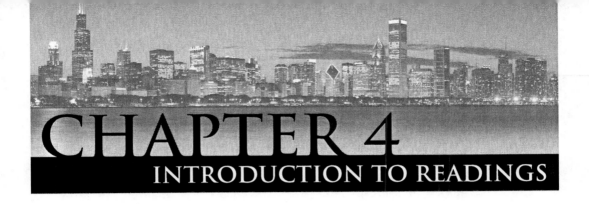

CHAPTER 4
INTRODUCTION TO READINGS

Taken together, these readings represent a variety of rhetorical situations that show highly varied approaches to argument. They are not texts that request a pro/con opinion on an issue; instead, they encourage an examination of the variables and objectives existing in the background when writing is first created, and ask you to foreground these concerns in your own writing. We hope that you will examine these readings as rhetoricians mapping out the intersections of appeals as they relate to audience and purpose, and then return to your own writing with a heightened understanding of your own rhetorical situation.

Despite their diverse origins, these readings divide into two main groups: primary source examples of writing, and secondary source analyses of how writing functions within a rhetorical environment. For instance, we have included a piece published in *TIME* magazine wherein Richard Dawkins and Francis Collins debate the intersection between God and science, as well as a piece by Whittenberger analyzing Dawkins' and Collins' respective strategies. Similar pairings include George Washington's Newburgh Address, which was given to convince a group of freezing, exhausted soldiers not to desert, and a rhetorical analysis of this same speech. There is also a primary source text about the mortality rates of mesothelioma, a type of cancer associated with asbestos exposure, accompanied by an essay by Stephen J. Gould describing his first-hand experience with such statistics. You'll also find several essays analyzing the rhetorical situations of various texts, as well as some primary texts without accompanying analyses.

This section of the textbook includes several grouped readings that (though they can stand alone) are designed to interconnect, providing readers with a chance to explore how a rhetorical situation shapes a text. Additionally, this section provides some thematic units that enhance concepts discussed in Part 1 of this book.

Here are some suggested groupings of texts, according to the type of literacy they represent. You can find further details about the contexts and authors for each of these pieces in their introductions.

RHETORICAL LITERACY

Texts: Selections from *Rhetoric* by Aristotle; Selections from *Institutio Oratoria* by Quintilian; *A Modest Proposal* by Jonathan Swift

This grouping emphasizes and models the theoretical underpinnings of argument, examining typical tools employed by speakers aiming to convince others to hold their point of view. They are all classics of the genre, and when grouped emphasize rhetoric's storied heritage and sustained relevance.

PUBLIC RELATIONS LITERACY

Texts: "Queen Elizabeth's Image Repair Discourse" by William L. Benoit and Susan L. Brinson; "President Bush Image Repair" by William L. Benoit and Jayne Henson; "Floyd Landis Doping Scandal" by Mark Glantz

These three texts evaluate uses of image repair discourse under heightened circumstances and model rhetorical analysis by drawing from three people facing a public relations crisis: the perception of Queen Elizabeth's dispassion at the death of Princess Diana; the public response to President George W. Bush's handling of Hurricane Katrina; and Floyd Landis' image issues following an accusation of steroid abuse. Each essay, after outlining the framework for examination, discusses strategies used by these individuals to repair their public personas, and the extent to which the combination of strategies was successful given their respective situations.

POLITICAL LITERACY

Texts: "How the Scapegoats Escaped" by William D. Cohan; "George Washington's Newburgh Address" by George Washington; "George Washington's Tear-Jerker" by John R. Miller; "Visceral has its Value" by Maureen Dowd; Selections from *The Prince* by Niccolò Machiavelli

Each of these texts is drawn from rhetoric in the realm of politics, which deals directly with persuasion and argument. Two of the texts—those centered around George Washington—are directly connected to one another, with the first being a speech by Washington compelling his men to remain loyal and the second being an analysis of this speech. We have also included "Visceral has its Value," which compares rhetorical strategies used by Sarah Palin to President Barack Obama's political style. Elsewhere, you can find an excerpt from Machiavelli's classic Renaissance text *The Prince*, which comments on whether it is better for a ruler to be loved or feared.

TECHNOLOGICAL LITERACY

Texts: "Give Employees Facebook Time" by Traci Armstrong; "The Closing of the American Mind" by Allan Bloom; "Do You Pass the Social Media Recruitment Test?" by Boris Epstein; "Colombia Uses Ads to Persuade Rebels to Turn Themselves In" by Laurel Wentz

> This section emphasizes how rhetoric functions within emerging discourse mediums, particularly non-literary ones. Two of the entries ("Give Employees Facebook Time" and "Do You Pass the Social Media Recruitment Test?") examine how social networks affect the persona of both employer and employee, and how this new dimension in the relationship is being managed (or should be managed). "The Closing of the American Mind" presents a similar value argument about how rock music impacts students' perception of culture. Finally, "Colombia Uses Ads to Persuade Rebels to Turn Themselves In" profiles an advertisement campaign in Colombia designed to persuade guerilla militants to defect from their positions.

SCIENTIFIC LITERACY

Texts: "God v. Science" by Francis Collins and Richard Dawkins; "The Dawkins v. Collins Debate" by Gary G. Whittenberger; "Senate Bill No. 561" by Senator Ben Nevers; "Greetings from Idiot America" by Charles P. Pierce; "What the Public Doesn't Get About Climate Change" by Bryan Walsh

> This album features sources about how scientific and religious topics intersect, and how adherents to both (or either) system of belief negotiate the discrepancies. "God v. Science" features a *TIME* interview with two scientists—one atheist and one Christian—about the role God plays in their respective worldviews, while the Whittenberger piece analyzes their arguments. "Greetings from Idiot America" is a provocative piece from *Esquire* that argues that the general dumbing down of America has led society away from scientific pursuits; "What the Public Doesn't Get about Climate Change" deals with similar material, but places much of the blame for this gap on how scientists communicate. Finally, we have included "Senate Bill No. 561" (the Louisiana Academic Freedom Act), which is a bill on teaching theories of evolution, formed as a response to public debate.

MEDICAL LITERACY

Texts: "Malignant Pleural Mesothelioma: Symptom Management" by Mary Ellen Cordes and Carol Brueggen; "The Median Isn't the Message" by Stephen J. Gould; "Malignant Mesothelioma Mortality" by the Center for Disease Control

Readings from this section are drawn from medical literacy, which asks students to consider how they might evaluate medical literature in a life-or-death situation. Each reading focuses on the condition of mesothelioma, a type of lung or abdominal cancer typically associated with exposure to asbestos. "Malignant Mesothelioma Mortality" is a government study describing the disease's morbidity rates, while "Symptom Management" describes its progression and treatment. As a counterpoint to these professional articles, we have also included "The Median Isn't the Message" by Stephen J. Gould, where Gould describes being diagnosed with the condition and how he interpreted the kinds of writings included elsewhere in this section.

ACADEMIC LITERACY

Texts: "Writing for the Public" by Mike Rose; "A Kind Word for Bullshit: The Problem of Academic Writing" by Philip Eubanks and John D. Schaeffer; "Cut this Story" by Michael Kinsley; "The Case for Short Words" by Richard Lederer; "Reading Philosophy with Background Knowledge and Metacognition" by David Concepción

These readings deal with how students engaging in academic discourse might effectively craft a credible academic persona—one that is confident without being brash, articulate without being condescending, and convincing without being bullshit (to borrow a term from Eubanks and Schaeffer). In "Writing for the Public," Mike Rose argues for a writing class that teaches experts how to communicate with non-experts. Similarly, Concepción presents a way to make academic writing accessible to students. "A Kind Word for Bullshit" grapples with questions of why so many people (students included) are often disdainful of academic writing, whether these reservations are legitimate, and what to do about it. "Cut this Story" and "The Case for Short Words" are more style-driven essays, focusing on how to create a concise writing style that still encourages individual ownership of writing decisions.

There are, of course, other combinations. For example, George Washington's speech (which implores his men to remain loyal) could be paired with the discussion of the Colombian rebels (who are being persuaded to desert). The gap between expert and layman described in "What the Public Doesn't Get about Climate Change" could be discussed in connection with the purely expert and distant tone of "Malignant Pleural Mesothelioma: Symptom Management." For that matter, we encourage you to use the theoretical models and analyses included here as springboards into more current topics. For example, the Image Repair Discourse theory outlined in the Public Relations texts could be applied to whoever finds themselves in the crisis spotlight at the time (Tiger Woods, BP, or Toyota Motors come to mind from recent events).

In order to allow you to explore the intersections between these works on your own, they are presented in alphabetical order. Discussion questions and activities follow each reading.

Excerpt from *Rhetoric*

Aristotle

Aristotle (384–322 B.C.E.) began his studies in medicine but soon found his way to Athens where he studied philosophy with Plato. He tutored Alexander the Great and later founded his own school of philosophy, the Lyceum. His writing considers a wide range of topics including science and politics as well as aesthetics. This passage from his Rhetoric (350 B.C.E) focuses on both the theory and practical applications of persuasive discourse, going beyond logic to consider all the appeals that can reach an audience. Aristotle remains one of the cornerstones of our study of rhetoric to this day. This selection highlights the importance of emotional literacy in persuasion. To follow up on this passage, you could consult the Stanford Encyclopedia of Philosophy: http://plato.stanford.edu/entries/aristotle-rhetoric/.

Book II

PART 1

We have now considered the materials to be used in supporting or opposing a political measure, in pronouncing eulogies or censures, and for prosecution and defence in the law courts. We have considered the received opinions on which we may best base our arguments so as to convince our hearers—those opinions with which our enthymemes deal, and out of which they are built, in each of the three kinds of oratory, according to what may be called the special needs of each.

But since rhetoric exists to affect the giving of decisions—the hearers decide between one political speaker and another, and a legal verdict is a decision—the orator must not only try to make the argument of his speech demonstrative and worthy of belief; he must also make his own character look right and put his hearers, who are to decide, into the right frame of mind. Particularly in political oratory, but also in lawsuits, it adds much to an orator's influence that his own character should look right and that he should be thought to entertain the right feelings towards his hearers; and also that his hearers themselves should be in just the right frame of mind. That the orator's own character should look right is particularly important in political speaking: that the audience should be in the right frame of mind, in lawsuits. When people are feeling friendly and placable, they think one sort of thing; when they are feeling angry or hostile, they think either something totally different or the same thing with a different intensity: when they feel friendly to the man who comes before them for judgement, they regard him as having done little wrong, if any; when they feel hostile, they take the opposite view. Again, if they are eager for, and have good hopes of, a thing that will be pleasant if it happens, they think that it certainly will happen and be good for them: whereas if they are indifferent or annoyed, they do not think so.

There are three things which inspire confidence in the orator's own character—the three, namely, that induce us to believe a thing apart from any proof of it: good sense, good moral character, and goodwill. False statements and bad advice are due to one or more of the following three causes. Men either form a false opinion through want of good sense; or they form a true opinion, but because of their moral badness do not say what they really think; or finally, they are both sensible and upright, but not well disposed to their hearers, and may fail in consequence to recommend what they know to be the best course. These are the only possible cases. It follows that any one who is thought to have all three of these good qualities will inspire trust in his audience. The way to make ourselves thought to be sensible and morally good must be gathered from the analysis of goodness already given: the way to establish your own goodness is the same as the way to establish that of others. Good will and friendliness of disposition will form part of our discussion of the emotions, to which we must now turn.

The Emotions are all those feelings that so change men as to affect their judgements, and that are also attended by pain or pleasure. Such are anger, pity, fear and the like, with their opposites. We must arrange what we have to say about each of them under three heads. Take, for instance, the emotion of anger: here we must discover (1) what the state of mind of angry people is, (2) who the people are with whom they usually get angry, and (3) on what grounds they get angry with them. It is not enough to know one or even two of these points; unless we know all three, we shall be unable to arouse anger in any one. The same is true of the other emotions. So just as earlier in this work we drew up a list of useful propositions for the orator, let us now proceed in the same way to analyse the subject before us.

PART 2

Anger may be defined as an impulse, accompanied by pain, to a conspicuous revenge for a conspicuous slight directed without justification towards what concerns oneself or towards what concerns one's friends. If this is a proper definition of anger, it must always be felt towards some particular individual, e.g. Cleon, and not 'man' in general. It must be felt because the other has done or intended to do something to him or one of his friends. It must always be attended by a certain pleasure—that which arises from the expectation of revenge. For since nobody aims at what he thinks he cannot attain, the angry man is aiming at what he can attain, and the belief that you will attain your aim is pleasant. Hence it has been well said about wrath,

> "Sweeter it is by far than the honeycomb
> "dripping with sweetness,
> "And spreads through the hearts of men."

It is also attended by a certain pleasure because the thoughts dwell upon the act of vengeance, and the images then called up cause pleasure, like the images called up in dreams.

Now slighting is the actively entertained opinion of something as obviously of no importance. We think bad things, as well as good ones, have serious importance; and we think the same of anything that tends to produce such things, while those which have little or no such tendency we consider unimportant. There are three kinds of slighting—contempt, spite, and insolence. (1) Contempt is one kind of slighting: you feel contempt for what you consider unimportant, and it is just such things that you slight. (2) Spite is another kind; it is a thwarting another man's wishes, not to get something yourself but to prevent his getting it. The slight arises just from the fact that you do not aim at something for yourself: clearly you do not think that he can do you harm, for then you would be afraid of him instead of slighting him, nor yet that he can do you any good worth mentioning, for then you would be anxious to make friends with him. (3) Insolence is also a form of slighting, since it consists in doing and saying things that cause shame to the victim, not in order that anything may happen to yourself, or because anything has happened to yourself, but simply for the pleasure involved. (Retaliation is not 'insolence,' but vengeance.) The cause of the pleasure thus enjoyed by the insolent man is that he thinks himself greatly superior to others when ill-treating them. That is why youths and rich men are insolent; they think themselves superior when they show insolence. One sort of insolence is to rob people of the honour due to them;

you certainly slight them thus; for it is the unimportant, for good or evil, that has no honour paid to it. So Achilles says in anger:

"He hath taken my prize for himself
"and hath done me dishonour,"
and
"Like an alien honoured by none,"

meaning that this is why he is angry. A man expects to be specially respected by his inferiors in birth, in capacity, in goodness, and generally in anything in which he is much their superior: as where money is concerned a wealthy man looks for respect from a poor man; where speaking is concerned, the man with a turn for oratory looks for respect from one who cannot speak; the ruler demands the respect of the ruled, and the man who thinks he ought to be a ruler demands the respect of the man whom he thinks he ought to be ruling. Hence it has been said

"Great is the wrath of kings, whose father is Zeus almighty,"
and
"Yea, but his rancour abideth long afterward also,"

their great resentment being due to their great superiority. Then again a man looks for respect from those who he thinks owe him good treatment, and these are the people whom he has treated or is treating well, or means or has meant to treat well, either himself, or through his friends, or through others at his request.

It will be plain by now, from what has been said, (1) in what frame of mind, (2) with what persons, and (3) on what grounds people grow angry. (1) The frame of mind is that of one in which any pain is being felt. In that condition, a man is always aiming at something.

Whether, then, another man opposes him either directly in any way, as by preventing him from drinking when he is thirsty, or indirectly, the act appears to him just the same; whether some one works against him, or fails to work with him, or otherwise vexes him while he is in this mood, he is equally angry in all these cases. Hence people who are afflicted by sickness or poverty or love or thirst or any other unsatisfied desires are prone to anger and easily roused: especially against those who slight their present distress. Thus a sick man is angered by disregard of his illness, a poor man by disregard of his poverty, a man aging war by disregard of the war he is waging, a lover by disregard of his love, and so throughout, any other sort of slight being enough if special slights are wanting. Each man is predisposed, by the emotion now controlling him, to his own particular anger. Further, we are angered if we happen to be expecting a contrary result: for a quite unexpected evil is specially painful, just as the quite unexpected fulfilment of our wishes is specially pleasant. Hence it is plain what seasons, times, conditions, and periods of life tend to stir men easily to anger, and where and when this will happen; and it is plain that the more we are under these conditions the more easily we are stirred.

These, then, are the frames of mind in which men are easily stirred to anger. The persons with whom we get angry are those who laugh, mock, or jeer at us, for such conduct is insolent. Also those who inflict injuries upon us that are marks of insolence. These injuries must be such as are neither retaliatory nor profitable to the doers: for only then will they be felt to be due to insolence. Also those who speak ill of us, and show contempt for us, in connexion with the things we ourselves most care about: thus those who are eager to win fame as philosophers get angry with those who show contempt for their philosophy; those who pride themselves upon their appearance get angry with those who show contempt for their appearance and so on in other cases. We feel particularly angry on this account if we suspect that we are in fact, or that people think we are, lacking completely or to any effective extent in the qualities in question. For when we are convinced that we excel in the qualities for which we are jeered at, we can ignore the jeering. Again, we are angrier with our friends than with other people, since we feel that our friends ought to treat us well and not badly. We are angry with those who have usually treated us with honour or regard, if a change comes and they behave to us otherwise: for we think that they feel contempt for us, or they would still be behaving as they did before. And with those who do not return our kindnesses or fail to return them adequately, and with those who oppose us though they are our inferiors: for all such persons seem to feel contempt for us; those who oppose us seem to think us inferior to themselves, and those who do not return our kindnesses seem to think that those kindnesses were conferred by inferiors. And we feel particularly angry with men of no account at all, if they slight us. For, by our hypothesis, the anger caused by the slight is felt towards people who are not justified in slighting us, and our inferiors are not thus justified. Again, we feel angry with friends if they do not speak well of us or treat us well; and still more, if they do the contrary; or if they do not perceive our needs, which is why Plexippus is angry with Meleager in Antiphon's play; for this want of perception shows that they are slighting us—we do not fail to perceive the needs of those for whom we care. Again we are angry with those who rejoice at our misfortunes or simply keep cheerful in the midst of our misfortunes, since this shows that they either hate us or are slighting us. Also with those who are indifferent to the pain they give us: this is why we get angry with bringers of bad news. And with those who listen to stories about us or keep on looking at our weaknesses; this seems like either slighting us or hating us; for those who love us share in all our distresses and it must distress any one to keep on looking at his own weaknesses. Further, with those who slight us before five classes of people: namely, (1) our rivals, (2) those whom we admire, (3) those whom we wish to admire us, (4) those for whom we feel reverence, (5) those who feel reverence for us: if any one slights us before such persons, we feel particularly angry. Again, we feel angry with those who slight us in connexion with what we are as honourable men bound to champion—our parents, children, wives, or subjects. And with those who do not return a favour, since such a slight is unjustifiable. Also with those who reply with humorous levity when we are speaking seriously, for such behaviour indicates contempt. And with those who treat us less well than they treat everybody else; it is another mark of contempt that they should think we do not deserve what every one else deserves. Forgetfulness, too, causes anger, as when our own names are forgotten, trifling as this may be; since forgetfulness is felt to be another sign that we are being slighted; it is due to negligence, and to neglect us is to slight us.

The persons with whom we feel anger, the frame of mind in which we feel it, and the reasons why we feel it, have now all been set forth. Clearly the orator will have to speak so as to bring his hearers into a frame of mind that will dispose them to anger, and to represent his adversaries as open to such charges and possessed of such qualities as do make people angry.

DISCUSSION *questions and activities*

1. How does Aristotle believe that rhetoric can create emotions in audience members?

2. Discuss the dangers and benefits of creating an emotion like anger in a reading or viewing audience. What kinds of rhetorical situations would justify making an audience angry?

3. What means does Aristotle use to prove his point about persuasive appeals?

4. Examine Aristotle's discussion of emotion in connection with Maureen Dowd's piece "Visceral Has Its Value." Does the use of emotion in politics as Dowd describes it seem effective or appropriate to you? Why or why not?

Give Employees Facebook Time
Six Ways Social-Media Freedom Benefits Employers

Traci Armstrong

Traci Armstrong wrote her article for Advertising Age, *a prominent trade publication in print and online for the advertising industry. She is the Director of Talent Acquisition for Organic and has published on recruiting and social networking. She uses both Twitter and blogging to create a presence in her field. Her article on giving employees Facebook time was published on March 31, 2009. You can follow her on Twitter @tannarmstrong.*

The social-media revolution is seeping into the workplace, and employers are nervous. According to social-web blogger David Armano, approximately 70% of organizations ban social networks. USA Today reports a lower amount, but still: An Oct. 22 survey shows 54% of businesses are banning social media from the workplace. Fears about decreased productivity and/or risk exposure seem to be resulting in censorship within workplaces.

Of course, banning social media is simply a bad idea. Many agencies report partnering with marketing clients to develop social-media strategies only to discover that clients themselves are unable to access key sites, such as Facebook and Twitter, from their work computers. Marketers are at a clear disadvantage when they don't have first-hand usage, insight, and experience with social-media channels.

Allowing employees to access social media could actually result in many other benefits for the employer:

Team-Building and Camaraderie

U.S. employers spend billions on employee team-building activities like picnics, holiday parties, and other exercises. Allowing employees to participate in the virtual water-cooler dialogue of social media gives them a chance to bond and find subjects with which they can relate to one another, free of cost to the employer. Studies show the main reason employees stay in jobs (or leave jobs) is based on their level of satisfaction with co-worker relationships. Social media enables employees to find a common bond and enhance the relationships with colleagues.

Productivity Benefits from Brain Breaks

A *Discovery* magazine article reports that neuroscientists at MIT have confirmed that taking breaks helps us learn and be more productive. A 2006 study observed rats pausing after exploring an unfamiliar maze. The neuroscientists theorized the rats were using the break to re-trace their steps in the maze for memory purposes—thus leading to better productivity during the next maze run. Another example: Educators can confirm first-hand the benefits of sending students to recess—and the chaotic results if kids don't get their downtime.

Social media is the equivalent of workplace recess. Mind breaks lead to employee satisfaction and better productivity. This results in increased morale, reduced employee stress, low absenteeism, and more engaged, healthier employees. All of these employee traits help the bottom line.

On-The-Job Training

Social media can serve as a virtual think tank. If an employee is embarking upon a new project and needs advice from her peers, it's as easy as posting a question to their social networks. Many professional groups are established on LinkedIn or Facebook and offer a venue for discussion and the opportunity to post specific questions. Polls and surveys enable virtual focus groups. Employees can easily follow subject-matter experts on a site like Twitter for an RSS-like feed of relevant content. While many companies offer organized mentoring programs, with social media employees can choose their own online advisor for guidance and knowledge sharing.

Trust and Transparency

If Facebook were a country, it would be the fourth largest. In September 2009, Facebook reached over 300 million active users. Gen Y-ers continue to rely less on e-mail and more on social media to communicate. Banning employees from this widespread communication tool is akin to telling your employees they can't use the phone for personal calls or e-mail friends and family. It's a signal your company is oppressive and in the Dark Ages. With the sale of smartphones on the rise, it's likely that employees would access their social-media sites on mobile devices anyway—creating an environment of concealment and mistrust.

Allowing employees to access social media communicates: "We trust you're mature and know when enough is enough." For employees that do abuse their time on social media, managers and HR departments should address the issue on an individual level—similar to any other performance problem like absenteeism, low productivity, or work quality.

Listening/Monitoring

Just as many brands are monitoring customers to address satisfaction issues, employers can apply the same model. If employees are complaining about their employer on social media, it might hurt a corporate brand—but it at least allows the employer a chance to address complaints or dissatisfaction.

Many companies conduct internal employee surveys to evaluate morale and employee satisfaction. As an alternative, HR or marketing staff could consider following and creating user lists/groups of employees on social sites to easily monitor conversations. Using a monitoring tool like Seesmic or Tweetdeck for Twitter allows an employer to continuously monitor keywords—like your company name—and immediately address unfavorable messaging. Caution: If your workplace doesn't offer a culture of transparency and openness, employees could misconstrue this as employer stalking.

Brand Evangelists

Just like unhappy employees complain about their jobs, happy employees love to share their positive workplace experience. And 78% of consumers trust peer recommendations over a brand's marketing efforts. That holds true for the workplace as well: Happy, well-performing employees will attract similar employees—a huge recruiting benefit.

The key for happy tweeps and happy tweets is creating a culture and environment in which an employee feels as though he can contribute and express himself. A satisfied employee will be an advocate for your company, might share job openings with friends and boast about the latest accomplishments. You can't buy that kind of press. Employers that embrace social media and provide employees with a simple policy, best practices, legal no-nos and basic usage/etiquette training will create an environment of openness with lower risk to the employer.

DISCUSSION *questions and activities*

1. What claim does Armstrong make about the place of social media in the workplace?
2. Describe Armstrong's style. What kind of connections do you see between the way she writes and her experience writing for blogs and Twitter?
3. If you were an employer, would you find Armstrong's argument convincing? Why or why not?

Queen Elizabeth's Image Repair Discourse:
Insensitive Royal or Compassionate Queen?

William L. Benoit and Susan L. Brinson

William Benoit received his Ph.D. from Wayne State University and teaches courses in crisis communication at the University of Missouri-Columbia. His co-author, Susan Brinson, teaches courses in mass communication at Auburn University and serves as the Editor of the Journal of Broadcasting and Electronic Media. *This essay appeared in 1999 in* Public Relations Review, *a long-standing journal that publishes work written by academics and professionals in several fields including social science research and public opinion formations. Benoit and Brinson examine four image repair strategies employed by Queen Elizabeth to quiet suspicions about the Royal Family's response to the sudden death of Princess Diana.*

Introduction

Our image, reputation, or face is vital to our social and emotional well-being. "Image" is the perception of a person (or group, or organization) held by others. One's image is influenced by one's own words and actions, as well as by the discourse and behavior of others. One's good name is very important to our emotional well-being, and having a positive reputation is very important in our dealings with others. Higgins and Snyder, for example, acknowledge that "people have a basic need to maintain positive images."[1] Threats to our reputation frequently compel us to attempt to repair our reputation: whenever we perceive that our image is at risk, we are inclined to take restorative action. Schlenker recognizes that predicaments can "damage" one's identity, "adversely affecting relationships" with others.[2] Accordingly, as Goffman explains, "When a face has been threatened, face-work must be done."[3] Face-work is persuasive discourse designed to restore a blemished image.

This phenomenon, motivation to repair a tarnished image, occurs throughout human behavior. Research has revealed that politicians,[4] corporations,[5] and sports/entertainment figures[6] all produce image restoration discourse when their image is threatened. But do Queens and other members of royalty need to concern themselves with the opinions of mere commoners?

The events following the death of Princess Diana—and the Royal family's response to suspicions, innuendo, and criticism—illustrate the claim that the need for public relations work is pervasive. Tragically, Diana, Princess of Wales, died of injuries sustained in an automobile accident in the early morning hours of Sunday, August 31, 1997. British citizens awoke Sunday morning to the shocking and completely unexpected news that Princess Diana was dead. In addition to explanations of the accident, the news media carried a brief statement issued by the Royal Family "confirming the death" of the Princess.[7]

While the Royal Family's initial public response to Diana's death may have been simple and muted, Britons responded with an enormous public demonstration of grief. Kensington Palace, Buckingham

Palace, and Westminster Abbey became instant shrines to Diana's memory and were deluged with flowers, cards, candles, and other remembrances of her. Stereotypes of the staid Briton with the "stiff upper lip" were replaced by video images of them weeping over their loss, and waiting in long lines to sign the books of condolence.

Their grief, however, was soon mixed with increasing anger directed toward the Queen and her family. News stories and letters to *The [London] Times* editor began to reveal public displeasure with the Royal Family's lack of response to Diana's death. One critique focused on the Queen's lack of public display of grief, and as the British newspaper *The Independent* put it, "if only the royals dared weep with the people."[8] Did the Royal Family even care about Princess Diana's tragic death?

The more stinging rebuke, however, chastised the Queen for failing to acknowledge her subjects' overwhelming grief.[9] Public judgments of inadequacy were stoked by several events. First, the Queen remained isolated in Balmoral Castle, Scotland, during the first several days following Diana's death, emerging only once on Sunday morning to attend church services and displaying no outward sign of grief over this tragedy. As one writer put it, "It is not understandable, indeed inexplicable, why…members of the Royal Family…should not have left Balmoral and talked directly to people.[10] The belief was that the Queen and her family should acknowledge their subjects' feelings. Second, the lack of a Royal Standard or Union Jack flying over Buckingham Palace in London also symbolized the Queen's lack of sensitivity to her subjects' grief.[11] In the other residence in Scotland, the flag flew, but not at half-mast. As *The Times* reported, "pictures of the Royal Standard flying at full-mast at Balmoral Castle…have further fueled a widespread feeling that the Royal Family is showing insufficient respect for the death of" Diana.[12] Although tradition holds that the Royal Standard is never flown at half-mast, even when a King or Queen dies, as *The Times* reported, Britons "were in no mood to observe the rules of royal protocol" regarding appropriate times for flying flags.[13] The clearest representations of public indignation were the headlines of London newspapers: "Your People Are Suffering. Speak to Us, Ma'am," "Where Is Our Queen? Where is Her Flag?," "Show Us You Care."[14] There was a widespread belief that the Royal Family was simply ignoring their subjects, creating a royal public relations nightmare.

According to the Queen's spokespersons she was genuinely hurt by the criticisms that suggested she was indifferent to Britons' suffering.[15] Nonetheless, the "ferocity" of the attacks[16] all but forced her to respond. Buckingham Palace "issued a statement acknowledging the enormous wave of public feeling for the Princess"[17] and several Royal Family members—including the Queen and Prince Philip—returned to London and engaged in a "burst of public activity" intended to communicate sympathy and solidarity.[18] In a significant break with Royal Protocol, the Queen also ordered the Royal Standard to fly at half-mast during Diana's funeral.

Even more remarkable than the decision to fly the Royal Standard at half-mast, however, was the Queen's agreement to address the British public on the evening before the funeral. As *The Times* put it, "The Palace has at last grasped the urgent need for a direct personal message."[19] In the United States we are accustomed to the President addressing the public frequently. This is decidedly not the case in England, where the Queen makes only two scheduled public addresses per year: the annual Christmas address and the Opening of Parliament. Indeed, in the 45 years since Queen Elizabeth ascended the British throne, she made only one other unscheduled public address to her subjects.[20] Further, while Britons certainly understood the importance of the Queen's address, television news anchors in the United States also "went out of their way to bridge the cultural gap and explain how historic the Queen's break with protocol was."[21] Queen Elizabeth's speech was thus an extraordinary response to the growing feeling of hostility among her subjects—and a clear signal of her concern over matters of public relations.

The circumstances leading to the public address Queen Elizabeth made on September 5, 1997, were virtually unprecedented. As Phillips explained, "The public and the press had so harshly scolded the royal family, and Queen Elizabeth in particular, for making no public expression…of its feelings that the Queen was forced to capitulate."[22] Thus, the address itself, designed to restore the Queen's damaged public image, deserves analysis to determine whether her response was appropriate and successful. The Royal Family is an institution that, like any corporation or other organization, must be concerned with public relations. However, rhetorical examinations of royal addresses are rare, perhaps owing to the infrequency with which these discourses occur. One of the few studies of this kind of situation is Ryan's evaluation of King Edward VIII's 1938 apologia following accusations by Prime Minister Stanley Baldwin over Edward's decision to marry a commoner.[23] To analyze Queen Elizabeth's public relations effort we first explain the theory of image restoration discourse. Then we describe and analyze the Queen's discourse. Finally, we evaluate the rhetorical effectiveness of her rhetorical response and discuss the implications of this analysis.

Theory of Image Restoration Discourse

The communication literature offers approaches to understanding image repair rhetoric.[24] Benoit's typology of image repair strategies synthesizes this material into a more comprehensive theory.[25] Because this typology has been described elsewhere we will briefly sketch the strategies available to rhetors here.

As Ryan correctly observes, image repair is best understood as a response to a prior attack (or to suspicions).[26] A persuasive attack has two key elements: (1) the accused must be seen as responsible for an act; (2) that act must be viewed as offensive by a salient audience.[27] Most of the rhetor's options stem directly from these two essential elements of an attack. There are five general forms of image repair, several with specific variants (see Table 1).

DENIAL
Simple denial has three forms. A person accused of wrong doing may deny that the offensive act occurred, deny that he or she committed the act, or deny that the act is harmful. Any of these forms of denial, if accepted by the audience, can help repair the rhetor's image. A related option is for the rhetor to attempt to shift the blame. If another person (or group, or organization) really committed the offensive act, the accused should not be blamed.

EVADE RESPONSIBILITY
Attempting to evade responsibility for the offensive act has four versions. One may claim the offensive act was a reasonable response to someone else's offensive act (usually an act of the alleged victim) and that this response is a reasonable reaction to that provocation. Defeasibility claims that the actor did

TABLE 1 IMAGE RESTORATION STRATEGIES

Denial	Reducing Offensiveness of Event
Simple Denial	Bolstering
Shifting the Blame	Minimization
Evasion of Responsibility	Differentiation
Provocation	Transcendence
Defeasibility	Attack Accuser
Accident	Compensation
Good Intentions	Corrective Action
	Mortification

not have the knowledge or ability to avoid committing the offensive act. One may also suggest that the offense occurred by accident. Fourth, the rhetor can explain that the act was performed with good intentions.

REDUCE OFFENSIVENESS

One can attempt to reduce the apparent offensiveness of the act in six ways. First, a rhetor can bolster his or her image so as to strengthen the audience's positive feelings toward him or her, hopefully offsetting the negative feelings arising from the wrongful act. Minimization suggests that the act in question is not as offensive as it seems. Differentiation is an attempt to distinguish the act from other similar but more offensive actions. In comparison, the act performed by the rhetor may not seem so bad. Transcendence attempts to justify the act by placing it in a more favorable context. One accused of wrong doing could attack his or her accusers, to reduce the credibility of the accusations (or suggest the victim deserved what happened). Compensation offers to give the victim money, goods, or services to help mitigate the negative feelings toward the rhetor.

CORRECTIVE ACTION

Corrective action is a commitment to repair the damage from the offensive act. This can take two forms: restoring the state of affairs before the offensive act and preventing the recurrence of the offensive act.

MORTIFICATION

The last strategy is to admit committing the offensive act and to ask for forgiveness. A sincere apology may help restore the rhetor's image. With a basic understanding of the concepts that guided our analysis of the Queen's speech in hand, we can turn to discussing the fruits of our analysis.

Queen Elizabeth's Image Repair Effort

The Queen's discourse[28] enacted four image repair strategies: two predominated (denial, bolstering), while two others played relatively minor roles (defeasibility, transcendence). We will discuss each strategy separately in this section.

DENIAL

First and foremost, the simple fact that the Queen gave this speech, unprecedented as it was, functioned to deny the accusation that the Royal Family did not care about Diana's death or about their subjects' feelings of grief. As such, this speech is an instance of rhetorical enactment.[29] As Campbell and Jamieson note, the fact that Barbara Jordan, an African-American woman, could be selected to give the keynote speech at a presidential nominating convention demonstrates that minorities have come a long way toward being integrated into the political mainstream. Similarly, the fact that Queen Elizabeth decided to give an unprecedented speech—before she ever spoke a word (or, as long as she wasn't offensive, almost regardless of what she said)—was a powerful rhetorical act expressing concern over Princess Diana and for her subjects' feelings. As in Campbell and Jamieson's explanation of Barbara Jordan's Democratic keynote, the sheer act of Queen Elizabeth delivering a speech on this topic "embodies the position she is arguing";[30] in this case, that position is that the Royal Family cares about Princess Diana and their subjects. Tradition-bound as the British monarchy is, surely it was not easy to make the decision to give such an unparalleled appearance. The British people could see on their televisions and hear on their radios that their Queen really did care about the Princess and about them and their feelings. The Queen was willing to break with tradition, to try something new, to reassure her subjects. This was a moment of high drama, and it functioned to deny the reproaches of the Royal Family.

Examination of the speech itself reveals that the Queen responded more directly to the criticisms. Several of her passages addressed the charge that the Royal Family did not care about Princess Diana's tragic death. The Queen characterized the news as "dreadful," thus revealing her attitude. She reassured her audience that she cared about the fallen Princess: "First, I want to pay tribute to Diana myself. She was an exceptional and gifted human being. In good times and bad, she never lost her capacity to smile and laugh, nor to inspire others with her warmth and kindness." Later, she explicitly declared that "I admired and respected her—for her energy and commitment to others, and especially for her devotion to her two boys." Similarly, Queen Elizabeth said, "I share in your determination to cherish her memory." These statements function directly to deny the accusations that the Royal Family was uncaring of Princess Diana.

Furthermore, the Queen set to rest suspicions that she did not care about her subjects' feelings. She was aware of the "overwhelming expression of sadness at Diana's death." The speech suggested that she and her subjects could share in the grieving process: "I hope that tomorrow we can all, wherever we are, join in expressing our grief at Diana's loss, and gratitude for her all-too-short life." Thus, the speech, in its specific details as well as being an unprecedented rhetorical act, directly denied the accusations directed toward the Royal Family.

Although not part of the address itself, the Queen's decision to lower the Royal Standard over Buckingham Palace to half-mast during Diana's funeral also functioned as a rhetorical act to deny charges of indifference. The Queen's actions communicated to her subjects that she cared about their perceptions of her, to the point of disregarding royal protocol.

BOLSTERING

Several passages in the message functioned to bolster the Queen's image. She assured her subjects of her sincerity, explaining, "What I say to you now, as your Queen and as a grandmother, I say from my heart." Queen Elizabeth revealed that the Royal Family had been at Balmoral to comfort Princess Diana's children: "This week at Balmoral, we have all been trying to help William and Harry come to terms with the devastating loss that they and the rest of us have suffered." She spoke directly to the bereaved viewers, thanking them for their outpouring of emotions for the entire Royal Family: "This is also an opportunity for me, on behalf of my family, and especially Prince Charles and William and Harry, to thank all of you who have brought flowers, sent messages, and paid your respects in so many ways to a remarkable person." These utterances function to display the Queen's, and the Royal Family's, heartfelt emotions, selfless motives, and gratitude, bolstering their image.

DEFEASIBILITY

Some of her audience might still have wondered why she didn't speak up sooner. At one point the Queen used the strategy of defeasibility to account for the lack of public response from the Royal Family. She explained, "It is not easy to express a sense of loss, since the initial shock is often succeeded by a mixture of other feelings: disbelief, incomprehension, anger—and concern for those who remain." Thus, these feelings—shock, disbelief, incomprehension, anger—were difficult to surmount, and are offered as an excuse for their initial reaction, or lack thereof.

TRANSCENDENCE

Finally, the Queen attempted to direct her viewers' attention toward a larger issue: the world's perception of the British people. She explained that this tragedy and Princess Diana's funeral "is a chance to show to the whole world the British nation united in grief and respect." This suggests that her subjects should band together to put on a united front to the rest of the world—rather than dwell on criticisms of the Royal Family. It gave them a reason to renew their bond with their monarch.

Evaluation of the Royal Image Repair Effort

We argue that this was a well-developed and appropriate response to the allegations and suspicions faced by the Royal Family. First, we believe the strategies are well chosen for this situation. It was incumbent upon the Queen to deny these charges. She couldn't simply offer an excuse or try to justify a lack of feelings for the Princess and her subjects. Denial was essential to this image repair effort. Furthermore, especially given growing concerns over the relevance and expense of the monarchy in recent years, it was appropriate for the Queen to bolster herself and the Royal Family in this address. Defeasibility is a potentially useful strategy, noting the interference of factors beyond one's control. Finally, attempting to transcend current events to focus on issues that were arguably more important is a plausible strategy. Other potential responses—like attempting to minimize the people's concerns, or attacking the Royal Family's accusers—were inappropriate and the Queen was wise to avoid them. Thus, we judge that the four strategies selected were appropriate.

A second issue is how well the strategies were operationalized in the discourse itself. Some denials, for example, are simply more believable than others. We judge that Queen Elizabeth did a good job implementing these image repair strategies in her response. As noted above, this speech was an instance of rhetorical enactment, wherein the discourse itself—apart from (or in addition to) what was said in it—embodied a response to the accusations. This was a highly dramatic and especially effective response to the accusations. Obviously, the Queen cared about her subjects: she was willing to take the risk of giving a virtually unprecedented speech to them! Her subjects responded well to this action. As Hamilton and McGrory revealed, "The Queen returned to London to face her people…, and they left her in do doubt that she was welcome."[31] Further, the specific instances of denial within the speech were appropriate as well. She sounded sincere and genuinely concerned about her people. She expressed her grief over Diana's death as well as her concern for her subjects' feelings. Again, Britons responded favorably to the Queen's denials, as "there was widespread praise…for the Queen's broadcast, ranging from members of the peerage to the crowd outside Buckingham Palace."[32] Apparently the speech's viewers found it persuasive as well.

Bolstering was also developed effectively in the speech. The Queen indicated that she was speaking from her heart. She mentioned the family's concerns for Princess Diana's two children, and expressed her appreciation for her subjects' support. Furthermore, defeasibility provided a plausible excuse for the Royal Family's apparent lack of response, and transcendence was a reasonable attempt to rally her subjects with an attractive appeal (a united Britain facing the world). It was also a good decision to mention these last two strategies without dwelling on either (which may have appeared too defensive). Therefore, each of the four strategies was developed well in the discourse. Many in England believed the Queen responded well to their concerns, and appreciated that she "opened her heart to her people…with a deeply-felt personal tribute to Diana."[33]

Implications

In a day and age in which it seems that almost everyone is apologizing for something (for ignoring atrocities committed in World War II; for experiments performed on minorities; for biting an opponent in a prize fight; for referring to African-Americans as "black jelly beans;"[3] for having an inappropriate sexual relationship with a White House intern), some people and institutions are comparatively silent. Elizabeth II, Queen of England, has never before given a speech to repair her image, or the Royal Family's image. Of course, she didn't apologize here, but her rhetorical action was especially dramatic in large part because she had never done it before. Of course, if tragedy strikes again and a similar situation faces her in the future, this approach will not work as well. Still, the mere fact that she gave a speech about Princess Diana's death (and the Royal Family's reaction, or apparent lack thereof) gave this speech a tremendous power. This does not mean that she could have said anything (an offensive stance could have robbed the moment of its significance), but the situation, including the fact that such a speech was unprecedented, favored the Queen.

She effectively denied the charges, provided a plausible excuse, and directed her viewers' attention to another, allegedly more important issue. She avoided strategies that would have caused resentment in her viewers (like minimization or attacking one's accusers). The speech was not simply adequate, not merely inoffensive, but positively well-crafted to succinctly but distinctly make her point. This image repair effort was aided by circumstances, but was extremely well-conceived as well.

The idea of rhetorical enactment is a significant one. There are occasional circumstances in which the sheer fact of a rhetorical act—regardless of its details—functions persuasively in a rhetorical situation. We suspect that it is no coincidence that Barbara Jordan's 1976 keynote speech (from an African-American woman) and Queen Elizabeth's image repair effort were unprecedented (in the case of King Edward VIII, his speech occurred when he had already abdicated, and his brother had already become King George VI).[34] These two rhetorical acts had more "power" or impact because they were unusual. However, for this very reason, if a second African-American woman, or another Queen, to give an image restoration discourse, it would not be as inherently effective. We speculate that there will probably be some spillover as well. When Katherine Ortega (a Hispanic woman) gave a Republican nominating convention keynote speech eight years after Barbara Jordan, even though she was a member of a different minority, we suspect the effect of rhetorical enactment was vastly dissipated from 1976. Rhetorical enactment can be powerful, but it may be a fleeting phenomenon.

Conclusion

After the tragic death of Princess Diana, the British people grew increasingly incensed as the Royal Family seemed to ignore first the fallen Princess and then their subjects. Criticism of the Monarchy grew very heated, creating an enormous public relations problem. Queen Elizabeth decided to make a historic, and completely unprecedented, rhetorical response to these accusations and criticisms. Her speech enacted one of her primary strategies, embodying a denial of the charge that the Royal Family did not care about Princess Diana or the British people and their grief. The Queen's speech was remarkably well-crafted: denying the accusations within the speech, bolstering her and the Royals, and briefly offering an excuse for their behavior and suggesting that the viewers turn their attention to another issue (the Britons united against the world). This case study clearly demonstrates that public relations are important concerns for the normally aloof royalty—and rightfully so.

References

1. R. L. Higgins and C. R. Snyder, "The Business of Excuses," in R. A. Giacalone and P. Rosenfeld (eds.), *Impression Management in the Organization* (Hillsdale, NJ: Lawrence Erlbaum, 1989), p. 74.
2. Barry R. Schlenker, *Impression Management: The Self-Concept, Social Identity, and Interpersonal Relations* (Monterey, CA: Brooks/Cole, 1980), p. 131.
3. Erving Goffman, *Relations in Public: Microstudies of the Public Order* (New York: Harper & Row, 1967), p. 27.
4. See, e.g., William L. Benoit, "Richard M. Nixon's Rhetorical Strategies in his Public Statements on Watergate," *Southern Speech Communication Journal* 47 (1982), pp. 192–211; William L. Be-

noit, "Senator Edward M. Kennedy and the Chappaquiddick Tragedy," in Halford R. Ryan (ed.), *Oratorical Encounters* (Westport, CT: Greenwood Press, 1988), pp. 187–199; William L. Benoit, Paul Gullifor, and Dan Panici, "Reagan's Discourse on the Iran-Contra Affair," *Communication Studies* 42 (1991), pp. 272–294; William L. Benoit and William T. Wells, *Candidates in Conflict: Persuasive Attack and Defense in the 1992 Presidential Debates* (Tuscaloosa: University of Alabama Press, 1996); Kimberly A. Kennedy and William L. Benoit "The Newt Gingrich Book Deal Controversy: Self-Defense Rhetoric," *Southern Communication Journal* 62 (1997), pp. 197–216; Robert A. Vartabedian, "Nixon's Vietnam Rhetoric: A Case Study of Apologia as Generic Paradox," *Southern Speech Communication Journal* 50 (1985), pp. 366–381.

5. See, e.g., William L. Benoit, "Sears' Repair of its Auto Repair Image: Image Restoration Discourse in the Corporate Sector," *Communication Studies* 46 (1995), pp. 89–109; William L. Benoit and Susan L. Brinson, "AT&T: Apologies Are not Enough," *Communication Quarterly* 42 (1994), pp. 75–88; William L. Benoit and Anne Czerwinski, "A Critical Analysis of USAir's Image Repair Discourse," *Business Communication Quarterly* 60 (1997), pp. 38–57; William L. Benoit and James J. Lindsey, "Argument Strategies: Antidote to Tylenol's Poisoned Image," *Journal of the American Forensic Association* 23 (1987), pp. 136–146; Susan L. Brinson and William L Benoit, "Dow Corning's Image Repair Strategies in the Breast Implant Crisis," *Communication Quarterly* 44 (1996), pp. 29–41; Sonya K. Foss, "Retooling an Image: Chrysler Corporation's Rhetoric of Redemption," *Western Journal of Speech Communication* 48 (1984), pp. 75–91; Keith M. Hearit, "Apologies and Public Relations crises at Chrysler, Toshiba, and Volvo," *Public Relations Review* 20 (1994), pp. 113–125; Keith M. Hearit, "The Use of Counter-Attack in Apologetic Public Relations Crises: The Case of General Motors vs. Dateline NBC," *Public Relations Review* 22 (1996), pp. 233–248; Keith M. Hearit, "On the Use of Transcendence as an Apologia Strategy: The Case of Johnson Controls and Its Fetal Protection Policy," *Public Relations Review* 23 (1997), pp. 217–231; Richard Ice, "Corporate Publics and Rhetorical Strategies: The Case of Union Carbide's Bhopal Crisis," *Management Communication Quarterly* 4 (1991), pp. 341–362.

6. See, e.g., William L. Benoit, "Hugh Grant's Image Restoration Discourse: An Actor Apologizes," *Communication Quarterly* 45 (1997), pp. 251–267; William L. Benoit and K. Kerby Anderson, "Blending Politics and Entertainment: Dan Quayle versus Murphy Brown," *Southern Communication Journal* 62 (1996), pp. 73–85; William L. Benoit and Robert S. Hanczor, "The Tonya Harding Controversy: An Analysis of Image Repair Strategies," *Communication Quarterly* 42 (1994), pp. 416–433; J. Nelson, "The Defense of Billie Jean King," *Western Journal of Speech Communication* 48 (1984), pp. 92–102.

7. Royal Press Releases, (1997, August 31), http://www.coi.gov.uk/coi/depts/GQB/GQB.html.

8. Warren Hoge, "Royal Family, Stung by Critics, Responds to Grieving Nation," *New York Times* (Sept. 4, 1997a), p. A1.

9. Alan Hamilton, Andrew Pierce, and Philip Webster, "Royal Family Is Deeply Touched by Public Support," *The [London] Times* (Sept. 4, 1997), p. 1.

10. "Royal Protocol and Public Grief," The [London] Times (Sept. 4, 1997), p. 19.

11. Hamilton, Pierce, and Webster, op. cit.

12. Hamilton, Pierce, and Webster, op. cit., p. A5.

13. Philip Webster and Alan Hamilton, "Queen to Make TV Broadcast," *The [London] Times* (Sept. 5, 1997), p. 1.

14. Warren Hoge, "Responding to Britain's Sorrow, Queen Will Address Nation," *New York Times* (Sept. 5, 1997b), p. A1.

15. Warren Hoge, "Elizabeth Returns to London to Bury, and Praise, Diana," *New York Times* (Sept. 6, 1997c), p. A1.

16. Hoge, op. cit., 1997b, p. A6.

17. Hamilton, Pierce, and Webster, op. cit, p. 1.

18. Webster and Hamilton, op. cit.

19. "Monarch and Media," *The [London] Times* (Sept. 5, 1997), p. 3.
20. Hoge, op. cit. (1997c).
21. Caryn James, "Windsors Through a Lens, Stiffly," *New York Times* (Sept. 6, 1997), p. A6.
22. Andrew Phillips, "Grief on Demand," *New York Times* (Sept. 7, 1997), Section 4, p. 16.
23. Halford R. Ryan, "Baldwin Versus Edward VIII: A Case Study in Kategoria and Apologia," *Southern Speech Communication Journal* 49 (1984), pp. 125–134; Halford R. Ryan, "Prime Minister Stanley Baldwin vs. King Edward VIII," in Halford R. Ryan (ed.), *Oratorical Encounters* (Westport, CT: Greenwood Press, 1988), pp. 53–62.
24. See, e.g., Kenneth Burke, *The Rhetoric of Religion* (Berkeley: University of California Press, 1970); B. L. Ware and Wil A. Linkugel, "They Spoke in Defense of Themselves: On the Generic Criticism of Apologia," *Quarterly Journal of Speech* 59 (1973), 273–283.
25. William L. Benoit, *Accounts, Excuses, Apologies: A Theory of Image Restoration Strategies* (Albany: State University of New York Press, 1995); William L. Benoit, "Image Repair Discourse and Crisis Communication," *Public Relations Review* 23 (1997), pp. 177–186.
26. Halford R. Ryan, "Kategoria and Apologia: On their Rhetorical Criticism as a Speech Set," *Quarterly Journal of Speech* 68 (1982), pp. 256–261.
27. William L. Benoit and Bruce Dorries, "Dateline NBC's Persuasive Attack of Wal-Mart," *Communication Quarterly* 44 (1996), pp. 463–477; Benoit and Wells, op. cit.
28. Queen Elizabeth, "The Queen's Message," http://www.coi.gov.ak/coi/depts/GQB/coi2175d.ok (Sept. 5, 1997).
29. Karlyn K. Campbell and Kathleen H. Jamieson, "Form and Genre in Rhetorical Criticism: An Introduction," in Karlyn K. Campbell and Kathleen H. Jamieson (eds.), *Form and Genre: Shaping Rhetorical Action* (Falls Church, VA: Speech Communication Association, 1978), pp. 9–32.
30. Ibid., p. 10.
31. Alan Hamilton and Daniel McGrory, "The Queen Shares her Sadness," *The [London] Times* (Sept. 6, 1997), p. 3.
32. Adrian Lee, "Generous Words Earn Universal Praise," *The [London] Times* (Sept. 6, 1997), p. 2.
33. Alan Hamilton, Philip Webster, and Daniel McGrory, "Queen Pays Tribute to 'Exceptional and Gifted Human Being," *The [London] Times* (Sept. 6, 1997), p. 1.
34. Ryan, op. cit. (1988).

DISCUSSION *questions and activities*

1. Describe the rhetorical situation that compelled the Queen of England to address her subjects after the death of Princess Diana. What expectations did the British audience hold that were thwarted by the Royal Family's response? Discuss the differences between this audience's expectations for its queen and those held by an American audience for its president after a national tragedy.

2. In small groups, analyze the authors' ability to support their claims that Queen Elizabeth is largely effective in her image repair efforts. Do you believe that the Queen's speech would change her audience's perception of her feelings about the loss of Princess Diana?

3. Read Benoit and Henson's article on President Bush's image repair discourse after Hurricane Katrina, and compare Bush's use of defeasibility and bolstering to Queen Elizabeth's use of these same tactics.

President Bush's Image Repair Discourse on Hurricane Katrina

William L. Benoit and Jayne R. Henson

William Benoit received his Ph.D. from Wayne State University and teaches courses in crisis communication at the University of Missouri-Columbia, where his co-author, Jayne Henson, was a doctoral student. Benoit has researched and published extensively in the area of image repair discourse; he and Henson now both teach courses in crisis communication. This essay appeared in 2009 in Public Relations Review, *a long-standing journal that publishes work written by academics and professionals in several fields including communication and public policy formation. Benoit and Henson analyze President Bush's attempts to regain the national trust after public critiques of his response to Hurricane Katrina, which took at least 1,836 lives and cost $81 billion in property damage.*

On August 29, 2005, Hurricane Katrina rocked the American gulf coast, in what the National Oceanic and Atmospheric Administration labeled "the most destructive storm ever to strike the USA" (Parker and Levin, 2005, 1A). In the following weeks, the death toll rose dramatically and assessment of the damage illustrated just how devastating a Category 4 hurricane could be. The coast lost nearly two-thirds of its housing, and Coast Guard officials warned of a massive oil spill comparable to the Exxon Valdez (Parker and Levin, 2005, 1A). The waters of Lake Ponchatrain spilled over the levies in several places, which was particularly problematic given that much of the city of New Orleans was situated below sea level. Of the 16 hospitals in New Orleans, only three remained open (Manning, 2005, 3A) and the staff who remained could do little but slowly watch patients die (Davis, 2005, 1A). City officials said that drinking water might be contaminated and they were helpless to warn remaining residents about health concerns (Parker and Frank, 2005, 1A). In addition to these concerns, massive looting plagued the city in the aftermath; a situation exacerbated by the alleged desertion of many police in the city's greatest hour of need (Levin, 2005, 5A). The current death toll stands at 964 (Johnson, 2005, 2C). Clearly, the human and economic toll from Hurricane Katrina was devastating.

Unfortunately, conditions continued to worsen for residents as response to this crisis was slow and fragmented. Senator John Kerry stated that citizens have doubts about "the competence and commitment of this administration" (Keen, 2005, 6A). Although the Senator could be expected to criticize the President (given that Kerry lost the 2004 presidential election to Bush), his concerns were echoed by others. For example, the Louisiana governor, Kathleen Babineaux Blanco, noted the federal government's failure while shouldering some responsibility herself (Governor, Mayor Admit Mistakes, 2005, 3A). In a radio interview that was played repeatedly, New Orleans mayor Ray Nagin expressed his frustration over the government's response: "Don't tell me 40,000 people are coming here! They're not here! It's too doggone late. Now get off your asses and let's do something! Let's fix the biggest God-damned crisis in the history of this country. People are dying" (Saulny, 2005, A13). President Bush's first trip to the region did not occur until September 2nd, 4 days after the hurricane made landfall.

Even Republicans had concerns about Bush's performance in the aftermath of Hurricane Katrina. Republican senator from Maine, Susan Collins, said that "we witnessed what appeared to be a sluggish initial response" and admitted that Katrina was proof of the inadequacy of the government's emergency-preparedness systems (Governor, Mayor Admit Mistakes, 2005, 3A). A National Journal, 2005 "insiders" poll of 31 congressional Republicans and 52 Republican political insiders revealed that both groups gave the President a C+ grade (2005). Some of the comments offered were "President Bush was slow to take charge"; "It took Bush way to long to react," and when he did he "did not set the right tone, such as his recollections of partying in New Orleans and looking forward to sitting on Trent Lott's new front porch"; and one should not appoint "anyone other than experienced professionals to emergency-management positions." The reactions of congressional Democrats and Democratic insiders were, of course, even more negative than these remarks.

The appointment of Michael D. Brown, director of the Federal Emergency Management Agency was controversial: His experience included work for a horse breeder's association. President Bush was accused of giving vital governmental offices to cronies instead of appointing qualified personnel. Brown publicly admitted ignorance of the unfolding situation in New Orleans where thousands were trapped and dying in the New Orleans convention center (Bumiller, 2005, A11). On September 9th the administration called him to Washington and he resigned on September 12th.

It appeared that the response from all levels of government was far too slow and poorly coordinated. This was particularly troubling at the federal level because our emergency-preparedness should have been high after the tragedy of 9/11. Thus, there was ample blame to go around, but President Bush came under particular attack for the government's inadequate response: painfully slow and at least initially ineffectual. An ABC News (2004) poll on September 2 reported that 76% of the people believed Bush should get some, a good amount, or a great deal of blame "for problems in the federal response" to Katrina. On September 15, over 2 weeks after Katrina struck, President Bush responded with a speech televised live from Jackson Square in New Orleans. This paper will critically analyze and evaluate his image repair effort in that speech. Although the president made other statements on Katrina (e.g., on August 30 in San Diego, August 31 in the Rose Garden, September 2 in Biloxi, MS), the Jackson Square speech was his major statement on Hurricane Katrina. We critically analyze that speech using the theory of image repair discourse. First, the method used in this analysis will be explicated. Then the rhetorical strategies employed in his speech will be analyzed, his image repair effort will be evaluated, and finally implications will be explored.

1. Critical Method: Image Repair Discourse

The task of understanding persuasive messages employed to repair a tarnished image has occupied many critics and theorists (see, e.g., Coombs, 1995; Hearit, 1994; Rowland and Jerome, 2004; Seeger, Sellnow, & Ulmer, 2003; Ware and Linkugel, 1973). The literature acknowledges that face, image, or reputation can be extremely important, that threats to image arise throughout human affairs, and that persuasive messages can help repair damage done to a reputation from accusations or suspicions of wrong-doing. Relying on previous scholarship in the area (e.g., Burke, 1970; Scott and Lyman, 1968; Ware and Linkugel, 1973). Benoit (1995, 1997, 2000) identified a variety of potential image repair strategies grouped under five general strategies (see also Blaney and Benoit, 2001; and the critique by Burns and Bruner, 2000). The first general category of image repair strategy is denial. Simple denial claims that the accused did not commit the offensive act or that the offensive act did not occur. Shifting blame goes a step further and attributes responsibility for the wrongful deed to another. The second general category of image repair, evading responsibility, can assume four forms. Provocation asserts that the offensive act should be viewed as an understandable response to another, prior wrongful act. Defeasibility claims that the accused should not be blamed because of a lack of information or control over the offensive act. Third, accident argues that the wrongful act was a mishap. Next, the accused can argue that he or she meant well, performing the act with good intentions. The third general category of image repair, reducing offensiveness, has six variants. Bolstering attempts to counterbalance the offensive act by accentuating the positive qualities or actions of the accused. Minimization is designed to reduce the severity of the consequences of the wrongful act. Differentiation works by comparing the act in question to similar but less desirable acts. Transcendence seeks to justify the offensive act with appeals to higher values or other more important ends. The accused can also attack the accuser, to reduce the credibility of the source of accusations and/or create the impression that the victim deserved his or her fate. The last version of reducing offensiveness occurs when the accused offers compensation to the victim. The last two general strategies are corrective action, which promises to repair and/or prevent recurrence of the problem, and mortification, which is Burke's term for an apology. With this critical method in hand, we can turn to an analysis of Bush's discourse on Katrina to see how he attempted to repair his image.

2. Critical Analysis of Bush's Image Repair Discourse

Careful analysis of the text of this speech reveals that President Bush (2005) used three strategies to repair his image: bolstering, defeasibility, and corrective action. His use of each of these strategies will be illustrated with excerpts from his speech.

2.1. BOLSTERING

This choice of location for this speech—Jackson Square in New Orleans—was surely deliberate. Bush was seen as physically present in the hurricane ravaged city, rather than far away inside the Washington beltway. This choice may have been intended to reinforce the idea that he cared about the victims. Furthermore, Jackson Square was obviously free from debris and flood waters, which may have been intended as a subtle attempt to minimize the damage, or to show the effects of clean-up efforts. However, given the tardiness of this discourse, and the visibly empty Square, it is unlikely that these factors made much difference to viewers. The setting visually bolstered the president: the speech occurred at night; Bush is the only person we see and in the background the St. Louis Cathedral is bathed in light.

Bush stressed his good character near the beginning of his speech by reminding the public that he is a man of faith. Religion refocuses attention from the destruction caused by the hurricane to a question of faith and resolve to turn this tragedy into positive moment. "Across the Gulf Coast, among people who have lost so much. . . we are seeing that same spirit—a core of strength that survives all hurt, a faith in God no storm can take away." Additionally, expression of his faith in this rhetoric may prompt the public to view him as a religious leader and a source of hope. Bush revealed his compassion for the suffering of others, supplementing his religious bolstering: The victims "remind us that we're tied together in this life, in this nation—and that despair of any touches us all." He also said that "You need to know that our whole nation cares about you, and in the journey ahead you're not alone" and he extended his "deepest sympathy" to the victims. This statement portrays his concern for the victims of the hurricane. Although Bush was physically far removed from the destruction in the Gulf Coast, his discourse indicated that he was sympathetic with the victims and empathized with the sense of loss experienced by survivors and loved ones: "I extend the deepest sympathy of your country." These and other similar statements functioned to bolster the president's image.

2.2. CORRECTIVE ACTION

In the middle portion of the address, Bush discussed actions designed to ameliorate the devastation of the hurricane. He described help that was already being delivered and assistance planned for the future. He also offered three general commitments for future relief.

First, the president promised to "meet the immediate needs of those who had to flee their homes." He asked for $60 billion from Congress for this purpose. Furthermore, he described several initiatives that had already begun by the time of his speech:

> The work of rescue is largely finished. . . In nearly all of Mississippi, electric power has been restored. . . The breaks in the levees have been closed, the pumps are running, and the water here in New Orleans is receding by the hour. Environmental officials are on the ground. . . And some very sad duties are being carried out by professionals who gather the dead.

Such actions as rescuing victims, restoring power, repairing levees, checking the environment, and caring for the dead are already helping to repair the damage created by hurricane Katrina and return New Orleans and the surrounding area to normalcy. The president also identified a number of actions being taken by federal officials in particular:

> The Department of Homeland Security is registering evacuees. . . The Department of Health and Human Services has sent more than 1,500 health professionals along with over 50 tons of medical supplies. The Social Security Administration is delivering checks. The Department of Labor is helping displaced persons apply for temporary jobs and unemployment benefits. And the Postal Service is registering new addresses.

All of these agencies of the federal government were already working toward helping the victims of Hurricane Katrina. He also explained that the government was bringing in mobile homes, doctors, and nurses and was providing money to pay local emergency personnel overtime.

Other actions, such as the generosity of "religious congregations and families" who "welcomed strangers and brothers and sisters and neighbors," were mentioned. The staff of the Tulane Children's Hospital "did not eat for days so patients could have food" and they "carried the patients on their backs up eight flights of stairs to helicopters." He also mentioned how members of local fire departments were going door-to-door "to search for survivors." Clearly, many people were participating in the relief efforts.

However, these efforts were not all we could expect: Bush's second major commitment was to "help the citizens of the Gulf Coast to overcome this disaster, put their lives back together, and rebuild their communities." He declared that "We will do what it takes, we will stay as long as it takes, to help citizens rebuild their communities and their lives." He described a "partnership" between federal, state, and local officials to "rebuild in a sensible, well-planned way." He promised that "federal funds will cover the great majority of the costs of repairing public infrastructure in the disaster zone, from roads and bridges to school and water systems." Thus, he promised to provide long-term relief to storm victims as well as to coordinate the resumption of normal life in the area.

The president proposed "Worker Recovery Accounts," up to $5000 for job training, education, and child care. Another law he recommended was the "Urban Homesteading Act," which would give federally owned property to low-income citizens who would build homes on this land. The Army Corps of Engineers would help strengthen the levee system to prevent future floods. Bush mentioned that Presidents Bush and Clinton have already "received pledges of more than $100 million" for hurricane relief.

Bush's third commitment was to rebuild communities so they are "even better and stronger than before the storm." This included assistance for minority-owned businesses and creation of a "Gulf Opportunity Zone," with tax relief, loans, and incentives for job creation. Bush also explained that he asked the USA Freedom Corps to create an information outlet for anyone seeking to help with the reconstruction.

Finally, he promised to improve future disaster response. First, he would study the response to Hurricane Katrina: "We're going to review every action and make necessary changes, so that we are better prepared for any challenge of nature, or act of evil men, that could threaten our people." Then, he declared that "our cities must have clear and up-to-date plans for responding to natural disasters and disease outbreaks or a terrorist attack." Thus, we would learn from this disaster so as to prevent similar problems in the future. It may have come as a surprise to some that years after 9/11 we lacked "clear and up-to-date plans" for terrorist attacks (and natural disasters).

At the end of his address he acknowledged that "it is hard to imagine a bright future," but declared nevertheless "that future will come."

> The streets of Biloxi and Gulfport will again be filled with lovely homes and the sound of children playing. The churches of Alabama will have their broken steeples mended and their congregations whole. And here in New Orleans, the street cars will once again rumble down St. Charles, and the passionate soul of a great city will return.

Thus, he predicted that the effect of the current and future initiatives would, in fact, restore the damage from Katrina. So, the president described the myriad of efforts, some already in place, some just proposals, to repair the damage from this storm.

One element that is noticeably absent from Bush's discussion of corrective action is the replacement of the head of FEMA. Much criticism had been leveled at Ron Brown and 3 days before this speech President Bush accepted his resignation. Ordinarily, one might expect the president to mention replacing the apparently ineffectual head of such an important organization in this crisis as a move to correct the problem, if not to prevent future problems. However, Bush does not mention his move to replace an individual widely viewed as inept in his speech. It is unclear why Bush chose not to mention this important instance of corrective action; it is possible that he did not want to remind people of his mistake in appointing a person with such dubious qualifications in the first place.

2.3. DEFEASIBILITY
The third strategy that Bush used, which was introduced at the beginning of his speech but mostly developed near the end of his speech, was defeasibility. He began the speech by acknowledging the huge magnitude of this disaster. New Orleans was "nearly empty, still partly under water, and waiting for life and hope to return" and "millions of lives were changed in a day by a cruel and wasteful storm." This disaster had terrible consequences for many people, who suffered

> desperation no citizen of this great and generous nation should ever have to know: fellow Americans calling out for food and water, vulnerable people left at the mercy of criminals who had no mercy, and bodies of the dead lying uncovered and untended in the street.

Clearly, this was a disaster with widespread and devastating consequences for the victims and their loved ones.

The president described this crisis as "unprecedented" and characterized the storm as "a massive flood" and "a major supply and security operation," with "an evacuation order affecting more than a million people." He explained that Katrina "was not a normal hurricane—and the normal disaster relief system was not equal to it." The president noted that "nature is an awesome force" and he called Katrina an extraordinary disaster. This implied that the disaster relief system would have done better if Katrina had been a normal disaster (which begs the question of what is a "normal" disaster). Bush asserted that "many of the men and women" of the disaster relief system "performed skillfully." Nevertheless, the system "at every level of government was not well-coordinated and was overwhelmed in the first few days." In hindsight, "It is now clear that a challenge on this scale requires greater federal authority." These statements all function as excuses, attempts to explain the inadequate governmental response as understandable given the severity of the storm. In short, conditions beyond our control—rather than ineptitude, lack of preparation, or inadequate concern—were responsible for the poor response to the storm. The system was "overwhelmed" by forces beyond our control by an "unprecedented" crisis and an "extraordinary" disaster. How could the president be blamed for poor disaster response if he lacked the necessary "federal authority" to deal with "a challenge on this scale"?

Of course, the president does say near the end of his speech that "When the federal government fails to meet such an obligation [emergency], I, as president, am responsible for the problem, and for the solution." This is a fairly transparent attempt to create the impression that he accepted responsibility (and blame) for a poor disaster response. However, the immediately preceding paragraph and much of the material earlier in the speech took some pains to argue that the situation was to blame (defeasibility) not him. This statement simply cannot be taken at face value, particularly given its placement in the speech. With this understanding of Bush's image repair effort on Hurricane Katrina in hand, we can turn to a critical evaluation of his persuasive discourse.

3. EVALUATION OF BUSH'S IMAGE REPAIR EFFORT

This section will evaluate the effectiveness of the image repair strategies that Bush utilized in his speech. First, his attempts to bolster his image were fairly ineffectual, most likely to be persuasive with those who still viewed the president favorably. His "man of the hour" approach, applauded after 9/11, was relatively ineffectual here because it does not answer questions about the slow federal response to the disaster. In fact, some audience members might have had some difficulty reconciling his attempt at bolstering with the impression of an uncaring president who appeared to virtually ignore the tragic hurricane for days. If he really cared so much about the victims of Katrina, why was his response so slow in coming?

The strategy of defeasibility was a poor choice. First, the magnitude of the storm might have justified a slow response and poor coordination emergency procedures if the threat from Katrina had not been known until the time it made landfall. However, anyone who had even glanced at the news in the days leading up to the disaster knew Katrina was a very powerful hurricane that was headed for the New Orleans area. One of the accusations against Bush was that the federal government did not begin to intervene until several days after Katrina struck the mainland. Defeasibility was not a very persuasive strategy in this situation; everyone knew the hurricane was headed for the Gulf Coast days before it struck. Surely some preparations should have been made (calling up the national guard, moving supplies into the region), which would have substantially reduced the delay in the relief efforts. In fact, we would argue that defeasibility is a dangerous choice for a president to use. Although we must acknowledge that there are limits on any president's ability to cope with serious problems. Using a lack of information or ability to excuse offensive actions (or inaction) emphasizes the president's inability to cope with problems. People do not want to believe our president is helpless. On the contrary, we want to believe that he can protect us from threats and danger, so it is highly problematic when a president's discourse intentionally undermines this important belief.

Considering other image repair problems can provide a useful context for viewing Bush's Katrina image repair effort. For example, Senator Edward Kennedy faced a threat to his image when a car he was driving went off a bridge and his passenger, Mary Jo Kopechne, drowned. He was suspected of driving while intoxicated and leaving the scene of an accident. The Senator gave a speech in which defeasibility played a large role (see Benoit, 1988; Ling, 1970). He argued that "the car that I was driving on an unlit road went off a narrow bridge which had no guard rails and was build on a left angle to the road" (Kennedy, 1969, p. 10). This passage employed defeasibility, because the situation (an unlit road, a narrow bridge, a bridge without guard rails, a bridge build at an angle to the road) is the "real" cause of the accident and Miss Kopechne's death. He also dealt with the problem of not reporting an accident by mentioning that he suffered a concussion, was in a state of shock, and was exhausted (from trying to rescue Miss Kopechne). Again, a lack of ability is the "true" cause of this offensive action. The consequences of his speech were that "his senate seat seems quite safe, his presidential hopes dimmed, but not entirely extinguished" (Benoit, 1988, p. 195). Kennedy's reliance on defeasibility may not have cost him his place in the senate, but it probably damaged his chances to become president. Bush's use of defeasibility is in some ways even more risky, because Bush argued that he was unable to perform *his duty as president* (to engage in effective and timely disaster relief).

Corrective action is often a desirable choice for image repair (e.g., Benoit, 1997), particularly when the damage or harm is real (e.g., not exaggerated). President Reagan, for example, had denied trading arms for hostages in the Iran-contra affair up until the Tower Commission Report made it clear he had in fact done so. However, Reagan ultimately admitted that "A few months ago I told the American people I did not trade arms for hostages. My heart and my best intentions still tell me that is true, but the facts and the evidence tell me it is not" (Reagan, 1987, p. A18). He further stated that "I take full responsibility for my own actions and for those of my Administration" and then he explained his corrective action (changes in personnel, national security policy, and the decision-making process). Benoit, Gullifor, and Panici (1991) observe that his approval rating dropped from 63% to 40%, rebounding after this speech. Clearly, the public responded favorably to a clear admission of wrong-doing and corrective action in this case.

Therefore, Bush's use of this strategy was generally a good idea. However, his use of corrective action had important limitations. First, he listed many actions taken by the federal government (e.g., Homeland Security, Health and Human Services, the Labor Department, the Social Security Administration, and the Postal Service), but he also listed many actions which probably had not been performed by the federal government (e.g., repairing levies, repairing gasoline pipelines, gathering the dead), as well as other efforts for which he was clearly not responsible (e.g., actions of the religious congregations, the Tulane Children's Hospital, local fire departments). Although he did not explicitly attempt to take credit for the actions of others, his decision to intertwine relief actions for which he was, and was not, responsible, could have been viewed as an unreasonable attempt by the president to take credit for relief efforts undertaken by others. Second, many of the specific *federal* actions discussed by the president were promises of future aid ($60 billion requested from Congress, the Urban Homesteading proposal, the Gulf Opportunity Zone proposal) rather than actions already in progress. Promises of (possible) future relief may not be as persuasive as reports of actions already being performed. Third, Bush left some important questions about the corrective action he proposed unanswered, such as whether the Federal or local government will ultimately be responsible for decisions about where and how to rebuild, or how he would pay for the expensive federal action he did promise. Finally, that President Reagan admitted having traded arms for hostages probably helped his image repair effort. People like to hear others accept responsibility for their mistakes. President Bush offered corrective action but he never really admitted any mistakes on his part. Remember that he failed to mention a change in the head of FEMA, presumably because he did not want to call attention to his mistake in selected Brown for this vital job.

It is unlikely an accident that the president waited to take responsibility for problems with the federal response until *after* he deployed the strategy of defeasibility (arguing that the response had been overwhelmed by an extraordinary disaster) and *after* he discussed current and future relief efforts (plans for corrective action). Near the end of his speech he stated that "When the federal government fails to meet such an obligation, I, as President, am responsible for the problem, and for the solution." However, careful reading of his speech reveals that apart from one passage ("the system at every level of government, was not well-coordinated, and was overwhelmed in the first few days") he does not admit *any* mistakes in the relief effort or in preparation in the days just before Katrina. Nor does the president apologize, for he made no errors; the only problems were ones caused by a system overwhelmed by an unprecedented, extraordinary hurricane. So, we evaluate his image repair effort as largely ineffectual.

A poll conducted on September 26–28, after this speech, revealed that only 40% of the public said they approved of how the president handled Hurricane Katrina (Benedetto, 2005). These data indicate that the public response to his speech was largely consistent with our evaluation. Unfortunately for those who lived in the Gulf Coast area, the president got an opportunity for a "do-over" with Hurricane Rita. He reacted to the second storm quite differently, with trips before, during, and after Rita (recall his first visit to Louisiana was 5 days after Katrina struck). Apparently he realized his response to Katrina had been ill-advised and learned from these mistakes: 71% of the public said they approved of how the president handled Rita (Benedetto, 2005). Therefore, most of the public was unpersuaded by Bush's image repair effort on Hurricane Katrina.

4. CONCLUSION

President Bush refused to admit any specific wrong-doing in his handling of the Hurricane Katrina disaster, choosing instead to rely heavily on defeasibility. This stance is consistent with his approach to other situations. For example, during the town hall debate of October 8, 2004, Linda Grabel asked the president to acknowledge three wrong decisions he had made during his first term in office:

Grabel: Please give three instances in which you came to realize you had made a wrong decision [during the last 4 years], and what you did to correct it.

In response, the president refused to identify any specific mistake in the previous 4 years:

Bush: I have made a lot of decisions, and some of them little, like appointments to boards you never heard of, and some of them big. And in a war, there's a lot of—there's a lot of tactical decisions that historians will look back and say: He shouldn't have done that. He shouldn't have made that decision. And I'll take responsibility for them. I'm human. But on the big questions, about whether or not we should have gone into Afghanistan, the big question about whether we should have removed somebody in Iraq, I'll stand by those decisions, because I think they're right. . . Now, you asked what mistakes. I made some mistakes in appointing people, but I'm not going to name them. I don't want to hurt their feelings on national TV. But history will look back, and I'm fully prepared to accept any mistakes that history judges to my administration, because the president makes the decisions, the president has to take the responsibility (Debate Two, 2005).

Of course, it is easy to accept responsibility for mistakes when you refuse to acknowledge making any. His vague claim to have made some mistakes in appointments is particularly ironic given his selection of Michael Brown to head FEMA (Brown's main qualification appeared to be work with a horse breeders' association).

Similarly, in Bush's interview with Tim Russert on *Meet the Press* the president refused to admit mistakes in justifying the invasion of Iraq on the basis of weapons of mass destruction or in his handling of the economy (Benoit, 2006). It appears as if Bush is simply unwilling to concede any specific mistakes made as president. Given this premise—that he will not admit wrong-doing or engage in mortification—defeasibility, making excuses, is the main option available in a situation such as this. Even corrective action may be more effective if coupled with mortification (e.g., Benoit, Gullifor, & Panici, 1991). Bush's reliance on defeasibility and his failure to employ mortification (admitting specific mistakes) may have been predictable from his other discourse, but it was not likely to be persuasive in this instance. We are unwilling to argue that no president should ever use defeasibility (the magnitude of the storm was a plausible excuse for some problems in the relief effort—but *not* for the unconscionable delay), but we do think presidents should think carefully before they admit that they lacked the ability to solve or prevent a problem.

Although we have argued that President Bush had a serious aversion to admission of wrong-doing (explaining why he designed the speech as he did), mortification would have almost certainly been a more effective approach to this situation. A major accusation in this tragedy was the unreasonable delay in the federal government's response effort (and, more subtly, Bush did not seem to take the crisis very seriously at first—a speech given over 2 weeks after the hurricane hit is one suggestion of his lack of concern). Listing the current relief efforts (which came too late) does nothing to deal with this allegation. However, the president had an obvious and reasonable scapegoat available in FEMA director Ron Brown. The president had even accepted Brown's resignation before the Jackson Square speech. It would have been easy to apologize (engage in mortification), blame Mr. Brown for delays, announce his replacement (corrective action for the delays), and then detail the current relief effort (corrective action for the damage). However, that would have required the president to admit he had made a serious error in appointing Brown head of FEMA in the first place, an admission he was apparently unwilling to make.

References

ABC News. (2004). Public opinion poll. Accessed 10/15/05: http://web.lexis-nexis.com/universe/document?_m=476e76e871bab44956d01412aa664ca7&_docnum=2&wchp=dGLzVzz-zSkVA&_md5=d7f3d7363e0058ebceb941e8cace4e87.

Benedetto, R. (2005, September 30). Rita response boosts Bush's poll ratings. *USA Today*, p. 12A.

Benoit, W. L. (1988). Senator Edward M. Kennedy and the Chappaquiddick tragedy. In H. R. Ryan (Ed.), *Oratorical encounters: Selected studies and sources of twentieth-century political accusations and apologies* (pp. 187–199). Westport, CT: Greenwood Press.

Benoit, W. L. (1995). *Accounts, excuses, apologies: A theory of image restoration strategies*. Albany: State University of New York Press.

Benoit, W. L. (1997). Image repair discourse and crisis communication. *Public Relations Review, 23,* 177–186.

Benoit, W. L. (2000). Another visit to the theory of image restoration strategies. *Communication Quarterly, 48,* 40–44.

Benoit, W. L. (2006). President Bush's image repair effort on *Meet the Press*: The complexities of defeasability. *Journal of Applied Communication Research, 34,* 285–306.

Benoit, W. L., Gullifor, P., & Panici, D. A. (1991). President Reagan's defensive discourse on the Iran-Contra affair. *Communication Studies, 42,* 272–294.

Blaney, J. R., & Benoit, W. L. (2001). *The Clinton scandals and the politics of image restoration*. Westport, CT: Praeger.

Bumiller, E. (2005, September 10). Casualty of a firestorm. *New York Times*, p. A11.

Burke, K. (1970). *The rhetoric of religion*. Berkeley: University of California Press.

Burns, J. P., & Bruner, M. S. (2000). Revisiting the theory of image restoration. *Communication Quarterly, 48,* 27–39.

Bush, G. W. (2005 September 15). President discusses hurricane relief in address to the nation. Accessed 10/19/05: http://www.whitehouse.gov/news/releases/2005/09/images/20050915-8_speech-515h.html.

Coombs, W. T. (1995). Choosing the right words: The development of guidelines for the selection of the "appropriate" response strategies. *Management Communication Quarterly, 8,* 447–475.

Davis, R. (2005, September 16). Hope turn to anguish as intensive-care unit. *USA Today*, p. 1A.

Debate Two. (2005 October 8). Accessed 11/8/05: http://www.debates.org/pages/trans2004c.html.

Governor, mayor acknowledge mistakes. (2005, September 15). *USA Today*, p. 3A.

Hearit, K. M. (1994). From "we didn't do it" to "it's not our fault": The use of apologia in public relations crises. In W. Elwood (Ed.), *Public relations inquiry as rhetorical criticism: Case studies of corporate discourse and social influence* (pp. 117–131). Westport, CT: Praeger.

Johnson, J. A. (2005, October 7). In aftermath of tragedy, Christians' duty is clear. *The Columbus Dispatch*, p. 2C.

Keen, J. (2005, September 16). Bullhorn or not, Bush aims for a boost. *USA Today*, p. 6A.

Kennedy, E. (1969, July 26). Kennedy's television statement to the people of Massachusetts. *New York Times*, p. 10.

Levin, A. (2005, September 28). New Orleans police chief quits. *USA Today*, p. 5A.

Ling, D. A. (1970). A pentadic analysis of Senator Edward Kennedy's address to the people of Massachusetts, July 25, 1969. *Central States Speech Journal, 21*, 81–86.

Manning, A. (2005, September 16). Accidents, infections new worry, clinics say. *USA Today*, 3A.

National Journal. (2005, September 10). Inside Washington: *National Journal* insiders poll. *National Journal, 37 (37)*, 2704–2705.

Parker, L., & Levin, A. (2005, September 16). City's coming back, but not to normal life. *USA Today*, p. 1A.

Parker, L., & Frank, T. (2005, September 19). Federal official, mayor disagree. *USA Today*, p. 1A.

Reagan, R. (1987, March 4). Transcript of Reagan's speech: "I take full responsibility for my actions." *New York Times*, p. A18.

Rowland, R. R., & Jerome, A. M. (2004). On organizational *apologia*: A reconceptualization. *Communication Theory, 14*, 191–211.

Saulny, S. (2005, September 3). Newcomer is struggling to lead a city in ruins. *New York Times*, p. A13.

Scott, M. S., & Lyman, S. M. (1968). Accounts. *American Sociological Review, 33*, 46–62.

Seeger, M. W., Sellnow, T. L., & Ulmer, R. R. (2003). *Communication and organizational crisis*. Westport, CT: Praeger.

Ware, B. L., & Linkugel, W. A. (1973). They spoke in defense of themselves: On the generic criticism of apologia. *Quarterly Journal of Speech, 59*, 273–283.

DISCUSSION *questions and activities*

1. Do some preliminary research on Hurricane Katrina and then describe the rhetorical context for the speech delivered by George W. Bush after this natural disaster.

2. Despite its publication in a peer-reviewed journal, Benoit and Henson's article has a few flaws including grammatical mistakes, errors in fact, and typos. Working in small groups, see if you can find some of these mistakes and discuss their impact, if any, on the authors' ethos.

3. Compare this article to one of the other two essays on image repair discourse. Based on your comparison, what would you say are the common features of this genre?

Excerpt From
The Closing of the American Mind

Allan Bloom

Allan Bloom (1930–1992) was a prominent American philosopher. Born in Indianapolis, he had lifelong roots in Chicago. After moving there at the age of fifteen, Bloom spent the rest of his life tied to the city, earning both an undergraduate degree and a Ph.D. from The University of Chicago. Bloom taught in France and Germany and later returned to the U.S. to teach at Cornell, Yale, and The University of Chicago. A prolific writer, he published both philosophical and popular pieces. The Closing of the American Mind, *from which this excerpt is taken, is a critique of the contemporary university and one of Bloom's most famous pieces.*

MUSIC

Though students do not have books, they most emphatically do have music. Nothing is more singular about this generation than its addiction to music. This is the age of music and the states of soul that accompany it. To find a rival to this enthusiasm, one would have to go back at least a century to Germany and the passion for Wagner's operas. They had the religious sense that Wagner was creating the meaning of life and that they were not merely listening to his works but experiencing that meaning. Today, a very large proportion of young people between the ages of ten and twenty live for music. It is their passion; nothing else excites them as it does; they cannot take seriously anything alien to music. When they are in school and with their families, they are longing to plug themselves back into their music. Nothing surrounding them—school, family, church—has anything to do with their musical world. At best that ordinary life is neutral, but mostly it is an impediment, drained of vital content, even a thing to be rebelled against. Of course, the enthusiasm for Wagner was limited to a small class, could be indulged only rarely and only in a few places, and had to wait on the composer's slow output. The music of the new votaries, on the other hand, knows neither class nor nation. It is available twenty-four hours a day, everywhere. There is the stereo in the home, in the car; there are concerts; there are music videos, with special channels exclusively devoted to them, on the air nonstop; there are the Walkmans so that no place—not public transportation, not the library—prevents students from communing with the Muse, even while studying. And, above all, the musical soil has become tropically rich. No need to wait for one unpredictable genius. Now there are many geniuses, producing all the time, two new ones rising to take the place of every fallen hero. There is no dearth of the new and the startling.

The power of music in the soul—described to Jessica marvelously by Lorenzo in the *Merchant of Venice*—has been recovered after a long period of desuetude. And it is rock music alone that has effected this restoration. Classical music is dead among the young. This assertion will, I know, be hotly disputed by many who, unwilling to admit tidal changes, can point to the proliferation on campuses of classes in classical music appreciation and practice, as well as performance groups of all kinds. Their presence is undeniable, but they involve not more than 5 to 10 percent of the students. Classical music is now a special taste, like Greek language or pre-Columbian archaeology, not a common culture of reciprocal communication and psychological shorthand. Thirty years ago, most middle-class families made some of the old European music a part of the home, partly because they liked it, partly because they thought it was good for the kids. University students usually had some early emotive association with Beethoven, Chopin, and Brahms, which was a permanent part of their makeup and to which they were likely to re- spond throughout their lives. This was probably the only regularly recognizable class distinction between educated and uneducated in America. Many, or even most, of the young people of that generation also swung with Benny Goodman, but with an element of self-consciousness—to be hip, to prove they weren't snobs, to show solidarity with the democratic ideal of a pop culture out of which would grow a new high culture. So there remained a class distinction between high and low, although private taste was beginning to create doubts about whether one really liked the high very much. But all that has changed. Rock music is as unquestioned and unproblematic as the air the students breathe, and very few have any acquaintance at all with classical music. This is a constant surprise to me. And one of the strange aspects of my relations with good students I come to know well is that I frequently introduce them to Mozart. This is a pleasure for me, inasmuch as it is always pleasant to give people gifts that please them. It is interesting to see whether and in what ways their studies are complemented by such music. But this is something utterly new to me as a teacher; formerly my students usually knew much more classical music than I did.

Music was not all that important for the generation of students preceding the current one. The romanticism that had dominated serious music since Beethoven appealed to refinements— perhaps overrefinements—of sentiments that are hardly to be found in the contemporary world. The lives people lead or wish to lead and their prevailing passions are of a different sort than those of the highly educated German and French bourgeoisie, who were avidly reading Rousseau and Baudelaire, Goethe and Heine, for their spiritual satisfaction. The music that had been designed to produce, as well as to please, such exquisite sensibilities had a very tenuous relation to American lives of any kind. So romantic musical culture in America had had for a long time the character of a veneer, as easily sus- ceptible to ridicule as were Margaret Dumont's displays of coquettish chasteness, so aptly exploited by Groucho Marx in *A Night At The Opera*. I noticed this when I first started teaching and lived in a house for gifted students. The "good" ones studied their physics and then listened to classical music. The stu- dents who did not fit so easily into the groove, some of them just vulgar and restive under the cultural tyranny, but some of them also serious, were looking for things that really responded to their needs. Al- most always they responded to the beat of the newly emerging rock music. They were a bit ashamed of their taste, for it was not respectable. But I instinctively sided with this second group, with real, if coarse, feelings as opposed to artificial and dead ones. Then their musical sans-culotteism won the revolution and reigns unabashed today. No classical music has been produced that can speak to this generation.

Symptomatic of this change is how seriously students now take the famous passages on musical education in Plato's *Republic*. In the past, students, good liberals that they always are, were indignant at the censorship of poetry, as a threat to free inquiry. But they were really thinking of science and politics. They hardly paid attention to the discussion of music itself and, to the extent that they even thought about it, were really puzzled by Plato's devoting time to rhythm and melody in a serious treatise on political philosophy. Their experience of music was as an entertainment, a matter of indifference to po- litical and moral life. Students today, on the contrary, know exactly why Plato takes music so seriously. They know it affects life very profoundly and are indignant because Plato seems to want to rob them of their most intimate pleasure. They are drawn into argument with Plato about the experience of music, and the dispute centers on how to evaluate it and deal with it. This encounter not only helps to illumi- nate the phenomenon of contemporary music, but also provides a model of how contemporary students can profitably engage with a classic text. The very fact of their fury shows how much Plato threatens what is dear and intimate to them. They are little able to defend their experience, which had seemed unquestionable until questioned, and it is most resistant to cool analysis. Yet if a student can—and this is most difficult and unusual—draw back, get a critical distance on what he clings to, come to doubt the ultimate value of what he loves, he has taken the first and most difficult step toward the philosophic conversion. Indignation is the soul's defense against the wound of doubt about its own; it reorders the cosmos to support the justice of its cause. It justifies putting Socrates to death. Recognizing indignation for what it is constitutes knowledge of the soul, and is thus an experience more philosophic than the study of mathematics. It is Plato's teaching that music, by its nature, encompasses all that is today most resistant to philosophy. So it may well be that through the thicket of our greatest corruption runs the path to awareness of the oldest truths.

Plato's teaching about music is, put simply, that rhythm and melody, accompanied by dance, are the barbarous expression of the soul. Barbarous, not animal. Music is the medium of the *human* soul in its most ecstatic condition of wonder and terror. Nietzsche, who in large measure agrees with Plato's analysis, says in *The Birth of Tragedy* (not to be forgotten is the rest of the title, *Out of the Spirit of Music*) that a mixture of cruelty and coarse sensuality characterized this state, which of course was religious, in the service of gods. Music is the soul's primitive and primary speech and it is *alogon*, without articulate speech or reason. It is not only not reasonable, it is hostile to reason. Even when articulate speech is added, it is utterly subordinate to and determined by the music and the passions it expresses.

Civilization or, to say the same thing, education is the taming or domestication of the soul's raw passions—not suppressing or excising them, which would deprive the soul of its energy—but forming and informing them as art. The goal of harmonizing the enthusiastic part of the soul with what develops later, the rational part, is perhaps impossible to attain. But without it, man can never be whole. Music, or poetry, which is what music becomes as reason emerges, always involves a delicate balance between passion and reason, and, even in its highest and most developed forms—religious, warlike and erotic— that balance is always tipped, if ever so slightly, toward the passionate. Music, as everyone experiences, provides an unquestionable justification and a fulfilling pleasure for the activities it accompanies: the soldier who hears the marching band is enthralled and reassured; the religious man is exalted in his prayer by the sound of the organ in the church; and the lover is carried away and his conscience stilled by the romantic guitar. Armed with music, man can damn rational doubt. Out of the music emerge the gods that suit it, and they educate men by their example and their commandments.

Plato's Socrates disciplines the ecstasies and thereby provides little consolation or hope to men. According to the Socratic formula, the lyrics—speech and, hence, reason—must determine the music—harmony and rhythm. Pure music can never endure this constraint. Students are not in a position to know the pleasures of reason; they can only see it as a disciplinary and repressive parent. But they do see, in the case of Plato, that that parent has figured out what they are up to. Plato teaches that, in order to take the spiritual temperature of an individual or a society, one must "mark the music." To Plato and Nietzsche, the history of music is a series of attempts to give form and beauty to the dark, chaotic, premonitory forces in the soul—to make them serve a higher purpose, an ideal, to give man's duties a fullness. Bach's religious intentions and Beethoven's revolutionary and humane ones are clear enough examples. Such cultivation of the soul uses the passions and satisfies them while sublimating them and giving them an artistic unity. A man whose noblest activities are accompanied by a music that expresses them while providing a pleasure extending from the lowest bodily to the highest spiritual, is whole, and there is no tension in him between the pleasant and the good. By contrast a man whose business life is prosaic and unmusical and whose leisure is made up of coarse, intense entertainments, is divided, and each side of his existence is undermined by the other.

Hence, for those who are interested in psychological health, music is at the center of education, both for giving the passions their due and for preparing the soul for the unhampered use of reason. The centrality of such education was recognized by all the ancient educators. It is hardly noticed today that in Aristotle's *Politics* the most important passages about the best regime concern musical education, or that the *Poetics* is an appendix to the *Politics*. Classical philosophy did not censor the singers. It persuaded them. And it gave them a goal, one that was understood by them, until only yesterday. But those who do not notice the role of music in Aristotle and despise it in Plato went to school with Hobbes, Locke and Smith, where such considerations have become unnecessary. The triumphant Enlightenment rationalism thought that it had discovered other ways to deal with the irrational part of the soul, and that reason needed less support from it. Only in those great critics of Enlightenment and rationalism, Rousseau and Nietzsche, does music return, and they were the most musical of philosophers. Both thought that the passions—and along with them their ministerial arts—had become thin under the rule of reason and that, therefore, man himself and what he sees in the world have become correspondingly thin. They wanted to cultivate the enthusiastic states of the soul and to re-experience the Corybantic possession deemed a pathology by Plato. Nietzsche, particularly, sought to tap again the irrational sources of vitality, to replenish our dried-up stream from barbaric sources, and thus encouraged the Dionysian and the music derivative from it.

This is the significance of rock music. I do not suggest that it has any high intellectual sources. But it has risen to its current heights in the education of the young on the ashes of classical music, and in an atmosphere in which there is no intellectual resistance to attempts to tap the rawest passions. Modern-day rationalists, such as economists, are indifferent to it and what it represents. The irrationalists are all for it. There is no need to fear that "the blond beasts" are going to come forth from the bland souls of our adolescents. But rock music has one appeal only, a barbaric appeal, to sexual desire—not love, not *eros*, but sexual desire undeveloped and untutored. It acknowledges the first emanations of children's emerging sensuality and addresses them seriously, eliciting them and legitimating them, not as little sprouts that must be carefully tended in order to grow into gorgeous flowers, but as the real thing. Rock gives children, on a silver platter, with all the public authority of the entertainment industry, everything their parents always used to tell them they had to wait for until they grew up and would understand later.

Young people know that rock has the beat of sexual intercourse. That is why Ravel's *Bolero* is the one piece of classical music that is commonly known and liked by them. In alliance with some real art and a lot of pseudo-art, an enormous industry cultivates the taste for the orgiastic state of feeling connected with sex, providing a constant flood of fresh material for voracious appetites. Never was there an art form directed so exclusively to children.

Ministering to and according with the arousing and cathartic music, the lyrics celebrate puppy love as well as polymorphous attractions, and fortify them against traditional ridicule and shame. The words implicitly and explicitly describe bodily acts that satisfy sexual desire and treat them as its only natural and routine culmination for children who do not yet have the slightest imagination of love, marriage, or family. This has a much more powerful effect than does pornography on youngsters, who have no need to watch others do grossly what they can so easily do themselves. Voyeurism is for old perverts; active sexual relations are for the young. All they need is encouragement.

The inevitable corollary of such sexual interest is rebellion against the parental authority that represses it. Selfishness thus becomes indignation and then transforms itself into morality. The sexual revolution must overthrow all the forces of domination, the enemies of nature and happiness. From love comes hate, masquerading as social reform. A worldview is balanced on the sexual fulcrum. What were once unconscious or half-conscious childish resentments become the new Scripture. And then comes the longing for the classless, prejudice-free, conflictless, universal society that necessarily results from liberated consciousness—"We Are the World," a pubescent version of *Alle Menschen werden Brüder*, the fulfillment of which has been inhibited by the political equivalents of Mom and Dad. These are the three great lyrical themes: sex, hate, and a smarmy, hypocritical version of brotherly love. Such polluted sources issue in a muddy stream where only monsters can swim. A glance at the videos that project images on the wall of Plato's cave since MTV took it over suffices to prove this. Hitler's image recurs frequently enough in exciting contexts to give one pause. Nothing noble, sublime, profound, delicate, tasteful, or even decent can find a place in such tableaux. There is room only for the intense, changing, crude, and immediate, which Tocqueville warned us would be the character of democratic art, combined with a pervasiveness, importance, and content beyond Tocqueville's wildest imagination.

Picture a thirteen-year-old boy sitting in the living room of his family home doing his math assignment while wearing his Walkman headphones or watching MTV. He enjoys the liberties hard won over centuries by the alliance of philosophic genius and political heroism, consecrated by the blood of martyrs; he is provided with comfort and leisure by the most productive economy ever known to mankind; science has penetrated the secrets of nature in order to provide him with the marvelous, lifelike electronic sound and image reproduction he is enjoying. And in what does progress culminate? A pubescent child whose body throbs with orgasmic rhythms; whose feelings are made articulate in hymns to the joys of onanism or the killing of parents; whose ambition is to win fame and wealth in imitating the drag-queen who makes the music. In short, life is made into a nonstop, commercially prepackaged masturbational fantasy.

This description may seem exaggerated, but only because some would prefer to regard it as such. The continuing exposure to rock music is a reality, not one confined to a particular class or type of child. One need only ask first-year university students what music they listen to, how much of it and what it means to them, in order to discover that the phenomenon is universal in America, that it begins in adolescence or a bit before and continues through the college years. It is *the* youth culture and, as I have so often insisted, there is now no other countervailing nourishment for the spirit. Some of this culture's power comes from the fact that it is so loud. It makes conversation impossible, so that much of friendship must be without the shared speech that Aristotle asserts is the essence of friendship and the only true common ground. With rock, illusions of shared feelings, bodily contact and grunted formulas, which are supposed to contain so much meaning beyond speech, are the basis of association. None of this contradicts going about the business of life, attending classes and doing the assignments for them. But the meaningful inner life is with the music.

This phenomenon is both astounding and indigestible, and is hardly noticed, routine and habitual. But it is of historic proportions that a society's best young and their best energies should be so occupied. People of future civilizations will wonder at this and find it as incomprehensible as we do the caste system, witch-burning, harems, cannibalism, and gladiatorial combats. It may well be that a society's greatest madness seems normal to itself. The child I described has parents who have sacrificed to provide him with a good life and who have a great stake in his future happiness. They cannot believe that the musical vocation will contribute very much to that happiness. But there is nothing they can do about it. The family spiritual void has left the field open to rock music, and they cannot possibly forbid their children to listen to it. It is everywhere; all children listen to it; forbidding it would simply cause them to lose their children's affection and obedience. When they turn on the television, they will see President Reagan warmly grasping the daintily proffered gloved hand of Michael Jackson and praising him enthusiastically. Better to set the faculty of denial in motion—avoid noticing what the words say, assume the kid will get over it. If he has early sex, that won't get in the way of his having stable relationships later. His drug use will certainly stop at pot. School is providing real values. And popular historicism provides the final salvation: there are new life-styles for new situations, and the older generation is there not to impose its values but to help the younger one to find its own. TV, which compared to music plays a comparatively small role in the formation of young people's character and taste, is a consensus monster—the Right monitors its content for sex, the Left for violence, and many other interested sects for many other things. But the music has hardly been touched, and what efforts have been made are both ineffectual and misguided about the nature and extent of the problem.

The result is nothing less than parents' loss of control over their children's moral education at a time when no one else is seriously concerned with it. This has been achieved by an alliance between the strange young males who have the gift of divining the mob's emergent wishes—our versions of Thrasymachus, Socrates' rhetorical adversary—and the record-company executives, the new robber barons, who mine gold out of rock. They discovered a few years back that children are one of the few groups in the country with considerable disposable income, in the form of allowances. Their parents spend all they have providing for the kids. Appealing to them over their parents' heads, creating a world of delight for them, constitutes one of the richest markets in the postwar world. The rock business is perfect capitalism, supplying to demand and helping to create it. It has all the moral dignity of drug trafficking, but it was so totally new and unexpected that nobody thought to control it, and now it is too late. Progress may be made against cigarette smoking because our absence of standards or our relativism does not extend to matters of bodily health. In all other things the market determines the value. (Yoko Ono is among America's small group of billionaires, along with oil and computer magnates, her late husband having produced and sold a commodity of worth comparable to theirs.) Rock is very big business, bigger than the movies, bigger than professional sports, bigger than television, and this accounts for much of the respectability of the music business. It is difficult to adjust our vision to the changes in the economy and to see what is really important. McDonald's now has more employees than U.S. Steel, and likewise the purveyors of junk food for the soul have supplanted what still seem to be more basic callings.

This change has been happening for some time. In the late fifties, De Gaulle gave Brigitte Bardot one of France's highest honors. I could not understand this, but it turned out that she, along with Peugeot, was France's biggest export item. As Western nations became more prosperous, leisure, which had been put off for several centuries in favor of the pursuit of property, the means to leisure, finally began to be of primary concern. But, in the meantime, any notion of the serious life of leisure, as well as men's taste and capacity to live it, had disappeared. Leisure became entertainment. The end for which they had labored for so long has turned out to be amusement, a justified conclusion if the means justify the ends. The music business is peculiar only in that it caters almost exclusively to children, treating legally and naturally imperfect human beings as though they were ready to enjoy the final or complete satisfaction. It perhaps thus reveals the nature of all our entertainment and our loss of a clear view of what adulthood or maturity is, and our incapacity to conceive ends. The emptiness of *values* results in the acceptance of the natural *facts* as the ends. In this case infantile sexuality is the end, and I suspect that, in the absence of other ends, many adults have come to agree that it is.

It is interesting to note that the Left, which prides itself on its critical approach to "late capitalism" and is unrelenting and unsparing in its analysis of our other cultural phenomena, has in general given rock music a free ride. Abstracting from the capitalist element in which it flourishes, they regard it as a people's art, coming from beneath the bourgeoisie's layers of cultural repression. Its antinomianism and its longing for a world without constraint might seem to be the clarion of the proletarian revolution, and Marxists certainly do see that rock music dissolves the beliefs and morals necessary for liberal society and would approve of it for that alone. But the harmony between the young intellectual Left and rock is probably profounder than that. Herbert Marcuse appealed to university students in the sixties with a combination of Marx and Freud. In *Eros and Civilization* and *One Dimensional Man* he promised that the overcoming of capitalism and its false consciousness will result in a society where the greatest satisfactions are sexual, of a sort that the bourgeois moralist Freud called polymorphous and infantile. Rock music touches the same chord in the young. Free sexual expression, anarchism, mining of the irrational unconscious and giving it free rein are what they have in common. The high intellectual life I shall describe in Part Two and the low rock world are partners in the same entertainment enterprise. They must both be interpreted as parts of the cultural fabric of late capitalism. Their success comes from the bourgeois' need to feel that he is not bourgeois, to have undangerous experiments with the unlimited. He is willing to pay dearly for them. The Left is better interpreted by Nietzsche than by Marx. The critical theory of late capitalism is at once late capitalism's subtlest and crudest expression. Anti-bourgeois ire is the opiate of the Last Man.

This strong stimulant, which Nietzsche called Nihiline, was for a very long time, almost fifteen years, epitomized in a single figure, Mick Jagger. A shrewd, middle-class boy, he played the possessed lower-class demon and teen-aged satyr up until he was forty, with one eye on the mobs of children of both sexes whom he stimulated to a sensual frenzy and the other eye winking at the unerotic, commercially motivated adults who handled the money. In his act he was male and female, heterosexual and homosexual; unencumbered by modesty, he could enter everyone's dreams, promising to do everything with everyone; and, above all, he legitimated drugs, which were the real thrill that parents and policemen conspired to deny his youthful audience. He was beyond the law, moral and political, and thumbed his nose at it. Along with all this, there were nasty little appeals to the suppressed inclinations toward sexism, racism and violence, indulgence in which is not now publicly respectable. Nevertheless, he managed not to appear to contradict the rock ideal of a universal classless society founded on love, with the distinction between brotherly and bodily blurred. He was the hero and the model for countless young persons in universities, as well as elsewhere. I discovered that students who boasted of having no heroes secretly had a passion to be like Mick Jagger, to live his life, have his fame. They were ashamed to admit this in a university, although I am not certain that the reason has anything to do with a higher standard of taste. It is probably that they are not supposed to have heroes. Rock music itself and talking about it with infinite seriousness are perfectly respectable. It has proved to be the ultimate leveler of intellectual snobbism. But it is not respectable to think of it as providing weak and ordinary persons with a fashionable behavior, the imitation of which will make others esteem them and boost their own self-esteem. Unaware and unwillingly, however, Mick Jagger played the role in their lives that Napoleon played in the lives of ordinary young Frenchmen throughout the nineteenth century. Everyone else was so boring and unable to charm youthful passions. Jagger caught on.

In the last couple of years, Jagger has begun to fade. Whether Michael Jackson, Prince, or Boy George can take his place is uncertain. They are even weirder than he is, and one wonders what new strata of taste they have discovered. Although each differs from the others, the essential character of musical entertainment is not changing. There is only a constant search for variations on the theme. And this gutter phenomenon is apparently the fulfillment of the promise made by so much psychology and literature that our weak and exhausted Western civilization would find refreshment in the true source, the unconscious, which appeared to the late romantic imagination to be identical to Africa, the dark and unexplored continent. Now all has been explored; light has been cast everywhere; the unconscious has been made conscious, the repressed expressed. And what have we found? Not creative devils, but show business glitz. Mick Jagger tarting it up on the stage is all that we brought back from the voyage to the underworld.

My concern here is not with the moral effects of this music—whether it leads to sex, violence, or drugs. The issue here is its effect on education, and I believe it ruins the imagination of young people and makes it very difficult for them to have a passionate relationship to the art and thought that are the substance of liberal education. The first sensuous experiences are decisive in determining the taste for the whole of life, and they are the link between the animal and spiritual in us. The period of nascent sensuality has always been used for sublimation, in the sense of making sublime, for attaching youthful inclinations and longings to music, pictures, and stories that provide the transition to the fulfillment of the human duties and the enjoyment of the human pleasures. Lessing, speaking of Greek sculpture, said "beautiful men made beautiful statues, and the city had beautiful statues in part to thank for beautiful citizens." This formula encapsulates the fundamental principle of the esthetic education of man. Young men and women were attracted by the beauty of heroes whose very bodies expressed their nobility. The deeper understanding of the meaning of nobility comes later, but is prepared for by the sensuous experience and is actually contained in it. What the senses long for as well as what reason later sees as good are thereby not at tension with one another. Education is not sermonizing to children against their instincts and pleasures, but providing a natural continuity between what they feel and what they can and should be. But this is a lost art. Now we have come to exactly the opposite point. Rock music encourages passions and provides models that have no relation to any life the young people who go to universities can possibly lead, or to the kinds of admiration encouraged by liberal studies. Without the cooperation of the sentiments, anything other than technical education is a dead letter.

Rock music provides premature ecstasy and, in this respect, is like the drugs with which it is allied. It artificially induces the exaltation naturally attached to the completion of the greatest endeavors—victory in a just war, consummated love, artistic creation, religious devotion, and discovery of the truth. Without effort, without talent, without virtue, without exercise of the faculties, anyone and everyone is accorded the equal right to the enjoyment of their fruits. In my experience, students who have had a serious fling with drugs—and gotten over it—find it difficult to have enthusiasms or great expectations. It is as though the color has been drained out of their lives and they see everything in black and white. The pleasure they experienced in the beginning was so intense that they no longer look for it at the end, or as the end. They may function perfectly well, but dryly, routinely. Their energy has been sapped, and they do not expect their life's activity to produce anything but a living, whereas liberal education is supposed to encourage the belief that the good life is the pleasant life and that the best life is the most pleasant life. I suspect that the rock addiction, particularly in the absence of strong counterattractions, has an effect similar to that of drugs. The students will get over this music, or at least the exclusive passion for it. But they will do so in the same way Freud says that men accept the reality principle—as something harsh, grim, and essentially unattractive, a mere necessity. These students will assiduously study economics or the professions and the Michael Jackson costume will slip off to reveal a Brooks Brothers suit beneath. They will want to get ahead and live comfortably. But this life is as empty and false as the one they left behind. The choice is not between quick fixes and dull calculation. This is what liberal education is meant to show them. But as long as they have the Walkman on, they cannot hear what the great tradition has to say. And, after its prolonged use, when they take it off, they find they are deaf.

DISCUSSION *questions and activities*

1. Bloom states, "Rock music encourages passions and provides models that have no relation to any kind of life the young people who go to universities can possibly lead. . ." Do you agree with this statement? Why or why not?

2. Should "young people who go to universities" have more realistic expectations about the kind of life they will lead? What would realistic expectations be?

3. How do you think Bloom would feel about reality television stars or news reports that feature celebrities? Why? Find examples from the text that support your position.

4. Much of Bloom's argument rests upon evidence that was current at the time, but has since become quaint (his heavy emphasis on Mick Jagger, for example). To what extent do his claims hold true when scaled against the lifestyle of today's music icons? What about in the context of new technology in music, like I-Pods and Mp3 players?

Malignant Mesothelioma Mortality— United States, 1999–2005

Center for Disease Control

"Malignant Mesothelioma Mortality" is a report on data compiled by the Center for Disease Control (CDC) regarding death rates from mesothelioma, a type of lung cancer associated with exposure to asbestos. This piece was published in the MMWR: Morbidity & Mortality Weekly Report. A trade publication, the MMWR is used by medical professionals (nurses, doctors, epidemiologists, and so on) to keep apprised of short- and long-term trends in infectious diseases, and to generate strategies and recommendations. Articles submitted to the MMWR are written by experts in the field, and heavily vetted by an editorial panel before being published. More information about the root publication for this source can be found at www.cdc.gov/mmwr.

Malignant mesothelioma is a fatal cancer primarily associated with exposure to asbestos. The latency period between first exposure to asbestos and clinical disease usually is 20–40 years (1). Although asbestos is no longer mined in the United States, the mineral is still imported, and a substantial amount of asbestos remaining in buildings eventually will be removed, either during remediation or demolition. Currently, an estimated 1.3 million construction and general industry workers potentially are being exposed to asbestos (2). To characterize mortality attributed to mesothelioma, CDC's National Institute for Occupational Safety and Health (NIOSH) analyzed annual multiple-cause-of-death records for 1999–2005, the most recent years for which complete data are available.[*] For those years, a total of 18,068 deaths of persons with malignant mesothelioma were reported, increasing from 2,482 deaths in 1999 to 2,704 in 2005, but the annual death rate was stable (14.1 per million in 1999 and 14.0 in 2005). Maintenance, renovation, or demolition activities that might disturb asbestos should be performed with precautions that sufficiently prevent exposures for workers and the public. In addition, physicians should document the occupational history of all suspected and confirmed mesothelioma cases.

Asbestos was used in a wide variety of construction and manufacturing applications through most of the 20th century. In the United States, asbestos use peaked at 803,000 metric tons in 1973 and then declined to approximately 1,700 metric tons in 2007 (Figure 1) (3).

For this report, malignant mesothelioma deaths were identified for 1999–2005 from death certificates and included any deaths for which *International Classification of Diseases, 10th Revision* (ICD-10) codes[†]

---

[*] Since 1968, CDC's National Center for Health Statistics (NCHS) has compiled multiple-cause-of-death data annually from death certificates in the United States. CDC's NIOSH extracts information on deaths from occupationally related respiratory diseases and conditions from the NCHS data and stores the information in the National Occupational Respiratory Mortality System, available at http://webappa.cdc.gov/ords/norms.html.

[†] Codes C45.0 (mesothelioma of pleura), C45.1 (mesothelioma of peritoneum), C45.2 (mesothelioma of pericardium), C45.7 (mesothelioma of other sites), and C45.9 (mesothelioma, unspecified).

FIGURE 1. ASBESTOS USE AND PERMISSIBLE EXPOSURE LIMITS*—UNITED STATES, 1900–2007

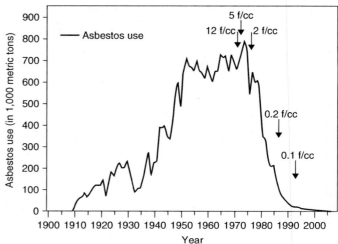

•Arrows indicate year when the Occupational Safety and Health Administration permissible exposure limits were put in place (12 fibers per cubic centimeter[f/cc] in 1971, 5 f/cc in 1972, 2 f/cc in 1976, 0.2 f/cc in 1986, and 0.1 f/cc in 1994.)

for malignant mesothelioma were listed in the multiple-cause-of-death mortality data entity axis.[§] Because mesothelioma predominantly is associated with occupational exposure and has a long latency, the analysis was restricted to deaths of persons aged ≥25 years. The annual death rate per 1 million persons aged ≥25 years was calculated using the July 1 population estimates for each year provided by the U.S. Census Bureau. Overall death rates were calculated based on the 2002 census population.

During 1999–2005, a total of 18,068 malignant mesothelioma deaths were reported in the United States; 14,591 (80.8%) occurred among males and 17,180 (95.1%) among whites (Table). Mesothelioma deaths were classified as mesothelioma of pleura (1,572; 8.7%), peritoneum (657; 3.6%), other anatomical site (2,605; 14.4%), and unspecified anatomical site (13,454; 74.5%).[¶] Mortality increased with age, with the greatest number of decedents aged ≥75 years; 311 deaths (1.7%) occurred in persons aged ≥44 years. From 1999 to 2005, the total number of malignant mesothelioma deaths increased 8.9%, from 2,482 in 1999 to 2,704 in 2005, but the annual death rate was stable (14.1 per million population in 1999 versus 14.0 in 2005). The death rate for males was 4.5 times that for females (23.2 versus 5.1 per million). During 1999–2005, the state death rate was greater than the national rate (13.8 per million population per year) in 26 states; in six states the rate exceeded 20 per million per year (Figure 2): Maine (173 deaths; rate: 27.5), Wyoming (50; 22.2), West Virginia (182; 21.0), Pennsylvania (1,210; 20.8), New Jersey (814; 20.2), and Washington (558; 20.1).

Reported by: *KM Bang, PhD, JM Mazurek, MD, E Storey, MD, MD Attfield, PhD, PL Schleiff, MS, JM Wood, MS, Div of Respiratory Disease Studies, JT Wassell, PhD, Div of Safety Research, National Institute for Occupational Safety and Health, CDC.*

Editorial Note: Despite regulatory actions and the sharp decline in use of asbestos, potential exposure to asbestos continues, but most deaths from mesothelioma in the United States derive from exposures decades ago. Because mesothelioma manifests 20–40 years after first exposure, the number of mesothelioma deaths will likely peak by 2010 (4). The analysis described in this report indicates that the annual number of mesothelioma deaths is still increasing, and future cases will continue to reflect the extensive past use of asbestos. New cases also might result through occupa-

[§] Entity axis includes information on all of the diseases, injuries, or medical complications, and the location (part, line, and sequence) of the information recorded on each certificate. Detail record layouts available at http://www.cdc.gov/nchs/about/major/dvs/mcd/msb.htm.

[¶] The sum of individual site death totals is greater than the total number of deaths because some decedents have more than one site of mesothelioma listed on their death certificates.

tional and environmental exposure to asbestos during remediation and demolition of existing asbestos in buildings if controls are insufficient to protect workers and the surrounding community.

The annual number of mesothelioma cases increased significantly from the late 1970s through the mid-1990s (4). Projections indicate that the number of mesothelioma cases involving males peaked during 2000–2004 at more than 2,000 cases and should be declining, with an expected return to background levels by 2055. The number of mesothelioma cases involving females (approximately 560 in 2003) is projected to increase slightly over time as a function of population size and shifting age distribution (4).

Previously, NIOSH examined industry and occupation data for 541 of the 2,482 mesothelioma deaths that occurred in 1999, the most recent year for which such data are available. After 1999, coding information for industry and occupation were no longer available. Of 130 industries reported, significant proportionate mortality ratios (PMRs) were found for ship and boat building and repairing (6.0; 95% confidence interval [CI] = 2.4–12.3); industrial and miscellaneous chemicals (4.8; CI = 2.9–7.5); petroleum refining (3.8; CI = 1.2–8.9); electric light and power (3.1; CI = 1.5–5.7); and construction (1.6; CI = 1.2–1.9). Of 163 occupations reported, significant PMRs were found for plumbers, pipefitters, and steamfitters (4.8; CI = 2.8–7.5); mechanical engineers (3.0; CI = 1.1–6.6); electricians (2.4; CI = 1.3–4.2); and elementary school teachers (2.1; CI = 1.1–3.6) (5).

Over the decades, the Occupational Safety and Health Administration (OSHA) and the Environmental Protection Agency have taken various regulatory actions to control occupational exposure to asbestos (6). OSHA established a permissible exposure limit (PEL) for asbestos in 1971. This standard set the PEL at 12 fibers per cubic centimeter (f/cc) of air.** This initial PEL was reduced to 5 f/cc in 1972, 2 f/cc in 1976, 0.2 f/cc in 1986, and 0.1 f/cc in 1994 (7). Inspection data for 1979–2003 show a general decline in asbestos exposure levels and in the percentage of samples exceeding designated occupational exposure limits in construction, manufacturing, mining, and other industries (5). However, in 2003, 20% of air samples collected in the construction industry exceeded the OSHA PEL (5).

The findings in this report are subject to at least three limitations. First, death certificates do not include information on exposure to asbestos or a specific work history. This limits identification of industries and occupations associated with mesothelioma. Second, the state of residence issuing death certificates might not always be the state in which the decedent's exposures occurred, which might affect state death rates. Finally, some mesothelioma cases might be misdiagnosed and assigned less

FIGURE 2. MALIGNANT MESOTHE-LIOMA DEATH RATE PER 1 MILLION POPULATION,* BY STATE—UNITED STATES, 1999–2005

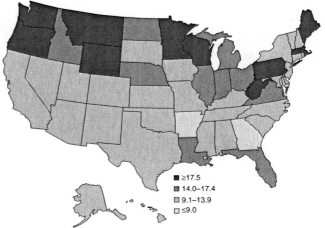

* Decedents for whom the *International Classification of Diseases, 10th Revision* codes C45.0 (mesothelioma of pleura), C45.1 (mesothelioma of peritoneum), C45.2 (mesothelioma of pericardium), C45.7 (mesothelioma of other sites), or C45.9 (mesothelioma, unspecified) were listed on death certificates were identified using CDC mortality data for 1999–2005.

■ ≥17.5
▨ 14.0–17.4
▨ 9.1–13.9
□ ≤9.0

** As an 8-hour time-weighted average based on the 1968 American Conference of Government Industrial Hygienists threshold limit value.

specific ICD codes (e.g., ICD-10 code C76, malignant neoplasm of other and ill-defined sites), and consequently not be captured in this analysis (8).

Although asbestos has been eliminated in the manufacture of many products, it is still being imported (approximately 1,730 metric tons in 2007) and used in the United States (3) in various construction and transportation products (6). Ensuring a future decrease in mesothelioma mortality requires meticulous control of exposures to asbestos and other materials that might cause mesothelioma. Recent studies suggest that carbon nanotubes (fiber-shaped nanoparticles), which are increasingly being used in manufacturing (9), might share the carcinogenic mechanism postulated for asbestos and induce mesothelioma (10), underscoring the need for documentation of occupational history in future cases. Capturing occupational history information for mesothelioma cases is important to identify industries and occupations placing workers at risk for this lethal disease.

ACKNOWLEDGMENTS

This report is based, in part, on contributions from G Syamlal, MBBS, and D Sharp, MD, National Institute for Occupational Safety and Health, CDC.

TABLE. NUMBER OF MALIGNANT MESOTHELIOMA DEATHS AMONG PERSONS AGED ≥ 25 YEARS, BY SELECTED CHARACTERISTICS—UNITED STATES, 1999–2005

Characteristic	No. of deaths, by year							
	1999	2000	2001	2002	2003	2004	2005	Total
Total	2,482	2,530	2,505	2,570	2,621	2,656	2,704	18,068
Death rate[*]	14.1	13.9	13.6	13.7	13.9	13.9	14.0	13.8
Age group (yrs)								
25–34	4	6	7	10	7	11	6	51
35–44	33	34	39	40	38	42	34	260
45–54	138	131	144	106	148	121	118	906
55–64	388	372	361	380	386	400	438	2,725
65–74	818	814	748	764	715	674	735	5,268
75–84	888	918	942	975	1,028	1,097	1,014	6,862
≥85	213	255	264	295	299	311	359	1,996
Median age (yrs)	*73*	*74*	*74*	*74*	*75*	*75*	*75*	*74*
Sex								
Male	1,993	2,043	2,019	2,126	2,122	2,140	2,148	14,591
Female	489	487	486	444	499	516	556	3,477
Race								
White	2,353	2,398	2,405	2,447	2,481	2,535	2,561	17,180
Black	104	109	75	99	109	97	114	707
Other	25	23	25	24	31	24	29	181
Anatomical site[†]								
Pleura	252	225	269	238	206	196	186	1,572
Peritoneum	92	84	83	95	95	101	107	657
Other	426	433	388	377	329	326	326	2,605
Unspecified	1,750	1,817	1,806	1,901	2,013	2,063	2,104	13,454

[*] Per 1 million population.

[†] The sum of anatomical site totals (18,288) is greater than the total number of deaths (18,068) because some decedents have more than one site listed on their death certificate.

References

1. Lanphear BP, Buncher CR. Latent period for malignant mesothelioma of occupational origin. J Occup Med 1992;34:718–21.
2. Occupational Safety and Health Administration. Safety and health topics: asbestos; 2009. Available at http://www.osha.gov/SLTC/asbestos.
3. Kelly TD, Matos GR. Historical statistics for mineral and material commodities in the United States. US Geological Survey data series 140. Reston, VA: US Department of the Interior, US Geological Survey; 2005. Available at http://minerals.usgs.gov/ds/2005/140.
4. Price B, Ware A. Mesothelioma trends in the United States: an update based on surveillance, epidemiology, and end results program data for 1973 through 2003. Am J Epidemiol 2004;159:107–12.
5. CDC. Work-related lung disease surveillance report 2007. Cincinnati, OH: US Department of Health and Human Services, CDC, National Institute for Occupational Safety and Health; 2008. Available at http://www.cdc.gov/niosh/docs/2008-143.
6. Environmental Protection Agency. EPA asbestos materials bans: clarification. Washington, DC: Environmental Protection Agency; 1999. Available at http://www.epa.gov/oppt/asbestos/pubs/asbbans2.pdf.
7. Martonik JF, Nash E, Grossman E. The history of OSHA's asbestos rule makings and some distinctive approaches that they introduced for regulating occupational exposure to toxic substances. AIHAJ 2001;62:208–17.
8. Gordon GJ, Jensen RV, Hsiao LL, et al. Translation of microarray data into clinically relevant cancer diagnostic tests using gene expression ratios in lung cancer and mesothelioma. Cancer Res 2002;62:4963–7.
9. CDC. Approaches to safe nanotechnology. Managing the health and safety concerns associated with engineered nanomaterials. Cincinnati, OH: US Department of Health and Human Services, CDC, National Institute for Occupational Safety and Health; 2009. Available at http://www.cdc.gov/niosh/docs/2009-125/pdfs/2009-125.pdf.
10. Takagi A, Hirose A, Nishimura T, et al. Induction of mesothelioma in p53+/– mouse by intraperitoneal application of multi-wall carbon nanotube. J Toxicol Sci 2008;33:105–16.

DISCUSSION *questions and activities*

1. Compare the presentation of mesothelioma here with one of the other mesothelioma texts, in terms of style, audience, appeals, or any other aspect of writing. What about each source's context might motivate any differences, and what is the effect of each strategy?

2. Think about this source from the perspective of someone recently diagnosed with mesothelioma (as Stephen Jay Gould describes in "The Median Isn't the Message"). As a layperson lacking medical background, how would you respond? What information would be accessible and what would not? What overall impression would you take away from the piece? If encountering this source in an attempt to understand your condition, what would be your next step in the process?

3. Below, you can find a link to the submissions guidelines for Full Reports to the MMWR. How does the Malignant Mesothelioma Mortality report conform to (or depart from) these editorial guidelines? What might have motivated any breaks with conventions of this genre? Guidelines can be found at http://www.cdc.gov/mmwr/author_guide.html.

How the Scapegoats Escaped

William D. Cohan

William D. Cohan is a former Wall Street banker and investigative journalist. He is currently a staff writer at Fortune *magazine and a frequent contributor to* The New York Times. *His book,* House of Cards: A Tale of Hubris and Wretched Excess on Wall Street *was published in 2009 to critical acclaim. This op-ed originally appeared in* The New York Times *in November of 2009 and is a scathing commentary on greed and banking.*

The quick "not guilty" verdict reached Tuesday afternoon by a Brooklyn jury in the federal criminal trial of two former Bear Stearns hedge fund managers was at once surprising—for its failure to comport with the zeitgeist—but also entirely understandable, based on a close reading of the prosecution's arguments and the evidence the judge allowed to be introduced. "There was a reasonable doubt on every charge," one juror told *The Times* afterward. "We just didn't feel that the case had been proven."

In short, the prosecution blew it—on two counts. First, in devising the original indictment for conspiracy and securities fraud against the two defendants, Ralph Cioffi and Matthew Tannin, it relied on damning snippets of lengthy e-mail messages that when viewed in their entirety proved to be highly ambiguous. Second, the prosecution made a reductionist opening argument claiming the men were nothing more than out-and-out liars, needlessly raising the bar in terms of what it had to prove to jurors.

In that opening speech, Patrick Sinclair, the assistant United States attorney for the Eastern District of New York, tried to head off all the confusing Wall Street jargon soon to be unleashed by claiming the defendants had simply been deceitful. He accused them of lying about the size of their personal investments in the funds and in their dealings with nervous investors who were considering getting out when subprime mortgages—in which the funds had invested heavily—began to rapidly lose value in March 2007.

"They did the best thing that they could think of to keep those investors in the fund and with any luck keep their bonuses coming: they lied," Mr. Sinclair told the jury. "They lied over and over again to lull those investors into a false sense of confidence and make them think that these failing funds continued to be a good investment when the exact opposite was true."

Unfortunately for the government, the evidence was not nearly as clear-cut as Mr. Sinclair portrayed it to be, and his strategy to make it seem so backfired. Consider the e-mail messages the prosecution placed at the center of its case.

In the indictment, the prosecution quoted from a note Mr. Tannin sent in April 2007 from his personal Gmail account to Mr. Cioffi's wife. The government made much of the fact that Mr. Tannin chose not to send it to Mr. Cioffi himself or from his Bear Stearns' e-mail account, suggesting he was trying to hide something. "The subprime market looks pretty damn ugly," Mr. Tannin wrote, adding that if a recent financial report was correct, "I think we should close the funds now…The entire subprime market is toast."

But the jury eventually saw the entire message, in which Mr. Tannin ruminated at length about various courses of action and seemed to be striving to make the soundest financial choice. In other words, it was just what you would hope your fund manager would be worrying about in a precarious time. In the end, he concluded he was feeling "pretty damn good" about what was happening at the funds and that "I've done the best possible job that I could have done." Any wonder the jurors came away with reasonable doubt?

The prosecution's misjudgments are doubly vexing because there was other evidence around which it might have built a stronger case. The prime example was a "talking points" memo in June 2007, sent by Bear Stearns's senior management to its brokers for use in discussions with hedge fund investors worried about a meltdown. The episode raised pretty clear doubts about whether Mr. Cioffi and Mr. Tannin had told investors the truth.

According to the memo, one of the questions deemed likely to be asked was: "I thought the fund was diversified, and now it turns out it seems to have had a fair amount of exposure to the subprime mortgage market. What exactly was the exposure?" The answer: "60 percent." The problem was that in all previous communications to the investors, the two fund managers had suggested that only about six percent of the funds were invested in subprime mortgages.

During the trial, a prominent former Bear Stearns broker, Shelly Bergman, testified about the damning nature of this talking points memo, which was as close to a smoking gun as prosecutors could have hoped for. Yet the prosecution never made much use of his testimony, and it did a poor job of rebutting the defense's claims that Mr. Bergman had a conflict of interest in testifying against the two fund managers.

So where does the verdict leave us? Word is that three federal grand juries are still investigating what went wrong at Lehman Brothers in 2007, but those prosecutors may be forced to tread lightly in the wake of what happened this week. Even though the facts and circumstances of the Lehman matter are very different from the Cioffi/Tannin episode, Tuesday's verdict may be the best news in more than a year for Richard Fuld, the former Lehman chief executive.

For now, Mr. Cioffi and Mr. Tannin remain the only bankers indicted for their professional behavior in what became one of the worst financial crises in our history. They became a symbol of greedy carelessness for a public intent on blaming someone—anyone—for Wall Street's folly. There must be some accountability for the Bear Stearns calamity, to say nothing of the $12 trillion of taxpayer money used to prop up capitalism, right? Not so fast, this Brooklyn jury declared. "The entire market crashed," one juror explained. "You can't blame that on two people."

DISCUSSION *questions and activities*

1. In a surprise verdict, two hedge fund managers are found "not guilty." Jurors are quoted saying, "we just didn't feel the case had been proven." The original emails had been taken out of context and did not represent the actual events. Can you find other examples of text out of context? What false impression did it give?

2. Another juror says, "The entire market crashed, you can't blame that on two people." Do you agree or disagree? Locate examples in the text that support your opinion.

Diffuse Malignant Pleural Mesothelioma: Symptom Management

Mary Ellen Cordes and Carol Brueggen

Mary Ellen Cordes and Carol Brueggen are registered nurses specializing in oncology and pulmonology. Cordes is an active member of the American Association of Critical-Care Nurses and teaches continuing education classes at the Mayo Clinic in Rochester, MN. Brueggen is the Vice-President of the Oncology Nursing Certification Corporation and a 2006 recipient of the Advanced Oncology Certified Nurse of the Year Award. This article explores the medical management of patients diagnosed with mesothelioma.

Diffuse malignant pleural mesothelioma (DMPM) is a rare disease that forms on the lining of the lungs. DMPM usually is associated with asbestos exposure and accounts for approximately 1% of all cancer deaths in the world (Peto, Decarli, LaVecchia, Levi, & Negri, 1999). The diagnosis of DMPM often is delayed because of nonspecific symptoms. Approximately 60%–90% of patients present with symptoms of dyspnea and chest pain (Grondin & Sugarbaker, 1999; Martin-Ucar, Edwards, Rengajaran, Muller, & Waller, 2001). Other common complaints at presentation include cough, fatigue, and weight loss, which can lead to anorexia or cachexia (Aisner, 1995; Grondin & Sugarbaker). Symptoms of DMPM can be present up to five months before a diagnosis is established (Merritt et al., 2001).

Patients diagnosed with DMPM have multiple disease- and treatment-related symptoms. The majority of patients with DMPM are diagnosed with advanced disease. Currently, no cure for DMPM exists and life expectancy usually is very limited. Aggressive multimodal therapy consisting of surgery, chemotherapy, and radiotherapy is used to treat DMPM. Supportive care is recommended for patients who are debilitated at diagnosis because they would not be able to tolerate aggressive therapy. The severity of symptoms increases as the disease progresses, putting patients at risk for anxiety and depression. Effective symptom management must be initiated early to assist in improving the quality of life for these patients.

Specific research about managing symptoms experienced by patients with DMPM is minimal. However, research findings about symptoms and symptom management in patients with lung cancer and patients with cancer in general are useful in identifying and describing possible interventions for patients with DMPM.

Dyspnea

Dyspnea, as defined by the American Thoracic Society (ATS) (1999), is "a subjective experience of breathing discomfort consisting of qualitatively distinct sensations that vary in intensity" (p. 322). Physiologic, psychological, cultural, and environmental factors contribute to patients' experience of dyspnea (ATS, 1999; Gift, 1990; Ripamonti & Bruera, 1997; West & Popkess-Vawter, 1994). Dyspnea was reported to be the number one presenting symptom in 46 of 101 patients with DMPM in a retrospective review (Merritt et al., 2001). In a study by Herndon and colleagues (1998), 70% of patients with DMPM (n = 337) reported that dyspnea was their chief complaint.

The subjective nature and multiple contributing factors make dyspnea a difficult symptom to assess. A variety of assessment tools for evaluation of dyspnea and interventions for relief exists. Available assessment tools include activity scales, such as the Pulmonary Function Status Scale, American Thoracic Standardized Questionnaire, Baseline and Transitional Dyspnea Indexes, and Therapy Impact Questionnaire for Quality of Life. Self-report measures, such as the Medical Research Council Dyspnea Scale, Dyspnea Interview Schedule, Oxygen Cost Diagram, Modified Borg Scale, Cancer Dyspnea Scale, and Visual Analog Scale, also are available (Mancini & Body, 1999; Tanaka, Akechi, Okuyama, Nishiwaki, & Uchitomi, 2002c; Wickham, 2002). The most commonly used tool is the visual analog scale, where patients rate their dyspnea on a horizontal or vertical line from no breathlessness to worst possible breathlessness (Ripamonti & Bruera, 1997).

Ideally, treating the underlying cause of dyspnea would eliminate this symptom; however, this is difficult to do in advanced-stage lung cancers (Gift, 1990). Dyspnea may be an indication of a phase in the illness in which resources should be shifted from acute intervention to palliative and supportive care measures (Ripamonti & Fusco, 2002). Goals of treatment are based on an assessment of subjective complaints and the limitations created for each patient.

The presence of pleural effusions and pleural thickening in DMPM contributes to dyspnea in this patient population. The prognosis for the majority of patients diagnosed with DMPM is poor, and multimodal treatment often is needed. A multimodal approach in treating this disease can assist in amelioration of the symptom of dyspnea. Surgical debulking of tumors and drainage of pleural effusions can allow for improved lung expansion and relief of dyspnea (Martin-Ucar et al., 2001; Soysal et al., 1997). Additional approaches to management of DMPM and the level of dyspnea that these patients experience include medical treatment using thoracentesis with pleurodesis, preventive radiotherapy, and chemotherapy (ATS, 2000). Palliative management of dyspnea is appropriate when treatment of the disease is unsuccessful.

Therapeutic thoracentesis is performed to remove fluid from the pleural space and allows greater expansion of the lungs. The rapid reaccumulation of fluid often requires repeat thoracentesis for symptom relief. Pleurodesis may be considered for management of symptomatic, recurrent pleural effusions. Also, patients may develop empyema secondary to repeat thoracentesis (Soysal et al., 1997). Placement of a large-bore chest tube, instillation of talc or other chemicals as sclerosing agents for pleurodesis, and an average four- to six-day hospitalization are considerations with this treatment that have financial and emotional costs to patients during end-of-life care (LeGrand, 2002).

Use of a small-bore catheter placed under fluoroscopy for drainage of pleural effusions and assessment of loculations has been evaluated as a less invasive technique. Small-bore catheters have been as effective as large thoracostomy tubes for drainage and pleurodesis, with no increase in complications such as infection (Marom et al., 1999; Parulekar, Di Primio, Matzinger, Dennie, & Bociek, 2001). Small-bore catheters can be placed without the use of general anesthesia and improve patients' dyspnea. However, thoracentesis with large- or small-bore catheters is not effective for long-term control of pleural effusions.

Repeat catheterization because of frequent reaccumulation of fluids has led to the development of a flexible, indwelling, pleural catheter (Pleurx®, Denver Biomedical, Golden, CO). This catheter is used to relieve dyspnea and allows patients to avoid frequent hospitalizations for drainage of pleural fluids. Patient selection is important. Patients who have experienced relief from drainage of pleural fluid and are able or have the support to manage the catheter are good candidates for this intervention (Brubacher

& Gobel, 2003; Taubert, 2001). The catheter is inserted in a hospital or an outpatient setting. Patients and caregivers are instructed to drain the fluid for symptom relief, and they can drain up to 1,000 ml at a time several times per week, if necessary. Drainage of pleural effusions in this manner provides timely symptom relief for dyspnea and cough. This intervention may increase exercise tolerance, as well (Pien, Gant, Washam, & Sterman, 2001). Mechanical pleurodesis may occur with frequent drainage and the introduction of the catheter, which serves as an irritant (Taubert). Patients who have dyspnea related to chronic pleural thickening are not improved by catheter placement (Putnam et al., 2000). As DMPM progresses, increasing lung encasement and invasion of mediastinal structures diminish symptomatic benefit of drainage by the pleural catheter (Pien et al.).

Supplemental oxygen can be used to enhance activity tolerance (ATS, 1999). Oxygen may create a placebo effect in some patients, and its use is controversial (Ripamonti, 1999). Airflow administered over the face and nasal mucosa may elicit the same subjective response of relief. For example, fans have been used to provide airflow over the face to decrease dyspnea (ATS, 1999).

Pharmacologic therapy in the treatment of dyspnea includes the use of opioids to alter patients' perception. Opioids systemically have the potential to relieve dyspnea by blunting perceptual responses (ATS, 1999). Dyspnea is worse in patients who require opioid medications to treat pain, and systemic opioid use by these patients may not decrease dyspnea (Smith et al., 2001). Side effects of systemic opioids include respiratory depression, altered mental status, constipation, nausea, vomiting, and drowsiness (Quelch, Faulkner, & Yun, 1997). Monitoring and managing these side effects will improve patients' tolerance of the treatment.

Nebulized morphine and fentanyl have been studied as a treatment for dyspnea in patients with cancer. Opioids delivered by this route have low systemic absorption with diminished side effects (Coyne, Viswanathan, & Smith, 2002; Quelch et al., 1997). When selecting patients who are appropriate for nebulized opioids, the following criteria are used: severe dyspnea, end-stage disease with no curative treatment options, no history of asthma, and ability to tolerate nebulized respiratory treatments (Chandler, 1999). A test dose must be administered in a closely monitored setting. Medication is administered via nebulizer, or a mask with mist, every four hours for 7–10 minutes. The dose varies significantly from patient to patient. Patients with a history of asthma are excluded from this treatment because of reports of fatal cardiac arrests secondary to bronchospasm when using nebulized opioids (Chandler; Quelch et al.). Nebulized furosemide also has been studied in clinical trials as a treatment for dyspnea in patients with cancer at the end stage of disease. Furosemide acts on the irritants and stretch receptors in the lungs to decrease dyspnea (Shimoyama & Shimoyama, 2002).

Other medications include bronchodilators and corticosteroids. Inhaled beta 2-adrenergic agonists may be of help, but patients must be monitored closely for adverse effects such as tachycardia, dysrhythmias, and possible increased anxiety (Wickham, 2002). Corticosteroids may decrease inflammation, allowing bronchodilation for dyspnea. Clinical trials have not established standard doses for this therapy (Wickham).

Psychological distress is associated significantly with dyspnea (Tanaka et al., 2002a). Providing psychological and social support is a key intervention. Anxiolytic agents assist in altering emotional responses to dyspnea and should be considered for a trial with patients who have severe dyspnea (ATS, 1999). Nonpharmacologic interventions, such as distraction, relaxation, guided imagery, symptom monitoring, and goal setting, can be beneficial (ATS, 1999). Teaching patients effective ways of coping with breathlessness as a result of progression of cancers of the lung and providing patients with an opportunity to talk about feelings and concerns may improve patients' quality of life by providing some sense of control (Bredin et al., 1999; Cox, 2002).

Exercise training to improve respiratory muscle strength increases activity tolerance and decreases dyspnea, leading to improved quality of life for patients with advanced lung cancers (Cox, 2002). Moderate levels of exercise could be considered as an intervention to delay or decrease the severity of dyspnea (LeGrand, 2002). A structured pulmonary rehabilitation program, combining education with exercise training and workout sessions, may decrease patients' perception of dyspnea and improve expectations and performance status (Scherer & Schmieder, 1997).

Pain

Pain and dyspnea coexist in patients with DMPM. The correlation between pain and dyspnea is controversial because pain may worsen dyspnea and dyspnea may worsen pain. Both symptoms tend to worsen as the disease progresses (Tanaka et al., 2002b). Pain is most common in patients with DMPM because of the invasion of the chest wall by the tumor. Palliative parietal pleurectomy controlled chest wall pain in 85% of patients when performed in early stages of the disease (Soysal et al., 1997). Pain relief was achieved early after palliative surgical intervention, but mortality at three months continued to be high (Martin-Ucar et al., 2001). Careful patient selection can maximize the benefits of palliative surgery in mesothelioma (Martin-Ucar et al.).

Radiotherapy is used to palliate chest wall pain, but its effectiveness has been disappointing (Merritt et al., 2001). In addition to radiotherapy, the use of opioids, nonopioid analgesics, and nonsteroidal anti-inflammatory medications is required. Around-the-clock dosing with medications is important to maintain adequate pain control. Use of adjuvant therapies is described in the step approach of the World Health Organization's analgesic ladder. (For details on this approach, see U.S. Department of Health and Human Services, Agency for Health Care Policy and Research [1994].)

Pain becomes more localized with disease progression as a result of entrapment of intercostal nerves (Grondin & Sugarbaker, 1999). Surgical debulking of tumors can relieve nerve compression and decrease pain symptoms (Martin-Ucar et al., 2001). If patients are not surgical candidates and are experiencing severe intractable pain, interpleural analgesia should be considered. Anesthetic agents such as bupivicaine can be instilled through a permanent, flexible catheter inserted in the pleural space (Irick & Hostetter, 2000). This treatment needs further research and may not be appropriate for patients at the end of life.

Distraction, relaxation, guided imagery, and symptom monitoring are interventions that can be taught to provide patients and caregivers with tools to help control the perception and experience of pain. Assessment of interventions is important to guide treatment. The numeric rating scale of 0 (no pain) to 10 (worst possible pain) or a faces pain-rating scale are commonly used assessment tools.

Cough

Donnelly and Walsh (1995) reported that chronic cough affects 37% of people with advanced cancer. Eighty percent of patients with advanced cancer and a chronic cough have lung cancer, and cough is a common symptom in DMPM (Knudson, Block, & Schulman, 1989). Infiltration of tumor into the pleura and hypersecretion of mucus may contribute to chronic cough. Chronic cough increases pain and fatigue, prevents adequate rest, and may cause rib fractures (Ingle, 2001). Coughing spasms can increase pain and trigger nausea and vomiting (Homsi, Walsh, & Nelson, 2001). A dry, irritating cough must be differentiated from a productive cough so that patients can be treated safely (Ingle). Treatment of underlying bacterial pneumonias with antibiotics also should be considered (Homsi et al., 2001). Patients' smoking history should be obtained, and patients should be counseled to stop smoking and advised on smoking cessation techniques (Ingle).

Empiric treatment with antitussive medications may be provided. Hydrocodone 5 mg every four to six hours is used commonly for chronic cough. Hydrocodone has less constipating and neuropsychologic side effects than codeine preparations (Homsi, Walsh, Nelson, LeGrand, & Davis, 2000). Homatropin is an anticholinergic additive found in some preparations of hydrocodone that may cause undesirable side effects of delirium and hallucinations (Homsi et al., 2001).

Nonopioids used for cough suppressants include drugs that act directly on cough receptors, such as benzonatate 100 mg three times per day. Side effects with this drug are infrequent (Homsi et al., 2001). A nebulized local anesthetic also may be used to decrease cough (Volker & Coward, 2003).

Providing warm, humidified air and instructing patients in deep breathing and coughing techniques are beneficial when secretions are present (Ingle, 2001). Mild hemoptysis is common, and patients can be monitored conservatively on an outpatient basis. Patients and families may fear massive hemoptysis and need reassurance that this is a rare event (Ripamonti & Fusco, 2002; Volker & Coward, 2003).

Fatigue

Patients with cancer, including those with cancers of the lung such as DMPM, identify fatigue as their most frequently experienced symptom (Chang, Hwang, Feuerman, & Kasimis, 2000; Degner & Sloan, 1995; Lobchuk, Kristjanson, Degner, Blood, & Sloan, 1997; Tishelman, Degner, & Mueller, 2000). Subjectively, fatigue is characterized as generalized weakness, exhaustion, and lack of energy (Aistars, 1987; Wu & McSweeney, 2001). The etiology of cancer-related fatigue is multifaceted and results from a variety of disease- and treatment-related physical and psychosocial factors (Nail & Winningham, 1995). Disease- and treatment-related factors include anemia, electrolyte imbalance, volume depletion, poor nutritional status, nausea and vomiting, dyspnea, pain, depression and sedation resulting from analgesics, hypoxia, and infection (Nail, 2001; Portenoy & Itri, 1999). Other contributing factors identified by Nail include sleep disturbance, increased requirements for physical activity, emotional stress, increased demands with personal relationships, and a need for increased concentration.

When evaluating patients' fatigue, subjective and objective data must be obtained. Symptom location, pattern, intensity, onset, and duration, along with any aggravating or alleviating factors, must be assessed. Differentiating between patients' and family members' or caregivers' perceptions of fatigue and the associated distress is important, as these may be very different (Rhodes & Watson, 1987). Healthcare providers also must consider patients' past and present medical history, review present prescription and nonprescription medications, and assess for the use of caffeine, vitamins, and alcohol to determine whether they may be contributing to sedation and fatigue (Kellum, 1985). Performance status, physical appearance, gait, etc., also should be assessed (Rhoton, 1982).

Several valid and reliable fatigue-measurement tools exist, such as the Piper Fatigue Scale, the Fatigue Symptom Inventory, and the Brief Fatigue Inventory (Hann et al., 1998; Mendoza et al., 1999; Piper et al., 1998). The use of a simple visual analog scale, in which 0 is no fatigue and 10 is the worst fatigue imaginable, is a good tool to use to open dialogue with patients and families regarding fatigue and their perceptions of its impact on quality of life (Rhoton, 1982). Self-report is the most effective fatigue measurement. (See Wu and McSweeney [2001] for a description and review of the major instruments used to measure cancer-related fatigue.)

Interventions begin with educating patients about the complexity of fatigue, its nature, options for therapy, and anticipated outcomes. To adequately care for patients with cancer experiencing fatigue, all symptoms being experienced must be assessed and managed. This includes reviewing current medications and determining whether they may be contributing to the fatigue, identifying and treating any sleep disturbances, reversing anemia or metabolic abnormalities, and managing major depression (Portenoy & Itri, 1999) (see Figure 1). Psychostimulants, such as methylphenidate, may be considered for the treatment of opioid-related somnolence and cognitive impairment in patients with a life expectancy of weeks to months. Improved mood and energy often are evident in 24 hours (Bruera, Brenneis, Paterson,

FIGURE 1. ALGORITHM FOR THE EVALUATION AND MANAGEMENT OF CANCER-RELATED FATIGUE

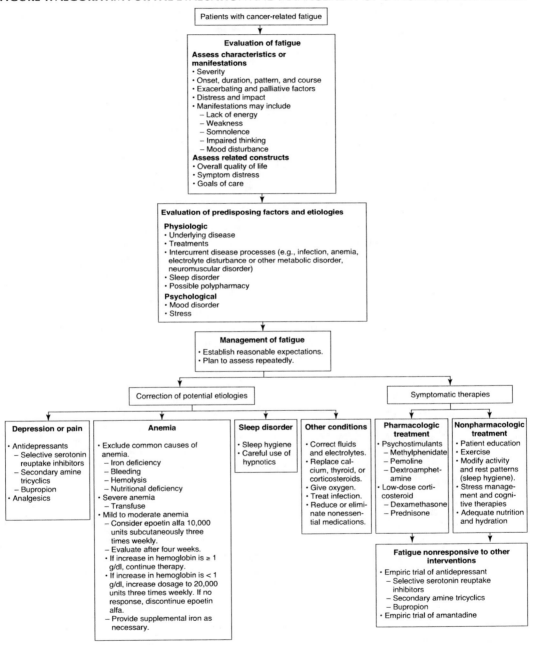

Figure from "Cancer-Related Fatigue: Guidelines for Evaluation and Management" by R.K. Portenoy and L.M. Itri in *The Oncologist*, 4. Copyright © 1999 by Alphamed Press, Inc. Reproduced with permission of Alphamed Press, Inc. via Copyright Clearance Center. Visit the journal's Web site at www.theoncologist.com

& MacDonald, 1989; Valentine & Meyers, 2001). Referrals for evaluation by physical and occupational therapy are important for providing information related to energy conservation and appropriate exercise. Patients also should be educated on practical tips for promoting sleep.

Depression

Feelings of sadness and grief are normal reactions to a life-threatening diagnosis such as DMPM. These responses are expected and may occur at the time of diagnosis and at various times throughout the cancer trajectory. Many patients with cancer experience distress. Distress and depression among patients with cancer can negatively affect length of survival, compliance with therapy, self-care ability, perception of pain, and quality of life (McDaniel, Musselman, Porter, Reed, & Nemeroff, 1995).

Patients diagnosed with DMPM experience many potential causes of psychosocial distress. For 60%–80% of patients with DMPM, asbestos exposure has been identified as the primary cause (Moskel, Urschel, Anderson, Antkowiak, & Takita, 1999). Many of these patients were exposed to asbestos prior to the implementation of occupational safety standards. For these patients and families, anger toward employers who did not inform them of the hazards of their environment is common. Distress mounts for patients and families who not only are dealing with a potentially life-threatening illness but also may face lengthy legal battles as they seek financial compensation for developing an occupationally associated illness (Munson, 1997).

Other causes of psychological distress include beginning treatment (surgery, chemotherapy, or radiotherapy), fear that the illness will result in death, extensive or painful medical procedures, loss of energy, and inability to work. Risk for depression may increase as patients become frustrated with their inability to maintain their normal level of functioning. Patients with cancers of the lung have been found to experience more symptom distress than patients with other types of cancer; these symptoms develop not only from the natural progression of the disease but also from treatment-related side effects (Lobchuk & Kristjanson, 1997).

When evaluating patients with cancer for depression, many things must be considered. Healthcare providers must assess whether patients have a history of depression, whether a family history of depression or suicide exists, what the life stressors are for each patient, and what supportive resources are available. The diagnostic criteria for major depression include the presence of depressed mood or loss of pleasure for more than two weeks in addition to at least three or four physical (weight gain or loss, sleep disturbance, loss of energy, psychomotor retardation) or psychological (difficulty concentrating, guilt or low self-esteem, thoughts of suicide or death) manifestations of depression (American Psychological Association, 2000).

Many of the symptoms associated with depression are similar to symptoms caused by many types of cancers and their corresponding treatment. In 1977, Plumb and Holland used the Beck Depression Inventory to separately study somatic items compared to psychological items and found that, in patients with cancer, depression is diagnosed best by the severity of dysphoric mood; the degree of guilt, hopelessness, and worthlessness; and the presence of suicidal thoughts. Endicott (1984) suggested that when physiologic symptoms of depression are caused by a medical condition, they are replaced by the following psychological symptoms.

- Fearful or depressed appearance
- Social withdrawal or decreased talkativeness
- Brooding, self-pity, or pessimism
- Nonreactive mood (cannot be cheered up, does not smile or react to good news)

Depression in patients with cancer can be managed successfully using a team approach of individual or group psychotherapy, cognitive or behavioral techniques, and antidepressant medications. Psychotherapy assists patients in identifying past strengths and previous techniques for coping. Cognitive-behavioral techniques assist patients in reframing inaccurate perceptions and assessments that can result in feelings of depression. Pharmacologic therapy has been helpful in reducing stress, increasing quality of life, and, in some cases, increasing survival (Fallowfield, Hall, Maguire, & Baum, 1990; Greer et al., 1992).

The primary treatment for depression in patients with cancer is psychopharmacologic therapy. Several categories of antidepressants are available to choose from: first- and second-generation tricyclic antidepressants, heterocyclics and monoamine oxidase inhibitors, selective serotonin reuptake inhibitors, serotonin and noradrenaline reuptake inhibitors, and dopamine antagonists. When choosing antidepressants, healthcare providers must consider their mechanism of action, potential side effects, existing comorbidities, existing depressive symptoms, and the response of patients if the antidepressants have been used in the past. When dosing antidepressants, prescribers also must take into consideration that patients with cancer experiencing depression often respond to lower doses than healthy individuals; thus, therapeutic dosing should be monitored via plasma levels. (See Lovejoy, Tabor, and Deloney [2000] and Lovejoy, Tabor, Matteis, and Lillis [2000] for an in-depth discussion of depression management.)

Healthcare professionals caring for patients with DMPM must diagnose depressive disorders accurately. Other symptoms experienced by patients with DMPM, such as pain, fatigue, dyspnea, and cough, may amplify their risk for depression. Thus, symptom management throughout the cancer experience is of great importance. Approximately 80% of patients with cancer who are diagnosed with depression can be successfully treated using psychotherapeutic and psychopharmacological interventions (Breitbart, Chochinov, & Passik, 1998).

Weight Loss, Anorexia, and Cachexia

Patients diagnosed with DMPM often present with cancer-related weight loss that increases as the disease progresses. Issues with anorexia and cachexia are common. Approximately 60%–90% of patients with cancer experience progressive weight loss at some point during the cancer continuum (Ottery, 2001). The paraneoplastic syndrome of anorexia-cachexia is characterized by loss of appetite, early satiety, severe involuntary weight loss, skeletal muscle wasting, weakness, fatigue, poor performance status, impaired immune function, serum protein depletion, and other metabolic abnormalities (Gill, Eldridge, & Rust, 2001; Puccio & Nathanson, 1997; Wilkes, 2003). The side effects of cancer treatment—pain, fatigue, and depression—also may contribute to anorexia-cachexia. As with other cancers of the lung, patients with advanced DMPM often experience severe dyspnea. This breathlessness can make the task of eating more difficult, resulting in patients wanting to avoid meals (Wilkes, 2003). Patients tend to eat less when they are forced, so they must maintain control of what and how much they eat (Gill et al.).

Patients experiencing malnutrition often have decreased quality of life. Many patients are unable to continue their usual activities as the resulting fatigue increases. From a psychological perspective, extreme weight loss is also a constant reminder of patients' cancer and mortality. Patients with DMPM, as well as other patients with cancer, who have anorexia may experience a heightened level of distress as concerned family members try to encourage and coax them to increase their nutritional intake (Wilkes, 2000).

According to Ottery (1994), preventing malnutrition is easier than reversing it. At the time of diagnosis, a thorough nutritional screening should be completed to assess for potential or existing problems in nutritional status. This will provide baseline data that needs to be reassessed during and after cancer treatment. A nutritional assessment generally begins with a discussion with patients regarding food preferences, usual dietary habits, attitudes about food, cultural factors, ability to obtain and prepare food, and psychological factors such as family support. Patients' preillness weight and weight at diagnosis should be obtained. When determining body weight, issues such as edema, ascites, dehydration, or tumor load should be considered (Klein et al., 1997). In general, nutritional intervention usually is deemed necessary if patients have a weight loss of 10% or more (Ottery, 1995). Once treatment has started, patients must be evaluated regularly for treatment side effects such as anorexia, nausea and vomiting, early satiety, or diarrhea. Taste changes must be considered as well. The use of medications, prescribed or over-the-counter, must be identified along with potential side effects that may have an impact on gastrointestinal function and result in decreased oral intake. The use of herbal supplements should be determined, as some may cause a decrease in appetite or result in side effects such as anorexia, diarrhea, or nausea and vomiting (Wilkes, 2000).

Hill (1992) recommended some fairly simple tests to assess for a decrease in muscle strength. Grip strength may be tested by asking patients to squeeze their index and middle fingers for ten seconds. Respiratory muscle strength may be tested by asking patients to blow on a strip of paper that is being held four inches (10 cm) away from their lips. Minimal to no movement suggests severe respiratory impairment. A Tendon-Bone Test and Finger-Thumb Test also can be completed to assess muscle wasting and loss of subcutaneous fat. The Tendon-Bone Test is performed by examining and palpating the patient's face, back, upper arms, and back of hands. Visible tendons and bones suggest a 30% or greater loss of total protein stores. The Finger-Thumb Test, which entails gently pinching the skin of the upper arm, may assess subcutaneous fat. If the triceps or biceps are felt, the test is positive and muscle body fat stores are potentially less than 10% (Hill, 1995; Wilkes, 2003).

Serum albumin is the most common laboratory study performed to assess nutritional status. The serum albumin level reflects the availability of protein within the past month (Gill et al., 2001). A normal range for serum albumin is 3.5–5 g/dl. A low serum albumin may indicate prolonged, severe protein deficiency and may be associated with cachexia and increased mortality (Dudak, 1997). Other laboratory tests that may be performed include transferrin, cholesterol, urinary urea nitrogen, hematocrit, total lymphocyte count, and absolute neutrophil count (Gill et al.).

A review of the elements of a well-balanced diet should be provided for patients who have good nutritional status. For patients who already are malnourished or at risk, a nutritional plan that includes ways to increase caloric intake and stabilize weight should be developed. Wilkes (2000) recommended that patients with cancer need 25–35 calories per kg per day (13–15 calories per pound) and 1–2 g/kg per day of protein.

Nonpharmacologic interventions include instructing patients to eat calorie- and protein-rich foods. Small, frequent meals usually are better tolerated. Different food textures, tastes, temperatures, seasonings, colors, etc., should be used to provide variety. High-calorie liquid supplements and a daily multivitamin without iron should be recommended (Gill et al., 2001). Evans, Roubenoff, and Schevitz (1998) reported that 15 minutes of gentle aerobic exercise 30 minutes before eating aids in stimulating the appetite and decreasing fatigue. Family and friends can be asked to assist with grocery shopping and food preparation so that patients can conserve energy. Previous dietary restrictions (i.e., diabetic, low cholesterol) should be reviewed. Many patients will be able to disregard previous restrictions and eat any foods that appeal to them.

Pharmacologic interventions for weight loss, anorexia, and cachexia begin with providing effective symptom management with antiemetics, antidiarrheals, and analgesics. Progestational agents such as megestrol acetate have been found to stimulate the appetite, increase oral intake, reduce nausea and vomiting, and promote nonfluid weight gain (Loprinzi, Schaid, Dose, Burnham, & Jensen, 1993; Ottery, 1994; Tchekmedyian et al., 1992). Patients taking megestrol acetate should be instructed to be observant for the signs of deep vein thrombosis because their risk for this increases when on this medication (Loprinzi et al., 1999). Corticosteroids such as dexamethasone can increase the appetite and assist in providing some patients with an improved sense of well-being. Some patients prefer not to take this medication because of the side effects of fluid retention, insomnia, and hyperglycemia (Ottery, 1995). Prokinetic agents such as metoclopramide can be used to decrease early satiety (Gill et al., 2001).

If patients are unable to take foods orally but have a functioning gut, enteral nutrition can be considered and is preferred over parenteral nutrition. Patients' prognoses must be considered when deciding whether to provide aggressive nutritional support. According to Gill et al. (2001), guidelines for the use of parenteral nutrition include a nonfunctioning gut, inadequate oral intake for more than 10 days, life expectancy of at least 40 days, and possible central line access. In advanced cancer, enteral and parenteral nutrition have not been shown to positively influence survival time (Foltz, 2000; Puccio & Nathanson, 1997).

Hospice

As DMPM progresses, the goal for care becomes supportive and a referral to hospice should be considered. The hospice staff is available to help patients, families, and caregivers address issues with symptom management and other psychological and spiritual issues. Nurses can help patients maintain their autonomy by encouraging them to participate in making end-of-life decisions through advanced care planning. Hospice staff also can assist patients and families in understanding what to expect as the disease progresses and prepare them for the process of dying. The support provided by hospice can aid not only in increasing the quality of patients' lives but also the quality of their death.

Conclusion

To date, advances in the treatment of DMPM have been limited and no curative treatment exists. The symptoms of dyspnea—cough, pain, fatigue, depression, weight loss, anorexia, and cachexia—if left untreated, can result in poor quality of life for patients with DMPM and their caregivers. Thorough, ongoing assessment is required. Nurses are in an excellent position to collaboratively work with other members of the healthcare team to assist patients with DMPM in attaining the goal of increased quality of life.

References

Aisner, J. (1995). Current approach to malignant mesothelioma of the pleura. *Chest, 107*(6 Suppl.), 332S–344S.

Aistars, J. (1987). Fatigue in the cancer patient: A conceptual approach to a clinical problem. *Oncology Nursing Forum, 14*(6), 25–30.

American Psychological Association. (2000). *Diagnostic and statistical manual of mental disorders* (4th ed.). Washington, DC: Author.

American Thoracic Society. (1999). Dyspnea: Mechanisms, assessment, and management: A consensus statement. *American Journal of Respiray and Critical Care Medicine, 159*, 321–340.

American Thoracic Society. (2000). Management of malignant pleural effusions. *American Journal of Respiratory Critical Care Medicine, 162*, 1987–2001.

Bredin, M., Corner, J., Krishnasamy, M., Plant, H., Bailey, C., & A'hern, R. (1999). Multicentre randomized controlled trial of nursing intervention for breathlessness in patients with lung cancer. *BMJ, 318*, 901–904.

Breitbart, W., Chochinov, H., & Passik, S. (1998). Psychiatric aspects of care. In D. Doyle, G.W.C. Hanks, & N. MacDonald (Eds.), *Oxford textbook of palliative medicine* (pp. 933–954). New York: Oxford Press.

Brubacher, S., & Gobel, B.H. (2003). Use of the Pleurx® pleural catheter for the management of malignant pleural effusions. *Clinical Journal of Oncology Nursing, 7*, 35–38.

Bruera, E., Brenneis, C., Paterson, A.H., & MacDonald, R.N. (1989). Use of methylphenidate as an adjuvant to narcotic analgesics in patients with advanced cancer. *Journal of Pain and Symptom Management, 4*, 3–6.

Chandler, S. (1999). Nebulized opioids to treat dyspnea. *American Journal of Hospice and Palliative Care, 16*, 418–422.

Chang, V.T., Hwang, S.S., Feuerman, M., & Kasimis, B. (2000). Symptom and quality of life survey of medical oncology patients at a veterans' affairs medical center. *Cancer, 88*, 1175–1183.

Cox, C. (2002). Non-pharmacological treatment of breathlessness. *Nursing Standard. 16*(24), 33–36.

Coyne, P.J., Viswanathan, R., & Smith, T.J. (2002). Nebulized fentanyl citrate improves patients' perception of breathing, respiratory rate, and oxygen saturation in dyspnea. *Journal of Pain and Symptom Management, 23*, 157–160.

Degner, L.F., & Sloan, J.A. (1995). Symptom distress in newly diagnosed ambulatory cancer patients and as a predictor of survival in lung cancer. *Journal of Pain and Symptom Management, 10*, 423–431.

Donnelly, S., & Walsh, D. (1995). The symptoms of advanced cancer. *Seminars in Oncology, 22* (3 Suppl. 3), 67–72.

Dudak, S.G. (1997). *Nutrition handbook for nursing practice* (3rd ed.). Philadelphia: Lippincott Williams and Wilkins.

Endicott, J. (1984). Measurement of depression in patients with cancer. *Cancer, 53*, 2243–2248.

Evans, W.J., Roubenoff, R., & Schevitz, A. (1998). Exercise and the treatment of wasting: Aging and human immunodeficiency virus infection. *Seminars in Oncology, 25*(2 Suppl. 6), 112–122.

Fallowfield, L.J., Hall, A., Maguire, G.P., & Baum, M. (1990). Psychological outcomes of different treatment policies in women with early breast cancer outside a clinical trial. *BMJ, 301*, 575–580.

Foltz, A. (2000). Nutritional disturbances. In C.H. Yarbro, M.H. Frogge, M. Goodman, & S. Groenwald (Eds.), *Cancer nursing: Principles and practice* (pp. 754–775). Boston: Jones and Bartlett.

Gift, A.G. (1990). Dyspnea. *Nursing Clinics of North America, 25*, 955–965.

Gill, C., Eldridge, B., & Rust, D. (2001). Nutritional support. In R.A. Gates & R.M. Fink (Eds.), *Oncology nursing secrets* (pp. 365–384). Philadelphia: Hanley and Belfus.

Greer, S., Moorey, S., Baruch, J.D., Watson, M., Robertson, B.M., Mason, A., et al. (1992). Adjuvant psychological therapy with cancer: A prospective randomized trial. *BMJ, 304*, 675–680.

Grondin, S.C., & Sugarbaker, D.J. (1999). Malignant mesothelioma of the pleural space. *Oncology, 13*, 919–932.

Hann, D., Jacobsen, P., Azzarello, L., Martin, S., Curran, S., Fields, K., et al. (1998). Measurement of fatigue in cancer patients: Development and validation of the Fatigue Symptom Inventory. *Quality of Life Research, 7*, 301–310.

Herndon, J.E., Green, M.R., Chahiniain, A.P., Corson, J.M., Yasunosuke, S., & Vogelzang, N. (1998). Factors predictive of survival among 337 patients with mesothelioma treated between 1984 and 1994 by the Cancer and Leukemia Group B. *Chest, 113*, 723–731.

Hill, G.L. (1992). Body composition research: Implications for the practice of clinical nutrition. *Journal of Parenteral and Enteral Nutrition, 16*, 197–218.

Hill, G.L. (1995). The clinical assessment of adult patients with protein energy malnutrition [Editorial]. *Nutrition in Clinical Practice, 10*, 129–130.

Homsi, J., Walsh, D., & Nelson, K.A. (2001). Important drugs for cough in advanced cancer. *Supportive Care in Cancer, 9*, 565–574.

Homsi, J., Walsh, D., Nelson, K.A., LeGrand, S.B., & Davis, M. (2000). Hydrocodone for cough in advanced cancer. *American Journal of Hospice and Palliative Care, 175*, 342–346.

Ingle, R. (2001). Lung cancer: Symptom management and supportive care. In C.H. Yarbro, M.H. Frogge, M. Goodman, & S. Groenwald (Eds.), *Cancer nursing: Principles and practice* (pp. 1298–1328). Boston: Jones and Bartlett.

Irick, N., & Hostetter, M.B. (2000). Interpleural analgesia for analgesia due to metastatic lung cancer. *Journal of Pharmaceutical Care in Pain and Symptom Control, 8*(3), 61–67.

Kellum, M.D. (1985). Fatigue. In M.M. Jacobs & W. Geels (Eds.), *Signs and symptoms in nursing: Interpretation and management* (pp. 103–118). Philadelphia: J.B. Lippincott.

Klein, S., Kinney, J., Jeejeebhoy, K., Alpers, D., Hellerstein, M., Murray, M., et al. (1997). Nutrition support in clinical practice: Review of published data and recommendations for future research directions. *Journal of Parenteral and Enteral Nutrition, 21*, 133–156.

Knudson, N., Block, K., & Schulman, S. (1989). Malignant pleural mesothelioma. *Oncology Nursing Forum, 16*, 845–851.

LeGrand, S.B. (2002). Dyspnea: The continuing challenge of palliative management. *Current Opinion in Oncology, 14*, 394–398.

Lobchuck, M.M., & Kristjanson, L.J. (1997). Perception of symptom distress in lung cancer patients: II. Behavioral assessment by primary family caregivers. *Journal of Pain and Symptom Management, 14*, 147–156.

Lobchuk, M.M., Kristjanson, L.J., Degner, L.F., Blood, P., & Sloan, J.A. (1997). Perceptions of symptom distress in lung cancer patients: I. Congruence between patients and family caregivers. *Journal of Pain and Symptom Management, 14*, 136–146.

Loprinzi, C., Kugler, J., Sloan, J., Mailliard, J., Krook, J., Wilwerding, M., et al. (1999). Randomized comparison of megestrol acetate versus dexamethasone versus fluoxymesterone for the treatment of cancer anorexia/cachexia. *Journal of Clinical Oncology, 17*, 3299–3306.

Loprinzi, C., Schaid, D., Dose, A., Burnham, N., & Jensen, M. (1993). Body composition changes in patients who gain weight receiving megestrol acetate. *Journal of Clinical Oncology, 11*, 152–154.

Lovejoy, N.C., Tabor, D., & Deloney, P. (2000). Cancer-related depression: Part II—Neurologic alterations and evolving approaches to psychopharmacology. *Oncology Nursing Forum, 27*, 795–808.

Lovejoy, N.C., Tabor, D., Matteis, M., & Lillis, P. (2000). Cancer-related depression: Part I—Neurologic alterations and cognitive behavioral therapy. *Oncology Nursing Forum, 27*, 667–678.

Mancini, I., & Body, J.J. (1999). Assessment of dyspnea in advanced cancer patients. *Supportive Care in Cancer, 7*, 229–232.

Marom, E.M., Patz, E.F., Erasmus, J.J., McAdams, H.P., Goodman, P.C., & Herndon, J.E. (1999). Malignant pleural effusions: Treatment with small-bore catheter thoracostomy and talc pleurodesis. *Radiology, 210*, 277–281.

Martin-Ucar, A.E., Edwards, J.G., Rengajaran, A., Muller, S., & Waller, D.A. (2001). Palliative surgical debulking in malignant mesothelioma: Predictors of survival and symptom control. *European Journal of Cardio-Thoracic Surgery, 20*, 1117–1121.

McDaniel, J.S., Musselman, D.C., Porter, M.R., Reed, D.A., & Nemeroff, C.B. (1995). Depression in patients with cancer: Diagnosis, biology and treatment. *Archives of General Psychiatry, 52*, 89–99.

Mendoza, T., Wang, X., Cleeland, C., Morrissey, M., Johnson, B., Wendt, J., et al. (1999). The rapid assessment of fatigue severity in cancer patients. Use of the Brief Fatigue Inventory. *Cancer, 85*, 1186–1196.

Merritt, N., Blewett, C.J., Miller, J.D., Bennett, W.F., Young, J.E.M., & Urschel, J.D. (2001). Survival after conservative (palliative) management of pleural malignant mesothelioma. *Journal of Surgical Oncology, 78*, 171–174.

Moskel, T.L., Urschel, J.D., Anderson, T.M., Antkowiak, J.G., & Takita, H. (1999). Malignant pleural mesothelioma: A problematic review. *Surgical Oncology, 7*, 5–12.

Munson, M. (1997). Mesothelioma. *Professional Nurse, 12*, 651–653.

Nail, L. (2001). Fatigue. In R.A. Gates & R.M. Fink (Eds.), *Oncology nursing secrets* (pp. 335–340). Philadelphia: Hanley and Belfus.

Nail, L., & Winningham, M.L. (1995). Fatigue and weakness in cancer patients: The symptom experience. *Seminars in Oncology Nursing, 11,* 272–278.

Ottery, F. (1994). Rethinking nutritional support in the cancer patient. *Seminars in Oncology, 24,* 277–287.

Ottery, F. (1995). Supportive nutrition to prevent cachexia and improve quality of life. *Seminars in Oncology, 22*(2 Suppl. 3), 98–111.

Ottery, F. (2001). Nutritional oncology: Planning a winning strategy [Live chat transcript]. Retrieved June 28, 2001, from http://www.cancersource.com/community/chat/archive.cfm?DiseaseID=1& Contentid=22873

Parulekar, W., Di Primio, G., Matzinger, F., Dennie, C., & Bociek, G. (2001). Use of small-bore vs. large-bore chest tubes for treatment of malignant pleural effusions. *Chest, 120,* 19–25.

Peto, J., Decarli, A., LaVecchia, C., Levi, F., & Negri, E. (1999). The European mesothelioma epidemic. *British Journal of Cancer, 79,* 666–672.

Pien, G.W., Gant, M., Washam, C.L., & Sterman, D.H. (2001). Use of an implantable pleural catheter for trapped lung syndrome in patients with malignant pleural effusion. *Chest, 119,* 1641–1646.

Piper, B.F., Dibble, S.L., Dodd, M.J., Weiss, M.C., Slaughter, R.E., & Paul, S.M. (1998). The revised Piper Fatigue Scale: Psychometric evaluation in women with breast cancer. *Oncology Nursing Forum, 25,* 677–684.

Plumb, M.M., & Holland, J. (1977). Comparative studies of psychological function in patients with advanced cancer. *Psychosomatic Medicine, 39,* 264–276.

Portenoy, R.K., & Itri, L.M. (1999). Cancer-related fatigue: Guidelines for evaluation and management. *Oncologist, 4,* 1–10.

Puccio, M., & Nathanson, L. (1997). The cancer cachexia syndrome. *Seminars in Oncology, 24,* 277–287.

Putnam, J.B., Walsh, G.L., Swisher, S.G., Roth, J.A., Suell, D.M., Vaporciyan, A.A., et al. (2000). Outpatient management of malignant pleural effusion by a chronic indwelling pleural catheter. *Annals of Thoracic Surgery, 69,* 369–375.

Quelch, P.C., Faulkner, D.E., & Yun, J.W.S. (1997). Nebulized opioids in the treatment of dyspnea. *Journal of Palliative Care, 13*(3), 48–52.

Rhodes, V.A., & Watson, P.M. (1987). Symptom distress—The concept: Past and present. *Seminars in Oncology Nursing, 3,* 242–247.

Rhoton, D. (1982). Fatigue and the postsurgical patient. In C.M. Norris (Ed.), *Concept clarification in nursing* (pp. 277–300). Rockville, MD: Aspen.

Ripamonti, C. (1999). Management of dyspnea in advanced cancer patients. *Supportive Care in Cancer, 7,* 233–243.

Ripamonti, C., & Bruera, E. (1997). Dyspnea: Pathophysiology and assessment. *Journal of Pain and Symptom Management, 13,* 220–232.

Ripamonti, C., & Fusco, F. (2002). Respiratory problems in advanced cancer. *Supportive Care in Cancer, 10,* 204–216.

Scherer, Y.K., & Schmieder, L.E. (1997). The effect of a pulmonary rehabilitation program on self-efficacy, perception of dyspnea, and physical endurance. *Heart and Lung, 26,* 15–22.

Shimoyama, N., & Shimoyama, M. (2002). Nebulized furosemide as a novel treatment for dyspnea in terminal cancer patients. *Journal of Pain and Symptom Management, 23,* 73–76.

Smith, E.L., Hann, D.M., Ahles, T.A., Furstenberg, C.T., Mitchell, T.A., Meyer, L., et al. (2001). Dyspnea, anxiety, body consciousness, and quality of life in patients with lung cancer. *Journal of Pain and Symptom Management, 21,* 323–329.

Soysal, O., Karaoglanoglu, N., Demircan, S., Topcu, S., Tastepe, I., Kaya, S., et al. (1997). Pleurectomy/decortication for palliation in malignant pleural mesothelioma: Results of surgery. *European Journal of Cardio-Thoracic Surgery, 11*, 210–213.

Tanaka, K., Akechi, T., Okuyama, T., Nishiwaki, Y., & Uchitomi, Y. (2002a). Factors correlated with dyspnea in advanced lung cancer patients: Organic causes and what else? *Journal of Pain and Symptom Management, 23*, 490–500.

Tanaka, K., Akechi, T., Okuyama, T., Nishiwaki, Y., & Uchitomi, Y. (2002b). Impact of dyspnea, pain and fatigue on daily life activities in ambulatory patients with advanced lung cancer. *Journal of Pain and Symptom Management, 23*, 417–423.

Tanaka, K., Akechi, T., Okuyama, T., Nishiwaki, Y., & Uchitomi, Y. (2002c). Prevalence and screening of dyspnea interfering with daily life activities in ambulatory patients with advanced lung cancer. *Journal of Pain and Symptom Management, 23*, 484–489.

Taubert, J. (2001). Management of malignant pleural effusion. *Nursing Clinics of North America, 36*, 665–683.

Tchekmedyian, N., Hickman, M., Siau, J., Greco, F., Keller, J., Browder, H., et al. (1992). Megestrol acetate in cancer anorexia and weight loss. *Cancer, 69*, 1268–1274.

Tishelman, C., Degner, L.F., & Mueller, B. (2000). Measuring symptom distress in patients with lung cancer: A pilot study of experienced intensity and importance of symptoms. *Cancer Nursing, 23*, 82–90.

U.S. Department of Health and Human Services, Agency for Health Care Policy and Research. (1994). Management of cancer pain. *Clinical Practice Guideline, 9*, 11–16.

Valentine, A.D., & Meyers, C.A. (2001). Cognitive and mood disturbance as cause and symptoms of fatigue in cancer patients. *Cancer, 92*(Suppl. 6), 1694–1698.

Volker, D.L., & Coward, D.D. (2003). End of life care. In M. Haas (Ed.), *Contemporary issues in lung cancer* (pp. 129–151). Boston: Jones and Bartlett.

West, N., & Popkess-Vawter, S. (1994). The subjective and psychosocial nature of breathlessness. *Journal of Advanced Nursing, 20*, 622–626.

Wickham, R. (2002). Dyspnea: Recognizing and managing an invisible problem. *Oncology Nursing Forum, 29*, 925–933.

Wilkes, G. (2000). Nutrition: The forgotten ingredient in cancer care. *American Journal of Nursing, 100*(4), 46–51.

Wilkes, G. (2003). Nutritional issues facing lung cancer individuals. In M. Haas (Ed.), *Contemporary issues in lung cancer: A nursing perspective* (pp. 153–174). Boston: Jones and Bartlett.

Wu, H., & McSweeney, M. (2001). Measurement of fatigue in people with cancer. *Oncology Nursing Forum, 28*, 1371–1384.

For More Information on this Topic, Visit the Following Web Sites.

Mesothelioma Web
 www.mesotheliomaweb.org
The Asbestos Cancer Resource
 www.mesoinfo.com
Mesothelioma Information Resource Group
 www.mirg.org
Links can be found using ONS Online at www.ons.org.

DISCUSSION *questions and activities*

1. The authors use charts to convey parts of the argument. How is this effective? What are the limitations of this component?

2. In diagram form, map out the primary and secondary claims in this argument.

3. What is the best way to read and digest this information? What are the advantages of being able to analyze a complicated piece of writing?

Reading Philosophy with Background Knowledge and Metacognition

David W. Concepción

David Concepción is an award winning professor at Ball State University, where he is the first person to receive all three of the university's teaching honors. Concepción earned his Ph.D. at the University of Wisconsin-Madison after completing his undergraduate work at Bates College in Maine. This essay was published in Teaching Philosophy, *a peer-reviewed journal devoted to addressing the pedagogical challenges faced by philosophy instructors in the classroom. The journal is a four-time recipient of the Mark Lenssen Prize for publishing and well respected by academics in the field. In this essay, Concepción offers both practical and theoretical insight to instructors and students struggling with the specialized language employed by writers in his field.*

This paper describes how and why I help students learn how to read philosophy. I argue that explicit reading instruction should be part of lower level philosophy courses. Specifically, students should be given metacognitively informed instruction that explicitly discusses relevant background knowledge. In the postscript, I note that student reactions to this type of instruction verify its necessity. The appendix contains a "How to Read Philosophy" handout that I use in my classes.

An Argument for Explicit Reading Instruction

Very few introductory books explain how to *read* primary philosophical texts. Much of the reading instruction that is available is either not entirely accessible to students or missing information that students want and need.[1] Students need reading instruction and part of what they need is not currently available.

A comment regarding how my "How to Read Philosophy" handout (see appendix) was developed will further illuminate what seems to be missing. I began by recognizing that there is a difference between what is familiar to professors and what should be obvious to students.[2] Students do not know what professors know about reading philosophy and what professors know will not be obvious to students. The task then was to write down what professors know about reading philosophy and to describe what professors do when they read. It is just this type of articulation of methods and assumptions that many students need to succeed. (See postscript)

The relative absence of appropriate "How to Read" material is peculiar. As years of listening to plaintive students teaches, intelligent and literate general studies and early major students lack the skills needed to read philosophy well. Students are not familiar with the folkways of academic philosophy and are too often left to learn them through trial and error. But we do our students a disservice if we let them flounder through with nothing but trial and error. Philosophy professors should not ask students in introductory or early major classes to spend three hours or more per week doing something they have never done before (i.e., read like a philosopher) without telling them how to do it. This is particularly true since we know they are likely to think reading philosophy is just like reading anything else.

Another reason to explicitly show students how to read philosophy is that reading primary texts well is *doing* philosophy, not merely *reading about* philosophy. If a student is truly engaged in reading she will be evaluating and making arguments. If we show students how to read philosophy well we will increase learning and when learning is increased, student enjoyment and retention tend to rise as well.

In sum, if (i) the skills required to read philosophy well are different from other reading skills, (ii) reading philosophy well is doing philosophy, and (iii) people build new skill more completely when they are explicitly shown *how* to perform the skill, then explicitly showing students how to read philosophy well will empower them to read philosophy in a more meaningfully way and thereby increase learning, enjoyment, and retention.

Reading Philosophy and Background Knowledge

There are multiple goals achieved by reading. There are also multiple methods of reading. Nevertheless, background knowledge and metacognition are central to expert reading in all settings.[3] In this section, background knowledge is discussed.

Readers understand a text when they construct a meaning by combining the result of decoding letters and words with what they already know. Readers with relatively little relevant background information read very slowly, in part because having so little background knowledge makes constructing the gist of a text difficult. As E. D. Hirsch noted, when "readers constantly lack crucial information, dictionaries and encyclopedias become quite impractical tools. A consistent lack of necessary information can make the reading process so laborious and uncommunicative that it fails to convey meaning."[4] Students confirm Hirsch's claim when they say, "I get nothing out of the reading."

To see how constructivist readers need background knowledge to develop an accurate and rich understanding, consider the following example.

> *A federal appeals panel today upheld an order barring foreclosure on a Missouri farm, saying that U.S. Agriculture Secretary John R. Block has reneged on his responsibilities to some debt ridden farmers. The appeals panel directed the USDA to create a system of processing loan deferments and of publicizing them as it said Congress had intended. The panel said that it is the responsibility of the agriculture secretary to carry out this intent. Not as a private banker, but as a public broker.*[5]

Hirsch notes that a great deal of background knowledge is necessary to fully understand this text. "What is a federal appeals panel? Where is Missouri and what about Missouri is relevant to the issue? Why are many farmers debt ridden? What is the USDA? What is a public broker?"[6] John T. Bruer expands Hirsch's insight:

> *We need background knowledge in reading for at least two reasons. First, background knowledge helps us make inferential links among the sentences that are written on the page.... Second, we need background information to construct and retain a text's gist. Given how our long-term memory works, to understand and remember what we read we have to relate the new information to schemas already in long-term memory. When background knowledge isn't active or available, we can remember very little of what we read.*[7]

Given how unfamiliar most general studies and early major students are with background information that is idiosyncratic to philosophy and philosophy course culture, we should not be surprised that many students do not manage to develop a rich understanding of some of the texts we ask them to read. One symptom of this inadequate understanding is the ubiquitous question: "Will this be on the test?" Many students do not realize that (much of) their grade is determined by their ability to perform skills beyond regurgitating information.

The need for relevant background information has implications for teaching philosophy courses.[8] Professors should give students as much background information as possible regarding the idiosyncrasies of philosophy generally as well as the special idiosyncrasies of the particular course being taught. Certainly no professor can give all of her students all of the relevant background knowledge needed to move beyond novice performance. However, no professor is completely powerless and each professor fails her students if she does not give what she can. The "How to Read Philosophy" handout in the appendix represents one manifestation of this background information.

Further, professors should help students gather more background information by requiring the mastery of relevant basic philosophical content, such as the definition of a sound argument. Exams should have a comprehensive short answer section to encourage this mastery. Simple mastery of information is an interactive prerequisite for the creation of rich understanding. Exams should also have essay sections because students actually create rich understanding in essays. However, explicit instruction regarding how to integrate knowledge effectively in an essay must also be offered. Without such essay writing instruction students are likely to (typically falsely) assume that essays are simply the location of comprehensive regurgitation of facts. Unless students are shown how to build reflective arguments from the information they have mastered they are likely to produce essays that seem to parrot the material. Purely "objective" exams are problematic because they do not give students the opportunity to create rich understanding. Exam essays are problematic when they are not accompanied by a requirement that facts be mastered. Dual format exams should encourage learning more fully than single format exams because dual format exams demand the mastery of information *and* encourage students to create their own rich understanding of the material.

The "How To" In "How to Read Philosophy"

The "How to Read Philosophy" handout (see appendix) begins with a description of some of the background information that instructors are apt to assume their students have. Good reading behaviors and unique features of philosophy texts are described. Also described are the differences between reading for enlightenment and reading for information, the differences between problem-based, historical, and figure-based philosophy classes, and the differences between primary and secondary sources. Next, three facets of the process of successful reading are delineated: stage setting, understanding, and evaluation.[9] The stage setting facet requires students to read the entire article quickly. The understanding facet requires students to re-read the entire article very carefully. During the stage setting read each student develops his or her own background information regarding the text. This particularized background information facilitates understanding during the careful re-read. Further, instructions regarding how to take notes while reading are provided, as are examples of note taking and key phrases. The dialogical nature of philosophical texts is also discussed. Finally, some frequently asked questions about reading philosophical texts are answered.

Of course, creating and distributing a handout alone does not typically solve learning problems. A number of scaffolding activities occur before and after students read the handout. First, students read, summarize, and evaluate a short passage in class. Second, students describe what they did while they read, summarized, and evaluated. Each student saves this pre-instructional self-reflection for comparison to post-instructional self-reflection. Third, students read the "How to Read Philosophy" handout. Fourth, students read, flag, summarize, and evaluate the passage again. Fifth, they compare their pre-instructional and post-instructional work to identify what they have learned. This second comparative self-assessment is turned in.[10] Sixth, to make further aspects of the learning process explicit, students examine the comparative post-instructional self-assessment of some of their classmates. Seventh, students turn in a formal summary of a complex text. In this summary students are expected to pull together what they have learned into a polished piece of writing. (Instructions for summary writing are provided to students separately.) Finally, this learning process is reinforced by the inclusion of questions regarding "How to Read" in the short answer portion of the exam.

These particular assignments may not fit well in every class. However, the underlying process may be used in a great many contexts. It may be useful then to describe the process in more general terms. We should (i) explicitly show students how to perform the desired skill, (ii) provide detailed models or examples, (iii) give students opportunities to practice the skill in a non-threatening (i.e., pass or fail) environment, (iv) show students how to engage in self-assessment of their performance and require them to do so, (v) evaluate students with very high standards on an attempt to perform the entire skill to the best of their ability, and (vi) reinforce the learning that has occurred by including exam questions regarding how to perform the skill.

Reading and Metacognition

Perhaps what is least familiar to philosophers about the procedure just described are its self-assessment and self-reflection aspects. Learning theorists refer to self-assessment and self-reflection as metacognition. Metacognition is "the ability to think about thinking, to be consciously aware of oneself as a problem solver, and to monitor and control one's mental processing."[11] In this section, metacognition is discussed in more detail.

Bruer concludes that the "most important implication [of recent educational research] is that *how* we teach is as important as what we teach….In short, high-order skills require extensive domain knowledge, understanding when to use the knowledge, and metacognitive monitoring and control. Students who have these things can solve novel, ambiguous problems; students who have high-order skills are intelligent novices."[12] It seems obvious that *how* we teach is important. However, if we unpack Bruer's conclusion we find that his insights recommend some not entirely obvious practices.

Bruer distinguishes between experts and novices.[13] Experts very skillfully work within a domain (e.g., philosophy) because they have extensive domain-specific knowledge and vast experience "chunking" that domain-specific knowledge. Experts are better than non-experts at grouping related information into a useful, accessible chunk that can be unpacked quickly. For example, experts in moral philosophy easily recognize the conceptual linkages among moral constructivism, subjectivism, intersubjectivism, and objectivism. Experts group these ideas into one intellectually manageable package of related but dissimilar ideas. Novices may not notice the conceptual linkages. Novices may attempt to memorize the meanings of these terms in isolation by rote. Such novices may be able to accurately identify these definitions on a multiple-choice exam. However, they are likely to have difficulty writing a sophisticated essay because they have not discerned the similarities and dissimilarities needed for rich understanding. To help students perform better, professors should do their best to explicitly describe how they chunk information.

Bruer also notes that among "the basic metacognitive skills are the ability to predict results of one's own problem-solving actions, to check the results of one's own actions (Did it work?), to monitor one's progress toward a solution (How am I doing?), and to test how reasonable one's actions and solutions are against the larger reality (Does this make sense?)."[14] Some novices have more metacognitive skill than others. Students differ in their ability to monitor and control their own learning progress. The meta-cognitive skills of juniors and seniors tend to be much more sharply honed than are those of first and second year students.

Importantly, students with better metacognitive skills learn new information more easily, accurately, and completely than students with weaker metacognitive skills. Good metacognition is a principle asset in learning.[15] If we want students to learn as much as possible, then we should help them improve their metacognitive skills.

Metacognition is involved in how I teach novices to read philosophy more successfully. Students have self-assessment questions to answer while reading. They must explicitly compare their self-reflection with the self-reflection of others. And, they must turn in written assignments to demonstrate their success.

There are other less obvious ways to encourage metacognition. For example, early in the semester students are *required* to pass notes to each other in class. At the end of class, each student must have contributed at least one question or answer to a written dialogue that took place in note passing during class. To receive credit, students must be on the lookout for material that they do not sufficiently understand and write a question or answer regarding it. In other words, students are given credit for being metacognitive during class.

One may worry that note passing is a dangerous practice because it provides cover to those who want to write off-topic notes and it distracts students from lecture. These worries seem unfounded. First, most students are quite good at multi-tasking. Students can write notes and pay attention to lecture at the same time. Second, the benefits outweigh the burdens: an improved ability to formulate a good question and a greater awareness of when one needs to ask a question. If the notes are turned in, instructors may receive the further benefit of valuable feedback regarding what is unclear to quiet students. Also, some students use the opportunity to have passionate debates with classmates. One day when the topic of the lecture was secular meta-ethics two students independently discovered the "Euthyphro" question about piety, moved to a discussion of God's attributes in an attempt to resolve it and finally discussed the problem of evil. Their thinking was not as rigorous as it should be by the end of the semester. Nevertheless, for two students to spontaneously generate an in-depth, on-task conversation in their second week of college is no small achievement. Further, even if students do goof-off during note passing time, they are only getting less out of the class if they are goofing-off more than they would have had note passing not been a part of the course.

Conclusion

By making familiar but not obvious background information explicit and making instruction more meta-cognitively aware we can improve student learning. Specifically, metacognitively informed instruction that explicitly discusses relevant background information assists philosophical novices to more fully develop the skills necessary to read and do philosophy well. Examples of how to provide this type of instruction include "How To" handouts, dual format exams, credited self-reflections, and note passing.

Postscript: A Comment on Student Reactions

Student reactions to the "How to Read Philosophy" handout further confirm the necessity of explicit instruction regarding metacognition, background knowledge, and "How To" information. Students were asked to write individual reflections about what they learned by reading the handout. Students compared their responses in groups and wrote down four things that at least one member of their group learned. In this unscientific survey, students most frequently reported that they learned that flagging, or abbreviated note taking, is superior to high-lighting. During discussion, one student said almost incredulously to the only group of students that did not include the importance of flagging on their list: "Flagging the article actually helps." The second most frequent response was that re-reading is important to develop understanding. As one student wrote, "There is a lot more reading involved than first thought." Another student summarized the third most frequent response by saying, "*Every* word is important."

What is most striking about these responses is that students *learned* that re-reading complex material is important for developing an accurate understanding of the text. Some students did not enter class knowing that re-reading is important for understanding. If students do not know that re-reading is important for understanding when they arrive in core curriculum and early major philosophy classes, then they are likely to think that the understanding garnered from a first read *is* a rich understanding. Without explicit reading instruction many students will not know that they did not fully understand a text that they just read. Consequently, many students will take no steps to increase their understanding. This fact is further evidence of the importance of explicit background information, metacognition, and "How To" instruction. Students need to be taught what constitutes rich understanding and how to assess how well they are doing in their attempts to develop it.

Appendix

HOW TO READ PHILOSOPHY
(*Warning: Do not use a highlighter when reading this. As you read on, you'll learn why.*)

INTRODUCTION
Even if you are very smart and very literate, as I assume you are, confusion and frustration may occur if you do not read philosophy in the way philosophers expect you to. There is more than one *way* to read. In this handout, I describe the basics of How to Read *Philosophy*.

WHAT TO EXPECT
Reading philosophy is an activity and, like any activity (e.g., playing volleyball), it takes practice to become good at it. As with any attempt to learn a new skill, you will make some mistakes along the way, get frustrated with the fact that you are progressing more slowly than you would like, and need to ask for help. You may become angry with authors because they say things that go against what you were brought up to believe and you may become frustrated because those same authors argue so well that you cannot prove them wrong. It is likely that you will find unfamiliar vocabulary, abstract ideas, complexly organized writing, and unsettling views. I mention this because it is normal to have certain reactions, such as confusion, outrage, and frustration, when first encountering philosophy. *Don't confuse these reactions with failure.* Many students who have come before you have had the same initial reactions and succeeded, even your professor.

THE ULTIMATE GOAL
Your aim is to develop, or become more confident in, your personal belief system, by building on what you already know about yourself and the world. By evaluating arguments regarding controversial issues, you should learn to take a well-justified stand that you are able to defend. When you read philosophy you should look for arguments, reasons, and conclusions, not facts, plot or character development, to help you reach your goal of evaluating the plausibility of various positions a person might take on some issue.

BASIC GOOD READING BEHAVIORS[16]

- Take care of yourself (take breaks, sit where you won't be distracted, give yourself enough time to read well, sit in an uncomfortable chair to avoid dozing off, etc.).
- Interact with the material (talk to your friends and classmates about what you have read, use a dictionary and philosophical encyclopedia while reading, remember you are reading one person's contribution to an ongoing debate, disagree with the author).
- Keep reasonable expectations (you may not understand everything without some effort, you may need to ask for help or clarification).
- Be able to state the author's conclusion and the gist of the argument for that conclusion BEFORE you come to class.
- Evaluate the gist of the author's argument BEFORE class.
- FLAG and TAKE NOTES. (Flagging is explained below)

IMPORTANT BACKGROUND INFORMATION
Reading for Information versus Reading for Enlightenment
You are familiar with reading for information: You pass your eyes over some words until some information about the world sticks in your head. Reading for enlightenment may be less familiar. When you read for enlightenment you use a text as an opportunity to *reflect* upon yourself and your beliefs. Part of the reason why reading for enlightenment is not easy is because self-evaluation often results in personal growth and sometimes when we grow, we experience growing pains.

Problem-Based, Historical, or Figure-Based Philosophy Classes
This is a problem-based class. In problem-based classes, students spend most of their time identifying, reflecting upon, and defending their beliefs. This is *not* a historical or figure-based course. In historical classes, students spend most of their time learning certain themes in the history of philosophy. In figure-based classes, students spend most of their time mastering what certain philosophers think.

In problem-based courses like this one, students read relatively short primary and secondary sources. A secondary source is a text that describes what other people have argued. The textbook for this class is a secondary source. A primary source is a text where a person actually argues that a certain position is correct. The course packet contains primary sources.

So, *you are in a problem-based course where you are supposed to read primary sources for enlightenment.* But how, exactly, does one read for enlightenment? Well, strong philosophy readers, people who read with care, do three things. As people increase their ability to read philosophy well they gradually become unaware that they do facet one and they combine facets two and three. However, it is a good idea for non-experts to do one thing at a time.

A THREE-PART READING PROCESS
Facet One—Stage Setting
(1) Pre-Read:
    For a very short time, examine the general features of the article. Look at the title, section headings, footnotes, bibliography, reading questions, and biography of the author. The goal of the pre-read is to get a basic idea of what the article is about. If you know what an article is about, it is easier to make sense of the individual sentences in it. Also, skim the first and last paragraph to see if you can easily identify a focal or thesis statement. A focal statement describes the topic of the text. Focal statements often begin with phrases such as "I will discuss X, Y, and Z." A thesis statement is a more specific description of the author's goal. Thesis statements often begin with phrases such as "I will show that X is true and Y and Z are false."

While doing the pre-read, ask yourself "How am I doing?" by answering the following questions:
Is this a primary or secondary text? Should I expect an argument or a description of an argument?
Am I reading for information or enlightenment?
What is the focal statement of the article? Is there a thesis statement? What is it?
What should I expect to find in the text in light of the title?
Are there section headings? If yes, what can I learn about the article from them?
Is there a bibliography? If yes, what can I learn about the article from it?
Are there footnotes? Are they essentially documentation or do they say something? (This lets you know
    whether you need to read them when you see a number in the text.)
Are there reading questions attached? If yes, in light of these questions, what can I expect to find in the
    text?

(2) Fast-Read:
    Read the entire article fairly quickly. The goal of the fast-read is to develop a basic understanding
    of the text. When doing the fast read, remember to do the following:
    •   Identify the thesis statement.
         Warning: You may not be able to do this until you reach the end of the article. Mark anything
         that seems like it might be a thesis statement or conclusion when you first notice it, then pick
         the one that seems most central when you are done. In some cases, the author may not even
         actually write a thesis statement down, so you may need to write one for the author.
    •   Look up definitions of words you don't know and write them in the margins. Warning: Don't
         get bogged down while doing this. If it is too difficult to figure out which meaning of a term
         an author seems to have in mind, or if you have to read an entire encyclopedia entry to figure
         out the meaning, just move on. (If you read near a computer see On-line Dictionary: http://
         dictionary.reference.com/ and Internet Encyclopedia of Philosophy: http://www.utm.edu/
         research/iep/.)
    •   FLAG the structure of the article in as much detail as possible without getting bogged down.
         When you flag a text you put marks in it that will allow you to reconstruct the meaning of the
         text without having to re-read the entire text again. *See below for specific suggestions on how
         to flag an article.*
    •   Don't let anything stop your progress. This is a fast read. You may skim long examples.

While doing the fast-read, ask yourself "How am I doing?" by answering the following questions:
Have I identified the thesis statement and written it down?
Do I know what the conclusion of the author's argument is and have I marked places in the text where
    important steps toward that conclusion occur?

Facet Two—Understanding
Develop a sophisticated understanding of the text. You should be able to explain to a friend how the au-
thor defends her/his conclusion. Once you are able to coherently explain the article in your own words,
you have truly internalized it—good job. When reading for understanding, remember to do the following:
•   Re-read the entire article VERY CAREFULLY.
•   Correct and add to your previous flagging.
•   Take lots of notes. In these notes, rephrase what the author says in your own words.
     Remember: You should practice the principle of charity when taking notes. Describe the author's
     view in the most favorable way possible. If you have trouble taking notes, stop at the end of every
     section or paragraph (sometimes even every sentence) and mentally rephrase the meaning of the
     text in your own words.

- Draw diagrams or flow charts of the major moves in the article if doing so helps you.
- Bring together all your work so far into a summary that is detailed enough that you won't have to re-read the article again to remind yourself of the author's argument.

While reading for understanding, ask yourself "How am I doing?" by answering the following questions:
Do I know *exactly* what the author is saying? Have I re-re-read passages that were confusing at first?
Can I connect the dots? Can I explain in my own words why the author concludes what she or he concludes? (In the fast-read you find the conclusion and do your best to figure out the steps to it. In the read-for-understanding, you come to fully understand each step in detail.)

Facet Three—Evaluating

Now that you have made yourself a concise and easy to articulate summary of the author's argument, it is time to evaluate it. When evaluating, your main tool is the summary you made, but you will need to re-re-read certain passages. At this stage, you are entering the debate, rather than simply learning about it. When evaluating a text, remember to do the following:
- Fix any mistaken flagging as you re-re-read important passages.
- Write down anything new that you discover as you go through the text again.

While evaluating a text, ask yourself "How am I doing?" by answering the following questions:
Have I looked to see if every conclusion in the text is well defended?
Have I thought about how an undefended conclusion could be defended? (Have I been charitable?)
Do I think the arguments for the conclusions are persuasive? Why or why not?
Can I think of any counter-examples to any assertion made by the author?
Can I put my finger on exactly what bothers me about what the author says? Can I explain where and why I think the author made a mistake?
Have I thought about how the author might respond to my criticism?
Have I identified some of my own beliefs that can't be true if the author is right?
Is there is a conflict between what I believe and what the author says? If so, to avoid being a hypocrite I must ultimately change my mind or show that the author's reasoning fails in some way. *Simply identifying a disagreement does not constitute an evaluation.*
Have I figured out, exactly, what the author got wrong so that I may continue to believe as I always have with confidence?
Have I figured out, exactly, which of my beliefs I must change in light of what I have learned from the author?
Have I looked for some point that the author did not consider that might influence what I think is true?

Two Important Details

(1) *Flagging*
When you flag a text you put short notes, preferably in pencil, in the margins of the text (unless you are using a library book) that will remind you of many details in the text so that you will not have to re-read an entire text to reconstruct its meaning in your head. Flagging marks allow you to pick out various important features of the text for further study.

Flagging is better than highlighting because flagging is more detailed than highlighting. If all you're interested in doing is distinguishing something that seems important from other stuff that doesn't seem important then highlighting is fine. But you want to do more than just distinguish important from unimportant. There is more than one kind of important thing in a philosophy text, and you want to mark your text in such a way that you can tell the difference. Another good thing **about flagging is that you can "unflag" and you can't "unhighlight."** The flexibility to change your notes is important because sometimes as you read further into a text, or read it a second time, you realize that something that seemed important really isn't important.

There are many ways to flag a text. You should develop your own method and notations. You should use whatever marks help you attain the goal of noting the different types of important parts of a text. A part of the text is important when it must be present for the author's conclusion to make sense. On some occasions important things are a sentence or a clause in length, but other times important things are a paragraph or a page long. The following are suggestions of abbreviations that have been particularly useful to me. But, again, feel free to use terms not on the list that you find helpful and ignore any, or all, of these if you find them unhelpful. In addition to these terms, I circle "list" words (e.g., First, second, [i], [ii]) and I underline definitions.

Tracking the Flow[17]

Focal	General topic this article will discuss
Thesis	Specific claim the author hopes to prove
Dfn	Definition
Dst	Distinction
e.g.	Example
Asn	Assertion of fact or an important claim the author will argue is true
Discuss	A discussion or explanation of a view, assertion, or problem
Rsn	Reason supporting an assertion or conclusion, a justification of a claim
Arg	An argument (combination of an assertion and a reason)
Obj	Objection to an argument or reason
Reply	Reply to an objection
Rejoin	Rejoinder or response to a reply
Con	Conclusion of an argument
Sum	Summary
Spost	A signpost or statement that explicitly marks an important transition in the text

Self-Monitoring

???	What? I don't get it. I must reread this passage carefully
=X?	This means what exactly?

Reader Evaluation

Why?	Why should someone agree with this?
[Underline]	This is important

Flagging should naturally evolve into note taking. If you are inclined to write "???" in a margin, it is a good idea to write out more fully what confused you. If you can articulate your confusion you are a good way down the road to figuring out what's going on. During your re-read for understanding make sure to spend as much time as necessary to fully grasp what is going on in the "???" section.

(2) Key Words

Some students find the following list of words or phrases that signal a significant moment in a text helpful. However, there are many texts where authors will not use any of these terms or phrases. These are words or phrases to be aware of so that if they come up you are ready, but you should not read a text as if you are on a treasure hunt for these words or phrases.

Focal statements are often signaled by phrases such as I will discuss Consideration will be given to My main concern is	*Thesis statements are often signaled by phrases such as* In this paper I argue that I hope to conclude that I will show that
Premises, Reasons, or Assertions are often signaled by words or phrases such as Because, Since, For, Whereas Secondly, It follows that Given that As shown or indicated by The reason is that	*Objections or criticisms are often signaled by words or phrases such as* Moreover, However It could be objected that Opponents of my view might claim Critics might say, On the other hand There is reason to doubt
Replies or Rejoinders are often signaled by words or phrases such as This criticism fails because My opponent does not notice that In response we should remember Nevertheless, On the other hand	*Conclusions are often signaled by words or phrases such as* In summary, Thus, Therefore, So, Hence, Accordingly, Consequently As a result We may infer, Which entails that

A FINAL COMPLICATION
Linear versus Dialogical Writing

Students sometimes ask me one or all of the following questions: (1) Why does the author contradict herself? (2) Why does the author repeat himself so much? (3) Why is this reading so wordy? Students ask these questions, I think, because they expect the reading to be linear when, in fact, philosophical writing is usually dialogical. So, let me tell you a little bit about dialogical writing and then I will answer each question individually.

Linear writing moves in a straightforward way from one idea to the next, without examining (m)any supporting or contradictory ideas. Dialogical writing explicitly acknowledges and responds to criticism. It may be helpful to think of philosophical writing as a monologue that contains a dialogue.[18] The author is speaking directly to you, delivering a monologue for your consideration. But in the monologue, the author is telling you about a dialogue or debate that she or he knows about, while giving you reasons for thinking that her or his understanding of that debate is right. As you know, in some debates there are more than two sides and sometimes people on the same side have different reasons for believing what they believe. Authors will take the time to tell you about as many sides, or different camps within one side, as they think you need to know about to understand, and be persuaded by, their view. This confuses people sometimes because it is hard to keep track of whether the author is arguing for their side or talking from another point of view or camp within the same side for the sake of (good) argument.

Points to remember about dialogical philosophical texts

- Authors sometimes support their views with thought-experiments (i.e., examples that ask you to imagine how things would be if something that is not true, were true).

- Authors sometimes argue that other thinkers haven't noticed an important difference between two things. Authors draw distinctions.

- Authors sometimes argue that another philosopher's views or arguments ought to be rejected. There is something really tricky here. Fair-minded writers will practice the principle of charity. According to the *principle of charity*, one should give one's opponents the benefit of the doubt; one should respond to the best thing that someone who disagrees with you could say, even if they didn't notice it. Sometimes attempts to abide by the principle of charity results in authors presenting arguments for the correctness of views they ultimately reject. That is, for the sake of (good) argument some authors will present reasons for thinking that their critics are right. *Try to avoid mistaking charitable elucidation for the author's main argument.*

Now that you are more familiar with dialogical texts I can answer the questions students sometimes ask about them.

Frequently Asked Questions

(1) Why does the author contradict herself?

Sometimes thinkers do unwittingly contradict themselves. Most of the time, however, people perceive a contradiction where there isn't one because they fail to notice a change in "voice." Authors will describe many sides, and camps within a side, but they will voice agreement with only one side or camp. If you lose track of the fact that the author is considering an alternative view, you will mistakenly think that a fair-minded examination of a different point of view is a contradiction. Keeping track of where you are in the argument is crucial to understanding. If you think you see a contradiction, double or triple check your flagging to make sure that you are not simply missing something.

(2) Why does the author repeat himself so much?

Usually philosophers do not repeat themselves all that much. Sometimes, however, they use examples that are so long, or discuss material that is interesting but ultimately tangential for such a long time, that they (correctly) assume that their readers have lost track of the point being made. In such cases, a simple repetition may occur for the benefit of the reader. More often, however, people lose track of where they are in an argument and consequently mistake something new for repetition. Again, keeping track of where you are in an argument is crucial to understanding and flagging really helps readers keep track of where they are.

(3) Why is the writing so wordy?

Some people think philosophers use all sorts of fancy words to intimidate their readers or show off. This reaction is understandable but mistaken in at least three ways. First, it is a mistake to become angry with an author because you have a limited vocabulary. There is an opportunity for learning here. Take it.

Second, there is an international community of philosophers, and like all specialized communities (such as you and your friends), there are certain patterns in the way members of that community talk to one another. Metaphorically, when you enrolled in philosophy class you walked into a room where a bunch of people have been having a conversation for a very long time. You need to adapt to their idiosyncratic ways of talking if you want to participate in their conversation. Of course, philosophers shouldn't be rude and intentionally try to exclude you with their words. But it is important to realize that they didn't know you were coming, so they might not have done everything possible to make your inclusion as easy as *you* would like. Whatever the author's faults, do your part—be open to what is being said, try your hardest to understand, and don't assume the worst about the author, even if the author doesn't always behave as you would like.

Third, and most importantly, not every complex idea can be stated in simple terms. Sometimes simplification is over-simplification, where the important nuances of what a person really thinks are lost. It is true that some philosophical writing is more complicated than it needs to be, but not all of it is. Some philosophical writing needs to be complicated to express a complicated idea. Part of the beauty of philosophy is its complexity. Do your best to appreciate the beauty of complexity.

SUMMARY: WHAT SUCCESSFUL PHILOSOPHY READERS DO
- Abide by the "Basic Good Reading Behaviors"
- Before class, complete all three facets of reading well
- Flag and Take Notes to keep track of where you are in the dialogue

References

I gratefully acknowledge support from the Lumina Foundation for Education, which allowed me to undertake this study. I have benefited from conversations with fellow grantees Bill McGrath, Dale Hahn, Reza Ahmadi, and Wendy Schmidt. I thank the students in my "Introduction to Philosophy" classes and the students of the Ball State University Philosophy Club for the invaluable feedback that only they could provide, especially Ryan Gessler. Improvements also came from responding to the kind critiques of Stephen Schulman, Paul Ranieri, and the editors of *Teaching Philosophy*.

1. Among the useful resources, however, are John Arthur, *Studying Philosophy: A Guide for the Perplexed* (2nd ed.) (Upper Saddle River, N.J.: Pearson/Prentice Hall, 2004); Gary Kessler, *Reading, Thinking, And Writing Philosophically* (2nd ed.) (Belmont, Calif.: Wadsworth, 2001); and Mark B. Woodhouse, *Reading and Writing About Philosophy* (Belmont, Calif.: Wadsworth, 1989).
2. I borrow here from Melinda Messineo, Robin Rufatto, Tom Talbert, and Dave Concepción, "Guide For New Faculty," Ball State University, Office of Teaching and Learning Advancement, Spring 2003.
3. John T. Bruer, *Schools for Thought: A Science for Learning in the Classroom* (Cambridge, Mass.: MIT Press, 1994), especially chapter 3, "Intelligent Novices: Knowing How To Learn," and chapter 6, "Reading: Seeing the Big Picture."
4. E. D. Hirsch, *Cultural Literacy* (Boston: Houghton Mifflin Co., 1987), 60.
5. Ibid., 13.
6. Ibid.
7. Bruer, *Schools for Thought*, 180–81.
8. Bruer makes a similar point. Bruer, *Schools for Thought*, 190, 194.
9. Similar methods are recommended by Kathryn Russell and Lyn Robertson. "Teaching Analytic Reading and Writing: A Feminist Approach," *Teaching Philosophy* 9:3 (September 1986): 207–17; Kessler, "Reading, Thinking, and Writing Philosophically." *op. cit.*; James Pryor, "How To Read A Philosophy Paper," www.princeton.edu/~jimpryor/general/reading.html; Jeff McLaughlin, "How to Read a Philosophy Paper (including this one)," www.cariboo.bc.ca/ae/php/phil/mclaughl/courses/howread.htm; and Letitia Meynell, "Reading Philosophy Actively," http://myweb.dal.ca/lt531391/readphil.pdf.
10. If time for grading is scarce, an instructor need only read a small number of the comparative self-assessments in detail and "grade" on a pass or fail basis. There are two reasons why it is important to initially give students credit for this work. First, the abruptness of the change in teaching and learning styles from high school to higher education is reduced. This reduction in abruptness eases student anxiety and builds student confidence. Second, giving credit for this work takes advan-

tage of the assumption made by some students that uncredited work is unimportant. To transfer responsibility for success firmly to the student, credit should not be given for such assignments as the semester progresses. For more on strategies for easing the transition from high school to higher education, see Ruth Beard and James Hartley, *Teaching and Learning in Higher Education* (4th ed.) (London: Harper and Row, 1984), Chapter 5: "Adjusting To Higher Education."

11. Bruer, *Schools for Thought*, 67.
12. Ibid., 77–78.
13. Ibid., 59ff.
14. Ibid., 72.
15. John D. Bransford, Ann L. Brown, and Rodney R. Cocking, eds., *How People Learn: Brain, Mind, Experience, and School* (expanded ed.) (Washington: National Academy Press, 2000); A. L. Brown "Domain-Specific Principles Affect Learning and Transfer in Children," *Cognitive Science* 14 (1990): 107–33; J. H. Flavell and H. M. Wellman, "Metamemory," in *Perspectives on the Development of Memory and Cognition*, ed. R. V. Kail, Jr., and J. W. Hagen (Hillside, N.J.: Erlbaum, 1977); J. H. Flavell, "Metacognition and Cognitive Monitoring: A New Area of Cognitive-Developmental Inquiry," *American Psychologist* 34:1 (1979): 906–11; A. L. Brown and J. S. DeLoache, "Skills, Plans, And Self-Regulation," in *Children's Thinking: What Develops?* ed. R. S. Siegler (Hillside, N.J.: Erlbaum, 1978); J. D. Bransford, R. Sherwood, N. Vye, and J. Rieser, "Teaching Thinking and Problem Solving," *American Psychologist* 41:10 (1986), 1078–89; J. D. Bransford, B. S. Stein, N. J. Vye, J. J. Franks, P. M. Auble, K. J. Mezynski, and G. A. Perfetto, "Differences in Approaches to Learning: An Overview," *Journal of Experimental Psychology: General* 111 (1982): 390–98; A. L. Brown, J. D. Bransford, R. A. Ferrara, and J. C. Camione, "Learning, Remembering, and Understanding," in *Handbook of Child Psychology, Vol. 2: Cognitive Development*, ed. P. H. Mussen (New York: Wiley, 1983); E. M. Markman, "Comprehension Monitoring: Developmental and Educational Issues," in *Thinking and Learning Skills, Vol. 2: Research and Open Questions*, ed. S. F. Chipman, J. W. Segal, and R. Glaser (Hillside, N.J.: Erlbaum, 1985).
16. I have borrowed from Jennifer McCrickerd in developing this material. Jennifer McCrickerd, "Reading Philosophy," www.drake.edu/artsei/philrel/fachomepages/jenhomepage/ReadingPhilosophy .html (site no longer active).
17. I have borrowed some flagging notation from Meynell, "Reading Philosophy Actively," *op. cit.*
18. I am grateful to Paul Ranieri for insisting that I put this idea this way.
    David W. Concepción, Philosophy and Religious Studies, Ball State University, Muncie, IN 47306; dwconcepcion@bsu.edu

DISCUSSION *questions and activities*

1. Make two lists that show what Concepción wants faculty to do and what he wants students to do in order to improve critical reading. Discuss with your classmates whether his ideas seem practical and effective.

2. Compare Concepción's style and tone in the Appendix which addresses students and the main article which addresses college faculty. Write an analysis of how he adapts his writing for these two audiences.

3. Use Concepción's Appendix as a guide to reading one of the texts in Part Two of this text. Write a short reflection on how his techniques affected the quality of your reading.

God vs. Science

Dan Cray

As the United States' first weekly magazine, TIME has covered news connected to important American political figures and celebrities since 1923. In 2006, TIME convened this debate between two of the great scientific minds of our time, Francis Collins and Richard Dawkins. As director of the National Center for Human Genome Research from 1993–2008, Collins presented a working draft of the human genome in 2000. The author of The Language of God: A Scientist Presents Evidence for Belief, *he now directs the National Institutes of Health. Prominent British biologist and outspoken atheist Richard Dawkins teaches at the University of Oxford. Dawkins has written several books, among them* The God Delusion, *which has prompted full-length book responses.*

We revere faith and scientific progress, hunger for miracles and for MRIs. But are the worldviews compatible? TIME convenes a debate.

There are two great debates under the broad heading of Science vs. God. The more familiar over the past few years is the narrower of the two: Can Darwinian evolution withstand the criticisms of Christians who believe that it contradicts the creation account in the Book of Genesis? In recent years, creationism took on new currency as the spiritual progenitor of "intelligent design" (I.D.), a scientifically worded attempt to show that blanks in the evolutionary narrative are more meaningful than its very convincing totality. I.D. lost some of its journalistic heat last December when a federal judge dismissed it as pseudoscience unsuitable for teaching in Pennsylvania schools.

But in fact creationism and I.D. are intimately related to a larger unresolved question, in which the aggressor's role is reversed: Can religion stand up to the progress of science? This debate long predates Darwin, but the antireligion position is being promoted with increasing insistence by scientists angered by intelligent design and excited, perhaps intoxicated, by their disciplines' increasing ability to map, quantify and change the nature of human experience. Brain imaging illustrates—in color!—the physical seat of the will and the passions, challenging the religious concept of a soul independent of glands and gristle. Brain chemists track imbalances that could account for the ecstatic states of visionary saints or, some suggest, of Jesus. Like Freudianism before it, the field of evolutionary psychology generates theories of altruism and even of religion that do not include God. Something called the multiverse hypothesis in cosmology speculates that ours may be but one in a cascade of universes, suddenly bettering the odds that life could have cropped up here accidentally, without divine intervention. (If the probabilities were 1 in a billion, and you've got 300 billion universes, why not?)

Roman Catholicism's Christoph Cardinal Schönborn has dubbed the most fervent of faith-challenging scientists followers of "scientism" or "evolutionism," since they hope science, beyond being a measure, can replace religion as a worldview and a touchstone. It is not an epithet that fits everyone wielding a test tube. But a growing proportion of the profession is experiencing what one major researcher calls "unprecedented outrage" at perceived insults to research and rationality, ranging from the alleged influence of the Christian right on Bush Administration science policy to the fanatic faith of the 9/11 terrorists to intelligent design's ongoing claims. Some are radicalized enough to publicly pick an ancient scab: the idea that science and religion, far from being complementary responses to the unknown, are at utter odds—or, as Yale psychologist Paul Bloom has written bluntly, "Religion and science will always clash." The market seems flooded with books by scientists describing a caged death match between science and God—with science winning, or at least chipping away at faith's underlying verities.

Finding a spokesman for this side of the question was not hard, since Richard Dawkins, perhaps its foremost polemicist, has just come out with *The God Delusion* (Houghton Mifflin), the rare volume whose position is so clear it forgoes a subtitle. The five-week *New York Times* best seller (now at No. 8) attacks faith philosophically and historically as well as scientifically, but leans heavily on Darwinian theory, which was Dawkins' expertise as a young scientist and more recently as an explicator of evolutionary psychology so lucid that he occupies the Charles Simonyi professorship for the public understanding of science at Oxford University.

Dawkins is riding the crest of an atheist literary wave. In 2004, *The End of Faith*, a multipronged indictment by neuroscience grad student Sam Harris, was published (over 400,000 copies in print). Harris has written a 96-page follow-up, *Letter to a Christian Nation*, which is now No. 14 on the *Times* list. Last February, Tufts University philosopher Daniel Dennett produced *Breaking the Spell: Religion as a Natural Phenomenon*, which has sold fewer copies but has helped usher the discussion into the public arena.

If Dennett and Harris are almost-scientists (Dennett runs a multidisciplinary scientific-philosophic program), the authors of half a dozen aggressively secular volumes are card carriers: In *Moral Minds*, Harvard biologist Marc Hauser explores the—nondivine—origins of our sense of right and wrong (September); in *Six Impossible Things Before Breakfast* (due in January) by self-described "atheist-reductionist-materialist" biologist Lewis Wolpert, religion is one of those impossible things; Victor Stenger, a physicist-astronomer, has a book coming out titled *God: The Failed Hypothesis*. Meanwhile, Ann Druyan, widow of archskeptical astrophysicist Carl Sagan, has edited Sagan's unpublished lectures on God and his absence into a book, *The Varieties of Scientific Experience*, out this month.

Dawkins and his army have a swarm of articulate theological opponents, of course. But the most ardent of these don't really care very much about science, and an argument in which one party stands immovable on Scripture and the other immobile on the periodic table doesn't get anyone very far. Most Americans occupy the middle ground: we want it all. We want to cheer on science's strides and still humble ourselves on the Sabbath. We want access to both MRIs and miracles. We want debates about issues like stem cells without conceding that the positions are so intrinsically inimical as to make discussion fruitless. And to balance formidable standard bearers like Dawkins, we seek those who possess religious conviction but also scientific achievements to credibly argue the widespread hope that science and God are in harmony—that, indeed, science is of God.

Informed conciliators have recently become more vocal. Stanford University biologist Joan Roughgarden has just come out with *Evolution and Christian Faith*, which provides what she calls a "strong Christian defense" of evolutionary biology, illustrating the discipline's major concepts with biblical passages. Entomologist Edward O. Wilson, a famous skeptic of standard faith, has written *The Creation: An Appeal to Save Life on Earth*, urging believers and non-believers to unite over conservation. But foremost of those arguing for common ground is Francis Collins.

Collins' devotion to genetics is, if possible, greater than Dawkins'. Director of the National Human Genome Research Institute since 1993, he headed a multinational 2,400-scientist team that co-mapped the 3 billion biochemical letters of our genetic blueprint, a milestone that then-President Bill Clinton honored in a 2000 White House ceremony, comparing the genome chart to Meriwether Lewis' map of his fateful continental exploration. Collins continues to lead his institute in studying the genome and mining it for medical breakthroughs.

He is also a forthright Christian who converted from atheism at age 27 and now finds time to advise young evangelical scientists on how to declare their faith in science's largely agnostic upper reaches. His summer best seller, *The Language of God: A Scientist Presents Evidence for Belief* (Free Press), laid out some of the arguments he brought to bear in the 90-minute debate TIME arranged between Dawkins and Collins in our offices at the Time & Life Building in New York City on Sept. 30. Some excerpts from their spirited exchange:

TIME: Professor Dawkins, if one truly understands science, is God then a delusion, as your book title suggests?

***DAWKINS*:**   The question of whether there exists a supernatural creator, a God, is one of the most important that we have to answer. I think that it is a scientific question. My answer is no.

TIME: Dr. Collins, you believe that science is compatible with Christian faith.

***COLLINS*:**   Yes. God's existence is either true or not. But calling it a scientific question implies that the tools of science can provide the answer. From my perspective, God cannot be completely contained within nature, and therefore God's existence is outside of science's ability to really weigh in.

TIME: Stephen Jay Gould, a Harvard paleontologist, famously argued that religion and science can coexist, because they occupy separate, airtight boxes. You both seem to disagree.

***COLLINS*:**   Gould sets up an artificial wall between the two worldviews that doesn't exist in my life. Because I do believe in God's creative power in having brought it all into being in the first place, I find that studying the natural world is an opportunity to observe the majesty, the elegance, the intricacy of God's creation.

***DAWKINS*:**   I think that Gould's separate compartments was a purely political ploy to win middle-of-the-road religious people to the science camp. But it's a very empty idea. There are plenty of places where religion does not keep off the scientific turf. Any belief in miracles is flat contradictory not just to the facts of science but to the spirit of science.

TIME: Professor Dawkins, you think Darwin's theory of evolution does more than simply contradict the Genesis story.

***DAWKINS*:**   Yes. For centuries the most powerful argument for God's existence from the physical world was the so-called argument from design: Living things are so beautiful and elegant and so apparently purposeful, they could only have been made by an intelligent designer. But Darwin provided a simpler explanation. His way is a gradual, incremental improvement starting from very simple beginnings and working up step by tiny incremental step to more complexity, more elegance, more adaptive perfection. Each step is not too improbable for us to countenance, but when you add them up cumulatively over millions of years, you get these monsters of improbability, like the human brain and the rain forest. It should warn us against ever again assuming that because something is complicated, God must have done it.

***COLLINS*:**   I don't see that Professor Dawkins' basic account of evolution is incompatible with God's having designed it.

TIME: When would this have occurred?

***COLLINS*:**   By being outside of nature, God is also outside of space and time. Hence, at the moment of the creation of the universe, God could also have activated evolution, with full knowledge of how it would turn out, perhaps even including our having this conversation. The idea that he could both foresee the future and also give us spirit and free will to carry out our own desires becomes entirely acceptable.

DAWKINS: I think that's a tremendous cop-out. If God wanted to create life and create humans, it would be slightly odd that he should choose the extraordinarily roundabout way of waiting for 10 billion years before life got started and then waiting for another 4 billion years until you got human beings capable of worshipping and sinning and all the other things religious people are interested in.

COLLINS: Who are we to say that that was an odd way to do it? I don't think that it is God's purpose to make his intention absolutely obvious to us. If it suits him to be a deity that we must seek without being forced to, would it not have been sensible for him to use the mechanism of evolution without posting obvious road signs to reveal his role in creation?

TIME: Both your books suggest that if the universal constants, the six or more characteristics of our universe, had varied at all, it would have made life impossible. Dr. Collins, can you provide an example?

COLLINS: The gravitational constant, if it were off by one part in a hundred million million, then the expansion of the universe after the Big Bang would not have occurred in the fashion that was necessary for life to occur. When you look at that evidence, it is very difficult to adopt the view that this was just chance. But if you are willing to consider the possibility of a designer, this becomes a rather plausible explanation for what is otherwise an exceedingly improbable event—namely, our existence.

DAWKINS: People who believe in God conclude there must have been a divine knob twiddler who twiddled the knobs of these half-dozen constants to get them exactly right. The problem is that this says, because something is vastly improbable, we need a God to explain it. But that God himself would be even more improbable. Physicists have come up with other explanations. One is to say that these six constants are not free to vary. Some unified theory will eventually show that they are as locked in as the circumference and the diameter of a circle. That reduces the odds of them all independently just happening to fit the bill. The other way is the multiverse way. That says that maybe the universe we are in is one of a very large number of universes. The vast majority will not contain life because they have the wrong gravitational constant or the wrong this constant or that constant. But as the number of universes climbs, the odds mount that a tiny minority of universes will have the right fine-tuning.

COLLINS: This is an interesting choice. Barring a theoretical resolution, which I think is unlikely, you either have to say there are zillions of parallel universes out there that we can't observe at present or you have to say there was a plan. I actually find the argument of the existence of a God who did the planning more compelling than the bubbling of all these multiverses. So Occam's razor—Occam says you should choose the explanation that is most simple and straightforward—leads me more to believe in God than in the multiverse, which seems quite a stretch of the imagination.

DAWKINS: I accept that there may be things far grander and more incomprehensible than we can possibly imagine. What I can't understand is why you invoke improbability and yet you will not admit that you're shooting yourself in the foot by postulating something just as improbable, magicking into existence the word God.

COLLINS: My God is not improbable to me. He has no need of a creation story for himself or to be fine-tuned by something else. God is the answer to all of those "How must it have come to be" questions.

DAWKINS: I think that's the mother and father of all cop-outs. It's an honest scientific quest to discover where this apparent improbability comes from. Now Dr. Collins says, "Well, God did it. And God needs no explanation because God is out-

	side all this." Well, what an incredible evasion of the responsibility to explain. Scientists don't do that. Scientists say, "We're working on it. We're struggling to understand."
COLLINS:	Certainly science should continue to see whether we can find evidence for multiverses that might explain why our own universe seems to be so finely tuned. But I do object to the assumption that anything that might be outside of nature is ruled out of the conversation. That's an impoverished view of the kinds of questions we humans can ask, such as "Why am I here?", "What happens after we die?", "Is there a God?" If you refuse to acknowledge their appropriateness, you end up with a zero probability of God after examining the natural world because it doesn't convince you on a proof basis. But if your mind is open about whether God might exist, you can point to aspects of the universe that are consistent with that conclusion.
DAWKINS:	To me, the right approach is to say we are profoundly ignorant of these matters. We need to work on them. But to suddenly say the answer is God—it's that that seems to me to close off the discussion.
TIME:	Could the answer be God?
DAWKINS:	There could be something incredibly grand and incomprehensible and beyond our present understanding.
COLLINS:	That's God.
DAWKINS:	Yes. But it could be any of a billion Gods. It could be God of the Martians or of the inhabitants of Alpha Centauri. The chance of its being a particular God, Yahweh, the God of Jesus, is vanishingly small—at the least, the onus is on you to demonstrate why you think that's the case.
TIME:	The Book of Genesis has led many conservative Protestants to oppose evolution and some to insist that the earth is only 6,000 years old.
COLLINS:	There are sincere believers who interpret Genesis 1 and 2 in a very literal way that is inconsistent, frankly, with our knowledge of the universe's age or of how living organisms are related to each other. St. Augustine wrote that basically it is not possible to understand what was being described in Genesis. It was not intended as a science textbook. It was intended as a description of who God was, who we are and what our relationship is supposed to be with God. Augustine explicitly warns against a very narrow perspective that will put our faith at risk of looking ridiculous. If you step back from that one narrow interpretation, what the Bible describes is very consistent with the Big Bang.
DAWKINS:	Physicists are working on the Big Bang, and one day they may or may not solve it. However, what Dr. Collins has just been—may I call you Francis?
COLLINS:	Oh, please, Richard, do so.
DAWKINS:	What Francis was just saying about Genesis was, of course, a little private quarrel between him and his Fundamentalist colleagues...
COLLINS:	It's not so private. It's rather public. [Laughs.]
DAWKINS:	...It would be unseemly for me to enter in except to suggest that he'd save himself an awful lot of trouble if he just simply ceased to give them the time of day. Why bother with these clowns?
COLLINS:	Richard, I think we don't do a service to dialogue between science and faith to characterize sincere people by calling them names. That inspires an even more dug-in position. Atheists sometimes come across as a bit arrogant in this regard, and characterizing faith as something only an idiot would attach themselves to is not likely to help your case.
TIME:	Dr. Collins, the Resurrection is an essential argument of Christian faith, but doesn't it, along with the virgin birth and lesser miracles, fatally undermine the scientific method, which depends on the constancy of natural laws?

COLLINS:	If you're willing to answer yes to a God outside of nature, then there's nothing inconsistent with God on rare occasions choosing to invade the natural world in a way that appears miraculous. If God made the natural laws, why could he not violate them when it was a particularly significant moment for him to do so? And if you accept the idea that Christ was also divine, which I do, then his Resurrection is not in itself a great logical leap.
TIME:	Doesn't the very notion of miracles throw off science?
COLLINS:	Not at all. If you are in the camp I am, one place where science and faith could touch each other is in the investigation of supposedly miraculous events.
DAWKINS:	If ever there was a slamming of the door in the face of constructive investigation, it is the word miracle. To a medieval peasant, a radio would have seemed like a miracle. All kinds of things may happen which we by the lights of today's science would classify as a miracle just as medieval science might a Boeing 747. Francis keeps saying things like "From the perspective of a believer." Once you buy into the position of faith, then suddenly you find yourself losing all of your natural skepticism and your scientific—really scientific—credibility. I'm sorry to be so blunt.
COLLINS:	Richard, I actually agree with the first part of what you said. But I would challenge the statement that my scientific instincts are any less rigorous than yours. The difference is that my presumption of the possibility of God and therefore the supernatural is not zero, and yours is.
TIME:	Dr. Collins, you have described humanity's moral sense not only as a gift from God but as a signpost that he exists.
COLLINS:	There is a whole field of inquiry that has come up in the last 30 or 40 years—some call it sociobiology or evolutionary psychology—relating to where we get our moral sense and why we value the idea of altruism, and locating both answers in behavioral adaptations for the preservation of our genes. But if you believe, and Richard has been articulate in this, that natural selection operates on the individual, not on a group, then why would the individual risk his own DNA doing something selfless to help somebody in a way that might diminish his chance of reproducing? Granted, we may try to help our own family members because they share our DNA. Or help someone else in expectation that they will help us later. But when you look at what we admire as the most generous manifestations of altruism, they are not based on kin selection or reciprocity. An extreme example might be Oskar Schindler risking his life to save more than a thousand Jews from the gas chambers. That's the opposite of saving his genes. We see less dramatic versions every day. Many of us think these qualities may come from God—especially since justice and morality are two of the attributes we most readily identify with God.
DAWKINS:	Can I begin with an analogy? Most people understand that sexual lust has to do with propagating genes. Copulation in nature tends to lead to reproduction and so to more genetic copies. But in modern society, most copulations involve contraception, designed precisely to avoid reproduction. Altruism probably has origins like those of lust. In our prehistoric past, we would have lived in extended families, surrounded by kin whose interests we might have wanted to promote because they shared our genes. Now we live in big cities. We are not among kin nor people who will ever reciprocate our good deeds. It doesn't matter. Just as people engaged in sex with contraception are not aware of being motivated by a drive to have babies, it doesn't cross our mind that the reason for do-gooding is based in the fact that our primitive ancestors lived in small groups. But that seems to me to be a highly plausible account for where the desire for morality, the desire for goodness, comes from.

COLLINS: For you to argue that our noblest acts are a misfiring of Darwinian behavior does not do justice to the sense we all have about the absolutes that are involved here of good and evil. Evolution may explain some features of the moral law, but it can't explain why it should have any real significance. If it is solely an evolutionary convenience, there is really no such thing as good or evil. But for me, it is much more than that. The moral law is a reason to think of God as plausible—not just a God who sets the universe in motion but a God who cares about human beings, because we seem uniquely amongst creatures on the planet to have this far-developed sense of morality. What you've said implies that outside of the human mind, tuned by evolutionary processes, good and evil have no meaning. Do you agree with that?

DAWKINS: Even the question you're asking has no meaning to me. Good and evil—I don't believe that there is hanging out there, anywhere, something called good and something called evil. I think that there are good things that happen and bad things that happen.

COLLINS: I think that is a fundamental difference between us. I'm glad we identified it.

TIME: Dr. Collins, I know you favor the opening of new stem-cell lines for experimentation. But doesn't the fact that faith has caused some people to rule this out risk creating a perception that religion is preventing science from saving lives?

COLLINS: Let me first say as a disclaimer that I speak as a private citizen and not as a representative of the Executive Branch of the United States government. The impression that people of faith are uniformly opposed to stem-cell research is not documented by surveys. In fact, many people of strong religious conviction think this can be a morally supportable approach.

TIME: But to the extent that a person argues on the basis of faith or Scripture rather than reason, how can scientists respond?

COLLINS: Faith is not the opposite of reason. Faith rests squarely upon reason, but with the added component of revelation. So such discussions between scientists and believers happen quite readily. But neither scientists nor believers always embody the principles precisely. Scientists can have their judgment clouded by their professional aspirations. And the pure truth of faith, which you can think of as this clear spiritual water, is poured into rusty vessels called human beings, and so sometimes the benevolent principles of faith can get distorted as positions are hardened.

DAWKINS: For me, moral questions such as stem-cell research turn upon whether suffering is caused. In this case, clearly none is. The embryos have no nervous system. But that's not an issue discussed publicly. The issue is, Are they human? If you are an absolutist moralist, you say, "These cells are human, and therefore they deserve some kind of special moral treatment." Absolutist morality doesn't have to come from religion but usually does.

We slaughter nonhuman animals in factory farms, and they do have nervous systems and do suffer. People of faith are not very interested in their suffering.

COLLINS: Do humans have a different moral significance than cows in general?

DAWKINS: Humans have more moral responsibility perhaps, because they are capable of reasoning.

TIME: Do the two of you have any concluding thoughts?

COLLINS: I just would like to say that over more than a quarter-century as a scientist and a believer, I find absolutely nothing in conflict between agreeing with Richard in practically all of his conclusions about the natural world, and also saying that I am still able to accept and embrace the possibility that there are answers that science isn't able to provide about the natural world—the questions about why instead of the questions about how. I'm interested in the whys. I find many of those answers in the spiritual realm. That in no way compromises my ability to think rigorously as a scientist.

DAWKINS: My mind is not closed, as you have occasionally suggested, Francis. My mind is open to the most wonderful range of future possibilities, which I cannot even dream about, nor can you, nor can anybody else. What I am skeptical about is the idea that whatever wonderful revelation does come in the science of the future, it will turn out to be one of the particular historical religions that people happen to have dreamed up. When we started out and we were talking about the origins of the universe and the physical constants, I provided what I thought were cogent arguments against a supernatural intelligent designer. But it does seem to me to be a worthy idea. Refutable—but nevertheless grand and big enough to be worthy of respect. I don't see the Olympian gods or Jesus coming down and dying on the Cross as worthy of that grandeur. They strike me as parochial. If there is a God, it's going to be a whole lot bigger and a whole lot more incomprehensible than anything that any theologian of any religion has ever proposed.

DISCUSSION *questions and activities*

1. Cray states, "We hunger for miracles and MRIs. But are the worldviews compatible?" After reading this debate, what is your position? Use examples from the text to support your claims.

2. This piece features two figures, Dawkins and Collins. Each makes a very unique claim and utilizes the rhetorical appeals in a different manner. Which argument is more effective? Why? Which appeals were used and why did they work?

3. Select and analyze the least successful argument. Where did it go wrong? How could the appeals have been used more effectively to improve this?

Visceral Has Its Value

Maureen Dowd

In 1999, Maureen Dowd won a Pulitzer Prize for her reporting on the Monica Lewinsky scandal. In addition to two books, she has written a regular column for The New York Times *Op-Ed page since 1995. A perfect example of Dowd's style, this op-ed piece juxtaposes two distinct approaches to politics, Barack Obama's and Sarah Palin's, to determine which connects with an audience saturated in American popular culture. Before it's over, Dowd tells us what Obama can learn from Palin's Old West approach to politics. For more information on Dowd, visit her columnist page at* The New York Times *online.*

It's easy to dismiss Sarah Palin.

She's back on the trail, with the tumbling hair and tumbling thoughts. The queen of the scenic strip mall known as Wasilla now reigns over thrilled subjects thronging to a politically strategic swath of American strip malls.

The conservative celebrity clearly hasn't boned up on anything, except her own endless odyssey of self-discovery. And she still has that Yoda-like syntax.

"And I think more of a concern has been not within the campaign the mistakes that were made, not being able to react to the circumstances that those mistakes created in a real positive and professional and helpful way for John McCain," she told Bill O'Reilly.

Yet Democrats would be foolish to write off her visceral power.

As Judith Doctor, a 69-year-old spiritual therapist, told *The Washington Post's* Jason Horowitz at Palin's book signing in Grand Rapids, Mich., "She's alive inside, and that radiates energy, and people who are not psychologically alive inside are fascinated by that."

Barack Obama, who once had his own electric book tour testing the waters for a campaign, could learn a thing or three from Palin. On Friday, for the first time, his Gallup poll approval rating dropped below 50 percent, and he's losing the independents who helped get him elected.

He's a highly intelligent man with a highly functioning West Wing, and he's likable, but he's not connecting on the gut level that could help him succeed.

The animating spirit that electrified his political movement has sputtered out.

People need to understand what the president is thinking as he maneuvers the treacherous terrain of a lopsided economic recovery and two depleting wars.

Like Reagan, Obama is a detached loner with a strong, savvy wife. But unlike Reagan, he doesn't have the acting skills to project concern about what's happening to people.

Obama showed a flair for the theatrical during his campaign, and a talent for narrative in his memoir, but he has yet to translate those skills to governing.

As with the debates, he seems resistant to the idea that perception, as well as substance, matters. Obama so values pragmatism, and is so immersed in the thorny details of legislative compromises, that he may be undervaluing the connective bonds of simpler truths.

Americans who are hurting get angry when they learn that Timothy Geithner, as head of the New York Fed before becoming Treasury secretary, caved to the insistence of Goldman Sachs and other A.I.G. trading partners that they get 100 cents on the dollar when he could have struck a far better bargain for taxpayers.

If we could see a Reduced Shakespeare summary of Obama's presidency so far, it would read:

Dither, dither, speech. Foreign trip, bow, reassure. Seminar, summit. Shoot a jump shot with the guys, throw out the first pitch in mom jeans. Compromise, concede, close the deal. Dither, dither, water down, news conference.

It's time for the president to reinvent this formula and convey a more three-dimensional person.

Palin can be stupefyingly simplistic, but she seems dynamic. Obama is impressively complex but he seems static.

She nurtures her grass roots while he neglects his.

He struggles to transcend identity politics while she wallows in them. As he builds an emotional moat around himself, she exuberantly pushes whatever she has, warts and all—the good looks, the tabloid-perfect family, the Alaska quirkiness, the kids with the weird names.

Just like the disastrous and anti-intellectual W., this Visceral One never doubts herself. The Cerebral One welcomes doubt.

On Afghanistan, Palin says, W-like, that the president should simply give Gen. Stanley McChrystal a blank check. But Afghanistan is a wrenching decision, and we do need the closest exit ramp. So the president should get credit for standing back and studying the issue, and for not rubber-stamping the generals' predictable urge to surge. But the way he has handled the perception part has allowed critics—including generals—to cast him as indecisive.

McChrystal and Gen. David Petraeus should have been giving their best advice to Obama—and airing their view against scaling down in Afghanistan—in confidence. Instead, McChrystal pushed his opinion in a speech in London, and Petraeus has discussed his feelings in private sessions with reporters. This creates a "Seven Days in May" syndrome, where the two generals are, in effect, lobbying against the president and undercutting him as he's trying to make a painfully complex, life-and-death decision.

This time, Obama should adopt Palin's straight-from-the-gut approach, call the generals into the Oval and tell them, "Your pie-holes you will shut or rise higher you will not. Because, dang it, the president I am!"

DISCUSSION *questions and activities*

1. Write a one-sentence statement of Dowd's stance. Compare your statement with those of at least three other students in your class. Discuss any differences in your readings and craft a brief negotiated summary of Dowd's argument.

2. Identify passages in Dowd's comparison of Obama and Palin that show her underlying values about rhetoric. Compare her image of the good rhetorician with the definition of Quintilian and/or of your own view of political rhetoric. In all of these cases, be sure to think about what you mean by the word "good."

3. Read George Washington's "Newburgh Address." Does he meet Dowd's call for visceral rhetoric?

Do You Pass the Social Media Recruitment Test?

Boris Epstein

This article was originally published on the blog mashable.com, an online news source for social media and web culture. The author, Boris Epstein, has a Bachelor's of Science from the University of California at Davis. He is the founder and current managing director of BINC, a staffing and recruiting firm in the San Francisco area. In this article, Epstein takes readers through a series of questions regarding their online presence, and whether human resources specialists think it is best for securing and maintaining employment.

With the emergence of social media sites like LinkedIn, Facebook, and Twitter, and their user bases growing by the millions, one would think that a headhunter's job just got much easier. I mean let's face it; nowadays we can find anybody whether it's on one of these social networking sites, on a blog, discussion board, alumni list or via true and tried headhunting techniques.

But it's not that simple. In the golden days of recruiting we would hunt for days to find a candidate with a degree from a top university who worked for a top notch company who of course was considered priceless and absolutely worth contacting. Today however, we run a simple search on LinkedIn and find hundreds that match that exact profile. Or we run a quick search on Twitter for anybody discussing a specific keyword and we now have hundreds more to contact. But with only a set number of hours in a day, we just don't have the bandwidth to contact everybody.

The problem of today completely flipped from the one of yesterday where we went from candidate scarcity and limited information to an overabundance of candidates and even more information available on each one.

So in today's world of information overload where talent is literally available by the truckloads, I thought it would be relevant to write a post about how we evaluate a candidate's social media footprint to determine (when all else is equal) which candidates we would contact and which ones get left by the wayside. I posed the following question to make it simple:

If all else were equal, like education, work history and general skill set, and I had to evaluate the social media footprints of two candidates to determine which one of them I would contact, which one would I contact and why? In my experience, I would contact the one who:

ON LINKEDIN
1. Has genuine recommendations from peers, managers and colleagues
2. Has the more complete profile
3. Is a member of more groups pertaining to their respective field

4. Has a picture
5. Lists interests, hobbies and other information related to their life outside of work
6. Participates and highlights their involvement in non-paid projects related to their field (open-source, community, volunteer, conference)
7. Updates their status more often
8. Asks and answers more questions
9. Links to their employer, blog and other projects of interest
10. Has the larger network

ON THEIR BLOG
1. Has interesting things to say about their respective profession and industry
2. Provides glimpses into their life outside of work—family, friends, hobbies, etc.
3. Does not bad-mouth their current or previous employer
4. Provides links to their other social networking profiles
5. Includes a link to their current resume
6. Updates with new posts regularly
7. Keeps it non-controversial—minimal discussion of sex, politics, religion and other such controversial topics
8. Is more genuine and honest
9. Has a blogroll with link to other interesting blogs

ON FACEBOOK
1. Respects the overlap between their personal and professional lives
2. Updates often
3. Posts pictures of friends and family but keeps them pg-13
4. Keeps it non-controversial—doesn't take extreme positions on sex, drugs, religion, politics or other topics that could cause an employer to be wary of hiring
5. Is a member of groups relevant to their profession

ON TWITTER
1. Tweets often (between 2–10 times per day is considered reasonable)
2. Has a healthy followers/following ratio
3. Has the biggest network
4. Keeps a healthy balance between personal and professional tweets
5. Doesn't just update, but also responds to others and generally seems to get Twitter

WHEN GOOGLED
1. Does not lead to something controversial like arrests
2. Leads to profession-related discussions and commentary on other social media sites
3. Leads me to their online blog, webpage or social media profiles
4. Doesn't come up blank

Why it matters

Now you might be asking yourself, if somebody has the skills that an employer requires, why are all of the above criteria important? The short answer is that nowadays employers rarely hire just skills and are looking for much more of a complete package — skills plus a well-rounded individual that fits well with their team and company. And a person's social media footprint gives employers (and others) the best insight into your passions, interests, communication styles, work habits, work/life balance and all sorts of other valuable information.

Simply put, it helps an employer get to know you and get comfortable with you before a single word has even been exchanged. So think about it, if you had the choice to consider a cold bland resume or an actual person with common interests, passions and work/life style, wouldn't the choice be obvious?

New to social media?

But what happens if you're new to the world of Social Media and aren't quite at the same pace as some of the veterans out there. Not to worry, just follow a few easy steps and you'll be right into the thick of the game in absolutely no time.

1. Start ASAP!
2. Create fully completed LinkedIn, Facebook and Twitter profiles.
3. Shed your preconceived notions of keeping your work and home life separate. Companies want people, not resumes. Start portraying yourself as the well-rounded individual that you are.
4. Use social media to its fullest — update often, connect with others and stay active.
5. Don't stop ever (even if you're happily employed and aren't looking for new work). Establishing and maintaining a social media footprint is not an act, it's a process. Just like your career evolves, so should your Social Media Footprint.

DISCUSSION *questions and activities*

1. Social media allows us to create a 'construct' of ourselves, to literally choose what we share and what we will decline to reveal. How does this impact the credibility of a social media source in research? Are social media postings, fan sites, or blogs ethical sources in academic research? Which ones are more reliable? Less? Why?

2. Epstein encourages users to embrace social media and to "evaluate your social media footprint" and think about the message you send to your audience. In what ways do you need to consider the message while crafting an academic argument?

3. Spend some time browsing through the comments for this article at www.mashable. com. What is the overall tone of the comments, and how do they change your perception of the article? Which ones seem in line with Epstein's advice about an online presence?

A Kind Word for Bullshit: The Problems with Academic Writing

Philip Eubanks and John D. Schaeffer

Philip Eubanks and John D. Schaeffer, professors of English at Northern Illinois University, teach a variety of rhetoric, writing, and literature classes. Their essay "A Kind Word for Bullshit: The Problems with Academic Writing" was published in the February 2008 edition of College Composition and Communication, *an academic journal that publishes current scholarship and research about writing pedagogy. In their argument, the authors apply concepts from Harry Frankfurt's book* On Bullshit *(2005) to academic writing in order to address the popular perception of a strong link between academic writing and bullshit.*

In 2005, Princeton University Press republished, in book form, Harry Frankfurt's classic essay "On Bullshit." Perhaps predictably, since most academic titles are not nearly so earthy, the book received more than the usual amount of public interest. *On Bullshit* garnered flattering attention in the *New York Times* and on *60 Minutes*, Frankfurt appeared on *The Daily Show*, and the book sold briskly. But for all the fanfare and commercial success, Frankfurt's essay is rather modest. He notes that bullshit is all around us, and yet "we have no clear understanding of what bullshit is, why there is so much of it, and what functions it serves" (1). Therefore, he proposes to "give a rough account of what bullshit is and how it differs from what it is not," and he cautions that he cannot offer anything "decisive" (2–3). This article proposes to take up where Frankfurt left off and to address the question of bullshit in a way that is especially pertinent to academics, even more pertinent to people in the humanities and social sciences, and most pertinent of all to those who specialize in rhetoric and writing.

Frankfurt is right that all of us are familiar with bullshit. We are also conflicted about it. In the United States, few words signal the same kind of ambivalence. Bullshit can be a bitter epithet: *the bullshit job*, words that are *a bunch of bullshit*, and people who are *nothing but bullshitters*. Yet the same word can be uttered with sly affection or charming self-deprecation. Think of the standard phrases: *I was just bullshitting. Never bullshit a bullshitter. If you can't dazzle 'em with brilliance, baffle 'em with bullshit.* Similar words don't allow for such playfulness. You cannot use *kidding* as a bitter epithet. You cannot say *I was just lying* and keep your self-respect.

In academe, we are if anything more conflicted than the public at large because of the scathing quality of the phrase *academic bullshit.* The most apt examples of academic bullshit come from the social sciences and humanities—not that anyone who produces this work is happy about it. After all, our work is serious, and we naturally take offense at critiques that call our writing and scholarship pretentious (which impugns our character) or nonrigorous (which impugns our minds). The flipside of that taking of offense is fear—fear that the critiques are right.

If you doubt that, try not to laugh at Dave Barry's advice to prospective English majors, advice "reprinted" on countless websites:

Suppose you are studying Moby-Dick. Anybody with any common sense would say that Moby-Dick is a big white whale, since the characters in the book refer to it as a big white whale roughly eleven thousand times. So in your paper, you say Moby-Dick is actually the Republic of Ireland....If you can regularly come up with lunatic interpretations of simple stories, you should major in English. (114)

Or abandon all restraint and become an English professor. Who more likely than a preeminent literary critic would provoke this scornful remark from a graduate student: "He's a total fraud—a complete *bullshitter*." Barry is just as dead-on in his parody of sociologists, who "spend most of their time translating simple, obvious observations into scientific-sounding code." You should be a sociologist, he says, if you can dress up the fact that children cry when they fall down in words like these: "Methodological observation of the sociometrical behavior tendencies of prematurated isolates indicates that a causal relationship exists between groundward tropism and lachrymatory, or 'crying,' behavior forms." And Barry is perhaps no more derisive than Richard Weaver, who observed decades ago that because of its overblown style social science "fails to convince us that it deals clearly with reality" (187). In other words, it sounded then, and sounds now, like bullshit.

Academics are thus in a peculiar spot with regard to bullshit. For us, it is not sufficient to observe, as Frankfurt does, that bullshit is "one of the most salient features of our culture" (1). Rather, we have to confront the fact that our culture often singles out academe as the mother lode of bullshit. Compositionists may be in the most peculiar and complicated spot of all—for at least three reasons. First, the writing style of composition research risks being called bullshit because it often has the timbre of abstruse literary criticism or of social science. Second, composition has taken up disciplinary writing as an important area of study and thus implicitly endorses it. It probably does not help that writing studies has often focused its attention on the rhetoric of science; that simply enlarges the number of suspect academic texts. Third, one major consequence of studying disciplinary writing has been the abandonment of the abstract ideal once called "good writing." The current mainstream of composition studies not only takes up academic writing as an object of study, but it also sees writing instruction as at least partly a matter of introducing undergraduates to the established practices of expert academic writers. Even though some composition scholars have critiqued academic discourse as a form of Enlightenment-inspired hegemony, almost no one advocates completely abandoning academic styles and standards. If academic writing is bullshit, then bullshit is what we teach.

Some or all of those reasons may seem profoundly unfair, but they nonetheless call for some reflection. The first part of that reflection ought to confront the problem of defining bullshit more usefully than Frankfurt has. As careful a job as Frankfurt does, he is right to say that he does not offer anything decisive. In fact, a major problem with Frankfurt's essay is that he assumes that lack of decisiveness is a shortcoming. But decisiveness is not the appropriate standard. There are better ways to wrestle with a word—ways that do not involve retreating into claims of indeterminacy, either. The second part of the reflection ought to confront how bullshit is and is not a part of the practice of composing academic arguments. It may well be that much academic rhetoric is, in fact, bullshit. But it may also be so that bullshit, in at least some senses, animates what is best in academic rhetoric. At least, that is the suggestion that will be made in this essay.

Method of Definition

Frankfurt makes it his project to say what bullshit means ("what bullshit is and how it differs from what it is not"), but he immediately finds that goal elusive. Bullshit is "often employed quite loosely," he says. But rather than accept that as a fundamental characteristic of the word, he attempts a tight definition that lays out the word's "essential" characteristics—a method that Charles Fillmore once called, not flatteringly, the "checklist" theory of definition (quoted in Coleman and Kay 26). Within the limitations of his method, though, Frankfurt's discussion is often illuminating. According to Frankfurt, bullshit does not *necessarily* involve a misrepresentation of facts but *must* involve a misrepresentation of the self—one's feelings, thoughts, or attitudes. In that way, a Fourth of July speaker may commit an act of bullshitting by exaggeratedly extolling the virtues of American history. American history may or may not be just as the speaker claims. But that is incidental. What matters to the speaker is the hyperbolic impression given of his or her own patriotism (16–18).

In that sense, bullshit is disconnected from the truth in a way that lying never is. Frankfurt argues,

> *It is impossible for someone to lie unless he thinks he knows the truth. Producing bullshit requires no such conviction. A person who lies is thereby responding to the truth, and he is to that extent respectful of it. When an honest man speaks, he says only what he believes to be true; and for the liar, it is correspondingly indispensable that he consider his statements to be false. For the bullshitter, however, all these bets are off: he is neither on the side of the true nor on the side of the false. His eye is not on the facts at all…except insofar as they may be pertinent to his interest in getting away with what he says. (55–56)*

In other words, bullshit may be false, and it may, by accident or by design, be true. But either way what really matters is that the bullshitter gets away with something, chiefly a misrepresentation of self and intention. That is the main reason, says Frankfurt, that we are generally more tolerant of bullshit than of lies. Unlike a lie, bullshit is not "a personal affront" (50) and yet is a greater enemy of truth than lies are (61).

The phrase *academic bullshit* thus presents a double insult to academics. It can mean academic writing that shows a reckless disregard for the truth—that it is almost certainly full of things that are false. That accusation stings. After all, the traditional aim of the university is to seek the truth without interference of politics or other loyalties. To what degree truth is objective or knowable has come under much scrutiny in the past few decades. But even that debate is a question of the truth about the Truth. If academic writing is seen as unconcerned about getting things right, that is problem enough. Yet an even worse problem may be that, as Frankfurt says, bullshit is not seen as a personal affront. Academic bullshit may bear no relationship to what is true or false, correct or incorrect. But no one is offended by academic irrelevancies anyway.

A tempting response to this might be to identify academic bullshitters and drum them out of the journals and academic presses, but that will not help. Some academic writing may stand out as bullshit. But—to many inside and outside of the academic world—almost all academic writing, and surely that produced in the humanities and social sciences, stands accused. What might help, though, would be to grapple with the meaning of bullshit differently than Frankfurt has.

Frankfurt himself nearly happens upon a better approach. He recounts a story about Wittgenstein in which a sick friend says, "I feel like a dog that has been run over." Wittgenstein responds, "You don't know what a dog that's been run over feels like." From that, Frankfurt draws the lesson that Wittgenstein was intolerant of anything that smelled of bullshit, no matter how faintly. But the lesson he should have drawn was that Wittgenstein was, at least in his later life, intolerant of unfounded speculations. Recall his dictum: "Don't think, but look!" (31). That was especially true when it came to definitions of words. For instance, Wittgenstein explains at some length that the word *game* refers to a set of loosely affiliated activities—board games, card games, ball games, Ring around the Rosy—that are not called by the same name because they share a fixed set of essential features but rather because they share in varying degrees *some* of the features typical of games. They are related by "family resemblances": "a complicated network of similarities overlapping and criss-crossing" (32). Like *game, bullshit* groups together acts that can be quite varied.

A similar approach to word definition is prototype semantics, which is based on a cognitive science view of categorization that says (1) that category members do not necessarily share a single set of distinguishing features and may exhibit features to greater or lesser degrees and (2) that some category members are more typical—that is, cognitively salient—than others. Linda Coleman and Paul Kay use prototype semantics to define the word *lie*. They demonstrate that, although lies may have identifiable features such as misrepresentation of belief, intent to deceive, falseness, and reprehensible motives, not all features are always present and not all features are equally prominent in every instance. In other words, *lie* is a graded category in which some examples are more easily and certainly recognized than others. In prototypical instances of *lie*, someone makes a false statement that he or she believes to be false for the purpose of deceiving another person. But other statements can also be called lies—such as when someone makes a statement that is factually true but is intended to conceal his or her motives or intentions. For instance, if your spouse asks you where you are going and you respond "to the store," he or she will very likely assume that you are going to the grocery store. If your intention is to go to the guitar shop, then you have—in a sense—lied. But it is not a *prototypical* lie.

Likewise, there are prototypical and nonprototypical instances of bullshit. So in defining *bullshit*, one task at hand is not to say what is bullshit and what is not but to distinguish what is prototypical bullshit from what is not. Another important task is to gain some sense of how the bullshit prototype rhetorically influences our attitudes about even very peripheral category members.

Prototypical Bullshit

Although Frankfurt makes no distinction between prototypical and nonprototypical cases, his discussion can be helpful in understanding what makes up the bullshit prototype. According to Frankfurt, the bullshitter attempts to misrepresent himself or herself, that is, to create an ethos that implies a character that the speaker does not possess. Furthermore, the misrepresentation aims to deceive; intentionality (the intention to misrepresent) is an essential part of bullshit. Both traits do seem to be especially characteristic of bullshit.

Once intentionality enters the definition, however, the difficulties begin because intentions are seldom if ever pure, seldom if ever entirely conscious. Nor is this a modern phenomenon. Isocrates, for example, urged his students to adopt a virtuous persona and offered to teach them how to do it, not merely because they might become successful pleaders, but because he thought they would soon see that the only way to persuade with a virtuous ethos was to actually have one. In short, acting virtuous would lead them to act virtuously. The case could be framed in modern terms: Is it deceptive to represent oneself as one actually aspires to be; to create an ethos one doesn't have yet but wants to have? Is such representation really misrepresentation? If so, what is the "sincere" alternative? Can one never speak out of a "better self" until one has a better self? And if so, when will one ever know that he or she has it? This difficulty requires refining the notion of misrepresentation.

First, Frankfurt's notion obviously runs afoul of current scholarship about rhetoric and the "constructed self." Some contemporary scholars might deny that there is a pre-existing self to which the bullshitter is not true. They might say that the self *is* bullshit. It is constructed out of bullshit and to believe that it exists independently of bullshit is, well, bullshit. The bullshitter thus could not misrepresent a self that does not exist outside of bullshit. A prototypical example might be sales representatives. Their goal is to sell the product, yet they are required to present themselves as benefactors of their potential customers, as persons with only the good of the client at heart. Is their sales pitch bullshit if they sincerely believe that their product really is what's best for their customers? Or does their biased position render them bullshitters no matter what their beliefs are? Actually, how a salesperson represents him or herself is suspect per se. The complexities described above indicate one of the serious limitations of Frankfurt's definition; namely, bullshit may be a defining aspect of rhetorical situations.

Bullshit may be essential to the kind of rhetorical situation that Walter Ong calls "ludic," that is, a situation in which certain rules and expectations permit behavior that would not be appropriate in "real life" situations (132–33); to prescind from the Latinate "ludic," these situations could be called "games" and the behavior appropriate to them called "gamesmanship." To continue with the salesman example: the client knows that the sales representative has his own agenda, that the salesman may be exaggerating the product's advantages and minimizing its shortcomings, but the client should expect nothing else. Likewise the salesman knows the client will ask questions and voice objections that he, the salesman, is expected to answer, not merely to demonstrate his knowledge of the product, but to demonstrate his knowledge of the client's problems, his sympathy with the client's situation—in short, to ingratiate himself with the client and establish his ethos as a knowledgeable and trustworthy colleague. The salesman/client situation clearly involves bullshit according to Frankfurt's definition, but the rhetorical situation, the game, makes bullshit far more complex than in Frankfurt's account.

The sales situation exemplifies bullshitting to convince someone, but bullshit can also aim to create an ethos for its own sake, to misrepresent the speaker simply for the pleasure of doing so. This activity is perhaps the most frequent kind of bullshitting, and it too participates in gamesmanship. The two prototypical examples of this kind of bullshit are the fish story and the sex story. The former usually concerns the one that got away; the latter the one that didn't. This bullshit aims to enhance the speaker's reputation as a sportsman or a lover and in the process entertain the auditors. It differs, however, from tall tales or fairy stories (although it may be as true) in that it purports to be the truth; it aims at belief, not the suspension of disbelief. Part of the game is to speak so convincingly that the auditors believe the bullshit and thus not only enhance the speaker's reputation as a fisherman or ladies' man, but also enhance his reputation as a skilled bullshitter. The truth of the account is secondary to the credibility that the speaker wins. The highest compliment, and most derogatory insult, that can be given to such a person is that he is *"full* of shit."

The above part of this essay slipped into the masculine pronoun—and with good reason. According to Ong, this ludic quality of bullshit is gender specific—it is almost exclusively a male game. Onglists a variety of such games: medieval disputants insulting or "flitting" their opponents, African Americans playing the dozens, primitive peoples engaging in ritual boasting, etc. (124–25). All these may be described as bullshitting insofar as they use language to establish an ethos of aggression and masculine superiority. This ethos can be highlighted by comparing it to the opposite of bullshit; not to "truth" or "sincerity" as Frankfurt would have it, but to "chicken shit."

The *locus classicus* for the use of this term is President Lyndon Johnson. When Johnson was in the Senate, he reputedly called Richard Nixon "chicken shit," implying that he was weak, petty, and untrustworthy, not because he was a bullshitter (Johnson himself had no equals) but because he was a liar. Later Nixon, while vice president, scored a public relations coup by standing up to an angry mob in Venezuela; Johnson embraced Nixon upon his return. When reminded by a reporter that he had called Nixon chicken shit, Johnson replied, "Son, you've got to learn that overnight chicken shit can turn to chicken salad" (Morgan 109). Finally, when Johnson was president, Charles Mohr asked him how pay raises to his staff were being distributed. Johnson replied, "Here you are, alone with the President of the United States and Leader of the Free World, and you ask a chicken-shit question like that" (Mohr).

In each instance, "chicken shit" connotes unmanliness, weakness, and pettiness. In Johnson's eyes, if Nixon had been a bullshitter, he would have been a far better man.

So "chicken shit" illustrates by contrast the masculine, aggressive, ludic qualities of "bullshit." These qualities are particularly important in light of Ong's insights into the nature of argument. He claims that argument, verbal conflict, was and is essentially a masculine endeavor fraught with ludic qualities. It is ritual combat in which the establishing of reputation is critical. Seen in that light, it is surely no accident that so many influential critiques of academic argument have come from a feminist perspective.

To sum up, prototypical bullshit has to do with a purposeful misrepresentation of self, has the quality of gamesmanship, and—contrary to what Frankfurt says—is at least potentially a lie. Frankfurt may be right to point out that some bullshit may possibly be true (e.g., the Fourth of July speech or the sales pitch), but it is not recognizable as bullshit because it may be truthful but rather because it is likely to be a lie. Most Fourth of July speeches are, in fact, chock-full of dubious historical claims, and sales pitches are all too often both biased *and* false. Moreover, Frankfurt's understanding of *lie* is too narrow ("It is impossible for someone to lie unless he thinks he knows the truth"). As Cole and Kay point out, the prototypical case of *lie* includes not just actual falsehoods but also statements made when there is an insufficient basis for knowing the truth.

One way to notice when bullshit is most bullshit-like is to look at the difference between the noun *bullshitter* versus the verb *to bullshit*. Consider Frankfurt's example in which Wittgenstein challenges the statement "I feel like a dog that has been run over." Someone who makes that statement may be bullshitting, but it is not the statement of a bullshitter. That is, it is not a statement to which a competent interlocutor can respond, "Bullshit!" Indeed, in the anecdote, apocryphal or not, Wittgenstein does not respond with anything like that but rather with a hyper-empirical rejoinder that demonstrates his meticulous cast of mind.

Prototypical bullshit is what a bullshitter tries to pull off—something that should provoke "Bullshit!" That may not always be "high-quality" bullshit. Frankfurt says that we are more tolerant of bullshit than of lies, citing the fatherly advice, "Never tell a lie when you can bullshit your way through" (48). That seems to be a recommendation not just to bullshit but to be very good at it. But we often grow weary of bullshit when it is both prototypical and of poor quality.

As good an example as any of prototypical and unsuccessful bullshit is found in the title of Laura Penny's book about corporate bullshit: *Your Call Is Important to Us*. The statement "Your call is important to us" has the usual qualities of self-misrepresentation (if corporations can be said to have a collective self). It is likely to be a lie because it greatly exaggerates the company's sincerity. And it is gamesmanship (or, to use Frankfurt's phrase, an "attempt to get away" with saying something). But it fails to play the game with skill or elegance. Part of gamesmanship in successful bullshit is that it is at once grandiose and difficult to be sure of: it gets away with something audacious while also putting it plainly on display. "Your call is important to us" is hardly audacious, and nobody believes it. So it grates. That is also true of the brand of bullshit sometimes called governmentese, which misrepresents intentions, is likely to be deceptive, and perpetrates, rather than plays, a game.

Of course, the ordinary defense for "Your call is important to us" and similar corporate banalities is that they are matters of politeness. But as many discourse analysts have pointed out, politeness is not without its complications. Norman Fairclough writes, "[P]articular politeness conventions embody, and their use implicitly acknowledges, particular social and power relations" (163). No doubt, part of the irritation people feel toward false politeness from corporations is that consumers are, all too apparently, powerless to avoid it or even respond to it—trapped on hold, with no choice but to be mollified again and again by a prerecorded "Your call is important to us." But it is not just a feeling of helplessness that bothers people; it is the bullshit quality of the corporate language. Its insincerity. Its smugness. The feebleness of its attempt to get away with something.

Both successful and unsuccessful bullshit can be found everywhere. But this essay is particularly concerned with the way bullshit is perceived and the way it operates in academe. Accordingly, the problem that will concern the remainder of this essay is this: What kinds of prototypical and nonprototypical bullshit characterize academic writing? And what difference does it make?

Academic Bullshit among Professors

For many non-academics, academic writing is not just bullshit but bullshit of the worst kind. That is a stinging condemnation, but one that would be easily dismissed if academics did not have their own reservations about academic discourse. The fact is: both non-academics and academics sometimes judge academic writing to be bullshit, but for reasons that are very different. At play in making these judgments are multiple prototypes and their contending rhetorical forces. Just as bullshit is a graded category centered on a prototype, some kinds of academic writing are more typical than others. Because of that, we have to investigate not whether academic writing is considered to be bullshit but whether or not *prototypical* academic writing is considered to be *prototypical* bullshit—and in whose estimation.

When non-academics call academic writing bullshit, they mean that it uses jargon, words whose meanings are so abstract and vague as to seem unrelated to anyone's experience. Such jargon seems to contribute nothing to the reader except confusion and serves only to enhance the ethos of the speaker, a strategy that the general public dislikes precisely because they suspect that academics are taken in by it. Academics, it is said, believe their own bullshit: They hide behind language that may be as slight, or exaggerated, or obfuscatory as any sales pitch or fish story.

Joseph Williams and Richard Lanham are perhaps the best-known commentators on the topic of overblown prose style. In *Style: Ten Lessons in Clarity and Grace*, Williams writes, "Generations of students have struggled with dense writing, many thinking they were not smart enough to grasp the writer's deep ideas. Some have been right about that, but more could have blamed the writer's inability (or refusal) to write clearly" (8). The key word here is "refusal." Often academic writers could be clearer but prefer to serve up something that sounds like bullshit. So begins a vicious cycle. As Lanham describes it, professors write prolix books and articles, students imitate their professors' style, and professors reward them for it—because professors often think that abstruse academic writing "sounds just right; it sounds professional" (17). Both Williams and Lanham point out the grammatical characteristics of unclear style: chiefly, agentless sentences and an overabundance of nominalizations. Or to put it more in academic-sounding words: The absence of agents in sentences and a corresponding abundance of abstract nominalizations characteristic of stylistic opaqueness figure prominently in Williams and Lanham's commentary.

But though we can surely identify typical grammatical features of unclear prose, the problem ultimately comes down to audience: When people consider writing to be not plain enough or deliberately obscure, what they really mean is that the writing does not appropriately address *them*. When discussing the essence of bullshit, Frankfurt does not specify an audience's character or expectations beyond those of the "average reader." Academic writing, however, is seldom meant for an average audience; it addresses an audience of specialists. Indeed, much academic publication, especially by young scholars, aims to qualify the author for membership in a group of specialists. When it comes to identifying what counts as prototypical academic writing, it matters who is making the judgment.

For the general public, the apotheosis of academic bullshit seems to be the interpretive paper in the humanities. Among those papers none suffers so much opprobrium as the ones delivered at the annual meeting of the Modern Language Association. Every year the daily press of the host city ridicules the conference papers. Titles such as "The Odor of Male Solitude," "Margaret Cavendish as Giant Cucumber," "Obviating the State by Stating the Obvious: Discourse-Analytical Linguistics and Anarchism," and

"Bestio-Scatological Politics in 'Go Dog, Go'" (actual titles) are reprinted gleefully in the mainstream press as evidence that the eggheads at our universities are not just loons but absolute bullshitters.

These egregious examples have the characteristics of prototypical bullshit. They apparently disregard the truth by delving wildly into the realm of interpretation. They use odd language in the service of building a false ethos. And they do both as a form of gamesmanship. Perhaps no one, including most academics, finds these titles bullshit-free. But they are irksomely bullshit-like *for a general audience*. Indeed, the general public takes them to be the prototype of academic writing in the humanities. Such writing is seen as gamesmanship in a game that is rigged. In the public mind, there is no admirable art or craft to bullshitting an audience of fellow academics who suspend disbelief so willingly.

However, what academics consider to be prototypical academic writing is far different from what the general public has in mind. In turn, academics have much different misgivings about it. They surely do not consider all academic writing to be bullshit but suspect that some of it—even some that they value—may not be entirely free of it. Consider here that gradedness of both categories: academic writing and bullshit. For academic insiders, the academic work that receives public scorn is recognizable as academic work but is not typical of it: the academic prototype is not characterized by outrageousness but rather by earnestness (indeed, by earnest tedium). Similarly, when insiders worry that academic writing may be bullshit, they are not concerned with prototypical bullshit: braggadocio or, worse, a pretense of gamesmanship in a rigged contest. Rather, they worry that even good academic writing, especially in the humanities and social sciences, is *something like* bullshit.

In other words, it is nonprototypical bullshit—in at least these ways: Academic writing very seldom aims to deceive the reader about its content, but it certainly is meant to enhance the reputation, the ethos, of the writer. Frequently academic publication aims to create an ethos that will result in tangible rewards for the academic: tenure, promotion, grants, etc. The academic knows that such rewards are distributed on the basis of reputation. Such a reputation is gained by publishing books and articles that have been peer reviewed before publication and positively reviewed afterward. Hence professional rewards come from academic reputation, and academic reputation comes from publication. This system seems to make academic publication a particularly rich field for bullshit. At least to some degree, the reward system encourages the academic writer to misrepresent him- or herself by emphasizing if not exaggerating the influence of what he or she has written. Yet there is nothing especially deceptive about this construction of ethos. Within the academic community, it is fully on display. Indeed, it is entirely conventional.

Academic publication is also coy about its argumentative—ludic—character. It generally aims to refute, qualify, or expand the positions taken in other academic publications, whether about the meaning of the white whale or the existence of a sub-atomic particle that lasts for billionths of a millisecond. But academics frequently describe publication as "entering the conversation" or with some other irenic descriptor. That turns successful academic writing into a complex game indeed—an art or craft in which arguments are forwarded, but more than just argumentative imperatives must be attended to. It follows the conventions of rhetorical argument familiar since the time of Aristotle. Yet it also follows certain discipline-specific conventions.

Consider the plethora of constraints to which the academic writer must conform. The academic writer must make claims and prove them according to the conventions of the discipline. The writer must marshal supporting information and arguments and present them in an approved format. The level of writing must be congruent with that of other publications in the field. Even if the writer profoundly disagrees with another position, it is an implicit rule that the opponent's professional reputation be respected. Abiding by these conventions creates a certain tone, the tone of the competent, often dispassionate, expert who is attempting to expand a fund of knowledge. Someone who can create this tone may indeed be playing the game of academic publication. This academic gamesmanship is liable to the charge of bullshit insofar as the persona or ethos created by that tone may be completely different from the "actual" disposition of the writer. In short, what academics would call *prototypical academic writing* may be bullshit, but it is not *prototypical bullshit*. It may, however, be a variant sort of bullshit—bullshit on the edge of the category.

Yet even peripheral sorts of bullshit suffer by association with the prototype. The prototype of bullshit is not just at the center of the category; it is the category's center of gravity. As Amos Tversky and Itamar Gati have shown, prototypes are the standard against which nonprototypes are unconsciously measured. In their experiments, participants in the United States consistently saw Mexico as more similar to the United States than the United States to Mexico. Once this phenomenon is pointed out, it seems obvious. We recognize ospreys as birds because they are something like robins; we do not recognize robins as birds because they are something like ospreys. Because of this unconscious phenomenon and the rhetoric it entails, academic writing may be nonprototypical bullshit, but all bullshit suffers from the gravitational pull of the prototype.

Moreover, part of academics' ambivalence derives from the feeling that *some* academic writing *is* prototypical. "Bullshit" within academia is an expletive that asserts loyalty and conviction about one's own ideological commitments while disvaluing those of others. While the academy constitutes a kind of specialized group, it is a group with subgroups and subspecialties organized according to a myriad of criteria: disciplines, historical periods, theoretical frameworks, etc. This latter criterion seems particularly vulnerable to accusations of bullshit both within and without the academy. Theoretical frameworks probably provoke more cries of "Bullshit!" than any other academic praxis: new criticism bullshit, Marxist bullshit, feminist bullshit, Marxist-feminist bullshit, deconstructionist bullshit, statistical bullshit, and the list goes on—and on. These epithets signify a final judgment of unintelligibility or bad faith leveled at the practitioners of one theory or discipline by practitioners of another, who not only disagree with the other theory or discipline but who, in some ultimate way, deny that it yields knowledge and assert that the whole discipline or theory qualifies as a prototypical case of bullshit. In the academy, to call something "Bullshit!" argues that the text does not merit a place in the academy, and it implies that its author does not deserve one either. It is an *argumentum ad hominem* that aims to excommunicate. And to a certain extent, the "average reader" may make a similar judgment about all our houses.

Academic Bullshit among Students

Compositionists will, of course, have already observed that composition theory explicitly advocates that students do just what makes academic writing seem to many like bullshit: to develop an identity within a community of discourse—that is, to gain "genre knowledge." This social understanding of writing and self is too familiar to rehearse at length here. Suffice it to say that whether we liken today's students to those of Isocrates, who were encouraged to create a persona that they wanted to inhabit, or whether we think of student writers along the lines of Lave and Wenger's apprentices, good writing is inseparable from the context in which it arises—and thus from the manipulations of self that contexts foist upon us all. Along the way to professional writing competence, there is bound to be some bullshit.

Yet, although it is easy enough to recognize apprentice writing as a peripheral type of bullshit, that's not what the word "bullshit" typically singles out in student writing. Rather, student bullshit is often brazenly prototypical. This problem is discussed well by William Perry in his essay "Examsmanship and the Liberal Arts." In the delicate language of 1963, Perry refers only to "bull" and to the practitioners of it as "bullsters." He defines bull as "relevancies, however relevant, without data" (65). That is to say, when a student can write intelligibly and intelligently about a book the student has not read, that is bull. It is interpretation by guesswork. Perry contrasts bull favorably with what he calls "cow": facts without interpretation. His point, charmingly made, is that becoming "a member of the community of scholars" depends at least as much on the ability to discuss matters about which one possesses few facts as upon knowledge of facts themselves.

Yet he also acknowledges that "bullsters" are usually seen as cynical. That is a key point. Perry's chief example—a student who receives an A– for an essay on a book that he has not read—is cynical, even if many, like Perry, are not overly offended by the achievement. Students are rewarded with grades, and everyone understands the temptation to subvert the system by means of bullshit. No one, not even the "bullster," would contend that bullshit can really substitute for well-informed and thoughtful writing. In that sense, the problem of prototypical student bullshit contains the seeds of its own solution.

Another kind of student bullshit constitutes a bigger problem. This bullshit subverts academic writing through competent but insincere cooperation. Jasper Neel calls this "anti-writing," writing that follows the conventions of academic writing but that conveys the sentiment "I care nothing about the truth" (85). Combine disregard for the truth with the inevitable classroom pretense that the writer truly cares about his or her academic development, and an insidious variety of bullshit is fashioned. The student has done all that is asked, except to be sincere—about the content of the writing and about his or her presentation of self. Just as bullshit is a greater threat to the truth than a lie, this docile form of bullshit is a greater threat to student writing than the cynical work of the bullster. The bullster is akin to the hoaxer, whose reward is in revealing (though probably just to peers) the successful exploit (compare Secor and Walsh). The cooperative bullshitter presents a "false" self but fails to recognize that the contingent self can lead to self-transformation. It is bullshit that aims to get by with something worse than a lie: disengagement.

A Brief Conclusion

At this point, convention would have us offer possible solutions to the problem of academic bullshit. But—taking a page from Frankfurt's essay—we will demur. Not because we do not want to be useful. As Frankfurt says, we operate in a world in which bullshit seems to be all around us. None of us can put an end to bullshit in the world, not even in our little corner of it. As scholars of rhetoric and writing, the most we can hope for is to avoid making the problem of academic bullshit larger than it is.

To do that, we need a more sophisticated understanding of *what bullshit is*—or, better yet, a more precise understanding of how *what bullshit is* varies. That will have more to do with acknowledging the graded category of bullshit. Most of what composition theory has advocated in recent years aims toward a pedagogy of bullshit—but not prototypical, masculinist ludic bullshit. And certainly not the cynical hoaxing of the bullster. Rather, most of us have in mind—for our students and for ourselves—a productive sort of bullshit: bullshit that ultimately produces better thought and better selves. We must acknowledge that benign bullshit is inevitable when people are attempting to write well.

But the category is graded, and the grade can be steep and slippery. The benign bullshit that is part of entry into the academic community comes conceptually bundled with the cynical gamesmanship of the bullster, the anti-writer, and the academic fraud. The structure of the category may encourage action that moves us closer to the prototype. Thus it is incumbent on us, the writing teachers, to be ever aware of the grades within the category and to move within and around those benign forms that are inescapable and even helpful, while resisting the gravitational pull of the prototypical. In doing so, we remain true to our discipline and to ourselves.

References

Barry, Dave. "College, Anyone? A Veteran's Crash Course in Campus Survival." *Chicago Tribune* 24 July 1983: 114.

Coleman, Linda, and Paul Kay. "Prototype Semantics: The English Word *Lie*." *Language* 57 (1981): 26–44.

Fairclough, Norman. *Discourse and Social Change*. Cambridge, UK: Polity, 1992.

Frankfurt, Harry G. *On Bullshit*. Princeton, NJ: Princeton UP, 2005.

Isocrates. *Antidosis*. Trans. George Norlin. Loeb Classical Library. Cambridge, MA: Harvard UP, 1952.

Lanham, Richard A. *Revising Prose*. 5th ed. New York: Pearson Longman, 2007.

Lave, Jean, and Etienne Wenger. *Situated Learning: Legitimate Peripheral Participation*. Cambridge: Cambridge UP, 1991.

Mohr, Charles. "Letter: Covering Washington." *New York Review of Books* 33.18 (20 November 1986): 58.

Morgan, Iwan W. *Nixon*. London: Arnold, 2002.

Neel, Jasper. *Plato, Derrida, and Writing*. Carbondale: Southern Illinois UP, 1988.

Ong, Walter J. *Fighting for Life: Contest, Sexuality, and Consciousness*. Ithaca, NY: Cornell UP, 1981.

Penny, Laura. *Your Call Is Important to Us: The Truth about Bullshit*. New York: Crown, 2005.

Perry, William. "Examsmanship and the Liberal Arts." *The Dolphin Reader*. Ed. Douglas Hunt. 6th ed. Boston: Houghton, 2003. 60–71.

Secor, Marie, and Lynda Walsh. "A Rhetorical Perspective on the Sokal Hoax: Genre, Style, and Context." *Written Communication* 21.1 (2004): 69–91.

Tversky, Amos, and Itamar Gati. "Studies of Similarity." *Cognition and Categorization*. Ed. Eleanor Rosch and Barbara B. Lloyd. Hillsdale, NJ: Erlbaum, 1978.

Weaver, Richard. "The Rhetoric of Social Science." *The Ethics of Rhetoric*. Chicago: H. Regnery, 1953.

Williams, Joseph. *Style: Ten Lessons in Clarity and Grace*. 8th ed. New York: Pearson Longman, 2005.

Wittgenstein, Ludwig. *Philosophical Investigations*. 3rd ed. Trans. G. E. M. Anscombe. New York: Macmillan, 1958.

DISCUSSION *questions and activities*

1. According to the authors, what relationship does bullshit have with the truth? Can you think of an example from your own academic experiences that reflects this relationship?

2. In what ways do the authors describe academic bullshit as being positive or useful? Do you agree with their evaluation?

3. Why do Eubanks and Schaeffer refrain from offering a solution to the problem of academic bullshit at the end of their argument? Can you offer a solution to the problem?

4. Are there any parts of the article that seem like bullshit to you? If so, explain how the definitions offered in the article itself do or do not inform your estimation.

The Floyd Landis Doping Scandal: Implications for Image Repair Discourse

Mark Glantz

Mark Glantz received his Masters of Arts in Communication from the State University of New York and his Ph.D. in Communication from the University of Missouri. He teaches for the Communications Department at Coker College in South Carolina. In this essay, Glantz analyzes Floyd Landis' attempts to repair damage caused to his public image after a drug-control test showed the presence of performance enhancing drugs, leading to his suspension from professional cycling and the removal of his 2006 Tour De France victory title.

1. Introduction

The dominant narrative to emerge from the 2006 Tour de France surrounded American cyclist Floyd Landis and his alleged use of performance enhancing substances to win that year's race. Reports of Landis' failed urine test began circulating on July 27, 2006. Although the original accusations against Landis were merely that an examination of his urine sample revealed peculiarities, it was not long before people took the next reasonable step and began to suspect that Floyd Landis had been using some sort of banned substance. Landis' situation grew even more troublesome when a second test from the Anti-Doping Agency confirmed that Landis had a prohibited amount of testosterone in his body. Moreover, the testosterone was said to be of the synthetic sort, and not naturally occurring as Landis originally argued. Ultimately, Landis made numerous efforts to repair his image in light of these accusations.

Landis, at the behest of his public relations team, launched an all out media blitz to try to repair his public image. This critical analysis will focus on several of Landis' televised appearances including the first press conference he held on July 28, 2006, in response to the accusations, his appearance on *Larry King Live* later that same day, and his early morning appearances on the *Today Show* and *Good Morning America* on August 7, 2006. Also analyzed here are his two appearances on the *Early Show* on June 26, 2007, and June 27, 2007, almost a full year after his initial image repair onslaught.

Under consideration here is an ineffective image repair effort. Landis was ultimately stripped of his Tour de France title, denounced by Tour de France director Christian Prudhomme, removed from the Phonak Hearing Systems racing team, and suspended from cycling for two years. When he returned to cycling in 2009, his name still carried baggage. The *Washington Times*, the *New York Daily News*, and the *Weekend Australian* all used the term "disgraced" to describe Landis when they reported his return (Knott, 2009, May 11; Kogoy, 2009, June 24; Thompson & Vinton, 2009, May 10), and the Ouch Pro Cycling Team immediately lost sponsors upon signing him (Macur, 2009, February 18). Throughout his trials, in both the court of law and the court of public opinion, Landis maintained his innocence, claiming that he has never been part of any doping process and that his Tour de France victory was completely legitimate.

Analysis of Floyd Landis' image repair efforts suggests numerous theoretical and practical implications. First, while some combinations of defense strategies work well together, others do not. Landis' use of denial, differentiation and evading responsibility was particularly convoluted and contradictory. This case demonstrates how denial strategies can leave rhetors with little else to say in their defense, and can place audiences in an either/or bind that forces them to judge accused parties as absolutely innocent or absolutely guilty. Second, there are considerable limitations to third party bolstering. Although several people spoke on Landis' behalf, their efforts, like his own, ultimately failed to clear his name. Finally, attacking one's accuser also has its limitations, particularly when one's accuser has empirical evidence of the accused party's guilt.

2. The theory of image repair discourse

Recurring attempts by individuals to defend their image, in combination with consistent scholarly interest in such discourse, has produced a wealth of literature on image repair discourse. Most important for the purposes of this essay is Benoit's (1995a) theory of image repair discourse, which was developed using important theoretical works by Burke (1961), Scott and Lyman (1968), and Ware and Linkugel (1973). All image repair studies are based on two assumptions (Benoit, 1995a). First, communication ought to be understood as a goal directed activity. Human beings have a purpose to their communicative endeavors. Whether written or spoken, their rhetoric is purposeful. Second, "maintaining a positive reputation is one of the central goals of communication" (p. 18). Because human beings often commit acts that are questioned or criticized by others, they feel the need to defend their image.

There are two components of attacks that must be present in order for them to warrant a response. First, an act must have occurred that is regarded as undesirable. Second, an actor must be viewed as responsible for the act. When these components are present, actors will defend themselves by relying on any number and combination of five broad strategies. These include denial, evading responsibility, minimization, mortification, and corrective action (Benoit, 1995a).

First, it is possible for actors to simply deny committing the act of which they are accused (Ware & Linkugel, 1973). One can either deny they are responsible for the act, deny the act occurred, or go a step further to blame another person or organization for the wrongful act (scapegoating).

If it is not possible or prudent for accused parties to deny that that they performed an offensive act, they may attempt to evade responsibility for the act, which can be done four ways. To claim provocation is to argue that an act was committed only because of some other equally wrongful prior act. Defeasibility is used when rhetors claim that they lacked the control that would have been necessary for preventing an objectionable act. Accused parties may also claim that what occurred was an accident. Finally, because people may be excused for committing an objectionable act if they are perceived to have been operating with the best of motives, rhetors can claim that they had good intentions.

A third category of image repair strategy, reducing offensiveness, is comprised of six sub-strategies. The accused can bolster their image (or have a third party boster their image) by associating themselves with something that is regarded positively by audiences. The accused may also try minimization, which attempts to make audiences feel less negative about the wrongful act.

In an effort to repair a threatened reputation, an accused party may find it prudent to take corrective action. Actors can take corrective action by contributing resources (time, money) to an effort to remedy the situation created by the wrongful act. Corrective action is also present when an individual promises to "clean up their act" or get help for whatever internal problems may have encouraged the objectionable act. Finally, those accused of wrongdoing can resort to mortification, which entails accepting responsibility for an act and acknowledging blame for their actions.

Benoit's scheme has been fruitfully applied to image repair discourse from politicians (Benoit & McHale, 1999; Benoit & Nill, 1998a; Benoit, Gullifor & Panici 1991; Blaney & Benoit, 2001; Len-Rios & Benoit, 2004), corporations (Benoit & Brinson, 1994; Benoit & Czerwinski, 1997; Benoit, 1995b; Brinson & Benoit, 1996; Coombs & Schmidt, 2000; King, 2006) and even entertainers (Benoit, 1997; Benoit & Nill, 1998b). There are also several studies that have investigated image repair in sports related contexts (Benoit & Hanczor, 1994; Brazeal, 2008; Jerome, 2008; Kruse, 1981; Nelson, 1984) such as the one analyzed here.

3. Floyd Landis' image repair strategies

Floyd Landis used numerous strategies in an attempt to defend his image. These strategies include differentiation, denial, evading responsibility, bolstering, and attacking the accuser.

3.1. DIFFERENTIATION

Although several image repair strategies are more prevalent in Landis' speech, differentiation is first chronologically. This is important because Landis clearly shifted his strategies over time. Later strategies were understood by the public in terms of his initial attempt at differentiation. Before even issuing a denial of wrongdoing, Landis differentiated the act of which he was accused from other, more heinous deeds. Upon initially acknowledging what he would later refer to as an "abnormality" in his test results, Landis said, "to start with, this result, which is no other than an alteration in relation of testosterone/epitestosterone, should not have made any kind of effect" (Press Conference). Although his speech was not fluent, this is a clear attempt to reframe the accusations against him. He conceded that something was curious about his test results, but he told *Larry King Live*, "It's not the positive test in the same criteria as finding something exogenous in the body." The unstated premise here is that getting caught with testosterone in your system is a far less serious offense than getting caught with performance enhancing drugs in your system.

Landis told the press that he and his lawyers and doctors were trying to decide how to "explain to the world why this is not a doping case" (Press Conference). Clearly, differentiation was important strategy for redefining the charges against the cyclist. He remained adamant that this was not a doping case. He boldly proclaimed at his press conference that, "In this particular case, nobody can talk about doping" and in a more humble moment requested, "that the case not be directly treated as a doping case" (Press Conference). Notably, Landis is unable or unwilling to craft language that suggests an affirmative understanding of what has transpired. Instead, he uses a "not doping" perspective that still includes a term with very negative connotations. Before denying that he has ever used banned substances, he uses differentiation to dispute that he is even being *charged* with using banned substances.

3.2. DENIAL

Although Landis made it clear that the case at hand is not a doping case, he still found it necessary to protect his image by denying any potential doping accusations. At his press conference he said, "I would like to leave absolutely clear that I am not in any doping process" (Press Conference). By denying that he had used restricted substances, Landis attempted to maintain his image as a drug-free athlete and imply that he did not cheat to win the Tour de France.

By the time Landis appeared on national television again, the accusations against him had already been worsened by a second test from the Anti-Doping Agency that confirmed the presence of synthetic testosterone in Landis' body. In other words, his initial defense was beginning to look less plausible. His differentiation defense was shot and he had to switch to denial. On ABC's *Good Morning America*, host Robin Roberts confronted Landis with what would be, for many, the most obvious question raised by

Landis' test results. She asked, "yes or no, did you use drugs to win the Tour de France?" To this Landis provided a brief and direct reply: "No, Robin, I did not." When Roberts followed up by asking if he had "ever, ever used any type of performance enhancing drug," he again replied with "no, I have not." Landis' brevity may have been intended to match the directness of Roberts' question, or it may have been an attempt to convey a confidence or conviction in his own innocence. Landis' interaction with Matt Lauer on the *Today Show* practically mirrored his conversation with Robin Roberts.

3.3. DEFEASIBILITY

Having flatly denied cheating to win the Tour de France, Landis still had to account for the presence of an abnormal ratio of testosterone in his body. When explaining the chemical irregularity, Landis claimed a lack of knowledge about how the testosterone got into his system, as well as a lack of control over the test results. At his press conference, he argued, "my physiological parameters of testosterone and epitestosterone are high, as of those of any other sportsman [*sic*]. And in special cases, as in mine, for natural reasons, this level is higher still." Although Landis is a bit vague about what makes his case "special," he proclaims that the abnormality in his test results is not of his own doing. Through the technique of defeasibility, Landis attempted to evade responsibility for his positive test results.

Landis continued to use defeasibility as a strategy for image repair during his conversation with Larry King. At this time an effort was made to provide some more specific reasons his testosterone levels were unusually high. Both he and his physician, Dr. Brent Kay, advanced the possibility that the skewed testosterone levels were the result of Landis consuming a number of alcoholic beverages the night before producing the questionable sample. Landis claimed that after having a particularly bad day of racing, he "did what a normal person would do on an ordinary bad day and had a beer and a little bit of Jack Daniels" (*Larry King Live*). Kay later alluded to some research that suggests alcohol can triple one's testosterone level.

Known by many to suffer from a serious hip problem as well as arthritis, Landis (and Kay) referenced the medication he had been taking for his injuries. The implication was that medication, just like alcohol, could be responsible for raising the natural levels of testosterone in Landis' body. By introducing several hypotheses into the public dialogue about what could have caused the spike in his testosterone, Landis and his associates attempted to reduce his culpability and evade responsibility for his own test results.

Shortly after the press conference and his appearance on *Larry King Live*, the media reported that the testosterone found in Landis' system was synthetic and therefore could not have been produced by his body. In other words, this news rendered the claim that Landis' testosterone was naturally, and accidentally increased due to alcohol intake or medication, far less plausible. Perhaps it is for this reason that Landis stopped using defeasibility as a defense strategy. In fact, his excuses regarding alcohol and medication actually became the media's focus as they accused him of lying and advancing bogus excuses for his positive test results.

3.4. BOLSTERING

Throughout his image repair discourse Landis also tried to reduce the offensiveness of the act of which he was accused by creating a favorable public opinion of himself. One of the primary grounds upon which Landis attempted to bolster his image was by touting his hard work and determination. He made references to his "many years of training," his "devotion to cycling" and "thousands of kilometers" that he cycled in preparation for the event (Press Conference).

This sort of rhetoric not only has the potential to make Landis look like a hard worker and a decent person, but it also suggests reasons other than drug abuse for Landis' victory in the Tour de France. Dr. Brent Kay also attempted to bolster Landis' image, arguing, "Floyd is about as tough as they come... I've seen that first hand. I've seen his training data. I've seen how hard he works. His training is legendary in the cycling area" (*Larry King Live*). Former Tour de France winner Lance Armstrong and Landis' wife, Amber, also appeared through Landis' image repair campaign to discuss Landis' determination and strength of character.

Landis' reaction to the charges against him should also be considered a form of bolstering. He portrayed himself as essentially naïve regarding matters of doping and drug testing, while at the same time attempting to seem proactive and cooperative. He claimed to be "equally surprised as everyone else" at the results of his doping test (Press Conference). He also expressed an ignorance of doping procedures and claimed that he would be willing to undergo any tests necessary for providing that he was not into doping. Even while maintaining his own innocence he managed to praise the strict anti-doping policies that were currently plaguing him, saying, "the good thing is that the people in this sport that makes mistakes aren't—aren't ignored" (*Larry King Live*).

3.5. ATTACKING THE ACCUSER

Landis and his supporters attacked both the competence and character of the Anti-Doping Agency. In doing so, he attempted to portray himself as the target of unjust accusations and wrongdoing. During a phone call to *Larry King Live*, Lance Armstrong suggested that the lab that analyzed Landis' failed sample was less than credible. He offered, "keep it in mind that the laboratory here that found this abnormal reading is the same lab that I've been involved in with all the allegations over in France." Armstrong referenced the problems that he had with the lab in the past as a means for demonstrating that the lab was untrustworthy and potentially even malicious. After all, the lab had made several accusations against him, but he had never been formally charged with breaking any rules because of the labs' presumed inefficiencies:

> and this is the same lab that through the independent investigation and that process would not answer the simplest of questions to the independent investigator about the ethics of what they did and who conducted the testing and what conditions were they done under. You know I'm a little skeptical of this particular laboratory and the report backs up that skepticism.

The lab, according to Armstrong, is unreliable and untrustworthy and he used his own personal experience to back this up. Dr. Kay also attacked the drug labs by arguing that the unexpected lab results could have been "due to a variety of other factors with handling and specimen contamination and various other things," thus raising doubts as to the legitimacy of the results (*Larry King Live*). He next argued that the results are undependable because the test itself lacks validity: "there is a long list of potential problems with the test. This is the original test that was designed and put into place 25 years ago and has not really been significantly altered during that time period" (*Larry King Live*). The lab and its procedures are simply not competent according to these statements. The idea here is that by reducing the credibility of the accuser, Landis and company can make the claims against him seem less serious and less convincing.

Importantly, competence is not the only component that makes up credibility, and so Landis also attacked the organization's character. He claimed that the United States Anti-Doping Association had privately offered to drop their case against him if he would testify against his friend and former teammate Lance Armstrong on similar charges from several years prior. This led Landis "to believe that there's something over and above them just trying to clean up sports" (*Early Show*). An interaction between Larry King and Lance Armstrong went so far as to suggest that anti-Americanism could be an impetus for the accusations against Landis. These sort of counter-accusations portray the Anti-Doping Agency as frivolous, wicked, and untrustworthy. If accepted, these charges could make Landis look like a victim of the Anti-Doping Agency's dirty tricks.

4. Evaluation of Landis' image repair effort

Generally speaking, Floyd Landis' image repair efforts ought to be judged a failure. Not only did his rhetoric fail to persuade authorities such as the USADA and the Phonak racing team of his innocence, but unscientific (non-random) poll data suggests Landis actually lost public support during this time. On August 12, 2006, 19% of the readers of the *Intelligencer Journal*, which is published in Landis' hometown of Lancaster, Pennsylvania, believed Landis had used banned substance to win the Tour de France ("People Poll," June 2). Nearly a year later on July 27, 2007, the *Intelligencer* reported that results of a similar poll saw that number jump to 45% ("People Poll," August 12). Of course, these numbers are not representative of the rest of America's or the world's perception of Landis. Still, it indicates that even after a major media blitz, Landis became less credible in the eyes of people from his own hometown.

Landis and his crisis management team butchered the image repair efforts so badly that Landis was actually forced to defend his defense (Zeigler, 2007, July 8). Robin Roberts of ABC challenged Landis by making remarks such as, "People feel that, in the beginning, some of the statements that you made, that you didn't vigorously defend yourself," and "it seems like you have contradicted yourself" (*Good Morning America*). Analysis of Landis' discourse in relation to theories of image repair suggests that Roberts was right: Landis contradicted himself.

Landis began his efforts to defend his image by using denial and differentiation. According to Ware and Linkugel (1973), this represents an "absolutive" stance intended to claim unconditional innocence and conclusively clear the accused of all charges. Although this strategy might seem the simple and clear choice of any guiltless individual, Landis severely complicated the way audiences might normally interpret an absolutive stance by incorporating defeasibility tactics as well. Benoit (1995a) reports that as a rhetorical strategy, evasion of responsibility is usually reserved "for those who are unable to deny performing the act in question" (p. 76). However, Landis had already denied that he performed any wrongful act. This leads to a problematic contradiction in the logic of Landis' defense. To include defeasibility strategies alongside denial and differentiation is to claim, "nothing happened, but if something did happen, here's how it happened." Careful analysis of Landis' claims reveals a rather complicated and ill-advised strategy that might not have been appreciated, accepted, or even understood by some of his audience. Landis' case speaks to the problems of using denial in tandem with evasion of responsibility. When anti-doping agencies produced further evidence in refutation of Landis' denial and differentiation, his attempt at evading responsibility made him look inconsistent and dishonest.

Importantly, Landis' execution of the defeasibility strategy was just as imprudent as his selection of the strategy in the first place. When attempting to account for his positive test results, he and his doctors offered several possibilities: maybe it was because of the alcohol he drank the night before, or maybe it was related to the medication he took for his bad hip. At the very least, these explanations could be said to lack plausibility. At the worst, they might be downright silly. On the *Today Show*, Matt Lauer confronted Landis about his litany of excuses, highlighting the fact that Landis' overall attempt to defend himself had been a relative failure:

> Well, let me—let me come up with some of those reasons and you tell me what was actually something that came from your mouth and what was just attributed to you. In the days following the first positive test I heard a lot of excuses, Floyd. One, that this is a flawed test. Another day I heard perhaps this was because of beer or Jack Daniels that you had consumed. And on another occasion that this was a naturally occurring phenomenon in your body. What's the truth?

Having had a week to evaluate and interpret Landis' original remarks, Lauer and much of the country appear to have begun to judge Landis a liar. Lauer, like other journalists, essentially asked Landis to defend his original defense. This is not a situation in which rhetors intent on repairing their image would wish to find themselves. Indeed, it ought to be considered an indication of the public's reluctance to alter their opinion about the offending individual.

Having discussed Landis' awkward combination of image repair strategies, this analysis now turns to a second major conclusion regarding Landis' failed rhetoric: his incorporation of third party bolstering was ill constructed. Landis' discourse therefore provides some important qualifiers to Nelson's (1984) contention that third party bolstering can be particularly effective for defending someone's image. Most of the third party bolstering utilized to improve Landis' image came from individuals who either lacked credibility or whose motives could be questioned. Most audiences likely recognized that Landis' doctors and lawyers had monetary incentive to aid their client, Landis, rather than objectively interpret the facts at hand. Despite their apparent authority, these sources may have been judged by some audiences as biased or untrustworthy. As for the sympathetic statements that Lance Armstrong made on Landis' behalf, those too lacked credibility because he had also been charged with doping in previous years. His words, like those of Landis' lawyers, could be interpreted by audiences as self-serving. When Armstrong attacks Landis' accusers, it might seem as though he is merely trying to settle a score.

The final argument presented here is that Landis' attacks against his accusers actually hurt his image repair efforts. He and his associates leveled numerous charges against both the USADA and the media. Although this was not by any means Landis' primary defense strategy (it rarely is for anyone), and although it makes sense to diminish an accuser's credibility, these attacks likely came off as spiteful and even childish. With so much evidence mounting against him, it did Landis little good to claim that everyone was out to get him. His claims that world doping agencies were anti-American and used sub-standard testing techniques lacked evidence and were likely viewed similarly to, and in combination with, his suggestion that whiskey may have been responsible for the presence of synthetic testosterone in his urine sample. When primary image repair strategies fail, secondary and tertiary strategies may exacerbate situations by encouraging tired audiences to make negative evaluations of the accused's character. Of course, the reverse is also possible here: Secondary and tertiary strategies, when poorly designed and executed, may actually detract from one's primary strategies. Landis' attempts at bolstering and attacking his accuser largely skirt the main issue in this case, which is, "How did synthetic testosterone get in Floyd Landis' urine?"

5. Conclusion

An evaluation of Landis' failed image repair efforts suggests numerous implications for image repair communication. First, this analysis suggests that it is in the best interest of those who wish to repair their image to keep their strategies relatively simple. The combination of denial, differentiation and evasion of responsibility can come off as complicated, inconsistent, and disorganized. It may have been wise of Landis to choose between either denial or evading responsibility, but these two strategies may contradict one another in the minds of audiences. If a person claims not to have committed an act, why then must he or she explain the act? Landis' strategies relied heavily on one another, meaning that if one strategy failed, all the rest would be put in jeopardy as well.

One of the primary reasons that Landis' image repair efforts failed is because during his attempt to clear his name, evidence surfaced that directly contradicted his explanations. Two suggestions could be made for those who wish to avoid similar problems in their own image repair efforts. One would be that people should make a prompt, initial response to charges of wrongdoing, but they should wait until all evidence concerning the accusations against them have been understood before communicating in too much detail to the public. Only after assessing the relevant facts should a defense strategy be put into action. Public relations specialists rightly preach the importance of immediate responses to image crises, but this should not come at the expense of the overall image repair effort. In some cases, it makes sense to proceed more carefully with one's image repair messages.

A second suggestion would be to simply admit wrongdoing through the strategy of mortification. Kruse's (1981) analysis of apologia and team sport suggested that apologies are a common and effective mode of defense for athletes, labeling the apology "a convention of the discourse" (p. 281). Importantly, an admission of guilt would have meant the same endgame for Landis as far as the anti-doping agency is concerned. He would have been stripped of his Tour de France title and banned from racing during some of his most competitive years. In some ways, the only thing Landis had to lose by denying the allegations was public support. Furthermore, very few athletes have confessed to the use of performance enhancing drugs. Barry Bonds, Mark McGuire, and Roger Clemens, just to name a few baseball players, have all been accused of steriod use, but have held fast to their innocence. This is certainly dubious company for Landis to keep, but at the very least, he avoids being cast out as a solitary whipping boy.

This analysis also suggests that third party bolstering is not unconditionally effective. If one wishes to benefit from the positive things that others have to say about them, it is best if those people appear as though they have little or nothing to gain by offering their assistance. Close friends and relatives who offer a personal perspective about the character of individuals accused of wrongful acts offer sentiments that resonate with audiences. Lawyers and doctors who may be regarded as "hired guns" by an audience have may have less ability to influence audiences despite their ostensible authority.

Additionally, it ought to be understood that as a defense strategy, attacking an accuser can only do so much to help a rhetor's image if other strategies are not chosen and executed properly. The most well implemented component of Landis' public relations effort was the way in which he attacked the credibility of the agency and laboratory responsible for determining and revealing his failed test results. Furthermore, his discussion of how the media has hounded him and his family may have also cultivated some sympathy and distracted audiences from the wrongdoing with which he was charged. However, these strategies may make a person look desperate or mean spirited if other strategies have not begun to sway the audience's opinions in his or her favor.

In addition to the three contributions to theory and criticism of image repair discourse that are offered above, this analysis derives additional importance from its subject matter. Although there have been several scholarly examinations of athlete's image repair efforts, none of them has dealt with accusations of performance enhancing drugs. In almost all professional sports, particularly Major League Baseball, charges of using steroids are becoming increasingly common.

This study presents an initial attempt at understanding the means by which athletes can defend themselves against such allegations. Due to both the innate qualities and learned skills that lead people to adopt certain vocations, there is reason to believe that professional athletes might be at a major disadvantage when called to defend themselves in public. Most image repair studies have focused on the communication of politicians, corporate officers, and entertainers, all of which have reputations as above average communicators. Athletes, who are far less likely to possess the skills or training necessary for communicating effectively to a diversity of audiences, may have a much greater challenge to meet when attempting to repair their public image. Image repair theory can certainly benefit from further study of athletes, particularly when they are accused of using performance enhancing substances.

References

Benoit, W. L. (1995a). *Accounts, excuses, and apologies: A theory of image restoration discourse.* Albany, NY: State University of New York Press.

Benoit, W. L. (1995b). Sears' repair of its auto repair image: Image restoration discourse in the corporate sector. *Communication Studies, 46,* 89–109.

Benoit, W. L. (1997). Hugh Grant's image restoration discourse: An actor apologizes. *Communication Quarterly, 45,* 251–267.

Benoit, W. L., & Brinson, S. L. (1994). AT&T: Apologies are not enough. *Communication Quarterly, 42,* 75–88.

Benoit, W. L., & Czerwinski, A. (1997). A critical analysis of USAir's image repair discourse. *Business Communication Quarterly, 60,* 38–57.

Benoit, W. L., & Hanczor, R. (1994). The Tonya Harding controversy: An analysis of image repair strategies. *Communication Quarterly, 42,* 416–433.

Benoit, W. L., & McHale, J. P. (1999). Kenneth Starr's image repair discourse viewed in 20/20. *Communication Quarterly, 47,* 265–280.

Benoit, W. L., & Nill, D. M. (1998a). A critical analysis of Judge Clarence Thomas's statement before the Senate Judiciary Committee. *Communication Studies, 49,* 179–195.

Benoit, W. L., & Nill, D. M. (1998b). Oliver Stone's defense of JFK. *Communication Quarterly, 46,* 127–143.

Benoit, W. L., Gullifor, P., & Panici, D. A. (1991). President Reagan's defensive discourse on the Iran-Contra affair. *Communication Studies, 42,* 272–294.

Blaney, J. R., & Benoit, W. L. (2001). *The Clinton scandals and the politics of image restoration.* Westport, CT: Praeger.

Brinson, S. L., & Benoit, W. L. (1996). Dow Corning's image strategies in the breast implant crisis. *Communication Quarterly, 44,* 29–41.

Burke, K. (1961). *Rhetoric of religion.* Berkeley, CA: University of California Press.

Coombs, T., & Schmidt, L. (2000). An empirical analysis of image restoration: Texaco's racism crisis. *Journal of Public Relations Research, 12,* 163–178.

King, G., III. (2006). Image restoration: An examination of the response strategies used by Brown and Williamson after allegations of wrongdoing. *Public Relations Review, 32,* 131–136.

Knott, T. (2009, May 11). Steroid cheaters are pregnant with excuses. *Washington Times,* C01.

Kogoy, P. (2009, January 24). Armstrong backs disgraced Landis. *Weekend Australian,* 55.

Kruse, N. W. (1981). Apologia in team sport. *Quarterly Journal of Speech, 67,* 270–283.

Len-Rios, M. E., & Benoit, W. L. (2004). Gary Condit's image repair strategies: Determined denial and differentiation. *Public Relations Review, 30,* 95–106.

Macur, J. (2009, February 18). Landis is on the road again, but detours from attention. *New York Times,* 17.

Nelson, J. (1984). The defense of Billie Jean King. *Western Journal of Speech Communication, 48,* 92–102.

People poll. (2006, August 12). People poll: Did Floyd Landis cheat? *Intelligencer Journal* [Electronic Version].

People poll. (2007, June 2). *Intelligencer Journal* [Electronic Version].

Scott, M. H., & Lyman, S. M. (1968). Accounts. *American Sociological Review, 33,* 46–62.

Thompson, T., & Vinton, N. (2009, May 10). Playing hardball: Manny ban shows commitment from MLB to catch drug cheats. *New York Daily News,* p54.

Ware, B. L., & Linkugel, W. A. (1973). They spoke in defense of themselves: On the generic criticism of apologia. *Quarterly Journal of Communication, 38,* 82–89.

Zeigler, M. (2007, July 8). *Under attack: Landis pedaling uphill against accusers.* San Diego: Union-Tribune.

DISCUSSION *questions and activities*

1. Write a one-sentence summary of Glantz's evaluation of Landis' efforts to repair his image. Compare your statement with those of three other students in your class. Discuss any differences in your readings and craft a negotiated summary of Glantz's argument.

2. In the section subtitled "the theory of image repair discourse," Glantz outlines five broad strategies that may be employed by rhetors. Working in small groups, define each category briefly and come up with examples from current American culture where a public figure has used these strategies. Do this for at least two of the categories.

3. In small groups, come up with a hypothetical public relations crisis for a fictitious character; your character could be a politician, an athlete, an actor, or another public figure. Once you've figured out the details of the crisis, write a brief speech that uses some of the strategies discussed in the article in order to repair the figure's image.

The Median Isn't the Message

Stephen Jay Gould

Stephen Jay Gould (1941–2002), one of the United States' most respected scientists, focused primarily on evolutionary science, fossil study, and diversity and change. He was noteworthy because he could translate the specialized language and thorny issues of science for an unspecialized audience. A Harvard professor and author of almost twenty books and hundreds of articles, he is also the only author in this book to have been animated on The Simpsons. A personal essay, "The Median Isn't the Message" focuses on Gould's experience with mesothelioma, a cancer associated with exposure to asbestos, and how his interpretation of the data influenced his approach to the illness.

My life has recently intersected, in a most personal way, two of Mark Twain's famous quips. One I shall defer to the end of this essay. The other (sometimes attributed to Disraeli), identifies three species of mendacity, each worse than the one before—lies, damned lies, and statistics.

Consider the standard example of stretching the truth with numbers—a case quite relevant to my story. Statistics recognizes different measures of an "average," or central tendency. The *mean* is our usual concept of an overall average—add up the items and divide them by the number of sharers (100 candy bars collected for five kids next Halloween will yield 20 for each in a just world). The *median*, a different measure of central tendency, is the half-way point. If I line up five kids by height, the median child is shorter than two and taller than the other two (who might have trouble getting their mean share of the candy). A politician in power might say with pride, "The mean income of our citizens is $15,000 per year." The leader of the opposition might retort, "But half our citizens make less than $10,000 per year." Both are right, but neither cites a statistic with impassive objectivity. The first invokes a mean, the second a median. (Means are higher than medians in such cases because one millionaire may outweigh hundreds of poor people in setting a mean; but he can balance only one mendicant in calculating a median).

The larger issue that creates a common distrust or contempt for statistics is more troubling. Many people make an unfortunate and invalid separation between heart and mind, or feeling and intellect. In some contemporary traditions, abetted by attitudes stereotypically centered on Southern California, feelings are exalted as more "real" and the only proper basis for action—if it feels good, do it—while intellect gets short shrift as a hang-up of outmoded elitism. Statistics, in this absurd dichotomy, often become the symbol of the enemy. As Hilaire Belloc wrote, "Statistics are the triumph of the quantitative method, and the quantitative method is the victory of sterility and death."

This is a personal story of statistics, properly interpreted, as profoundly nurturant and life-giving. It declares holy war on the downgrading of intellect by telling a small story about the utility of dry, academic knowledge about science. Heart and head are focal points of one body, one personality.

In July 1982, I learned that I was suffering from abdominal mesothelioma, a rare and serious cancer usually associated with exposure to asbestos. When I revived after surgery, I asked my first question of my doctor and chemotherapist: "What is the best technical literature about mesothelioma?" She replied, with a touch of diplomacy (the only departure she has ever made from direct frankness), that the medical literature contained nothing really worth reading.

Of course, trying to keep an intellectual away from literature works about as well as recommending chastity to *Homo sapiens*, the sexiest primate of all. As soon as I could walk, I made a beeline for Harvard's Countway medical library and punched mesothelioma into the computer's bibliographic search program. An hour later, surrounded by the latest literature on abdominal mesothelioma, I realized with a gulp why my doctor had offered that humane advice. The literature couldn't have been more brutally clear: mesothelioma is incurable, with a median mortality of only eight months after discovery. I sat stunned for about fifteen minutes, then smiled and said to myself: so that's why they didn't give me anything to read. Then my mind started to work again, thank goodness.

If a little learning could ever be a dangerous thing, I had encountered a classic example. Attitude clearly matters in fighting cancer. We don't know why (from my old-style materialistic perspective, I suspect that mental states feed back upon the immune system). But match people with the same cancer for age, class, health, socioeconomic status, and, in general, those with positive attitudes, with a strong will and purpose for living, with commitment to struggle, with an active response to aiding their own treatment and not just a passive acceptance of anything doctors say, tend to live longer. A few months later I asked Sir Peter Medawar, my personal scientific guru and a Nobelist in immunology, what the best prescription for success against cancer might be. "A sanguine personality," he replied. Fortunately (since one can't reconstruct oneself at short notice and for a definite purpose), I am, if anything, even-tempered and confident in just this manner.

Hence the dilemma for humane doctors: since attitude matters so critically, should such a sombre conclusion be advertised, especially since few people have sufficient understanding of statistics to evaluate what the statements really mean? From years of experience with the small-scale evolution of Bahamian land snails treated quantitatively, I have developed this technical knowledge—and I am convinced that it played a major role in saving my life. Knowledge is indeed power, in Bacon's proverb.

The problem may be briefly stated: What does "median mortality of eight months" signify in our vernacular? I suspect that most people, without training in statistics, would read such a statement as "I will probably be dead in eight months"—the very conclusion that must be avoided, since it isn't so, and since attitude matters so much.

I was not, of course, overjoyed, but I didn't read the statement in this vernacular way either. My technical training enjoined a different perspective on "eight months median mortality." The point is a subtle one, but profound—for it embodies the distinctive way of thinking in my own field of evolutionary biology and natural history.

We still carry the historical baggage of a Platonic heritage that seeks sharp essences and definite boundaries. (Thus we hope to find an unambiguous "beginning of life" or "definition of death," although nature often comes to us as irreducible continua.) This Platonic heritage, with its emphasis in clear distinctions and separated immutable entities, leads us to view statistical measures of central tendency wrongly, indeed opposite to the appropriate interpretation in our actual world of variation, shadings, and continua. In short, we view means and medians as the hard "realities," and the variation that permits their calculation as a set of transient and imperfect measurements of this hidden essence. If the median is the reality and variation around the median just a device for its calculation, the "I will probably be dead in eight months" may pass as a reasonable interpretation.

But all evolutionary biologists know that variation itself is nature's only irreducible essence. Variation is the hard reality, not a set of imperfect measures for a central tendency. Means and medians are the abstractions. Therefore, I looked at the mesothelioma statistics quite differently—and not only because I am an optimist who tends to see the doughnut instead of the hole, but primarily because I know that variation itself is the reality. I had to place myself amidst the variation.

When I learned about the eight-month median, my first intellectual reaction was: fine, half the people will live longer; now what are my chances of being in that half. I read for a furious and nervous hour and concluded, with relief: damned good. I possessed every one of the characteristics conferring a probability of longer life: I was young; my disease had been recognized in a relatively early stage; I would receive the nation's best medical treatment; I had the world to live for; I knew how to read the data properly and not despair.

Another technical point then added even more solace. I immediately recognized that the distribution of variation about the eight-month median would almost surely be what statisticians call "right skewed." (In a symmetrical distribution, the profile of variation to the left of the central tendency is a mirror image of variation to the right. In skewed distributions, variation to one side of the central tendency is more stretched out—left skewed if extended to the left, right skewed if stretched out to the right.) The distribution of variation had to be right skewed, I reasoned. After all, the left of the distribution contains an irrevocable lower boundary of zero (since mesothelioma can only be identified at death or before). Thus, there isn't much room for the distribution's lower (or left) half—it must be scrunched up between zero and eight months. But the upper (or right) half can extend out for years and years, even if nobody ultimately survives. The distribution must be right skewed, and I needed to know how long the extended tail ran—for I had already concluded that my favorable profile made me a good candidate for that part of the curve.

The distribution was indeed, strongly right skewed, with a long tail (however small) that extended for several years above the eight month median. I saw no reason why I shouldn't be in that small tail, and I breathed a very long sigh of relief. My technical knowledge had helped. I had read the graph correctly. I had asked the right question and found the answers. I had obtained, in all probability, the most precious of all possible gifts in the circumstances—substantial time. I didn't have to stop and immediately follow Isaiah's injunction to Hezekiah—set thine house in order for thou shalt die, and not live. I would have time to think, to plan, and to fight.

One final point about statistical distributions. They apply only to a prescribed set of circumstances —in this case to survival with mesothelioma under conventional modes of treatment. If circumstances change, the distribution may alter. I was placed on an experimental protocol of treatment and, if fortune holds, will be in the first cohort of a new distribution with high median and a right tail extending to death by natural causes at advanced old age.

It has become, in my view, a bit too trendy to regard the acceptance of death as something tantamount to intrinsic dignity. Of course I agree with the preacher of Ecclesiastes that there is a time to love and a time to die—and when my skein runs out I hope to face the end calmly and in my own way. For most situations, however, I prefer the more martial view that death is the ultimate enemy—and I find nothing reproachable in those who rage mightily against the dying of the light.

The swords of battle are numerous, and none more effective than humor. My death was announced at a meeting of my colleagues in Scotland, and I almost experienced the delicious pleasure of reading my obituary penned by one of my best friends (the so-and-so got suspicious and checked; he too is a statistician, and didn't expect to find me so far out on the right tail). Still, the incident provided my first good laugh after the diagnosis. Just think, I almost got to repeat Mark Twain's most famous line of all: the reports of my death are greatly exaggerated.

DISCUSSION *questions and activities*

1. What argumentative techniques does Gould use to convince readers how statistics and data should be perceived? Which ones strike you as most effective?

2. Gould is admired for his ability to make scientific concepts accessible to a novice audience. Identify moments in the text where he seems to place his scientific persona aside and reach out to the common reader. Do you think this is an appropriate choice, or does it compromise his credibility as a scientist?

3. Many students overvalue statistics in research, weighting them higher than other methods of proof. To what extent do you see this habit in your own writing, and what might be the reason? What larger implications might Gould's discussion have on using statistics in argumentation?

Cut This Story!
Newspaper Articles are Too Long.

Michael Kinsley

Michael Kinsley is a lawyer, journalist, and media figure who specializes in political reporting. He has been a host of the television talk show Crossfire *and was a founder of* Slate, *an online magazine that covers current affairs. This article was written for the January/February 2010 State of the Union issue of* The Atlantic, *a magazine of political and intellectual life founded in Boston in 1857. Kinsley's critique of journalistic discourse comes at a time when newpapers are closing across the country and the future of print media is a subject of debate. The Atlantic's website is www.theatlantic.com.*

One reason seekers of news are abandoning print newspapers for the Internet has nothing directly to do with technology. It's that newspaper articles are too long. On the Internet, news articles get to the point. Newspaper writing, by contrast, is encrusted with conventions that don't add to your understanding of the news. Newspaper writers are not to blame. These conventions are traditional, even mandatory.

Take, for example, the lead story in *The New York Times* on Sunday, November 8, 2009, headlined "Sweeping Health Care Plan Passes House." There is nothing special about this article. November 8 is just the day I happened to need an example for this column. And there it was. The 1,456-word report begins:

Handing President Obama a hard-fought victory, the House narrowly approved a sweeping overhaul of the nation's health care system on Saturday night, advancing legislation that Democrats said could stand as their defining social policy achievement.

Fewer than half the words in this opening sentence are devoted to saying what happened. If someone saw you reading the paper and asked, "So what's going on?," you would not likely begin by saying that President Obama had won a hard-fought victory. You would say, "The House passed health-care reform last night." And maybe, "It was a close vote." And just possibly, "There was a kerfuffle about abortion." You would not likely refer to "a sweeping overhaul of the nation's health care system," as if your friend was unaware that health-care reform was going on. Nor would you feel the need to inform your friend first thing that unnamed Democrats were bragging about what a big deal this is—an unsurprising development if ever there was one.

Once upon a time, this unnecessary stuff was considered an advance over dry news reporting: don't just tell the story; tell the reader what it means. But providing "context," as it was known, has become an invitation to hype. In this case, it's the lowest form of hype—it's horse-race hype—which actually diminishes a story rather than enhancing it. Surely if this event is such a big, big deal—"sweeping" and "defining" its way into our awareness—then its effect on the next election is one of the less important things about it. There's an old joke about the provincial newspaper that reports a nuclear attack on the nation's largest city under the headline "Local Man Dies in NY Nuclear Holocaust." Something similar happens at the national level, where everything is filtered through politics. ("In what was widely seen as a setback for Democrats just a year before the midterm elections, nuclear bombs yesterday obliterated seven states, five of which voted for President Obama in the last election…")

It could be worse. Here is *The Washington Post's* lead on the same health-care story:

> *Hours after President Obama exhorted Democratic lawmakers to "answer the call of history," the House hit an unprecedented milestone on the path to health-care reform, approving a trillion-dollar package late Saturday that seeks to overhaul private insurance practices and guarantee comprehensive and affordable coverage to almost every American.*

Give *The Post* points for at least attempting to say what the bill does, but take them away again for the bungled milestone metaphor (you don't "hit" a milestone if you hope to reach the next one), and for allowing Obama to fill the first 13 words of the piece with tired rhetoric. The *Times* piece, by contrast, waits until the third paragraph to quote Representative George Miller, who said, "This is our moment to revolutionize health care in this country." That is undeniably true. If there was ever a moment to revolutionize health care, it would be the moment when legislation revolutionizing health care has just passed. But is this news? Did anybody say to anybody else, "Wait'll you hear what George Miller just said"? The quote is 11 words, while identifying Miller takes 16. And there's more:

> *"Now is the chance to fix our health care system and improve the lives of millions of Americans," Representative Louise M. Slaughter, Democrat of New York and chairwoman of the Rules Committee, said as she opened the daylong proceedings.*

(Quote: 18 words; identification: 21 words.)

Meanwhile, Republicans oppose the bill. Yes, they do. And if you haven't surmised this from the duly reported fact that all but one of them voted against it, perhaps you will find another quote informative.

> *"More taxes, more spending and more government is not the plan for reform the people support," said Representative Virginia Foxx, Republican of North Carolina and one of the conservatives who relentlessly criticized the Democrats' plan.*

(Quote: 16 words; identification, 19 words.)

Quotes from outside experts or observers are also a rich source of unnecessary verbiage in newspaper articles. Another *New York Times* story from the November 8 front page provides a good example here. It's about how the crackdown on some Wall Street bonuses may have backfired. Executives were forced to take stock instead of cash, but then the stock went up, damn it. This is an "enterprise" story—one the reporter or an editor came up with, not one dictated by events. And the reporter clearly views the information it contains as falling somewhere between ironic and appalling, which seems about right. But it's not her job to have a view. In fact, it's her job to *not* have a view. Even though it's her story and her judgment, she must find someone else—an expert or an observer—to repeat and endorse her conclusion. These quotes then magically turn an opinionated story into an objective one. And so:

> *"People have to look at the sizable gains that have been made since stock and options were granted last year, and the fact is this was, in many ways, a windfall," said Jesse M. Brill, the chairman of CompensationStandards.com, a trade publication. "This had nothing to do with people's performance. These were granted at market lows."*

Those are 56 words spent allowing Jesse M. Brill to restate the author's point. Yet I, for one, have never heard of Jesse M. Brill before. He may be a fine fellow. But I have no particular reason to trust him, and he has no particular reason to need my trust. *The New York Times*, on the other hand, does need my trust, or it is out of business. So it has a strong incentive to earn my trust every day (which it does, with rare and historic exceptions). But instead of asking me to trust it and its reporter about the thesis of this piece, *The New York Times* asks me to trust this person I have never heard of, Jesse M. Brill.

Of course this attempt to pass the hot potato to a total stranger doesn't work, because before I can trust Jesse M. Brill about the thesis of the piece, I have to trust *The New York Times* that this Jesse M. Brill person is trustworthy, and the article under examination devotes many words to telling me who he is so that I will trust him. (By contrast, it tells me nothing about the reporter.) Why not cut out the middleman? The reason to trust this story, if you choose to do so, is that it is in *The New York Times*. What Jesse M. Brill may think adds nothing. Yet he is only one of several experts quoted throughout, basically telling the story all over again.

In the current financial crisis, *The New York Times* and other papers seem to have given reporters more leeway than ever before to express their opinions directly. Editors may have realized that these issues are hard enough to explain without running into roadblocks at every turn labeled warning: opinion territory ahead. But the old wordy conventions survive. Quotes from strangers restating the reporter's opinion are one. Another is adding protective qualifiers to statements about which there is no real doubt (as when I wrote above that the bonus restrictions "may have" backfired). A third—illustrated by the headline on that story, "Windfall Seen as Bonuses Are Paid in Stock"—is to attribute the article's conclusion to unnamed others. Somebody sees a windfall. We're just telling you about it.

The software industry has a concept known as "legacy code," meaning old stuff that is left in software programs, even after they are revised and updated, so that they will still work with older operating systems. The equivalent exists in newspaper stories, which are written to accommodate readers who have just emerged from a coma or a coal mine. Who needs to be told that reforming health care (three words) involves "a sweeping overhaul of the nation's health care system" (nine words)? Who needs to be reminded that Hillary Clinton tried this in her husband's administration without success? Anybody who doesn't know these things already is unlikely to care. (Is, in fact, unlikely to be reading the article.)

Then there is "inverted-pyramid style"—an image I have never quite understood—which stands for the principle of putting the most-crucial information at the top of a story and leaving the details for below. Pyramid style is regarded as a bit old-fashioned these days, hence all those florid subordinate clauses at the top of both the *Times* and the *Post* versions of the health-care story. The revolt against pyramid style is also why you get those you'll-never-guess-what-this-is-about, faux-mystery narrative leads about Martha Lewis, a 57-year-old retired nurse, who was sitting in her living room one day last month watching *Oprah* when the FedEx delivery man rang her doorbell with an innocent-looking envelope…and so on. (The popularity of this device is puzzling, since the headline—"Oprah Arrested in FedEx Anthrax Plot"—generally gives the story away.) But ruthless adherence to classic inverted-pyramid style can also lead to repetition of the story again and again, with one or two more nuggets of information each time.

And then, finally, comes the end, or "tag." Few writers can resist the lure of closure—some form of summing-up or leave-taking. Often this is a quote that repeats the central point one last time, perhaps combining it with some rueful irony about the limits of human agency. The *Times* health-care article does this. "'Our plan is not perfect, but it is a good start toward providing affordable health care to all Americans,' said Representative Peter A. DeFazio of Oregon." The same day's story in *The Post* does it too, with a quote too long to quote.

On the first day of my first real job in journalism—on the copy desk at the *Royal Oak Daily Tribune* in Royal Oak, Michigan—the chief copy editor said, "Remember, every word you cut saves the publisher money." At the time, saving the publisher money didn't strike me as the world's noblest ideal. These days, for anyone in journalism, it's more compelling.

DISCUSSION *questions and activities*

1. What does Kinsley criticize about the way that contemporary news stories are written?
2. Do you read print journalism on a regular basis? Explain your choices.
3. What kind of solution does Kinsley propose for making news stories more readable and informative for contemporary audiences? Would any of his ideas apply to college writing?

The Case for Short Words

Richard Lederer

Richard Lederer spent the first 27 years of his career as a high school English teacher and has since become a popular and prolific author. His books, such as Verbivore *and* Get Thee to a Punnery, *often take a playful approach to the English language. "The Case for Short Words" is a chapter from his 1991 book* The Miracle of Language. *He also writes a syndicated newspaper column called "Looking at Language."*

When you speak and write, there is no law that says you have to use big words. Short words are as good as long ones, and short, old words—like *sun* and *grass* and *home*—are best of all. A lot of small words, more than you might think, can meet your needs with a strength, grace, and charm that large words do not have.

Big words can make the way dark for those who read what you write and hear what you say. Small words cast their clear light on big things—night and day, love and hate, war and peace, and life and death. Big words at times seem strange to the eye and the ear and the mind and the heart. Small words are the ones we seem to have known from the time we were born, like the hearth fire that warms the home.

Short words are bright like sparks that glow in the night, prompt like the dawn that greets the day, sharp like the blade of a knife, hot like salt tears that scald the cheek, quick like moths that flit from flame to flame, and terse like the dart and sting of a bee.

Here is a sound rule: Use small, old words where you can. If a long word says just what you want to say, do not fear to use it. But know that our tongue is rich in crisp, brisk, swift, short words. Make them the spine and the heart of what you speak and write. Short words are like fast friends. They will not let you down.

The title of this chapter and the four paragraphs that you have just read are wrought entirely of words of one syllable. In setting myself this task, I did not feel especially cabined, cribbed, or confined. In fact, the structure helped me to focus on the power of the message I was trying to put across.

One study shows that twenty words account for twenty-five percent of all spoken English words, and all twenty are monosyllabic. In order of frequency they are: *I, you, the, a, to, is, it, that, of, and, in, what, he, this, have, do, she, not, on,* and *they*. Other studies indicate that the fifty most common words in written English are each made of a single syllable.

For centuries our finest poets and orators have recognized and employed the power of small words to make a straight point between two minds. A great many of our proverbs punch home their points with pithy monosyllables: "Where there's a will, there's a way," "A stitch in time saves nine," "Spare the rod and spoil the child," "A bird in the hand is worth two in the bush."

Nobody used the short word more skillfully than William Shakespeare, whose dying King Lear laments:

And my poor fool is hang'd! No, no, no life! Why should a dog, a horse, a rat have life, And thou no breath at all?...Do you see this? Look on her, look, her lips. Look there, look there!

Shakespeare's contemporaries made the King James Bible a centerpiece of short words—"And God said. Let there be light: and there was light. And God saw the light, that it was good." The descendants of such mighty lines live on in the twentieth century. When asked to explain his policy to Parliament, Winston Churchill responded with these ringing monosyllables: "I will say: it is to wage war, by sea, land, and air, with all our might and with all our strength that God can give us." In his "Death of the Hired Man" Robert Frost observes that "Home is the place where, when you go there,/They have to take you in." And William H. Johnson uses ten two-letter words to explain his secret of success: "If it is to be,/It is up to me."

You don't have to be a great author, statesman, or philosopher to tap the energy and eloquence of small words. Each winter I ask my ninth graders at St. Paul's School to write a composition composed entirely of one-syllable words. My students greet my request with obligatory moans and groans, but, when they return to class with their essays, most feel that, with the pressure to produce high-sounding polysyllables relieved, they have created some of their most powerful and luminous prose. Here are submissions from two of my ninth graders:

What can you say to a boy who has left home? You can say that he has done wrong, but he does not care. He has left home so that he will not have to deal with what you say. He wants to go as far as he can. He will do what he wants to do.

This boy does not want to be forced to go to church, to comb his hair, or to be on time. A good time for this boy does not lie in your reach, for what you have he does not want. He dreams of ripped jeans, shorts with no starch, and old socks.

So now this boy is on a bus to a place he dreams of, a place with no rules. This boy now walks a strange street, his long hair blown back by the wind. He wears no coat or tie, just jeans and an old shirt. He hates your world, and he has left it. — Charles Shaffer

For a long time we cruised by the coast and at last came to a wide bay past the curve of a hill, at the end of which lay a small town. Our long boat ride at an end, we all stretched and stood up to watch as the boat nosed its way in.

The town climbed up the hill that rose from the shore, a space in front of it left bare for the port. Each house was a clean white with sky blue or grey trim; in front of each one was a small yard, edged by a white stone wall strewn with green vines.

As the town basked in the heat of noon, not a thing stirred in the streets or by the shore. The sun beat down on the sea, the land, and the back of our necks, so that, in spite of the breeze that made the vines sway, we all wished we could hide from the glare in a cool, white house. But, as there was no one to help dock the boat, we had to stand and wait.

At last the head of the crew leaped from the side and strode to a large house on the right. He shoved the door wide, poked his head through the gloom, and roared with a fierce voice. Five or six men came out, and soon the port was loud with the clank of chains and creak of planks as the men caught ropes thrown by the crew, pulled them taut, and tied them to posts. Then they set up a rough plank so we could cross from the deck to the shore. We all made for the large house while the crew watched, glad to be rid of us. — Celia Wren

You too can tap into the vitality and vigor of compact expression. Take a suggestion from the highway department. At the boundaries of your speech and prose place a sign that reads "Caution: Small Words at Work."

DISCUSSION *questions and activities*

1. How did you react to reading the first four paragraphs of the essay? Did you notice the consistent use of one syllable words before Lederer himself mentioned the pattern?
2. Lederer points out many benefits to using short words. Are there any potential disadvantages that might arise from using many "short, old words"?
3. Do you think you would feel "cabined, cribbed, or confined" if you tried to write an essay using only one-syllable words? Why or why not?

Chapter XVII from *The Prince*,

"Concerning Cruelty And Clemency, And Whether It Is Better To Be Loved Than Feared"

Niccolò Machiavelli

Niccolò Machiavelli (1469–1527) wrote The Prince *as a manual on how to obtain and keep political power in the context of tumultuous civic struggles in what is now the nation of Italy. His advice is coldly realistic in its embrace of practices like bribery and torture. His work was famous in its own day: Shakespeare quoted Machiavelli. In our own time, Tupac Shakur referred to himself as a "Machiavel."*

Coming now to the other qualities mentioned above, I say that every prince ought to desire to be considered clement and not cruel. Nevertheless he ought to take care not to misuse this clemency. Cesare Borgia was considered cruel; notwithstanding, his cruelty reconciled the Romagna, unified it, and restored it to peace and loyalty. And if this be rightly considered, he will be seen to have been much more merciful than the Florentine people, who, to avoid a reputation for cruelty, permitted Pistoia to be destroyed. Therefore a prince, so long as he keeps his subjects united and loyal, ought not to mind the reproach of cruelty; because with a few examples he will be more merciful than those who, through too much mercy, allow disorders to arise, from which follow murders or robberies; for these are wont to injure the whole people, whilst those executions which originate with a prince offend the individual only.

And of all princes, it is impossible for the new prince to avoid the imputation of cruelty, owing to new states being full of dangers. Hence Virgil, through the mouth of Dido, excuses the inhumanity of her reign owing to its being new, saying:

Res dura, et regni novitas me talia cogunt Moliri, et late fines custode tueri.[1]

Nevertheless he ought to be slow to believe and to act, nor should he himself show fear, but proceed in a temperate manner with prudence and humanity, so that too much confidence may not make him incautious and too much distrust render him intolerable.

Upon this a question arises: whether it be better to be loved than feared or feared than loved? It may be answered that one should wish to be both, but, because it is difficult to unite them in one person, is much safer to be feared than loved, when, of the two, either must be dispensed with. Because this is to be asserted in general of men, that they are ungrateful, fickle, false, cowardly, covetous, and as long as you succeed they are yours entirely; they will offer you their blood, property, life and children, as is said above, when the need is far distant; but when it approaches they turn against you. And that prince who, relying entirely on their promises, has neglected other precautions, is ruined; because friendships

---

1 . . . against my will, my fate,
  A throne unsettled, and an infant state,
  Bid me defend my realms with all my pow'rs,
  And guard with these severities my shores.

that are obtained by payments, and not by greatness or nobility of mind, may indeed be earned, but they are not secured, and in time of need cannot be relied upon; and men have less scruple in offending one who is beloved than one who is feared, for love is preserved by the link of obligation which, owing to the baseness of men, is broken at every opportunity for their advantage; but fear preserves you by a dread of punishment which never fails.

Nevertheless a prince ought to inspire fear in such a way that, if he does not win love, he avoids hatred; because he can endure very well being feared whilst he is not hated, which will always be as long as he abstains from the property of his citizens and subjects and from their women. But when it is necessary for him to proceed against the life of someone, he must do it on proper justification and for manifest cause, but above all things he must keep his hands off the property of others, because men more quickly forget the death of their father than the loss of their patrimony. Besides, pretexts for taking away the property are never wanting; for he who has once begun to live by robbery will always find pretexts for seizing what belongs to others; but reasons for taking life, on the contrary, are more difficult to find and sooner lapse. But when a prince is with his army, and has under control a multitude of soldiers, then it is quite necessary for him to disregard the reputation of cruelty, for without it he would never hold his army united or disposed to its duties.

Among the wonderful deeds of Hannibal this one is enumerated: that having led an enormous army, composed of many various races of men, to fight in foreign lands, no dissensions arose either among them or against the prince, whether in his bad or in his good fortune. This arose from nothing else than his inhuman cruelty, which, with his boundless valour, made him revered and terrible in the sight of his soldiers, but without that cruelty, his other virtues were not sufficient to produce this effect. And shortsighted writers admire his deeds from one point of view and from another condemn the principal cause of them. That it is true his other virtues would not have been sufficient for him may be proved by the case of Scipio, that most excellent man, not of his own times but within the memory of man, against whom, nevertheless, his army rebelled in Spain; this arose from nothing but his too great forbearance, which gave his soldiers more licence than is consistent with military discipline. For this he was upbraided in the Senate by Fabius Maximus, and called the corrupter of the Roman soldiery. The Locrians were laid waste by a legate of Scipio, yet they were not avenged by him, nor was the insolence of the legate punished, owing entirely to his easy nature. Insomuch that someone in the Senate, wishing to excuse him, said there were many men who knew much better how not to err than to correct the errors of others. This disposition, if he had been continued in the command, would have destroyed in time the fame and glory of Scipio; but, he being under the control of the Senate, this injurious characteristic not only concealed itself, but contributed to his glory.

Returning to the question of being feared or loved, I come to the conclusion that, men loving according to their own will and fearing according to that of the prince, a wise prince should establish himself on that which is in his own control and not in that of others; he must endeavour only to avoid hatred, as is noted.

DISCUSSION *questions and activities*

1. How would you explain the enduring power of Machiavelli's argument? Why do you think people keep reading his work?
2. Look up a definition of "machiavellian" in a dictionary. Do you think this adjective fairly applies to the text of *The Prince*?
3. Write a dialogue between Quintilian and Machiavelli about the definition of a rhetorician.

George Washington's Tear-Jerker

John R. Miller

John R. Miller has served as a senior fellow for the Discovery Institute, a conservative think tank and lobbying group. He is the author of a book on George Washington. This piece examines the rhetorical context and lasting relevance of Washington's Newburgh Address, which also appears in this book. His essay was printed in the Op- Ed section of The New York Times *on February 14, 2009, as the future of the war in Afghanistan was under debate in Congress.*

Civilian control of the military is a cherished principle in American government. It was President Obama who decided to increase our involvement in Afghanistan, and it is Congress that will decide whether to appropriate the money to carry out his decision. It is the president and Congress, not the military, that will decide whether our laws should be changed to allow gays and lesbians to serve in our armed forces. The military advises, but the civilian leadership decides.

Yet if not for the actions of George Washington, whose birthday we celebrate, sort of, this month, America might have moved in a very different direction.

In early 1783, with Revolutionary War victory in sight but peace uncertain, Washington and the Continental Army bivouacked at Newburgh, N.Y. Troops were enraged by Congress's failure to provide promised back pay and pensions. Rumors of mutiny abounded.

On March 10, an anonymous letter appeared, calling for a meeting of all officers the next day to discuss the grievances. Within hours came a second anonymous letter, in which the writer, later revealed as Maj. John Armstrong Jr., an aide to top Gen. Horatio Gates, urged the troops, while still in arms, to either disengage from British troops, move out West and "mock" the Congress, or march on Philadelphia and seize the government.

When Washington learned of the letters, he quickly called for the meeting to be held instead on March 15—to give time, he said, for "mature deliberation" of the issues. He ordered General Gates to preside and asked for a report, giving the impression that a friend of the instigators would run the show and that Washington himself wouldn't even attend. He spent the next few days planning his strategy and lining up allies.

But just as the meeting of approximately 500 officers came to order, Washington strode into the hall and asked permission to speak. He said he understood their grievances and would continue to press them. He said that many congressmen supported their claims, but that Congress moved slowly. And he warned that to follow the letter writer would only serve the British cause.

The officers had heard all this before—the letter writer had even warned against heeding Washington's counsel of "more moderation and longer forbearance." The crowd rustled and murmured with discontent. Washington then opened a letter from a sympathetic congressman, but soon appeared to grow distracted. As his men wondered what was wrong, Washington pulled out a pair of glasses, which even his officers had never seen before. "Gentlemen," he said, "you must pardon me, for I have grown not only gray but blind in the service of my country."

The officers were stunned. Many openly wept. Their mutinous mood gave way immediately to affection for their commander.

After finishing the letter, Washington appealed to the officers' "patient virtue" and praised the "glorious example you have exhibited to mankind." He then strode from the hall. His appearance probably lasted less than 15 minutes.

An officer quickly made a motion to thank the commander for his words and appoint a committee—all trusted Washington aides—to prepare a resolution carrying out the general's wishes. The motion passed, and the committee soon returned with a resolution damning the anonymous letter and pledging faith in Congress. The resolution was adopted by roaring acclamation and the meeting adjourned.

This wasn't the end of the Army's intransigence: several weeks later, Pennsylvania militiamen marched on Philadelphia and forced Congress to flee to Princeton, N.J. But with the story from Newburgh fresh in their minds, the mutineers quickly developed second thoughts and went home. True to his word, Washington pursued the Army's grievances, though with mixed results—Congress voted a lump-sum pension payment and disbanded the force.

Given Washington's near universal popularity, word of his speech spread rapidly, and civilian control of the military soon became a central priority in the formation of the young Republic. Six years later the new country adopted a Constitution that implicitly recognized civilian control.

But powerful armies often make their own rules, and many nations have succumbed to military control despite strong constitutions. In the United States, it was the story of Newburgh and Washington's iconic status in our early years that so firmly established a tradition of civilian control in the minds of both our military and civilians. That tradition continues, a testament to our first, finest and most political general.

DISCUSSION *questions and activities*

1. How does Miller connect Washington's speech to the political situation in 2009?
2. What does Miller see as the most persuasive aspect of Washington's presentation? Do you agree? How did you reach this conclusion?
3. Do you think that Miller supports his claim about the reasons that the U.S. military is under civilian control?

Senate Bill 561

Ben Nevers

Drafted by the Louisiana Family Forum, Senate Bill 561, the "Louisiana Science Education Act," was sponsored by Ben Nevers and signed into law by Governor Bobby Jindal in June 2008. The law grants teachers, students, and administrators greater freedom to include literature that challenges the tenets of widely accepted scientific theories like Darwinism. Supporters of the bill note its emphasis on "critical thinking skills, logical analysis, and open and objective discussion of scientific theories." The bill has inspired similar legislation in Florida, Alabama, Missouri, Michigan, and South Carolina. See the Louisiana Science Coalition's analysis of SB 561 at: http://lasciencecoalition.org/2008/05/22/sb_733_analysis/.

TEACHERS. Provides for the Louisiana Academic Freedom Act. (gov. sig.)

An act

To enact R.S. 17:2118, relative to public elementary and secondary schools; to provide that no public elementary or secondary school governing authority, superintendent, administrator, or principal shall prohibit any teacher from discussing certain scientific evidence; to prohibit certain content-based censorship; to provide for notice of such to local school systems and employees; and to provide for related matters.

Be it enacted by the Legislature of Louisiana:

Section 1. R.S. 17:2118 is hereby enacted to read as follow:

§2118. Discussion of certain scientific evidence; prohibitions; limitations; dissemination to local school systems

A.   The Louisiana Legislature finds and declares all of the following:

  (1) The Preamble of the Louisiana Constitution declares that the promotion of education is one of the legitimate ends of government.

  (2) That the Louisiana Board of Elementary and Secondary Education has promulgated the "Louisiana Science Framework" which states that "the process of scientific inquiry involves 'thinking critically and logically about the relationships between evidence and explanations, constructing and analyzing alternative explanations, and communicating scientific arguments.'"

  (3) That an important purpose of science education is to inform students about scientific evidence and to help students develop critical thinking skills that they need in order to become intelligent, productive, and scientifically informed citizens.

(4) That the teaching of some scientific subjects, such as biological evolution, the chemical origins of life, global warming, and human cloning, can cause controversy, and that some teachers may be unsure of the expectations concerning how they should present information on such subjects.

(5) That this Act shall be known as the "Louisiana Academic Freedom Act."

B. The Louisiana Department of Education, public elementary and secondary school governing authorities, superintendents of schools, school system administrators, and public elementary and secondary school principals and administrators shall endeavor to create an environment within public elementary and secondary schools that encourages students to explore scientific questions, learn about scientific evidence, to help students develop critical thinking skills, and respond appropriately and respectfully to differences of opinion about controversial issues. Such educational authorities in Louisiana shall also endeavor to assist teachers to find more effective ways to present the science curriculum where it addresses scientific controversies. Toward this end, teachers shall be permitted to help students understand, analyze, critique, and review in an objective manner the scientific strengths and scientific weaknesses of existing scientific theories pertinent to the course being taught.

C. Neither the Louisiana Department of Education, nor any public elementary or secondary school governing authority, superintendent of schools, or school system administrator, nor any public elementary or secondary school principal or administrator shall prohibit any teacher in a public school system of this state from helping students understand, analyze, critique, and review in an objective manner the scientific strengths and scientific weaknesses of existing scientific theories pertinent to the course or courses being taught. Such topics may include those topics listed in Paragraph A(4) of this Section.

D. Neither the Louisiana Department of Education, nor any public elementary or secondary school governing authority, superintendent of schools, or school system administrator, nor any public elementary or secondary school principal or administrator or teacher, in the course and scope of his duties in such capacity, shall censor or suppress in any way any writing, document, record, or other content of any material which references topics listed in Paragraph A(4) of this Section.

E. This Section only protects the teaching of scientific information, and this section shall not be construed to promote any religious doctrine, promote discrimination for or against a particular set of religious beliefs, or promote discrimination for or against religion or non-religion.

F. By no later than the start of the 2008–2009 school term, the state superintendent of elementary and secondary education shall notify all public school system superintendents of the provisions of this Section. Each superintendent shall then disseminate to all employees within his school system a copy of the provisions of this Section.

Section 2. This Act shall become effective upon signature by the governor or, if not signed by the governor, upon expiration of the time for bills to become law without signature by the governor, as provided by Article III, Section 18 of the Constitution of Louisiana. If vetoed by the governor and subsequently approved by the legislature, this Act shall become effective on the day following such approval.

The original instrument and the following digest, which constitutes no part of the legislative instrument, were prepared by Carla S. Roberts.

Digest

<u>Proposed law</u> creates the Louisiana Academic Freedom Act.
  <u>Proposed law</u> specifies legislative findings as follows:
  (1)   The Preamble of the Louisiana Constitution declares that the promotion of education is one of the legitimate ends of government.
  (2)   That the Louisiana Board of Elementary and Secondary Education has promulgated the "Louisiana Science Framework" which states that "the process of scientific inquiry involves 'thinking critically and logically about the relationships between evidence and explanations, constructing and analyzing alternative explanations, and communicating scientific arguments.'"
  (3)   That an important purpose of science education is to inform students about scientific evidence and to help students develop critical thinking skills that they need in order to become intelligent, productive, and scientifically informed citizens.
  (4)   That the teaching of some scientific subjects, such as biological evolution, the chemical origins of life, global warming, and human cloning, can cause controversy, and that some teachers may be unsure of the expectations concerning how they should present information on such subjects.

<u>Proposed law</u> provides that the Louisiana Department of Education, public elementary and secondary school governing authorities, superintendents of schools, school system administrators, and public elementary and secondary school principals and administrators shall endeavor to create an environment within public elementary and secondary schools that encourages students to explore scientific questions, learn about scientific evidence, to help students develop critical thinking skills, and respond appropriately and respectfully to differences of opinion about controversial issues.

<u>Proposed law</u> provides that the Louisiana Department of Education, nor any school official shall not prohibit any teacher in a public school system from helping students understand, analyze, critique, and review, in an objective manner, the scientific strengths and weaknesses of existing scientific theories pertinent to the course or courses being taught. Such topics may include biological evolution, the chemical origins of life, global warming, and human cloning.

<u>Proposed law</u> prohibits the Louisiana Department of Education or any school official from prohibiting, censoring or suppressing writing, document, record, or other content of any material about biological evolution, the chemical origins of life, global warming, and human cloning.

<u>Proposed law</u> provides that the legislation only protects the teaching of scientific information, and this section shall not be construed to promote any religious doctrine, promote discrimination for or against a particular set of religious beliefs, or promote discrimination for or against religion or non-religion.

<u>Proposed law</u> provides that, no later than the start of the 2008–2009 school term, the state superintendent of elementary and secondary education shall notify all public school system superintendents of the provisions of this Section. Each superintendent shall then disseminate to all employees within his school system a copy of the provisions of this Section.

Effective upon signature of the governor or lapse of time for gubernatorial action.
(Adds R.S. 17:2118)

DISCUSSION *questions and activities*

1. The language used to write public policy is often value-laden. After reading this bill, describe its intended audience and find the terms you believe are used to connect with their values.

2. Read this bill alongside Charles Pierce's "Greetings from Idiot America." Pretending you are writing from Pierce's perspective, write a response to this bill that duplicates his writing style.

3. The title "The Louisiana Science Education Act" implies that education is its core value and suggests respect for scientific disciples in particular. Conduct research on bills under consideration by your state's legislature and perform a brief rhetorical analysis on their titles.

Greetings from Idiot America

Charles P. Pierce

Charles P. Pierce received his degree in journalism from Marquette University and went on to complete two full days of graduate school at Boston College. His work on sports and politics has appeared in The New York Times Magazine, LA Times Magazine, *and* The Chicago Tribune. *This article was written for* Esquire, *an award-winning magazine for men that counts the 2007 National Magazine Award for Reporting among its accolades. In 2009, Pierce published a book titled,* Idiot America: How Stupidity Became a Virtue in the Land of the Free, *which grew out of the article appearing here. His complete biography is available at www.charlespierce.net.*

There is some undeniable art—you might even say design—in the way southern Ohio rolls itself into northern Kentucky. The hills build gently under you as you leave the interstate. The roads narrow beneath a cool and thickening canopy as they wind through the leafy outer precincts of Hebron—a small Kentucky town named, as it happens, for the place near Jerusalem where the Bible tells us that David was anointed the king of the Israelites. This resulted in great literature and no little bloodshed, which is the case with a great deal of Scripture.

At the top of the hill, just past the Idlewild Concrete plant, there is an unfinished wall with an unfinished gate in the middle of it. Happy, smiling people are trickling in through the gate this fine morning, one minivan at a time. They park in whatever shade they can find, which is not much. It's hot as hell this morning.

They are almost uniformly white and almost uniformly bubbly. Their cars come from Kentucky and Tennessee and Ohio and Illinois and as far away as New Brunswick, Canada. There are elderly couples in shorts, suburban families piling out of the minivans, the children all Wrinkle-Resistant and Stain-Released. There is a clutch of Mennonite women in traditional dress—small bonnets and long skirts. All of them wander off, chattering and waving and stopping every few steps for pictures, toward a low-slung building that seems from the outside to be the most finished part of the complex.

Outside, several of them stop to be interviewed by a video crew. They have come from Indiana, one woman says, two toddlers toddling at her feet, because they have been home-schooling their children and they have given them this adventure as a kind of field trip. The whole group then bustles into the lobby of the building, where they are greeted by the long neck of a huge, herbivorous dinosaur. The kids run past that and around a corner, where stands another, smaller dinosaur.

Which is wearing a saddle.

It is an English saddle, hornless and battered. Apparently, this was a dinosaur used for dressage competitions and stakes races. Any working dinosaur accustomed to the rigors of ranch work and herding other dinosaurs along the dusty trail almost certainly would wear a sturdy western saddle.

This is very much a show dinosaur.

The dinosaurs are the first things you see when you enter the Creation Museum, which is very much a work in progress and the dream child of an Australian named Ken Ham. Ham is the founder of Answers in Genesis, an organization of which the museum one day will be the headquarters. The people here today are on a special tour. They have paid $149 to become "charter members" of the museum.

"Dinosaurs," Ham laughs as he poses for pictures with his visitors, "always get the kids interested."

AIG is dedicated to the proposition that the biblical story of the creation of the world is inerrant in every word. Which means, in this interpretation and among other things, that dinosaurs coexisted with man (hence the saddles), that there were dinosaurs in Eden, and that Noah, who certainly had enough on his hands, had to load two brachiosaurs onto the Ark along with his wife, his sons, and their wives, to say nothing of green ally-gators and long-necked geese and humpty-backed camels and all the rest.

(Faced with the obvious question of how to keep a three-hundred-by-thirty-by-fifty-cubit ark from sinking under the weight of dinosaur couples, Ham's literature argues that the dinosaurs on the Ark were young ones, and thus did not weigh as much as they might have.)

"We," Ham exclaims to the assembled, "are taking the dinosaurs back from the evolutionists!" And everybody cheers.

Ham then goes on to celebrate the great victory won in Oklahoma, where, in the first week of June, Tulsa park officials announced a decision (later reversed) to put up a display at the city zoo based on Genesis so as to eliminate the "discrimination" long inflicted upon sensitive Christians by a statue of the Hindu god Ganesh that decorated the elephant exhibit.

This is a serious crowd. They gather in the auditorium and they listen intently, and they take copious notes as Ham draws a straight line from Adam's fall to our godless public schools, from Darwin to gay marriage. He talks about the triumph over Ganesh, and everybody cheers again.

Ultimately, the heart of the museum will be a long walkway down which patrons will be able to journey through the entire creation story. This, too, is still in the earliest stages of construction. Today, for example, one young artist is working on a scale model of the moment when Adam names all the creatures. Adam is in the delicate process of naming the saber-toothed tiger while, behind him, already named, a woolly mammoth seems to be on the verge of taking a nap.

Elsewhere in the museum, another Adam figure is full-size, if unpainted, and waiting to be installed. This Adam is reclining peacefully; eventually, if the plans stay true, he will be placed in a pool under a waterfall. As the figure depicts a prelapsarian Adam, he is completely naked. He also has no penis.

This would seem to be a departure from Scripture inconsistent with the biblical literalism of the rest of the museum. If you're willing to stretch Job's description of a "behemoth" to include baby brachiosaurs on Noah's Ark, as Ham does in his lectures, then surely, since we are depicting him before the fall, Adam should be out there waving unashamedly in the paradisaical breezes. For that matter, what is Eve doing there, across the room, with her hair falling just so to cover her breasts and midsection, as though she's doing a nude scene from some 1950s Swedish art-house film?

After all, Genesis 2:25 clearly says that at this point in their lives, "And the man and his wife were both naked, and they were not ashamed." If Adam courageously sat there unencumbered while he was naming saber-toothed tigers, then why, six thousand years later, should he be depicted as a eunuch in some family-values Eden? And if these people can take away what Scripture says was rightfully his, then why can't Charles Darwin and the accumulated science of the past 150-odd years take away all the rest of it?

These are impolite questions. Nobody asks them here by the cool pond tucked into a gentle hillside. Increasingly, nobody asks them outside the gates, either. It is impolite to wonder why our parents sent us all to college, and why generations of immigrants sweated and bled so their children could be educated, if it wasn't so that we would all one day feel confident enough to look at a museum filled with

[handwritten margin notes: "stupid to believe this new "history"" ; "crazy, psychotic people" ; "More examples: ridiculous statements" ; "support w/ examples most political leaders exploit "the gut"" ; "u.u against the people"]

dinosaurs rigged to run six furlongs at Belmont and make the not unreasonable point that it is all batshit crazy and that anyone who believes this righteous hooey should be kept away from sharp objects and his own money. → *crazy, psychotic people*

Dinosaurs with saddles?

Dinosaurs on Noah's Ark?

Welcome to your new Eden.

Welcome to Idiot America.

Past → present

Let's take a tour, shall we? For the sake of time, we'll just cover the last year or so.

A federally funded abstinence program suggests that HIV can be transmitted through tears. An Alabama legislator proposes a bill to ban all books by gay authors. The Texas House passes a bill banning suggestive cheerleading. And nobody laughs at any of it, or even points out that, in the latter case, having Texas ban suggestive cheerleading is like having Nebraska ban corn.

James Dobson, a prominent conservative Christian spokesman, compares the Supreme Court to the Ku Klux Klan. Pat Robertson, another prominent conservative preacher, says that federal judges are a more serious threat to the country than is Al Qaeda and, apparently taking his text from the Book of Gambino, later sermonizes that the United States should get with it and snuff the democratically elected president of Venezuela.

The Congress of the United States intervenes to extend into a televised spectacle the prolonged death of a woman in Florida. The majority leader of the Senate, a physician, pronounces a diagnosis based on heavily edited videotape. The majority leader of the House of Representatives argues against cutting-edge research into the use of human stem cells by saying that "an embryo is a person....We were all at one time embryos ourselves. So was Abraham. So was Muhammad. So was Jesus of Nazareth." Nobody laughs at him or points out that the same could be said of Hitler, Stalin, Pol Pot, or whoever invented the baby-back rib.

And, finally, in August, the cover of *TIME*—for almost a century the dyspeptic voice of the American establishment—clears its throat, hems and haws and hacks like a headmaster gagging on his sherry, and asks, quite seriously: "Does God have a place in science class?"

Fights over evolution—and its faddish new camouflage, intelligent design, a pseudoscience that posits without proof or method that science is inadequate to explain existence and that supernatural causes must be considered—roil up school districts across the country. The president of the United States announces that he believes ID ought to be taught in the public schools on an equal footing with the theory of evolution. And in Dover, Pennsylvania, during one of these many controversies, a pastor named Ray Mummert delivers the line that both ends our tour and, in every real sense, sums it up:

"We've been attacked," he says, "by the intelligent, educated segment of the culture."

And there it is.

Idiot America is not the place where people say silly things. It's not the place where people believe in silly things. It is not the place where people go to profit from the fact that people believe in silly things. Idiot America is not even those people who believe that Adam named the dinosaurs. Those people pay attention. They take notes. They take the time and the considerable mental effort to construct a worldview that is round and complete.

The rise of Idiot America is essentially a war on expertise. It's not so much antimodernism or the distrust of intellectual elites that Richard Hofstadter deftly teased out of the national DNA forty years ago. Both of those things are part of it. However, the rise of Idiot America today represents—for profit mainly, but also, and more cynically, for political advantage and in the pursuit of power—the breakdown of a consensus that the pursuit of knowledge is a good. It also represents the ascendancy of the notion that the people whom we should trust the *least* are the people who best know what they're talking about. In the new media age, everybody is a historian, or a preacher, or a scientist, or a sage. And if everyone is an expert, then nobody is, and the worst thing you can be in a society where everybody is an expert is, well, an actual expert.

In the place of expertise, we have elevated the Gut, and the Gut is a moron, as anyone who has ever tossed a golf club, punched a wall, or kicked an errant lawn mower knows. We occasionally dress up the Gut by calling it "common sense." The president's former advisor on medical ethics regularly refers to the "yuck factor." The Gut is common. It is democratic. It is the rolling repository of dark and ancient fears. Worst of all, the Gut is faith-based.

It's a dishonest phrase for a dishonest time, "faith-based," a cheap huckster's phony term of art. It sounds like an additive, an artificial flavoring to make crude biases taste of bread and wine. It's a word for people without the courage to say they are religious, and it is beloved not only by politicians too cowardly to debate something as substantial as faith but also by Idiot America, which is too lazy to do it.

After all, faith is about the heart and soul and about transcendence. Anything calling itself faith-based is admitting that it is secular and profane. In the way that it relies on the Gut to determine its science, its politics, and even the way it sends its people to war, Idiot America is not a country of faith; it's a faith-based country, fashioning itself in the world, which is not the place where faith is best fashioned.

Hofstadter saw this one coming. "Intellect is pitted against feeling," he wrote, "on the ground that it is somehow inconsistent with warm emotion. It is pitted against character, because it is widely believed that intellect stands for mere cleverness, which transmutes easily into the sly or the diabolical."

The Gut is the basis for the Great Premises of Idiot America. We hold these truths to be self-evident:

1) Any theory is valid if it sells books, soaks up ratings, or otherwise moves units.

2) Anything can be true if somebody says it on television.

3) Fact is that which enough people believe. Truth is determined by how fervently they believe it.

How does it work? This is how it works. On August 21, a newspaper account of the "intelligent design" movement contained this remarkable sentence: "They have mounted a politically savvy challenge to evolution as the bedrock of modern biology, propelling a fringe academic movement onto the front pages and putting Darwin's defenders firmly on the defensive."

A "politically savvy challenge to evolution" is as self-evidently ridiculous as an agriculturally savvy challenge to euclidean geometry would be. It makes as much sense as conducting a Gallup poll on gravity or running someone for president on the Alchemy Party ticket. It doesn't matter what percentage of people believe they ought to be able to flap their arms and fly, none of them can. It doesn't matter how many votes your candidate got, he's not going to turn lead into gold. The sentence is so arrantly foolish that the only real news in it is where it appeared.

On the front page.

Of *The New York Times.*

Within three days, there was a panel on the subject on *Larry King Live,* in which Larry asked the following question:

"All right, hold on. Dr. Forrest, your concept of how can you out-and-out turn down creationism, since if evolution is true, why are there still monkeys?"

And why do so many of them host television programs, Larry?

This is how Idiot America engages the great issues of the day. It decides, en masse, with a thousand keystrokes and clicks of the remote control, that because there are two sides to every question, they both must be right, or at least not wrong. And the poor biologist's words carry no more weight than the thunderations of some turkey-neck preacher out of the Church of Christ's Own Parking Facility in DeLand, Florida. Less weight, in fact, because our scientist is an "expert" and, therefore, an "elitist." Nobody buys his books. Nobody puts him on cable. He's brilliant, surely, but his Gut's the same as ours. He just ignores it, poor fool.

This is a great country, in no small part because it is the best country ever devised in which to be a public crank. Never has a nation so dedicated itself to the proposition that not only should its people hold nutty ideas but they should cultivate them, treasure them, shine them up, and put them right there on the mantelpiece. This is still the best country ever in which to peddle complete public lunacy. The right to do so is there in our founding documents.

After all, the Founders were men of the Enlightenment, fashioning a country out of new ideas—or out of old ones that they excavated from centuries of religious internment. Historian Charles Freeman points out that in Europe, "Christian thought...often gave irrationality the status of a universal 'truth' to the exclusion of those truths to be found through reason. So the uneducated was preferred to the educated, and the miracle to the operation of natural laws."

In America, the Founders were trying to get away from all that, to raise a nation of educated people. In pledging their faith to intellectual experimentation, however, the Founders set freedom free. They devised the best country ever in which to be completely around the bend. It's just that making a respectable living out of it used to be harder work.

They call it the Infinite Corridor, which is the kind of joke you tell when your day job is to throw science as far ahead as you can and hope that the rest of us can move fast enough to catch up. It is a series of connecting hallways that run north through the campus of the Massachusetts Institute of Technology. The hallways are lined with cramped offices, their doors mottled thickly with old tape and yellowing handbills. The Infinite Corridor is not a straight line. It has branches and tributaries. It has backwaters and eddies. You can get lost there.

One of the offices belongs to Professor Kip Hodges, a young and energetic North Carolinian who studies how mountain ranges develop and grow. Suffice it to say that Hodges's data do not correspond to the six-thousand-year-old earth of the creationists, whereupon dinosaurs and naked folks doth gambol together.

Hodges is recently returned from Nepal, where he rescued his research from encroaching Maoist rebels, who were not interested in the least in how the Himalayas became the Himalayas. They were interested in land, in guns, in power, and in other things of the Gut. Moreover, part of Hodges's duties at MIT has been to mentor incoming freshmen about making careers in science for themselves.

"Scientists are always portrayed in the literature as being above the fray intellectually," Hodges says. "I guess to a certain extent that's our fault, because scientists don't do a good enough job communicating with people who are nonscientists—that it's not a matter of brainiacs doing one thing and nonbrainiacs doing another."

Americans of a certain age grew up with science the way an earlier generation grew up with baseball and even earlier ones grew up with politics and religion. America cured diseases. It put men on the moon. It thought its way ahead in the cold war and stayed there.

"My earliest memory," Hodges recalls, "is watching John Glenn go up. It was a time that, if you were involved in science or engineering—particularly science, at that time—people greatly respected you if you said you were going into those fields. And nowadays, it's like there's no value placed by society on a lot of the observations that are made by people in science.

"It's more than a general dumbing down of America—the lack of self-motivated thinking: clear, creative thinking. It's like you're happy for other people to think for you. If you should be worried about, say, global warming, well, somebody in Washington will tell me whether or not I should be worried about global warming. So it's like this abdication of intellectual responsibility—that America now is getting to the point that more and more people would just love to let somebody else think for them."

The country was founded by people who were fundamentally curious; Thomas Jefferson and Benjamin Franklin, to name only the most obvious examples, were inveterate tinkerers. (Before dispatching Lewis and Clark into the Louisiana Territory, Jefferson insisted that the pair categorize as many new plant and animal species as they found. Considering they were also mapping everything from Missouri to Oregon, this must have been a considerable pain in the canoe.) Further, they assumed that their posterity would feel much the same as they did; in 1815, appealing to Congress to fund the building of a national university, James Madison called for the development of "a nursery of enlightened preceptors."

It is a long way from that to the moment on February 18, 2004, when sixty-two scientists, including a clutch of Nobel laureates, released a report accusing the incumbent administration of manipulating science for political ends. It is a long way from Jefferson's observatory and Franklin's kite to George W. Bush, in an interview in 2005, suggesting that intelligent design be taught alongside the theory of evolution in the nation's science classes. "Both sides ought to be properly taught," said the president, "so people can understand what the debate is about."

The "debate," of course, is nothing of the sort, because two sides are required for a debate. Nevertheless, the very notion of it is a measure of how scientific discourse, and the way the country educates itself, has slipped through lassitude and inattention across the border into Idiot America—where fact is merely that which enough people believe, and truth is measured only by how fervently they believe it.

If we have abdicated our birthright to scientific progress, we have done so by moving the debate into the realm of political and cultural argument, where we all feel more confident, because it is there that the Gut rules. Held to this standard, any scientific theory is rendered mere opinion. Scientific fact is no more immutable than a polling sample. This is how there's a "debate" over the very existence of global warming, even though the preponderance of fact among those who actually have studied the phenomenon renders the "debate" quite silly. The debate is about making people feel better about driving SUVs. The debate is less about climatology than it is about guiltlessly topping off your tank and voting in tax incentives for oil companies.

The rest of the world looks on in cockeyed wonder. The America of Franklin and Edison, of Fulton and Ford, of the Manhattan project and the Apollo program, the America of which Einstein wanted to be a part, seems to be enveloping itself in a curious fog behind which it's tying itself in knots over evolution, for pity's sake, and over the relative humanity of blastocysts versus the victims of Parkinson's disease.

"Even in the developing world, where I spend lots of time doing my work," Hodges says, "if you tell them that you're from MIT and you tell them that you do science, it's a big deal. If I go to India and tell them I'm from MIT, it's a big deal. In Thailand, it's a big deal. If I go to Iowa, they could give a rat's ass. And that's a weird thing, that we're moving in that direction as a nation."

Hence, Bush was not talking about science—not in any real sense, anyway. Intelligent design is a theological construct, a faith-based attempt to gussy up creationism in a lab coat. Its fundamental tenets cannot be experimentally verified—or, most important, falsified. That it enjoys a certain public cachet is irrelevant; a higher percentage of Americans believes that a government conspiracy killed John F. Kennedy than believes in intelligent design, but there is no great effort abroad in the land to include that conspiracy theory in sixth-grade history texts. Bush wasn't talking about science. He was talking about the political utility of putting saddles on the dinosaurs and breaking Ganesh's theological monopoly over the elephant paddock.

"The reason the creationists have been so effective is that they have put a premium on communication skills," explains Hodges. "It matters to them that they can talk to the guy in the bar, and it's important to them, and they are hugely effective at it."

It is the ultimate standard of Idiot America. How does it play to Joe Six-Pack in the bar? At the end of August 2004, the Zogby people discovered that 57 percent of undecided voters would rather have a beer with George Bush than with John Kerry. Now, how many people with whom you've spent time drinking beer would you trust with the nuclear launch codes? Not only is this not a question for a nation of serious citizens, it's not even a question for a nation of serious drunkards.

If even scientific discussion is going to be dragged into politics, then the discussion there at least ought to exist on a fairly sophisticated level. Again, the Founders thought it should. They considered self-government a science that required an informed and educated and enlightened populace to make all the delicate mechanisms run. Instead, today we have the Kabuki politics and marionette debates best exemplified by cable television. Instead, the discussion of everything ends up in the bar.

(It wasn't always this way. Theodore Roosevelt is reckoned to be the manliest of our manly-man presidents. He also was a lifelong science dweeb, cataloging songbirds, of all things. Of course, he shot them first, so maybe that makes all the difference.)

It is, of course, television that has allowed Idiot America to run riot within the modern politics and all forms of public discourse. It is not that there is less information on television than there once was. (That there is less news is another question entirely.) In fact, there is so much information that fact is now defined as something that so many people believe that television notices it, and truth is measured by how fervently they believe it.

"You don't need to be credible on television," explains Keith Olbermann, the erudite host of his own show on MSNBC. "You don't need to be authoritative. You don't need to be informed. You don't need to be honest. All these things that we used to associate with what we do are no longer factors.

"There is an entire network [the Fox News Channel] that bills itself as news that is devoted to reinforcing people's fears and saying to them, 'This is what you should be scared of, and here's whose fault it is,'" Olbermann says. "And that's what they get—two or three million frustrated paranoids who sit in front of the TV and go, 'Damn right, it's those liberals' fault.' Or, 'It's those—what's the word for it?—_college graduates_' fault.' "

The reply, of course, is that Fox regularly buries Olbermann and the rest of the MSNBC lineup in breaking off a segment of a smidgen of a piece of the television audience. Truth is what moves the needle. Fact is what sells.

Idiot America is a bad place for crazy notions. Its indolent tolerance of them causes the classic American crank to drift slowly and dangerously into the mainstream, wherein the crank loses all of his charm and the country loses another piece of its mind. The best thing about American crackpots used to be that they would stand proudly aloof from a country that, by their peculiar lights, had gone mad. Not today. Today, they all have book deals, TV shows, and cases pending in federal court.

Once, it was very hard to get into the public square and very easy to fall out of it. One ill-timed word, even a whiff of public scandal, and all the hard work you did in the grange hall on all those winter nights was for nothing. No longer. You can be Bill Bennett, gambling with both fists, but if your books still sell, you can continue to scold the nation about its sins. You can be Bill O'Reilly, calling up subordinates to proposition them both luridly and comically—loofahs? falafels?—and if more people tune in to watch you than tune in to watch some other blowhard, you can keep your job lecturing America about the dangers of its secular culture. Just don't be boring. And keep the ratings up. Idiot America wants to be entertained.

Because scientific expertise was dragged into political discussion, and because political discussion is hopelessly corrupt, the distrust of scientific expertise is now as general as the distrust of politicians is. Everyone is an expert, so nobody is. For example, Sean Hannity's knowledge of, say, stem-cell research is measured precisely by his ratings book. His views on the subject are more well known than those of the people doing the actual research.

The credibility of Senator Rick Santorum of Pennsylvania on the subject of the cultural anthropology of the American family ought to be, well, minimal. He spent the summer promoting a book in which he propounded theories on the subject that were progressively loopier. "For some parents," he writes, "the purported need to provide things for their children simply provides a convenient rationalization for pursuing a gratifying career outside the home." He goes on later to compare a woman's right to choose an abortion unfavorably with the institution of slavery. Nevertheless, he's welcome in the mainstream, at least until either he's defeated for reelection or his book doesn't sell.

"Somewhere along the line, we stopped rewarding intelligence with success and stopped equating intelligence with success," Olbermann says. We're all in the bar now, where everybody's an expert, where the Gut makes everyone so very sure. All opinions are of equal worth. No voice is more authoritative than any others; some are just louder. Of course, the problem in the bar is that sooner or later, for reasons that nobody will remember in the clear light of the next morning, some noisy asshole picks a fight. And it becomes clear that the rise of Idiot America has consequences.

On the morning of September 11, 2001, nobody in the American government knew more than Richard Clarke did on the subject of a shadowy terrorist network called Al Qaeda. He had watched it grow. He had watched it strike—in New York and in Africa and in the harbor in Yemen. That morning, in the Situation Room in the White House, Clarke watched the buildings burn and fall, and he recognized the organization's signature as well as he'd recognize his own. Instead, in the ensuing days a lot of people around him—people who didn't know enough about Al Qaeda to throw to a cat—wanted to talk about Iraq. What they believed trumped what Clarke knew, over and over again. He left the government.

"In the 1970s and 1980s, when the key issue became arms control, the traditional diplomats couldn't do the negotiating because that negotiating involved science and engineering," Clarke recalls. "Interagency decision papers were models of analysis, where assumptions were laid out and tested.

"That's the world I grew up in. [The approach] still applied to issues, even terrorism. Then these people come in, and they already have the answers, how to spin it, how to get the rest of the world on board. I thought, Wait a minute. That isn't analysis. It's the important issues where we really need analysis.

"In the area of terrorism, there is a huge potential for emotional reaction. The one thing I told my team [on September 11]—they were mad and they were crying, the whole range of emotions—was that we didn't have time for emotion that day."

Nothing that the administration of George W. Bush has done has been inconsistent with the forces that twice elected it. The subtle, humming engine of its success—against John Kerry, surely, but most vividly against poor, cerebral Al Gore—was a celebration of instinct over intellect, a triumph of the Gut. No campaigns in history employed the saloon question with such devastating success or saw so clearly the path through the deliberate inexpertise of the national debate. No politician in recent times has played to the Gut so deftly.

So it ought not shock anyone when the government suddenly found itself at odds with empirical science. It ought not shock anyone in the manner in which it would go to war. Remember the beginning, when it was purely the Gut—a bone-deep call for righteous revenge for which Afghanistan was not sufficient response. In Iraq, there would be towering stacks of chemical bombs, a limitless smorgasbord of deadly bacteria, vast lagoons of exotic poisons. There would be candy and flowers greeting our troops. The war would take six months, a year, tops. Mission Accomplished. Major combat operations are over.

"Part of the problem was that people didn't want the analytic process because they'd be shown up," Richard Clarke says. "Their assumptions would be counterfactual. One of the real areas of expertise, for example, was failed-state reconstruction. How to go into failed states and maintain security and get the economy going and defang ethnic hatred. They threw it all out.

"They ignored the experts on the Middle East. They ignored the experts who said it was the wrong target. So you ignore the experts and you go in anyway, and then you ignore all the experts on how to handle the postconflict."

One of those experts was David Phillips, a senior advisor on what was called the Future of Iraq program for the State Department. Phillips was ignored. His program was ignored. Earlier, Phillips had helped reconstruct the Balkans after the region spent a decade tearing itself apart with genocidal lunacy. Phillips knew what he knew. He just didn't believe what they believed.

"You can just as easily have a faith-based, or ideologically driven, policy," he says today. "You start with the presumption that you already know the conclusion prior to asking the question. When information surfaces that contradicts your firmly entrenched views, you dismantle the institution that brought you the information."

There was going to be candy and flowers, remember? The war was going to pay for itself. Believe.

"We went in blindfolded, and we believed our own propaganda," Phillips says. "We were going to get out in ninety days, spend $1.9 billion in the short term, and Iraqi oil would pay for the rest. Now we're deep in the hole, and people are asking questions about how we got there.

"It's delusional, allowing delusion to be the basis of policy making. Once you've told the big lie, you have to substantiate it with a sequence of lies that's repeated. You can't fix a policy if you don't admit it's broken."

Two thousand American lives later, remember the beginning. One commentator quite plainly made the case that every few years or so, the United States should "throw a small nation up against the wall" to prove that it means business. And Idiot America, which is all of us, cheered.

Goddamn right. Gimme another. And see what the superpowers in the back room will have.

August 19, 2005, was a beautiful day in Idiot America.

In Washington, William Frist, a Harvard-trained physician and the majority leader of the United States Senate, endorsed the teaching of intelligent design in the country's public schools. "I think today a pluralistic society," Frist explained, "should have access to a broad range of fact, of science, including faith."

That faith is not fact, nor should it be, and that faith is not science, nor should it be, seems to have eluded Doctor Senator Frist. It doesn't matter. He was talking to the people who believe that faith is both those things, because Bill Frist wants to be president of the United States, and because he believes those people will vote for him specifically because he talks this rot, and Idiot America will take it as an actor merely reciting his lines and let it go at that. Nonsense is a no-lose proposition.

On the same day, across town, a top aide to former secretary of state Colin Powell told CNN that Powell's pivotal presentation to the United Nations in which he described Iraq's vast array of deadly weapons was a farrago of stovepiped intelligence, wishful thinking, and utter bullshit.

"It was the lowest point in my life," the aide said.

That it has proven to be an even lower point for almost two thousand American families, and God alone knows how many Iraqis, seems to have eluded this fellow. It doesn't matter. Neither Frist with his pandering nor this apparatchik with the tender conscience—nor Colin Powell, for all that—will pay a substantial price for any of it because the two stories lasted one day, and, after all, it was a beautiful day in Idiot America.

Idiot America is a collaborative effort, the result of millions of decisions made and not made. It's the development of a collective Gut at the expense of a collective mind. It's what results when politicians make ridiculous statements and not merely do we abandon the right to punish them for it at the polls, but we also become too timid to punish them with ridicule on a daily basis, because the polls say they're popular anyway. It's what results when leaders are not held to account for mistakes that end up killing people.

And that's why August became a seminal month in Idiot America.

In its final week, a great American city drowned and then turned irrevocably into a Hieronymus Bosch painting in real time and on television, and with complete impunity, the president of the United States wandered the landscape and talked like a blithering nitwit.

First, he compared the violence surrounding the writing of an impromptu theocratic constitution in Baghdad to the events surrounding the Constitutional Convention in Philadelphia in 1787. Undaunted, he later compared the war he'd launched in Iraq to World War II. And then he compared himself to Franklin Roosevelt. One more public appearance and we might have learned that Custer was killed by Hezbollah.

Finally, we saw the apotheosis of the end of expertise, when New Orleans was virtually obliterated as a functional habitat for human beings, and the country discovered that the primary responsibility for dealing with the calamity lay with a man who'd been dismissed as an incompetent from his previous job as the director of a luxury-show-horse organization.

And the president went on television and said that nobody could have anticipated the collapse of the unfortunate city's levees. In God's sweet name, engineers anticipated it. Politicians anticipated it. The poor bastards in the Ninth Ward certainly anticipated it. Hell, four generations of *folksingers* anticipated it.

And the people who hated him went crazy and the people who loved him defended him. But where were the people who heard this incredible, staggeringly stupid bafflegab, uttered with conscious forethought, and realized that whatever they thought of the man, the president had gotten behind a series of podiums and done everything but drop his drawers and dance the hootchie-koo? They were out there, lost in Idiot America, where it was still a beautiful day.

Idiot America took it as a bad actor merely bungling his lines. Nonsense is a no-lose proposition. For Idiot America is a place where people choose to live. It is a place that is built consciously and deliberately, one choice at a time, made or (most often) unmade. A place where we're all like that statue of Adam now, reclining in a peaceful garden of our own creation, brainless and dickless, and falling down on the job of naming the monsters for what they are, dozing away in an Eden that, every day, looks less and less like paradise.

DISCUSSION *questions and activities*

1. Write a one-sentence statement of Pierce's main claim. Compare your statement with those of at least three other students in your class. Discuss any differences in your readings and craft a negotiated summary of Pierce's argument.

2. Write a brief description of Pierce's writing style and find three examples in the essay that support your description. Based on what you have learned about his style, who do you think constitutes his intended audience?

3. Read the "God V. Science" debate hosted by *TIME*. Where do Charles Pierce's ideas fit into the debate between Francis Collins and Richard Dawkins?

Excerpt from
Institutio Oratoria Book XII, Chapter 1

Quintilian

Quintilian (35-100 AD) is the better known name for Marcus Fabius Quintilianus who came from the Roman territory that is modern-day Spain. He studied in Rome and worked for a series of emperors, including Vespasian, who made him a consul. In addition to his government work and his appearances in the law courts, he conducted a public school of rhetoric. The great orator Cicero was one of his major influences, and he advocated a simpler, clearer style of rhetoric than was popular in his time. His Institutio Oratoria *(95 AD) deals not only with how to speak but also outlines a program for the education of rhetoricians. Several university websites publish the full work online, including http://penelope.uchicago.edu.*

1 I now come to what is by far the most arduous portion of the task which I have set myself to perform. Indeed had I fully realised the difficulties when I first designed this work, I should have considered betimes whether my strength was sufficient to support the load that now weighs upon me so heavily. But to begin with, I felt how shameful it would be to fail to perform what I had promised, and later, despite the fact that my labour became more and more arduous at almost every stage, the fear of stultifying what I had already written sustained my courage through every difficulty. 2 Consequently even now, though the burden that oppresses me is greater than ever, the end is in sight and I am resolved to faint by the wayside rather than despair. But the fact that I began with comparatively trivial details deceived me. Subsequently I was lured still further on my voyage by the temptations of the favouring breeze that filled my sails; but the rules which I was then concerned to give were still of a familiar kind and had been already treated by most writers of rhetorical textbooks: thus far I seemed to myself to be still in sight of shore and I had the company of many who had ventured to entrust themselves to the self-same winds. 3 But presently when I entered on the task of setting forth a theory of eloquence which had been but newly discovered and rarely essayed, I found but few that had ventured so far from harbour. And finally now that the ideal orator, whom it was my design to mould, has been dismissed by his masters and is either proceeding on his way borne onward by his own impetus, or seeking still mightier assistance from the innermost shrine of wisdom, I begin to feel how far I have been swept into the great deep. 4 Now there is

"Nothing before and nothing behind but the sky and the Ocean."[1]

One only can I discern in all the boundless waste of waters, Marcus Tullius Cicero, and even he, though the ship in which he entered these seas is of such size and so well found, begins to lessen sail and to row a slower stroke, and is content to speak merely of the kind of speech to be employed by the perfect orator. But my temerity is such that I shall essay to form my orator's character and to teach him his duties. Thus I have no predecessor to guide my steps and must press far, far on, as my theme may demand. Still an honourable ambition is always deserving of approval, and it is all the less hazardous to dare greatly, when forgiveness is assured us if we fail.

1 The orator then, whom I am concerned to form, shall be the orator as defined by Marcus Cato, "a good man, skilled in speaking."[2] But above all he must possess the quality which Cato places first and which is in the very nature of things the greatest and most important, that is, he must be a good man. This is essential not merely on account of the fact that, if the powers of eloquence serve only to lend arms to crime, there can be nothing more pernicious than eloquence to public and private life alike, while I myself, who have laboured to the best of my ability to contribute something of value to oratory, shall have rendered the worst of services to mankind, if I forge these weapons not for a soldier, but for a robber. 2 But why speak of myself? Nature herself will have proved not a mother, but a stepmother with regard to what we deem her greatest gift to man, the gift that distinguishes us from other living things, if she devised the power of speech to be the accomplice of crime, the foe to innocency and the enemy of truth. For it had been better for men to be born dumb and devoid of reason than to turn the gifts of providence to their mutual destruction. 3 But this conviction of mine goes further. For I do not merely assert that the ideal orator should be a good man, but I affirm that no man can be an orator unless he is a good man. For it is impossible to regard those men as gifted with intelligence who on being offered the choice between the two paths of virtue and of vice choose the latter, nor can we allow them prudence, when by the unforeseen issue of their own actions they render themselves liable not merely to the heaviest penalties of the laws, but to the inevitable torment of an evil conscience. 4 But if the view that a bad man is necessarily a fool is not merely held by philosophers, but is the universal belief of ordinary men, the fool will most assuredly never become an orator. To this must be added the fact that the mind will not find leisure even for the study of the noblest of tasks, unless it first be free from vice. The reasons for this are, first, that vileness and virtue cannot jointly inhabit in the selfsame heart and that it is as impossible for one and the same mind to harbour good and evil thoughts as it is for one man to be at once both good and evil: 5 and secondly, that if the intelligence is to be concentrated on such a vast subject as eloquence it must be free from all other distractions, among which must be included even those preoccupations which are free from blame. For it is only when it is free and self-possessed, with nothing to divert it or lure it elsewhere, that it will fix its attention solely on that goal, the attainment of which is the object of its preparations. 6 If on the other hand inordinate care for the development of our estates, anxiety over household affairs, passionate devotion to hunting or the sacrifice of whole days to the shows of the theatre, rob our studies of much of the time that is their due (for every moment that is given to other things involves a loss of time for study), what, think you, will be the results of desire, avarice, and envy, which waken such violent thoughts within our souls that they disturb our very slumbers and our dreams? 7 There is nothing so preoccupied, and distracted, so rent and torn by so many and such varied passions as an evil mind. For when it cherishes some dark garden, it is tormented with hope, care and anguish of spirit, and even when it has accomplished its criminal purpose, it is racked by anxiety, remorse and the fear of all manner of punishments. Amid such passions as these what room is there for literature or any virtuous pursuit? You might as well look for fruit in land that is choked with thorns and brambles. 8 Well then, I ask you, is not simplicity of life essential if we are to be able to endure the toil entailed by study? What can we hope to get from lust or luxury? Is not the desire to win praise one of the strongest stimulants to a passion for literature? But does that mean that we are to suppose that praise is an object of concern to bad men? Surely every one of my readers must by now have realised that oratory is in the main concerned with the treatment of what is just and honourable? Can a bad and unjust man speak on such themes as the dignity of the subject demands? 9 Nay, even if we exclude the most important aspects of the question now before us, and make the impossible concession that the best and worst of men may have the same talent, industry and learning, we are still confronted by the question as to which of the two is entitled to be called the better orator. The answer is surely clear enough: it will be he who is the better man. Consequently, the bad man and the perfect orator can never be identical.

10 For nothing is perfect, if there exists something else that is better. However, as I do not wish to appear to adopt the practice dear to the Socratics of framing answers to my own questions, let me assume the existence of a man so obstinately blind to the truth as to venture to maintain that a bad man equipped with the same talents, industry and learning will be not a whit inferior to the good man as an orator; and let me show that he too is mad. 11 There is one point at any rate which no one will question, namely, that the aim of every speech is to convince the judge that the case which it puts forward is true and honourable. Well then, which will do this best, the good man or the bad? The good man will without doubt more often say what is true and honourable. 12 But even supposing that his duty should, as I shall show may sometimes happen, lead him to make statements which are false, his words are still certain to carry greater weight with his audience. On the other hand bad men, in their contempt for public opinion and their ignorance of what is right, sometimes drop their mask unawares, and are impudent in the statement of their case and shameless in their assertions. 13 Further, in their attempt to achieve the impossible they display an unseemly persistency and unavailing energy. For in lawsuits no less than in the ordinary paths of life, they cherish depraved expectations. But if often happens that even when they tell the truth they fail to win belief, and the mere fact that such a man is its advocate is regarded as an indication of the badness of the case.

14 I must now proceed to deal with the objections which common opinion is practically unanimous in bringing against this view. Was not Demosthenes an orator? And yet we are told that he was a bad man. Was not Cicero an orator? And yet there are many who have found fault with his character as well. What am I to answer? My reply will be highly unpopular and I must first attempt to conciliate my audience. 15 I do not consider that Demosthenes deserves the serious reflexions that have been made upon his character to such an extent that I am bound to believe all the charges amassed against him by his enemies; for my reading tells me that his public policy was of the noblest and his end most glorious. 16 Again, I cannot see that the aims of Cicero were in any portion of his career other than such as may become an excellent citizen. As evidence I would cite the fact that his behaviour as consul was magnificent and his administration of his province a model of integrity, while he refused to become one of the twenty commissioners,[3] and in the grievous civil wars which afflicted his generation beyond all others, neither hope nor fear ever deterred him from giving his support to the better party, that is to say, to the interests of the common weal. 17 Some, it is true, regard him as lacking in courage. The best answer to these critics is to be found in his own words, to the effect that he was timid not in confronting peril, but in anticipating it. And this he proved also by the manner of his death, in meeting which he displayed a singular fortitude. 18 But even if these two men lacked the perfection of virtue, I will reply to those who ask if they were orators, in the manner in which the Stoics would reply, if asked whether Zeno, Cleanthes or Chrysippus himself were wise men. I shall say that they were great men deserving our veneration, but that they did not attain to that which is the highest perfection of man's nature. 19 For did not Pythagoras desire that he should not be called a wise man, like the sages who preceded him, but rather a student of wisdom?[4] But for my own part, conforming to the language of every day, I have said time and again, and shall continue to say, that Cicero was a perfect orator, just as in ordinary speech we call our friends good and sensible men, although neither of these titles can really be given to any save to him that has attained to perfect wisdom. But if I am called upon to speak strictly and in accordance with the most rigid laws of truth, I shall proclaim that I seek to find that same perfect orator whom Cicero also sought to discover. 20 For while I admit that he stood on the loftiest pinnacle of eloquence, and can discover scarcely a single deficiency in him, although I might perhaps discover certain superfluities which I think he would have pruned away (for the general view of the learned is that he possessed many virtues and a few faults, and he himself[5] states that he has succeeded in suppressing much of his youthful exuberance), none the less, in view of the fact that, although he had by no means a low opinion of himself, he never claimed to be the perfect sage, and, had he been granted longer life and less troubled conditions for the composition of his works, would doubtless have spoken better still, I shall not lay

myself open to the charge of ungenerous criticism, if I say that I believe that he failed actually to achieve that perfection to the attainment of which none have approached more nearly, 21 and indicate had I felt otherwise in this connexion, I might have defended my point with greater boldness and freedom.[6] Marcus Antonius declared that he had seen no man who was genuinely eloquent (and to be eloquent is a far less achievement than to be an orator), while Cicero himself has failed to find his orator in actual life and merely imagines and strives to depict the ideal. Shall I then be afraid to say that in the eternity of time that is yet to be, something more perfect may be found than has yet existed? 22 I say nothing of those critics who will not allow sufficient credit for eloquence to Cicero and Demosthenes, although Cicero himself does not regard Demosthenes as flawless, but asserts that he sometimes nods,[7] while even Cicero fails to satisfy Brutus and Calvus (at any rate they criticised his style to his face), or to win the complete approval of either of the Asinii, who in various passages attack the faults of his oratory in language which is positively hostile.

Endnotes

[1] *Aen.* III.193.
[2] cp. I. *Pr.* 9.
[3] For the distribution of the Campanian lands.
[4] *i.e.* φιλόσοφος, a term of which he was reputed the inventor.
[5] *Brut.* xci.316; *Orat.* xxx.107.
[6] Quintilian's reverence for Cicero is such that he feels hampered in maintaining his thesis.
[7] See X.1.24.

DISCUSSION *questions and activities*

1. Quintilian argues that an orator must be morally good as well as skilled in the art of rhetoric. What reasons does he give for taking this stand?
2. What are the objections that Quintilian imagines his audience might raise to his argument?
3. How do you think your own character and values affect your writing?

Writing for the Public

Mike Rose

Mike Rose is a writer and researcher who teaches in the University of California at Los Angeles' Graduate School of Education and Information Studies. He has published extensively on education, literacy, and teaching remedial writers. A renowned scholar in his field, Rose has frequently been recognized by his colleagues through awards and fellowships, including a Guggenheim Fellowship, the Grawemeyer Award in Education, and the Commonwealth Club of California Award for Literary Excellence in Nonfiction. "Writing for the Public" is an opinion piece written for the January 2010 issue of College English, *an academic journal geared toward university-level scholars and teachers of English and literature.*

For the past twenty years or so, I have been fortunate to write for a fairly broad audience. While I was teaching, or running an educational program, or doing research, I was also composing opinion pieces or commentaries about the work I was doing. This process of writing with part of my attention on the classroom or research site and part of it on the public sphere forced me—would force anyone—out of familiar rhetorical territory. As a result, I've been thinking a lot about both the challenge and the importance of academics and other specialists communicating with the general public—and I certainly have been thinking about how hard it is to do this. Our languages of specialization can be so opaque, and mass media are becoming all the more sound-bite and entertainment oriented. Serious consideration of serious issues is difficult to achieve.

Let me offer two moments from my own writing life that represent some of the tensions inherent in trying to write for a wider readership today.

Lives on the Boundary, a book about educational underpreparation published in 1989, was my first attempt to write about educational issues for the general public. When I began circulating early chapters to publishers in 1987, I received one form-letter rejection after another...at least a dozen in all. Then I lucked out and got an agent—though he didn't have much success either until he got a longtime acquaintance, an editor at the *Free Press*, to sit down with the thing. My agent told me later that the first question he typically got when he told editors I worked at the University of California-Los Angeles (UCLA) and did my research on education and literacy was some variation of, "Okay, but can he write?"

Media need experts in and out of the academy for their knowledge and opinion, but there is an odd relationship here. Those in broadcast media, in trade publishing, in the world of newspapers and magazines are reliant on expertise but, as a rule, are wary, even disdainful, of the expert's ability to communicate it. And not without reason. As so many of all ideological persuasions, in and out of the academy, have hammered home (see Patricia Nelson Limerick's "Dancing with Professors" for a classic treatment), we academic types can be long-winded, reliant on jargon, and given to tangent or an endless loop of qualification and nit-picking. Caught in the linguistic bubble of our specializations, we are often impervious to our inability to connect with a more general audience of listeners and readers. When all those editors knew of me came from a brief professional biography, they had reason to be cautious.

This leads me to my second vignette, which offers another piece of the story.

Not too long ago, I sent a commentary on the No Child Left Behind Act (NCLB) to a magazine of social and political commentary, in which I had published before. So much had been written about NCLB that either dealt with it strictly on the political and policy level, or energetically championed or damned it, that I wanted to try a piece that, though critical, would consider the legislation from multiple perspectives and also explain in plain language the problems with some of its core mechanisms, like the standardized test.

To the editor's credit, I got a quick, personal response, affirming the importance of the topic. But my treatment of it was "too wonky." Could I write something that is "faster" as to what works, what doesn't, and why? The piece I sent was "too cautious."

A "wonk" is someone who is taken by the details of a subject—in this case, education-al policy—and the implication is of narrow preoccupation, getting lost in detail, a grind. I was trying to explain the key elements of a piece of public policy and reflect on its implications, but to this editor, what I was doing came across as tedious, boring, the domain of the policy wonk but not the general public. We were at an impasse.

The editor's comments highlight several characteristics of contemporary media's treatment of public policy and social issues, all of which have been much discussed, often by media people themselves.

The first has to do with the definition of *news* itself. The process by which an event gets tagged as newsworthy is influenced by a host of variables, from novelty, conflict, and sensationalism ("If it bleeds, it leads") to an editor's tastes and beliefs. A central issue here involves the scripts or narratives typically used to frame a story. In my case, the editor wanted a "what works/what doesn't" structure, a kind of ledger sheet that, I'll admit, would make for a quicker read. (The equivalent, if we were looking at the politics of NCLB, would be a "who's winning/who's losing" story line.) Scripts like these contribute to what gets defined as a good news story. Pertinent here is a troubling finding in the Project for Excellence in Journal-ism's *The State of the News Media* 2008: the agenda of the American news media continues to narrow, not broaden. This is true, the report adds, for new media as well. Sadly, education gets a tiny percent of total news coverage, and that coverage will tend toward certain kinds of stories rather than others.

The second issue involves the increasing influence of an entertainment orientation on news and commentary. The length of stories is shrinking, as is their informational content. One example of many can be found in the average length of a presidential candidate's television sound bite. During the 1968 election it was 42 seconds; by 2004 it had been clipped to 7.6 seconds.[1] Newspapers and news magazines reflect the same impulse. Sam Zell, the real estate tycoon who owns the *Chicago Tribune* and *Los Angeles Times*, has been slashing and burning his papers to become, in his words, spicier, flashier, and easier to read.[2]

And all this is affected by the explosion of new media. As words decrease, images proliferate, amped up via digital technology. To be sure, images can contribute to powerful inquiry, depending on how they're sequenced and integrated with spoken or written text. But as Glynda Hull, a researcher of literacy and new media, observes, "Instead of examination of an issue, we tend to get simplification. The visual substitutes for narrative and analysis" (personal communication).

I've also noticed in print media, even in outlets pitched as highbrow, a rising value given to style that is arch or edgy. Liberal columnist Bob Herbert gets slammed in the liberal *Washington Monthly* because, though he's on the side of the magazine's angels, he's "boring."[3] Snap and sizzle. The quick over the deliberative. "Surprise me," an impatient public radio producer tells me as I pitch an idea for a Labor Day commentary.

If academics limit themselves through their specialized language, editors are limited as well by their own definitions of a newsworthy story and can overreact to the mere hint of scholarship, rejecting anything that, as one editor told me, "looks like a study."

***

I want to suggest some ways for academics to write successfully within this communicative tangle. I'll do so by describing two courses I developed to help graduate students write for broader audiences. These courses are housed in the place where I work, a graduate school of education, but, like education, rhetoric and composition is widely interdisciplinary and has a long reach into practice. The reader will see many parallels.

Education includes areas of study as diverse as history and developmental biology and psychology...as well as economics, linguistics, anthropology, political science, sociology, statistics, and more. It is not uncommon for a student to study several of these disciplines, acquiring their vocabularies and modes of argument along the way, acquiring as well the authority of disciplinary membership. But education is also intimately connected to broad public concerns, and the majority of students in education very much want to affect educational policy and practice. How do they turn, and tune, their voices from the seminar room to the public sphere? As they try to do so, they find themselves smack in the middle of a whole set of questions about communication: about writing, voice, audience, and the tension between the language of specialization and the language of public discourse. The school of education becomes a rhetorical laboratory.

I hadn't been in UCLA's School of Education for very long before these tensions became a focus of my teaching. Student after student in child development, or language policy, or the study of higher education sat in my office expressing a desire to make a difference in the world, to communicate with the public about educational issues that mattered deeply to them. But they didn't know how to do it, or, to be more exact, they worried that the specialized language of learning theory, or critical social thought, or organizational behavior that they had worked so hard to acquire both certified their authority in the academy and tongue-tied them when it came to writing for nonspecialists. Some also worried that these new languages—the syntax and vocabulary, the conventions and stance—left no room for a personal mark, for the deeply felt beliefs that brought them into education, for passion.

The first course I developed helps students become more effective scholarly writers. And while it certainly addresses everything from conventions of citation to summarizing a body of research literature, it also assists students in framing a tight argument and questioning it, in thinking hard about audience, in appropriating stylistic devices and considering the grace as well as informational content of their sentences.

The course is structured like a workshop, and each student begins by reading aloud a piece of his or her writing, even if half of it is charts and statistical tables. Because so many students in education come out of the social or psychological sciences, they have rarely, if ever, had the opportunity to think about their writing as *writing* and not just a vehicle to hold information. I want them to *hear* their writing. I urge them to find other scholarly and non-scholarly writers they like and read them like a writer, noting and analyzing what it is they do that works—and then incorporating those writers' techniques into their own work. At the end of the quarter, I think that the primary thing students acquire is a rhetorical sense of their writing; style and audience are more on their minds. As one student put it so well, "The course got me to think of my writing as strategic. Who am I writing to? Where do I want to take them with my argument? How can I get them there?" (For a fuller discussion of this course, see Rose and McClafferty.)

The second course shares a good deal with the workshop on scholarly writing, but is designed to help students in education write for the general public. The goal is to produce two pieces of writing: the newspaper op-ed piece and the magazine article. Students can vary these for online media, but the purpose remains the same: to draw on one's studies and research to write for a wide audience a 700- to 800-word opinion piece and a 1,500- to 2,500-word magazine article. Students are also required to familiarize themselves with appropriate outlets and submit to them.

To streamline our discussion here, I'll focus on the opinion piece, though my students and I go through the same process and make some of the same discoveries in writing the magazine article.

On the first day of class, I distribute a variety of opinion pieces—and encourage students to subsequently bring in ones they find that catch their fancy. We operate inductively, reading the selections and looking for characteristics and commonalities. Students immediately notice the brevity and conciseness of the opinion piece (versus the longer, more elaborated writing of their disciplines). Claims and arguments are made quickly and without heavy citation or marshalling of other research relevant to the topic.

Evidence is present in the opinion piece, of course, but it will be one or two key statistics or examples or reports, or a telling and crisp quotation from another expert. The length of this essay won't allow for many examples, but let me offer one here that my students liked. Writing about the plight of temp workers, labor policy analyst Laura Jones warns, "When it comes to benefits, temps better take their vitamins and look both ways before crossing the street: Only 5% receive employer-provided health insurance" (B5). The question that then emerges is, how does one select a sample of evidence that is vibrant yet still representative? Or, more challenging, how does one deal with conflicting evidence within constraints?

Students also notice features of the op-ed genre, particularly the "hook," the linking of the piece onto an event in the news. And, in some pieces, the "turn," that point where the writer, having summarized current policy or perception, turns the tables and offers another way—the way the writer prefers—to think about the issue at hand.

Opinion pieces are written in all kinds of styles and voices—from polemical to didactic to ironic—but students comment on the commonalities in language, the accessible vocabulary, the lack of jargon (or the judicious use of it, always defined), the frequent use of colloquial speech—always for rhetorical effect. Along with diction, they note the syntax of sentences—often not as complicated as they find in scholarly prose—and the short paragraphs (versus paragraphs that in scholarly writing can go on for a page).

This attention to style leads to experimentation: incorporating metaphor, varying sentence length, strategically shortening paragraphs. It also contributes to a heightened appreciation of revision and a commitment to it. "By the time I got done with my piece," one student said, "every sentence was changed. It does you no good to hold onto your precious words."

One thing I love about teaching this course—or the one focused more on scholarly writing—is how easily, readily big topics emerge, topics central to the kind of work the students envision for themselves. We might be talking in class about the kind of evidence to provide, and that discussion balloons to the issue of authority, of demonstrating expertise. Or we're down to the level of the sentence, mixing long sentences with short ones, or even the effective use of the semicolon or the dash, and suddenly we're talking about how someone wants to sound, to come across to a reader.

This concern about how one comes across has a lot to do with identity, a fundamental issue at this stage of a graduate student's development. What kind of work do I want to do? How can I sound at least a little bit distinctive while appropriating the linguistic conventions of my discipline? Whom do I want to write for; how narrowly or broadly will I think of my audience or audiences? Who am I as a scholar?

Another gratifying element of the course is the crossover effect that always emerges: These young scholars begin to apply the lessons learned in this class on popular writing to their academic prose. I encourage a kind of bilingualism, the continued development of facility with both scholarly writing and writing for nonspecialists. But there is playback, as well, from the opinion piece and magazine article onto the writing students do for their disciplines.

They learn, for example, to present their argument quickly, tersely, without the scaffolds of jargon, catchphrases, and a swarm of citations. This honing of language can have a powerful effect on a writer's conceptualization of the argument itself. What *exactly* am I trying to say here? What is the problem I'm trying to solve? What is the fundamental logic of my study? Writing the opinion piece, one student observed, "helped me think deeply about my topic. It's so easy to string a lot of fancy words together that look really important, but don't really have substance to them."

I've been writing about the crossover from the opinion piece to scholarly writing, but the crossover works in both directions. Students gain a heightened sense of the potential relevance of their work to issues of public concern. This awareness can vitalize scholarship.

The fostering of a hybrid professional identity—the life lived both in specialization and in the public sphere—is something I think we as a society need to nurture. The more opinion is grounded on rich experience and deep study, the better the quality of our public discourse about the issues that matter to us.

***

Even as I am helping young scholars write the newspaper opinion piece, newspapers themselves are in flux and being wrenched toward various blends with new media. "How can you convey profundity," a public relations friend of mine asks me, "through Twitter?" Though he used an extreme example with Twitter—the microblogging service where messages are limited to 140 characters—he was pressing a legitimate point. Am I preparing my students for a vanishing world? Is even the 600- to 700-word opinion piece becoming irrelevant?

Though my students are way savvier about new media than I am, I try to provide some guidance in writing for online outlets and in strategically blending image with text. Still, opinion pieces are published online, and many of the abilities students develop working on them carry over to newer genres: the rhetorical sensibility, the linguistic facility, the push toward conciseness.

It *is* hard for specialists to make their way in our complex and evolving media world. Lord knows, this world has handed me my fair share of rejections. But though difficult, it is not closed by any means, and the blogosphere offers its own wide range of options and entry points. One clear thing the history of technology shows us is that while a new technology does change things, sometimes dramatically, it also blends and morphs into existing technologies and social practices.

It is important then to keep in mind that various forms of media are not hermetic, not sealed off from each other. Many users shift from YouTube to a radio podcast, to Google Scholar, to a paperback recommended by a friend...possibly on Facebook. And skills learned in one form can transfer to another, and hybrid forms can emerge. A generative interaction. Here are a few quick examples from my own experience.

I mentioned earlier the importance of being concise without sacrificing your core claim or argument. At about the same time I wrote my first opinion piece, I was also beginning to do radio interviews. One medium is print-based and static, the other oral and interactive, but each in its way pushed me to refine the ability to state a point quickly. Also, talk radio—especially those shows with call-ins—really helped me develop a richer, more concrete sense of the audience out there, of possible misunderstandings or elaborations of a claim of mine or counter-arguments to it. And this experience with real and unpredictable audiences was certainly valuable when I sat down to compose something for the unknown readers of the opinion page.

Long inept with all things computeresque, I recently entered the blogosphere, and, probably because I didn't know better, I wrote in a traditional mode for this new medium. Millions of active blogs are out there, of all imaginable content and style, but few in the (admittedly) small sample I saw looked like what I had in mind.

Our national discussion of education has gotten terribly narrow, a discourse of economic competitiveness and test scores. So I wanted a blog that encouraged a more reflective, deliberative discussion of the purpose of education, and the essay more so than the typical blog post seemed the right genre. I wanted to use this new medium to write old-school, small essays about school. What is interesting is the degree to which the readers of the blog have responded in kind. Some of their comments are paragraphs long, crafted and thoughtful. A community college instructor writes a meditation on teaching and the purpose of education: "I love to pull my teaching cart out into the dark, smelling all the trees and flowers that are now only shadows, knowing that I and my students are tired from doing something worthwhile." Essayist literacy a mouse-click away from Twitter.

***

Rhetoric and composition is deeply connected to matters of broad public interest—literacy, teaching, undergraduate education—and for a while now, some within our field have been seeking public connection through service-learning, courses in civic rhetoric, or involvement in workplace and community literacy projects. There is talk of a "public turn" in composition studies, and several new journals are directly addressing public and community literacy. But the huge, clattering irony is that our field, a field that has rhetoric at its core, offers little or no graduate-level training for public writing or speaking. English and education don't either. Yet many in rhetoric and composition (and in education) are yearning to speak to wider audiences, to insert our various bodies of knowledge and perspectives into the public record.

We academics easily develop a tin ear to the sound of our own language. We talk too much to each other, and not beyond. We risk linguistic, intellectual, and political isolation. Many good things have come of rhetoric and composition's move toward disciplinary status. But with disciplinarity also comes a turn inward, a concentration on the mechanics of the profession, on internal debates and intellectual display, on a specific kind of career building—and it is all powerfully reinforced, materially and symbolically, by the academy.

There's nothing wrong with watching out for one's livelihood, of course not. And there's real value in a tradition that demands intellectual scrutiny within ranks. But, as Lisa Ede smartly observed a while back, there is a tendency for disciplines, for us, to create, or at least amp up, our debates by reducing and reifying one another's positions—then opposing them. This is the academic engine and, yes, it can contribute to more intense thinking. But it also keeps our attention focused on ourselves while all hell breaks loose in public policy and the broader public sphere.

I wonder how we might continue to turn outward through our disciplinary debates. How can we attend to both our field and the public domain...and find something generative in considering the two together?

The field of rhetoric and composition is grounded on the art of persuasion, is multidisciplinary, and has a foundational connection to teaching practice and education policy. It is the ideal place, as a number of people have been arguing lately, to imagine a different kind of disciplinary and institutional life.

We could begin in our graduate programs. Here's one small suggestion. We could offer training—through a course or some other curricular mechanism—in communicating to broader audiences, the *doing* of rhetoric. The training could include analysis of public policy and media to heighten sophistication about how they work and how one might find or create an entry point. And such training could also include rhetorical theory and history that enhances the understanding of such public intellectual work—I think here, as one example, of Jacqueline Jones Royster's *Traces of a Stream,* which offers a rich account of nineteenth-century African American women moving into and affecting public life with a rhetorically attuned public writing. Students would learn a lot about media and persuasion and the sometimes abstract notion of audience. And they would understand rhetoric, the rhetorical impulse and practice, in a way that is both grounded and fresh.[4]

Endnotes

1. These statistics come from two sources: Thomas E. Patterson's 1994 book *Out of Order* (160) and Erik P. Bucy and Maria Elizabeth Grabe's paper "Image Bite News" (20).
2. Zell is quoted by media reporter Richard Perez-Pena on WNYC's "On the Media," June 13, 2008.
3. See the very title of T.A. Frank's *Washington Monthly* article "Why Is Bob Herbert Boring?" *Washington Monthly*, October, 2007, 16–20.
4. I would like to thank the following people for their comments on an earlier version of this essay: Richard Lee Colvin, Ellen Cushman, Casandra Harper, Linda Kao, Elham Kazemi, Rema Reynolds, and Kerri Ullucci.

References

Bucy, Erik P., and Maria Elizabeth Grabe. "Image Bite News: An Underappreciated Source of Political Information." American Political Science Association. Marriott, Loew's Philadelphia, and the Pennsylvania Convention Center, Philadelphia. 31 Aug. 2006. Address.

Ede, Lisa. "Reading the Writing Process." *Taking Stock: The Writing Process Movement in the '90s.* Ed. Lad Tobin and Thomas Newkirk. Portsmouth: Boynton/Cook, 1994. 31–43. Print.

Hull, Glynda. Personal Communication. 13 June 2008.

Jones, Laura. "For Temps, There Are No Holidays." *Los Angeles Times* 6 Sept. 1999: B5. Print.

Limerick, Patricia Nelson. "Dancing with Professors: The Trouble with Academic Prose." *New York Times Book Review* 31 Oct. 1993: 3, 23–24. Print.

Patterson, Thomas E. *Out of Order.* New York: Knopf, 1993. Print.

Project for Excellence in Journalism. *The State of the News Media 2008: An Annual Report on American Journalism.* Project for Excellence in Journalism, 17 Mar. 2008. Web. 9 July 2009.

Rose, Mike. *Lives on the Boundary: The Struggles and Achievements of America's Underprepared.* New York: Free Press, 1989. Print.

Rose, Mike, and Karen McClafferty. "A Call for the Teaching of Writing in Graduate Education." *Educational Researcher* 30.2 (2001): 27–33. Print.

Royster, Jacqueline Jones. *Traces of a Stream: Literacy and Social Change among African American Women.* Pittsburgh: U of Pittsburgh P, 2000. Print.

DISCUSSION *questions and activities*

1. In the first part of his commentary, Rose describes having to split his attention between an academic audience and a general audience. Have you ever felt as though you were trying to write to two or more distinct audiences at once? If so, how did you manage it?

2. Does Rose take his own advice in this argument and apply his principles to help academics write more accessibly?

3. Compare Rose's perspective on academic language and writing to that taken by Eubanks and Shaeffer in "A Kind Word for Bullshit: The Problems with Academic Writing." How are their attitudes and analyses similar or different?

A Modest Proposal

Jonathan Swift

Jonathan Swift (1667-1745) is best known for Gulliver's Travels. He is considered one of the giants of eighteenth century literature, a period known for the rise of satire as a dominant genre. As the Dean of St. Patrick's Cathedral in Dublin, Ireland, Swift was deeply invested in the welfare of the Irish people who were facing food shortages under the policies of the British government. "A Modest Proposal" addresses these social conditions in the voice of an early social scientist. Its tone is completely reasonable; its argument is monstrous.

It is a melancholy object to those, who walk through this great town, or travel in the country, when they see the streets, the roads and cabbin-doors crowded with beggars of the female sex, followed by three, four, or six children, all in rags, and importuning every passenger for an alms. These mothers instead of being able to work for their honest livelihood, are forced to employ all their time in stroling to beg sustenance for their helpless infants who, as they grow up, either turn thieves for want of work, or leave their dear native country, to fight for the Pretender in Spain, or sell themselves to the Barbadoes.

I think it is agreed by all parties, that this prodigious number of children in the arms, or on the backs, or at the heels of their mothers, and frequently of their fathers, is in the present deplorable state of the kingdom, a very great additional grievance; and therefore whoever could find out a fair, cheap and easy method of making these children sound and useful members of the commonwealth, would deserve so well of the publick, as to have his statue set up for a preserver of the nation.

But my intention is very far from being confined to provide only for the children of professed beggars: it is of a much greater extent, and shall take in the whole number of infants at a certain age, who are born of parents in effect as little able to support them, as those who demand our charity in the streets.

As to my own part, having turned my thoughts for many years, upon this important subject, and maturely weighed the several schemes of our projectors, I have always found them grossly mistaken in their computation. It is true, a child just dropt from its dam, may be supported by her milk, for a solar year, with little other nourishment: at most not above the value of two shillings, which the mother may certainly get, or the value in scraps, by her lawful occupation of begging; and it is exactly at one year old that I propose to provide for them in such a manner, as, instead of being a charge upon their parents, or the parish, or wanting food and raiment for the rest of their lives, they shall, on the contrary, contribute to the feeding, and partly to the cloathing of many thousands.

There is likewise another great advantage in my scheme, that it will prevent those voluntary abortions, and that horrid practice of women murdering their bastard children, alas! too frequent among us, sacrificing the poor innocent babes, I doubt, more to avoid the expence than the shame, which would move tears and pity in the most savage and inhuman breast.

The number of souls in this kingdom being usually reckoned one million and a half, of these I calculate there may be about two hundred thousand couple whose wives are breeders; from which number I subtract thirty thousand couple, who are able to maintain their own children, (although I apprehend there cannot be so many, under the present distresses of the kingdom) but this being granted, there will remain an hundred and seventy thousand breeders. I again subtract fifty thousand, for those women who miscarry, or whose children die by accident or disease within the year. There only remain an hundred and twenty thousand children of poor parents annually born. The question therefore is, How this number shall be reared, and provided for? which, as I have already said, under the present situation of affairs, is utterly impossible by all the methods hitherto proposed. For we can neither employ them in handicraft or agriculture; we neither build houses, (I mean in the country) nor cultivate land: they can very seldom pick up a livelihood by stealing till they arrive at six years old; except where they are of towardly parts, although I confess they learn the rudiments much earlier; during which time they can however be properly looked upon only as probationers: As I have been informed by a principal gentleman in the county of Cavan, who protested to me, that he never knew above one or two instances under the age of six, even in a part of the kingdom so renowned for the quickest proficiency in that art.

I am assured by our merchants, that a boy or a girl before twelve years old, is no saleable commodity, and even when they come to this age, they will not yield above three pounds, or three pounds and half a crown at most, on the exchange; which cannot turn to account either to the parents or kingdom, the charge of nutriments and rags having been at least four times that value.

I shall now therefore humbly propose my own thoughts, which I hope will not be liable to the least objection.

I have been assured by a very knowing American of my acquaintance in London, that a young healthy child well nursed, is, at a year old, a most delicious nourishing and wholesome food, whether stewed, roasted, baked, or boiled; and I make no doubt that it will equally serve in a fricasie, or a ragoust.

I do therefore humbly offer it to publick consideration, that of the hundred and twenty thousand children, already computed, twenty thousand may be reserved for breed, whereof only one fourth part to be males; which is more than we allow to sheep, black cattle, or swine, and my reason is, that these children are seldom the fruits of marriage, a circumstance not much regarded by our savages, therefore, one male will be sufficient to serve four females. That the remaining hundred thousand may, at a year old, be offered in sale to the persons of quality and fortune, through the kingdom, always advising the mother to let them suck plentifully in the last month, so as to render them plump, and fat for a good table. A child will make two dishes at an entertainment for friends, and when the family dines alone, the fore or hind quarter will make a reasonable dish, and seasoned with a little pepper or salt, will be very good boiled on the fourth day, especially in winter.

I have reckoned upon a medium, that a child just born will weigh 12 pounds, and in a solar year, if tolerably nursed, encreaseth to 28 pounds.

I grant this food will be somewhat dear, and therefore very proper for landlords, who, as they have already devoured most of the parents, seem to have the best title to the children.

Infant's flesh will be in season throughout the year, but more plentiful in March, and a little before and after; for we are told by a grave author, an eminent French physician, that fish being a prolifick dyet, there are more children born in Roman Catholick countries about nine months after Lent, the markets will be more glutted than usual, because the number of Popish infants, is at least three to one in this kingdom, and therefore it will have one other collateral advantage, by lessening the number of Papists among us.

I have already computed the charge of nursing a beggar's child (in which list I reckon all cottagers, labourers, and four-fifths of the farmers) to be about two shillings per annum, rags included; and I believe no gentleman would repine to give ten shillings for the carcass of a good fat child, which, as I have said, will make four dishes of excellent nutritive meat, when he hath only some particular friend, or his own family to dine with him. Thus the squire will learn to be a good landlord, and grow popular among his tenants, the mother will have eight shillings neat profit, and be fit for work till she produces another child.

Those who are more thrifty (as I must confess the times require) may flea the carcass; the skin of which, artificially dressed, will make admirable gloves for ladies, and summer boots for fine gentlemen.

As to our City of Dublin, shambles may be appointed for this purpose, in the most convenient parts of it, and butchers we may be assured will not be wanting; although I rather recommend buying the children alive, and dressing them hot from the knife, as we do roasting pigs.

A very worthy person, a true lover of his country, and whose virtues I highly esteem, was lately pleased, in discoursing on this matter, to offer a refinement upon my scheme. He said, that many gentle-men of this kingdom, having of late destroyed their deer, he conceived that the want of venison might be well supply'd by the bodies of young lads and maidens, not exceeding fourteen years of age, nor under twelve; so great a number of both sexes in every country being now ready to starve for want of work and service: And these to be disposed of by their parents if alive, or otherwise by their nearest relations. But with due deference to so excellent a friend, and so deserving a patriot, I cannot be altogether in his sentiments; for as to the males, my American acquaintance assured me from frequent experience, that their flesh was generally tough and lean, like that of our school-boys, by continual exercise, and their taste disagreeable, and to fatten them would not answer the charge. Then as to the females, it would, I think, with humble submission, be a loss to the publick, because they soon would become breeders themselves: And besides, it is not improbable that some scrupulous people might be apt to censure such a practice, (although indeed very unjustly) as a little bordering upon cruelty, which, I confess, hath always been with me the strongest objection against any project, how well soever intended.

But in order to justify my friend, he confessed, that this expedient was put into his head by the famous Salmanaazor, a native of the island Formosa, who came from thence to London, above twenty years ago, and in conversation told my friend, that in his country, when any young person happened to be put to death, the executioner sold the carcass to persons of quality, as a prime dainty; and that, in his time, the body of a plump girl of fifteen, who was crucified for an attempt to poison the Emperor, was sold to his imperial majesty's prime minister of state, and other great mandarins of the court in joints from the gibbet, at four hundred crowns. Neither indeed can I deny, that if the same use were made of several plump young girls in this town, who without one single groat to their fortunes, cannot stir abroad without a chair, and appear at a play-house and assemblies in foreign fineries which they never will pay for; the kingdom would not be the worse.

Some persons of a desponding spirit are in great concern about that vast number of poor people, who are aged, diseased, or maimed; and I have been desired to employ my thoughts what course may be taken, to ease the nation of so grievous an incumbrance. But I am not in the least pain upon that matter, because it is very well known, that they are every day dying, and rotting, by cold and famine, and filth, and vermin, as fast as can be reasonably expected. And as to the young labourers, they are now in almost as hopeful a condition. They cannot get work, and consequently pine away from want of nourishment, to a degree, that if at any time they are accidentally hired to common labour, they have not strength to perform it, and thus the country and themselves are happily delivered from the evils to come.

I have too long digressed, and therefore shall return to my subject. I think the advantages by the proposal which I have made are obvious and many, as well as of the highest importance.

For first, as I have already observed, it would greatly lessen the number of Papists, with whom we are yearly over-run, being the principal breeders of the nation, as well as our most dangerous enemies, and who stay at home on purpose with a design to deliver the kingdom to the Pretender, hoping to take their advantage by the absence of so many good Protestants, who have chosen rather to leave their country, than stay at home and pay tithes against their conscience to an episcopal curate.

Secondly, The poorer tenants will have something valuable of their own, which by law may be made liable to a distress, and help to pay their landlord's rent, their corn and cattle being already seized, and money a thing unknown.

Thirdly, Whereas the maintainance of an hundred thousand children, from two years old, and upwards, cannot be computed at less than ten shillings a piece per annum, the nation's stock will be thereby encreased fifty thousand pounds per annum, besides the profit of a new dish, introduced to the tables of all gentlemen of fortune in the kingdom, who have any refinement in taste. And the money will circulate among our selves, the goods being entirely of our own growth and manufacture.

Fourthly, The constant breeders, besides the gain of eight shillings sterling per annum by the sale of their children, will be rid of the charge of maintaining them after the first year.

Fifthly, This food would likewise bring great custom to taverns, where the vintners will certainly be so prudent as to procure the best receipts for dressing it to perfection; and consequently have their houses frequented by all the fine gentlemen, who justly value themselves upon their knowledge in good eating; and a skilful cook, who understands how to oblige his guests, will contrive to make it as expensive as they please.

Sixthly, This would be a great inducement to marriage, which all wise nations have either encouraged by rewards, or enforced by laws and penalties. It would encrease the care and tenderness of mothers towards their children, when they were sure of a settlement for life to the poor babes, provided in some sort by the publick, to their annual profit instead of expence. We should soon see an honest emulation among the married women, which of them could bring the fattest child to the market. Men would become as fond of their wives, during the time of their pregnancy, as they are now of their mares in foal, their cows in calf, or sow when they are ready to farrow; nor offer to beat or kick them (as is too frequent a practice) for fear of a miscarriage.

Many other advantages might be enumerated. For instance, the addition of some thousand carcasses in our exportation of barrel'd beef: the propagation of swine's flesh, and improvement in the art of making good bacon, so much wanted among us by the great destruction of pigs, too frequent at our tables; which are no way comparable in taste or magnificence to a well grown, fat yearly child, which roasted whole will make a considerable figure at a Lord Mayor's feast, or any other publick entertainment. But this, and many others, I omit, being studious of brevity.

Supposing that one thousand families in this city, would be constant customers for infants flesh, besides others who might have it at merry meetings, particularly at weddings and christenings, I compute that Dublin would take off annually about twenty thousand carcasses; and the rest of the kingdom (where probably they will be sold somewhat cheaper) the remaining eighty thousand.

I can think of no one objection, that will possibly be raised against this proposal, unless it should be urged, that the number of people will be thereby much lessened in the kingdom. This I freely own, and 'twas indeed one principal design in offering it to the world. I desire the reader will observe, that I calculate my remedy for this one individual Kingdom of Ireland, and for no other that ever was, is, or, I think, ever can be upon Earth. Therefore let no man talk to me of other expedients: Of taxing our absentees at five shillings a pound: Of using neither cloaths, nor houshold furniture, except what is of our own growth and manufacture: Of utterly rejecting the materials and instruments that promote foreign luxury: Of curing the expensiveness of pride, vanity, idleness, and gaming in our women: Of introducing a vein of parsimony, prudence and temperance: Of learning to love our country, wherein we differ even from Laplanders, and the inhabitants of Topinamboo: Of quitting our animosities and factions, nor acting any longer like the Jews, who were murdering one another at the very moment their city was taken: Of being a little cautious not to sell our country and consciences for nothing: Of teaching landlords to have at least one degree of mercy towards their tenants. Lastly, of putting a spirit of honesty, industry, and skill into our shop-keepers, who, if a resolution could now be taken to buy only our native goods, would immediately unite to cheat and exact upon us in the price, the measure, and the goodness, nor could ever yet be brought to make one fair proposal of just dealing, though often and earnestly invited to it.

Therefore I repeat, let no man talk to me of these and the like expedients, 'till he hath at least some glympse of hope, that there will ever be some hearty and sincere attempt to put them into practice.

But, as to my self, having been wearied out for many years with offering vain, idle, visionary thoughts, and at length utterly despairing of success, I fortunately fell upon this proposal, which, as it is wholly new, so it hath something solid and real, of no expence and little trouble, full in our own power, and whereby we can incur no danger in disobliging England. For this kind of commodity will not bear exportation, and flesh being of too tender a consistence, to admit a long continuance in salt, although perhaps I could name a country, which would be glad to eat up our whole nation without it.

After all, I am not so violently bent upon my own opinion, as to reject any offer, proposed by wise men, which shall be found equally innocent, cheap, easy, and effectual. But before something of that kind shall be advanced in contradiction to my scheme, and offering a better, I desire the author or authors will be pleased maturely to consider two points. First, As things now stand, how they will be able to find food and raiment for a hundred thousand useless mouths and backs. And secondly, There being a round million of creatures in humane figure throughout this kingdom, whose whole subsistence put into a common stock, would leave them in debt two million of pounds sterling, adding those who are beggars by profession, to the bulk of farmers, cottagers and labourers, with their wives and children, who are beggars in effect; I desire those politicians who dislike my overture, and may perhaps be so bold to attempt an answer, that they will first ask the parents of these mortals, whether they would not at this day think it a great happiness to have been sold for food at a year old, in the manner I prescribe, and thereby have avoided such a perpetual scene of misfortunes, as they have since gone through, by the oppression of landlords, the impossibility of paying rent without money or trade, the want of common sustenance, with neither house nor cloaths to cover them from the inclemencies of the weather, and the most inevitable prospect of intailing the like, or greater miseries, upon their breed for ever.

I profess, in the sincerity of my heart, that I have not the least personal interest in endeavouring to promote this necessary work, having no other motive than the publick good of my country, by advancing our trade, providing for infants, relieving the poor, and giving some pleasure to the rich. I have no children, by which I can propose to get a single penny; the youngest being nine years old, and my wife past child-bearing.

DISCUSSION *questions and activities*

1. The narrator is making a proposal argument. Summarize his plan for the economic improvement of poor Irish families.
2. How does the author make cannibalism sound completely reasonable? Does he use any of the techniques that you are learning in your writing course?
3. Irony is defined as a rhetorical strategy where the literal meaning is the opposite of what the author intends the audience to understand. In small groups, discuss the advantages and dangers of presenting an argument ironically.

What the Public Doesn't Get About Climate Change

Bryan Walsh

Bryan Walsh is an environmental writer and a contributor to Ecocentric, a TIME blog focusing on diverse subjects related to environmentalism and the green movement. "What the Public Doesn't Get About Climate Change" was published in TIME *in October 2008. In the article, Walsh responds to the results of a study that had been recently published in* Science, *a peer-reviewed academic journal sponsored by the American Association for the Advancement of Science.*

As I report on climate change, I come across a lot of scary facts, like the possibility that thawing permafrost in Siberia could release gigatons of carbon dioxide into the atmosphere or the risk that Greenland could pass a tipping point and begin to melt rapidly. But one of the most frightening studies I've read recently had nothing to do with icebergs or mega-droughts. In a paper that came out Oct. 23 in *Science,* John Sterman—a professor at Massachusetts Institute of Technology's (MIT) Sloan School of Management— wrote about asking 212 MIT grad students to give a rough idea of how much governments need to reduce global greenhouse gas emissions by to eventually stop the increase in the concentration of carbon in the atmosphere. These students had training in science, technology, mathematics and economics at one of the best schools in the world—they are probably a lot smarter than you or me. Yet 84% of Sterman's subjects got the question wrong, greatly underestimating the degree to which greenhouse gas emissions need to fall. When the MIT kids can't figure out climate change, what are the odds that the broader public will?

The shocking study reflects the tremendous gap that exists regarding global warming. On the one hand are the scientists, who with few exceptions think climate change is very serious and needs to be dealt with immediately and ambitiously. On the other side is the public, which increasingly believes that climate change is real and worries about it, but which rarely ranks it as a high priority. A 2007 survey by the U.N. Development Programme found that 54% of Americans advocate taking a "wait and see" approach to climate-change action—holding off on the deep and rapid cuts in global warming that would immediately impact their lives. (And it's not just SUV-driving Americans who take this position— similar majorities were found in Russia, China and India.) As a result, we have our current dilemma: a steady drumbeat of scientific evidence of global warming's severity and comparatively little in the way of meaningful political action. "This gap exists," says Sterman. "The real question is why."

That's where Sterman's research comes in. "There is a profound and fundamental misconception about climate," he says. The problem is that most of us don't really understand how carbon accumulates in the atmosphere. Increasing global temperatures are driven by the increase in the concentration of carbon in the atmosphere. Before the industrial age, the concentration was about 280 parts per million (p.p.m.) of carbon in the atmosphere. After a few centuries of burning coal, oil and other fossil fuels, we've raised that concentration to 387 p.p.m., and it continues to rise by about 2 p.p.m. every year.

Many scientists believe that we need to at least stabilize carbon concentrations at 450 p.p.m. to ensure that global temperatures don't increase more than about 2 degrees Celsius above the pre-industrial level. To do that, we need to reduce global carbon emissions (which hit about 10 billion tons last year) until they are equal to or less than the amount of carbon sequestered by the oceans and plant life (which removed about 4.8 billion tons of carbon last year). It's just like water in a bathtub—unless more water is draining out than flowing in from the tap, eventually the bathtub will overflow.

That means that carbon emissions would need to be cut drastically from current levels. Yet almost all of the subjects in Sterman's study failed to realize that, assuming instead that you could stabilize carbon concentration simply by capping carbon emissions at their current level. That's not the case—and in fact, pursuing such a plan for the future would virtually guarantee that global warming could spin out of control. It may seem to many like good common sense to wait until we see proof of the serious damage global warming is doing before we take action. But it's not—we can't "wait and see" on global warming because the climate has a momentum all its own, and if we wait for decades to finally act to reduce carbon emissions, it could well be too late. Yet this simply isn't understood. Someone as smart as Bill Gates doesn't seem to get it. "Fortunately climate change, although it's a huge challenge, it's a challenge that happens over a long period of time," he said at a forum in Beijing last year. "You know, we have time to work on it." But the truth is we don't.

If élite scientists could simply solve climate change on their own, public misunderstanding wouldn't be such a problem. But they can't. Reducing carbon emissions sharply will require all 6.5 billion (and growing) of us on the planet to hugely change the way we use energy and travel. We'll also need to change the way we vote, rewarding politicians willing to make the tough choices on climate. Instead of a new Manhattan Project—the metaphor often used for global warming—Sterman believes that what is needed is closer to a new civil rights movement, a large-scale campaign that dramatically changes the public's beliefs and behaviors. New groups like Al Gore's We Campaign are aiming for just such a social transformation, but "the reality is that this is even more difficult than civil rights," says Sterman. "Even that took a long time, and we don't have that kind of time with the climate."

The good news is that you don't need a Ph.D. in climatology to understand what needs to be done. If you can grasp the bathtub analogy, you can understand how to stop global warming. The burden is on scientists to better explain in clear English the dynamics of the climate system, and how to affect it. (Sterman says that the Intergovernmental Panel on Climate Change's landmark report last year was "completely inadequate" on this score.) As for the rest of us, we should try to remember that sometimes common sense isn't a match for science.

DISCUSSION *questions and activities*

1. Is the support Walsh presents for his claim convincing? Why or why not?
2. Do you think Walsh considers his primary audience as part of the public that "doesn't get" climate change? Use specific passages from the article to explain your response.
3. In his last paragraph, Walsh suggests that "if you can grasp the bathtub analogy, you can understand how to stop global warming." Do you think using metaphors to describe global warming would assist scientists in communicating its severity? Why or why not?
4. Walsh puts much of the blame for the public's lack of understanding of climate change on how the scientists themselves communicate. Consider this piece in connection with Pierce's *Greetings from Idiot America*. How might the scientific community need to change their approach on communicating climate change to the audience that Pierce describes?

Newburgh Address

George Washington

George Washington (1732–1799) may seem like an untouchable icon today in his role as the first president of the United States. In his time, however, the outcome of the revolutionary struggle was often in doubt. His Newburgh Address in 1783 came at the end of the Revolutionary War when the troops he commanded had not been paid for months. He appeared unexpectedly and turned the mood from mutinous to supportive, largely on account of his ethos. Another selection in this book ("George Washington's Tear-Jerker") analyzes the context and reception of this speech. For further information on Washington: www.whitehouse.gov/about/presidents/georgewashington.

By an anonymous summons, an attempt has been made to convene you together. How inconsistent with the rules of propriety, how unmilitary and how subversive of all order and discipline let the good sense of the army decide.

In the moment of this summons, another anonymous production was sent into circulation, addressed more to the feelings of passions than to the reason and judgment of the army. The author of the piece is entitled to much credit for the goodness of his pen, and I could wish he had as much credit for the rectitude of his heart. For, as men, we see through different optics, and are induced by the reflecting faculties of the mind to use different means to attain the same end. The author of the address should have had more charity than to mark with suspicion the man who would recommend moderation or longer forbearance, or, in other words, who should not think as he thinks and act as he advises. But, he had another plan in view, in which candor and liberality of sentiment, regard for justice, and love of country have no part. And, he was right to insinuate the darkest suspicion to effect the blackest designs.

That the address is drawn with great art and is designed to answer the most insidious purposes, that it is calculated to impress the mind with an idea of premeditated injustice to the sovereign power of the United States and rouse all those resentments which must unavoidably flow from such a belief, that the secret mover of this scheme (whoever he may be) intended to take advantage of the passions while they were warmed by the recollection of past distresses without giving time for cool, deliberative thinking and that composure of mind which is so necessary to give dignity and stability to measures is rendered too obvious by the mode of conducting the business to need other proof than a reference to the preceding.

Thus much, Gentlemen, I have thought it incumbent on me to observe to you, to show upon what principles I opposed the irregular and hasty meeting which was proposed to have been held on Tuesday last, and not because I wanted a disposition to give you every opportunity, consistent with your honor and the dignity of the army, to make known your grievances. If my conduct heretofore has not evinced to you that I have been a faithful friend to the army, my declaration of it at this time would be equally unavailing and improper. But, as I was among the first who embarked in the cause of our common country, as I have never left your side one moment but when called on public duty, as I have been the constant companion and witness of your distresses and not among the last to feel and acknowledge your merits, as I have ever considered my own military reputation as inseparably connected with that of the army, as my heart has ever expanded with joy when I heard its praises and my indignation has arisen when the mouth of detraction has been opened against it, it can scarcely be supposed, at this late stage of the war, that I am indifferent to its interests.

But, how are they to be promoted? The way is plain, says the anonymous addresser. If war continues, remove into the unsettled country, there establish yourselves, and leave an ungrateful country to defend itself. But, who are they to defend? Our wives, our children, our farms, and other property which we leave behind us. Or, in this state of hostile separation, are we to take the first two (the latter cannot be removed) to perish in a wilderness with hunger, cold and nakedness? If peace takes place, never sheath your sword, says he, until you have obtained full and ample justice. This dreadful alternative, of deserting our country in the extremest hour of her distress or turning our arms against it (which is the apparent object unless Congress can be compelled into instant compliance) has something so shocking in it that humanity revolts at the idea. My God! What can this writer have in view by recommending such measures? Can he be a friend to the army? Can he be a friend to this country? Rather is he not an insidious foe, some emissary, perhaps, from New York, plotting the ruin of both by sowing the seeds of discord and separation between the civil and military powers of the continent? And, what compliment does he pay to our understandings when he recommends measures in either alternative impracticable in their nature?

But here, Gentlemen, I will drop the curtain. And, because it would be as imprudent in me to assign my reasons for this opinion as it would be insulting to your conception to suppose you stood in need of them, a moment's reflection will convince every dispassionate mind of the physical impossibility of carrying either proposal into execution.

There might, Gentlemen, be an impropriety in my taking notice in this address to you of an anonymous production, but the manner in which that performance has been introduced to the army, the effect it was intended to have, together with some other circumstances, will amply justify my observations on the tendency of that writing. With respect to the advice given by the author to suspect the man who shall recommend moderate measures and longer forbearance—I spurn it, as every man who regards that liberty and reveres that justice for which we contend undoubtedly must. For if men are to be precluded from offering their sentiments on a matter which may involve the most serious and alarming consequences that can invite the consideration of mankind, reason is of no use to us. The freedom of speech may be taken away and, dumb and silent, we may be led like sheep to the slaughter.

I cannot, in justice to my own belief and what I have great reason to conceive is the intention of Congress, conclude this address without giving it as my decided opinion that that Honorable body entertain exalted sentiments of the services of the army and, from a full conviction of its merits and sufferings, will do it complete justice. That their endeavors to discover and establish funds for this purpose have been unwearied and will not cease till they have succeeded, I have no doubt. But, like all other large bodies where there is a variety of different interests to reconcile, their deliberations are slow. Why then should we distrust them and, in consequence of that distrust, adopt measures which may cast a shadow over that glory which has been so justly acquired and tarnish the reputation of an army which is celebrated through all Europe for its fortitude and patriotism? And for what is this done? To bring the object we seek nearer? No! Most certainly, in my opinion, it will cast it at a greater distance.

For myself (and I take no merit in giving the assurance, being induced to it from principles of gratitude, veracity and justice), a grateful sense of the confidence you have ever placed in me, a recollection of the cheerful assistance and prompt obedience I have experienced from you under every vicissitude of fortune, and the sincere affection I feel for an army I have so long had the honor to command, will oblige me to declare in this public and solemn manner that in the attainment of complete justice for all your toils and dangers and in the gratification of every wish, so far as may be done consistently with the great duty I owe my country and those powers we are bound to respect, you may freely command my services to the utmost of my abilities.

While I give you these assurances and pledge myself in the most unequivocal manner to exert whatever ability I am possessed of in your favor, let me entreat you, Gentlemen, on your part, not to take any measures which, viewed in the calm light of reason, will lessen the dignity and sully the glory you have hitherto maintained. Let me request you to rely on the plighted faith of your country and place a full confidence in the purity of the intentions of Congress that, previous to dissolution as an army, they will cause all your accounts to be liquidated as directed in their resolutions which were published to you two days ago, and that they will adopt the most effectual measures in their power to render ample justice to you for your faithful and meritorious services. And, let me conjure you in the name of our common country, as you value your own sacred honor, as you respect the rights of humanity, as you regard the military and national character of America, to express your utmost horror and detestation of the man who wishes, under any specious pretenses, to overturn the liberties of our country and who wickedly attempts to open the floodgates of civil discord and deluge our rising empire in blood.

By thus determining, and thus acting, you will pursue the plain and direct road to the attainment of your wishes. You will defeat the insidious designs of our enemies, who are compelled to resort from open force to secret artifice. You will give one more distinguished proof of unexampled patriotism and patient virtue, rising superior to the pressure of the most complicated sufferings. And you will, by the dignity of your conduct, afford for posterity to say, when speaking of the glorious example you have exhibited to mankind: "Had this day been wanting, the world had never seen the last stage of perfection to which human nature is capable of attaining."

DISCUSSION *questions and activities*

1. What is Washington's stance in regard to the back pay issue for the troops?
2. How does Washington deal with his audience's negative feelings for the government?
3. What sense does the speech give you of Washington's character?
4. Compare Washington's use of pathos and propaganda techniques with another speech from contemporary American politics. Do you see the same strategies in place? Why or why not?

Colombia Uses Ads to Persuade Rebels to Turn Themselves In

Laurel Wentz

Laurel Wentz is the international and multicultural affairs editor for Advertising Age, *a prominent trade publication for the media and marketing industry. Wentz's career as a reporter has placed her in several countries in Latin America including Mexico, Argentina, and Brazil. Her article was originally published in* AdAge *on November, 16, 2009. The online version included the video of the original ad that the Colombian government used to persuade guerillas to give themselves up. You can access it on the AdAge website: www.adage.com.*

Not a lot of ad campaigns target armed guerrillas who live in the jungle. But it's an established strategy in Colombia.

Wracked by years of guerrilla warfare, the Colombian government has been steadily slashing the number of fighters from groups like the Revolutionary Armed Forces of Colombia, better known as FARC. An ad campaign by Bogota-based Lowe SSP3 is helping to encourage armed insurgents to defect from the jungle using advertising built around what disillusions them about life as a revolutionary, supported with a media plan that leans heavily on soccer games they like to watch.

Jose Miguel Sokoloff, chief creative officer of Lowe SSP3, said his creative team spent weeks with former guerrilla fighters interviewing and getting to know them. The big insight that emerged was that those who defected felt as if they had become as much a prisoner as their hostages, lacking any personal freedom and deprived of all family life. Asked what they do in the jungle when not fighting, the rebels responded: "We watch soccer."

A plan was born. TV and radio spots air during soccer games such as Colombia's Nov. 12 match against Switzerland, which the guerrillas listen to on the radio or watch on DirecTV (funded by drug operations, groups like FARC can easily afford satellite TV). Lowe's first TV spots were mostly re-enactments of true stories—a young woman forced to abort her baby, a young man ordered to kill his comrades—accompanied by a voice-over from the guerrilla who told the story. Newer radio and TV spots are testimonials, filmed on a camcorder by Lowe or army officials, from guerrillas who have just turned themselves in. Sounding awkward but strikingly genuine, they talk about their reasons for leaving and why they became disillusioned. Ads end with the tagline: "Think about it. There's another life. Demobilization is the way out."

It's not easy. Rebels seeking a way out have to escape from the guerrilla camp in the jungle and then turn themselves in to Colombian soldiers who have been told not to harm them. One defector ensured his welcome by showing up with a severed hand, Mr. Sokoloff said. He had executed his comandante, a senior rebel leader.

Demobilization

The Colombian government started trying to get guerrillas to defect back in 2002, but Sergio Jaramillo, Colombia's vice minister for defense, recognized the need for an organized, strategic ad campaign to drive the ongoing demobilization effort, and Lowe SSP3 was approached in 2006.

Lowe SSP3's work is pro bono but Colombia's Ministry of Defense has an annual paid media budget of about $800,000 for the campaign, used to distribute fliers in rural towns visited by fighters and buy airtime during soccer games and the news programs watched by higher-level insurgents. Of course, even if all the guerrillas tuned in, most of the soccer audience is made up of ordinary Colombians.

"The Ministry of Defense said the advertising had to do two things: get people out of the guerrilla [forces], but also let the rest of the country understand we're winning this war," Mr. Sokoloff said.

When a senior rebel commander defects, for instance, an ad is quickly made with the defector's story, to encourage all Colombians to believe the tide has turned, as well as to pinpoint the remaining rebels.

About 11,405 armed insurgents were demobilized between 2002 and 2008, including 3,461 in 2008, an increase of about 8% over the year before. Mr. Sokoloff said the percentage is probably higher this year, judging from the steadily declining ranks of fighters.

Declining ranks

A decade ago, Colombia's terrorist groups had as many as 30,000 members. Despite new recruits, that number is now down to an estimated 3,000 to 8,000 armed rebels, following Colombian President Alvaro Uribe's aggressive moves against them since he took office in 2002. Estimates are difficult because fighters vanish by burying their weapons and dressing as villagers, then reappearing later. Even counting dead guerrillas is a challenge; rebels bury the bodies to make it harder for the government to claim victories.

So return on investment, so to speak, from the campaign is hard to calculate. But in a sign that people may be leaving now because the campaign's message has sunk in, defections are no longer as directly correlated to military strikes against the insurgents as they used to be, Mr. Sokoloff said. "With the number of defections, they are very weakened, and their lack of military power is very real."

The campaign makes sure that message gets out. One flier, distributed last year in rural towns where fighters go on their days off, says "Demobilization is your way out. More than 8,900 of your compañeros have done it." Like any good direct-response piece, the flier includes a guerrilla hotline number, and two smiling pictures of bearded former rebels who didn't seize the opportunity—one was killed by the army, and the other by his own men.

As the campaign has gained momentum, other Colombians, from international pop star Shakira to local newspaper El Espectador, have joined in, usually checking with Lowe SSP3 and the Colombian government first to make sure they're on-message. "Other brands and voices have joined this fight," Mr. Sokoloff said. "It's something we Colombians believe in."

One moving TV spot, for instance, features real footage of a FARC hostage released after almost seven years in the jungle as his two now-teenage sons leap to hug him. That spot was done by El Espectador at the suggestion of Lowe SSP3's media-buying agency BEAT. A creative who has since joined Lowe put it together, and the ad ends with the daily's own tagline. Two well-known local singers wrote a song about leaving the jungle that became a hit, and Shakira made an appeal to the armed groups to release their hostages and demobilize.

Another sign that the program is working is the increasing seniority of the rebel fighters who are demobilizing, Mr. Sokoloff said. Now that so many of the underage combatants have fled the jungle, one goal is to keep targeting the remaining high-ranking commanders, who have the ability to recruit new kids. And maybe enter a few award shows.

DISCUSSION *questions and activities*

1. Go to the adage.com website and view the commercial that is the subject of this article. How does seeing this material affect your reaction to the Colombian government's strategy?

2. What is Wentz's point of view about this commercial? Does she display a political stance herself? Why might readers of *Advertising Age* be interested in her point of view?

The Dawkins v. Collins Debate

Gary J. Whittenberger

Dr. Gary J. Whittenberger earned his PhD in clinical psychology at Florida State University. The bulk of his career has been spent working in prisons where he designed and evaluated addictions programs. Whittenberger currently resides in Tallahassee, Florida, where he works as a consulting psychologist. In The Dawkins vs. Collins Debate, *Whittenberger provides lively commentary on a famous debate on evolution.*

A "GOD v. SCIENCE" DEBATE WAS featured in the November 13, 2006, issue of *TIME* magazine between well-known scientists Francis Collins, who is a Christian, and Richard Dawkins, who is an atheist. The article reported a lively exchange between these two scientific heavyweights who answered questions from a moderator about various controversies involving religion and science. Skeptics and believers alike should read the original article. However, this essay will summarize the important points of the *TIME* article and provide commentary from a skeptical perspective.

In the first exchange, Dawkins and Collins apparently agreed that the proposition "God exists" is either true or false. Dawkins indicated that science is appropriate to the task of answering the question, but Collins disagreed: "From my perspective, God cannot be completely contained within nature, and therefore God's existence is outside of science's ability to really weigh in."

Collins started on the wrong foot by doing a little question begging; he assumed God's existence from the outset without presenting any evidence for the inference. But he also left the backdoor open for science to weigh in on God's existence. By saying that "God cannot be completely contained within nature," he implied that God can be *partly contained* within nature, which makes God open to scientific analysis. On the other hand, Collins implied that God is partly contained outside nature. Since we are part of nature, how could we ever get outside of it to see whether there is anything on the other side? It is common for religious apologists like Collins to talk about things "outside nature" or "the supernatural," but they always seem to fall short in presenting any evidence that anything "supernatural" exists. By inventing a category called "supernatural" and relegating hypothetical things to it, they apparently hope to protect those things from the requirement of evidence.

Dawkins indicated that before the theory of evolution it was thought that the idea of God was required to explain the complexity, purpose, beauty, and elegance of living things. But the theory of evolution showed that the God hypothesis was unnecessary for the explanation. Collins responded by saying that a God, being "outside of nature" and therefore "outside of space and time," could have designed and activated evolution itself at the moment of his creation of the universe. Collins fails to consider all the consequences of inventing a realm or a being "outside of nature." One important feature of nature is its orderliness. If God were "outside of nature," wouldn't he be "outside of orderliness"? If so, then this would preclude him from having all the wonderful behavioral tendencies, such as perfect goodness, which are often ascribed to him. Collins is fond of saying that God is "outside of space and time." What does this mean? Does it make any sense to say that something exists outside of space and time? When we apply the word "exists" to something, don't we mean that we can observe it or its effects in space and time? Have we *ever* observed anything outside space and time? Collins seems to be caught in the quicksand of contradiction. Even if one entertains for a moment the odd notion that God could exist "outside time," this seems to lead to a conclusion that he couldn't do anything, including the particularly spectacular act attributed to him, i.e., creating the universe.

Time is the measure of change. If there is no time, there is no change. If there is no change, there is no action. If there is no action, there is no creation. If God were to exist outside of time, he would be impotent to do anything at all! By insisting that God exists "outside of nature," Collins nearly makes his supernatural compartment so small that there isn't enough room for God.

In response, Dawkins indicated that it would be odd if God chose to create humans through a 14-billion-year process of evolution. Collins responded by saying that this roundabout way of producing humans would not be an odd course of action for a God not having the purpose of making "his intention absolutely obvious to us." Collins postulates a sort of subtle God who doesn't want to give us too much information about his existence. Responding further to Dawkins, Collins said "If it suits him to be a deity that we must seek without being forced to, would it not have been sensible for him to use the mechanism of evolution without posting obvious road signs to reveal his role in creation?" What would be so wrong with God's "posting obvious road signs?" Collins implies the answer, i.e., by doing so, God would simply be forcing us to believe in him!

Collins seems to endorse the dubious notion that giving clear unambiguous information to people would be forcing them to take a certain course of action. If we were to emulate the God whom Collins envisions, we would dispense with any "obvious road signs" and would withhold dear information from adolescents about the connection between smoking cigarettes and getting lung cancer so that they wouldn't be forced to forgo smoking. Rather than addressing the subtle God that Collins imagines, Dawkins challenges the traditional God. He is certainly correct that the inefficiency of evolution, not to mention its "errors of design," is inconsistent with the traditional idea of God as an omniscient, omnipotent, and omnibenevolent being. This traditional kind of God would be more likely to operate through creationism, but this hyothesized mode of operation is not supported by the evidence of biology, genetics, geology, and cosmology.

Collins and Dawkins then offered their differing views on the "free-tuning" of our universe. According to this idea, if the value of any one of a half dozen of the "physical constants" of our universe had differed slightly from what it actually is, then life as we know it, including human life, would not exist. The terminology gets a little confusing here. How can something that is a constant be different from what it is? When physicists and cosmologists talk about a "physical constant," they mean a physical factor which has a certain value (represented by a particular number) which is constant throughout all times and places in our universe but which might possibly vary across different universes, if there were other universes. A physical constant would have the same value throughout any given universe, but might vary from one universe to another.

Dawkins proposed two possible explanations for the values of the physical constants we find in our universe. One is that these constants couldn't be any different from what they are; they simply are what they are. The other is that our universe is just one of a very large population of universes. Within this great multiverse environment, there are bound to be some universes that have the physical constants at just the right values to support the development of life, and we find ourselves in one of them. Collins dealt with the improbability of the physical constants, life, and human life by suggesting that a super-being selected the physical constants to be what they are. God "tuned" the universe to make life possible. In supporting his own explanation, Collins ignored the first hypothesis mentioned by Dawkins and attempted to dismiss the second. He said that the application of Occam's razor leads him to favor the God-as-tuner hypothesis. Dawkins responded by saying that the God hypothesis, although not impossible, is actually more improbable than the universe which it is designed to explain. Nevertheless, he advocated keeping an open mind when he said "It's an honest scientific quest to discover where this apparent improbability comes from."

Although Dawkins seems to present the two best currently available alternatives to Collins' God hypothesis to explain the life-enabling values of the physical constants of our universe, he and Collins both seem to accept without any skepticism the proposition that our universe is improbable. But how can they just assume this? In my opinion, they do this through a misapplication of probability theory. In the debate they used the "gravitational constant" as an example. They correctly noted that if the universal gravitational constant (G) were different by one part in a hundred million million, then life, as we know it, would not be possible in our universe. One can imagine a range of values from X to Y, within which G is included (X Y) for which life is not possible in our universe. Dawkins and Collins jump to the conclusion that, since the former range of values is so small compared to the latter set of values, our universe must be really rare or improbable.

Not only do they ignore the idea that some other kind of life ("life as we do not know it") might be possible outside the X-to-Y range, they also ignore the idea that there are an infinite number of values between X and Y for which life might be possible in our universe. Even more significantly, they also assume that they know something very important about the population of universes. In order to conclude that a particular item with some feature is improbable, one must know at least two facts about the population from which the item is drawn as a sample. One must know how many items *with* the feature are in the population *and* how many items *without* the feature are in that same population (or alternatively, how many items altogether are in the population). One can then draw valid inferences about the probabilities of different samples. The problem is that neither Dawkins nor Collins nor anyone else knows these facts about any possible population of universes from which our particular one might have been drawn as a sample.

In fact, we do not know that any other universes exist at all! Without knowledge of other universes, Dawkins and Collins misuse probability theory to conclude that our universe is rare. Because they start with an unwarranted assumption, their further speculations along these lines can't go very far. Even if we knew that a universe supportive of life was improbable, which we don't know, purposeful selection among possible universes (the God hypothesis) is a worse explanation of our particular universe than is random selection.

More must be said about Collins' contention that the application of Occam's razor supports the God hypothesis over the multiverse hypothesis. It doesn't. The God hypothesis is less parsimonious than the multiverse hypothesis for two reasons: 1) it invents a totally new type of entity, a supernatural being "outside time and space," which is not necessary with the latter hypothesis, and 2) it leads to the classic problem of infinite regress. If there must be something outside our universe, i.e., God, to explain the existence of our universe, then there must be something outside of God, i.e., "Z," to explain God. Then something is needed to explain "Z," and so on.

At one point in the debate Collins said that those who interpret Genesis in a literal way reach conclusions at odds with the findings of science, especially on the age of the Earth and the way in which species are related. Alluding to St. Augustine and commenting on the book of Genesis, Collins said "It was not intended as a science textbook. It was intended as a description of who God was, who we are and what our relationship is supposed to be with God." It is just as likely or more likely that the writer of Genesis intended his narrative to be an accurate account of what happened during creation than that he intended his narrative to be metaphorical, figurative, or allegorical. Collins is able to avoid the conclusion that the Bible is very likely not the "word of God" by adopting a nonliteral interpretation. Dawkins suggested that in defending evolution from his fundamentalist colleagues Collins was simply having an in-house quarrel, something he should just avoid.

The debate then turned to a discussion of miracles. The *TIME* moderator asked: "Dr. Collins, the Resurrection is an essential argument of Christian faith, but doesn't it, along with the virgin birth and lesser miracles, fatally undermine the scientific method?" It would have been better had he phrased his questions the other way around and asked if the scientific method undermines or challenges the claims of the Resurrection, the virgin birth, and other miracles. Nevertheless, Collins responded that if one accepts God's existence, then it is not unreasonable to expect that God might occasionally intervene in the world in a miraculous way, and that if one accepts that Jesus was divine then the Resurrection is "not a great logical leap." But these are big "ifs," and although Collins tries to show that they are plausible, he offers no good evidence to show that they are probable.

The debaters expressed different views on the origin of altruistic feelings and behavior. Collins said that there is a good explanation for some altruism; it either involves helping family members who share our DNA or it involves helping others whom we expect to help us later in return. But he said that there is not a good naturalistic explanation for altruism of the type exhibited by people such as Oskar Schindler who provided safety to Jews during the reign of the Nazis. It appears that people sometimes risk their lives and in the process also their genes in order to help strangers from whom they have no expectations of help in return. Collins implied that this altruism is a sign of God's existence and a gift from him. Dawkins asserted that altruism in these cases is a kind of carry-over from ancient times when altruism had survival value for people living in small clans. Going beyond altruism, Collins then pointed to the existence of "moral law" or the "absolutes...of good and evil" within the human species as evidence for the existence of God. This morality among humans is supposed to show that beyond just being a creator of the universe, God cares about us. Dawkins responded that good and evil don't exist as independent entities but that good and bad things simply happen to people.

Collins' "moral law" argument is another variation on the "God of the Gaps" theme. If science doesn't yet have a complete description of a phenomenon, then there must be a super-being behind the scenes who is responsible for whatever is in the gaps. A big problem with this approach is that it tends to put a damper on further investigation. Besides that, Collins has an obligation to present a positive case for God's existence and not just rely on the current apparent weaknesses of rival hypotheses. Collins' idea of a "moral law" is premature and far too rigid when one considers the variability in moral rules across different geographic areas, cultures, ethnicities, and religions. There are moral principles because humans are constantly deciding on how they should behave, especially towards each other, and there are some commonalities in these moral principles, but there is hardly a "moral law." In fact, the absence of a "moral law," a universally agreed upon set of moral rules, is more compatible with God's nonexistence than with his existence. Wouldn't an all-knowing, all-powerful, perfectly good God have revealed a universal moral code to all peoples from the very beginning of our species and reinforced it with booster training sessions each generation?

When he tried to explain why he supports the opening of new stem cell lines, in contrast to a great many other religious people, Collins presented a confusing, almost incoherent discussion of the relationship of faith and reason: "Faith is not the opposite of reason. Faith rests squarely upon reason, but with the added component of revelation." Part of the difficulty here is that "faith" has several different meanings and unfortunately Collins isn't clear about which meaning he intends. "Faith" may refer to a religion or worldview, as in "My faith is Islam." It may refer to an attitude of trust or confidence, as in "I have faith in my physician." Or it may refer to believing propositions without evidence or out of proportion to the available evidence. It is this latter meaning that goes against Collins' platitude that "Faith is not the opposite of reason." Reason involves believing propositions on the basis of evidence or in proportion to the available evidence. Thus, if not strictly the opposite of one another, faith and reason are certainly incompatible. And how does adding revelation to the mix help at all? Revelation is not a separate way of knowing immune from the light of reason. One must still look at the evidence to evaluate a claim that a "holy book" contains "revelations" from a supreme being.

In his concluding remarks Collins indicated that he is interested in many "why" questions for which he believes answers may not come from science but from the "spiritual realm." In his concluding remarks Dawkins indicated his doubt that the future discoveries of science would support any of the beliefs of the traditional religions, beliefs that he regards as parochial, but nevertheless worthy of some respect. And on that conciliatory note, the debate was concluded.

Who won the debate? From the perspective of style or mode of expression, perhaps Collins won. At times, Dawkins seemed to come across as a bit testy and abrasive. He not only referred to fundamentalists as "clowns," but several times he accused Collins of presenting "cop outs." Collins, on the other hand, seemed more self-assured and gentlemanly in his interpersonal style. From the perspective of content or validity of argument, Dawkins won the debate hands-down. He made many points that Collins seemed helpless to rebut. Collins failed to show that he has found a satisfactory conciliation between religion and science, between faith and reason, or even that such a project is possible. Overall, the debate provided useful insights into the currently hot, but perennial issue of science versus religion.

DISCUSSION *questions and activities*

1. Compare and contrast this commentary on the debate to the article *God vs. Science.* Which piece is a stronger argument? Why? Do you agree with Whittenberger's view that Collin's won the debate based on his style and self-expression?

2. Compare and contrast the style in this piece vs. the actual debate. What similarities do you find? Differences? Are they useful? Why or why not?

3. Examine Whittenberger's tone in this essay. Is it is skeptical? Weary? Leary? Why? Use examples from the text to support your stance.